The Town's Game

The Origins of Rugby and Association Football in Southport (1872-1889)

Daniel J Hayes

Foreword by Michael Braham

First edition July 2022

Paperback: ISBN 9798836541293
Hardback: ISBN 9798837198267

Independently published

www.southportfootballclub.co.uk

Acknowledgements

I am grateful for the support of friends at both Southport Football Club and Southport Rugby Football Club for the encouragement I have received whilst I have been on this journey of discovery.

I would like to place on record my thanks to the staff at Crosby Library for their assistance, and to the community of the Football Historians Research Group on Facebook for the many responses I have received to questions raised over the past couple of years.

I would also like to specifically thank David Walshe for his assistance in helping to find some of the more obscure characters and places in this story, and to James Cave, James Cook and Enda Rylands for their encouragement to undertake the project in the first place.

I am most grateful however for the contributions and encouragement of two men, Michael Braham and the late Geoff Wilde, without whom this book would never have been possible. Geoff and Michael set the benchmark and wrote the gold-standard of football club history books. Both men gave me mountains of support as I pursued my goal to give this period of history equal weight, firstly via my website and latterly via this book.

It would be remiss of me not to mention the many years of hard work and dedication that the late Graham Ellis gave to Southport Rugby Football Club as club historian. What saddens me as I publish this book is that neither Graham nor Geoff are here to see it. I never had the opportunity to meet Graham, but Geoff was a dear friend. Any errors in the writing of this book are, of course, entirely my own as without Geoff here to proofread and correct me, I'm sure one or two will have crept in.

I must say that I am indebted to my father, Mike Hayes, for reading through the numerous rough drafts and versions of this book that he offered to read as I got towards the end of the project. As caffeine kept me up pouring thoughts out through my pen, he helped to shape what might otherwise have been a book without a front page and a missing storyline into something I hope will be of interest to sports fans and local historians alike.

Contents

Foreword

Congratulations to the Southport Rugby Club on their 150th anniversary. It has a proud history being one of the oldest clubs in the Northwest and today is a vibrant and thriving community club. Until now little has been known about its formation but thanks to Dan Hayes we now have a complete record of their early history and the personalities involved in the development of rugby in the town.

I am glad to have been given the opportunity to contribute the Foreword of this book and feel qualified to do so on two counts. I have been a supporter of Southport Football Club for almost sixty-five years and a vice president for the past forty-eight years, and I was also a schoolboy member of Southport RUFC for several years and I learnt the rudiments of the game playing at Waterloo Road. Back in those days I would on occasions sit in the wooden stand on Saturday afternoons cheering on the team.

Both Southport RUFC and Southport FC have played a significant part in the sporting life of the town. With Saturday afternoons becoming a half holiday for many, sports began to prosper in the town. Southport Rugby Club from its inception provided the principal outdoor recreation in the winter.

Dan Hayes' thorough research has done both Southport RUFC and Southport FC a great service. His book affords us the opportunity to look back at the formative years of both clubs telling the story of how Southport Football Club forsook the handling code and resulted in the birth of Southport Association Football Club in 1881. He has unearthed much fascinating information and debunked many myths relating to the foundation and early history of both clubs.

Dan has brought to life the difficulties experienced by the original rugby club, how it evolved, and the expansion of the game in Southport during the 1870s which saw the proliferation of several clubs – not all of whom prospered. Indeed, thanks to Dan we now know that the original Southport club folded some years after its formation only to make a brief come back in 1881 before switching to association football.

Dan has given a fresh perspective on the role played by Ralph Rylance whose status as the driving force behind the inauguration of the association game has been perpetuated for one hundred and forty-one years largely because of claims made by his son Walter. Thomas Burnett at last receives due recognition as being the catalyst for the change of codes. Whilst Ralph Rylance may not have been the founder of Southport Football Club, having previously played for Blackburn Law, he certainly played a part in establishing association football in the town. Almost a hundred years later I represented Blackburn Young Lawyers which was the successor to Blackburn Law.

Hours of research at Crosby library browsing through newspaper microfilms aided by the national newspaper archives have enabled Dan to plot the line ups for games played by not only the titular rugby and football clubs but also the clubs with whom they were later associated. Geoff Wilde looking down from the penalty area in the sky would wholeheartedly approve of Dan's meticulous approach to this aspect of the book!

The personalities involved in the establishment of the winter game in Southport are given due prominence and brief biographies of civic leaders and prominent townspeople who associated themselves with both rugby and football club are included.

The advent of professional football following the establishment of Southport Central in 1888 and the signing of 'foreign talent' is well documented right up to Central's admission to the Lancashire League the following season, when three years later they were to be joined by the embryonic Liverpool FC!

I trust that this book whets the appetite for further study of Southport's sporting past. Certainly, Dan Hayes has provided a vast amount of raw material for future publications.

Michael Braham

Preface

The research that has led to this book has been a labour of love over many years, although when I started it, I hadn't even considered that it would end up in print.

Ever since I first read 'The Sandgrounders: The Complete League history of Southport Football Club' by Michael Braham and Geoff Wilde, I wanted to know more about the early years of Southport Football Club and have obsessed over their pre-Football League history ever since.

What started out as an idea to add a bit more information to my website (www.southportfootballclub.co.uk), very quickly became a detailed study into the story of football, and rugby, in this town. I'm a bit of a completist when it comes to information, I'm never really satisfied until I know as much as is possible about something that interests me and have exhausted every angle, argument and counter-argument. It became clear that you simply could not cover the early years of 'association' football in Southport without first covering 'the rugby years' in as much detail, nor could you cover either without also touching upon Cricket such is the uniqueness of the pattern sport has woven into this town.

Much of what I once took for granted I have discovered is not entirely correct. I make no apologies that on occasion, in this book, I make corrections to previously accepted fact, and where I do so, I hope you will agree that the justification for doing so is legitimate.

A lot of research has gone into the production of this book and therefore in the back, I have included the fixtures and results, with line-ups wherever available, for Southport Football Club (Rugby), Southport Olympic (Rugby), Southport Wasps (Rugby), Southport Hornets (Rugby), Southport Football Club (Association), Southport Wanderers (Association) and Southport Recreation (Association), between the years 1872 and 1889. For some of these clubs, this period covers the entirety of their history. For the others, this presents the start of a longer journey.

A good friend of mine used to always correct someone if they referred to him as a 'historian' by stating that no, he was a 'statistician'. I do the opposite. Whilst I do keep statistical records, my interest is in the *story* and *meaning* behind those statistics. I therefore include the results in this book as a reference to reassure the reader that the history presented has been thoroughly researched.

I would hesitate to ever call these records, or this history, a complete picture, not because research wasn't thorough but because we did not live through the period in question and therefore can be no more certain of the accuracy of historical reports than anyone reading them at the time might have been. It is however as complete a picture as has been possible, given the historical resources available at the current time. What I am confident of however is that this is, at the time of writing, the most complete record published of any of these clubs for the period concerned. For authenticity, I have included many of these early reports in their original words.

Coming up with a title for this book I actually found quite difficult. I did not set out to write one, and certainly did not intend for it to be a book covering the earliest years of *two* prominent local clubs. For a while, simply 'The Early Years' was my working title but that changed as the project progressed. The fact that the book covered the early years was pretty obvious, so I wanted a title that gave a clue to the story within. I chose 'Switching Codes' at first because the notion that the original Southport Football Club switched from rugby to association football was so woven into the histories of both clubs that I felt it hit the nail on the head, but as I began to understand more about the town, the clubs, and the people it became more than a story about a single decision. 'The Town's Game' was a name I arrived at quite late, but I chose it because this book tells the story of a game (or two!) that was initially an unassuming winter pastime for a select few but underwent a fascinating evolution to become the most popular activity in the town. 'The Town's Game' was a term first used by the Southport Guardian in 1886 when they too had arrived at the conclusion that it had finally captured the public's imagination and attention.

I hope that as you read this story you will share in the excitement that I have had as I have researched this period of history. The story of the first 17 years of football in this town is an engrossing one and whilst there are distinct sections within this book for association and rugby, I would encourage you not to focus simply on the one you think you ought to read as a fan of either today's rugby or football clubs, but to read both, and whilst doing so acknowledge and appreciate the hard work and dedication of some of those long forgotten characters that gave this town something to be proud of.

Daniel J. Hayes

Part I - Origins

Introduction

For anyone to understand the early history of Southport Football Club, they first need to understand that society, and the game of football itself, was evolving.

Before 1870 the only guaranteed national holidays were Christmas and Easter, meaning that for the working classes there was little time for recreational sport. By 1850 the Factory Act had begun to limit the working week to sixty hours with the week ending earlier on a Saturday. With Sundays being set aside for Church this naturally led to Saturday afternoons being given over to leisure. Skilled workers were first to exploit this limited leisure time, and those towns given over to manufacturing industries such as Sheffield were quick to make the most of the new Saturday half day holiday. By the 1860s other industries began to follow, with the railways providing more of the lower middle-class workers.

In Southport, Saturday afternoon recreation was still far from the minds of the majority. Indeed, the Southport News and Independent reported that there were still on-going discussions in the town regarding the 'early closing' that had begun to happen across the country, as an enabler for such activities.

Our readers will observe, by announcement in our advertisement columns, a public meeting will be held in the Town Hall on Thursday evening next, to consider the question of a general uniform closing of the shops in the town, and to form an early closing association similar to those already formed in towns of Lancashire and Yorkshire. It is hoped that there will be a large attendance of tradesmen to consider so important a question

(Southport News & Independent, 30th November 1872)

The meeting was considered a success in Southport in terms of establishing a time where leisure activities could be more easily pursued. This was a most significant development in creating an opportunity for people to engage in organised activities to alleviate the burden of their working lives.

The Early Closing Movement has at last taken some shape in this town. We have the subject fairly launched, and it now rests with the tradesmen of the town to say how the matter shall succeed. An opportunity now presents itself for a combination which cannot fail, to be productive of much good. The meeting on Thursday evening, we are well aware, was largely composed of assistants, and their enthusiasm in the matter could not be misapprehended. Of course, the circumstances may give the impression that the whole question is affecting the assistants only, but the facts gleaned from the employers, who really did the business, and who were the speakers on that occasion, sufficiently show that they are evidently alive to the fact the question is one of equal moment to themselves. Indeed, Southport must be a remarkable exception to the rule if masters do not derive an equal advantage with the assistants from the adoption of shorter hours. One fact much overlooked, was brought prominently forward – that if the tradesmen act only upon the supposition that the hours at which a certain class of customers at present do their shopping is to be the rule when the shops are to be closed, no satisfactory result will ever be arrived at. Of course it is impossible but that some little inconvenience may accrue to a few individuals. This will be the case in every movement for the public good.

(Southport News & Independent, 7th December 1872)

'Football' is a term that originally covered an array of different games ranging from local kick-abouts to organised public school affairs, and the word itself has been on a transformational journey from its first use in the modern sense back in the 1400s (yes, really) to that which we understand today. Prior to this there were stories of Greeks and Romans kicking heads up and down streets for 'fun' but in 1424 there is the first record of football in law as King James of Scotland banned the playing of 'Foot-ball' by his soldiers as it was causing a distraction from their duties. Furthermore, its almost exclusive use to describe association football is only very recent, and it wasn't until well into the 1900s that the term stopped being used to describe both rugby and association football interchangeably.

In the 1630s we find evidence of the first documented set of rules, written in Latin by the head teacher of the Aberdeen Grammar School. These are largely ignored by football scholars in favour of the rules of the 'Eton field game' first documented in 1815. In truth, the Eton field game, a game involving a round ball that you were not allowed to handle, scrums (referred to as 'rouges' at the time) and tries, more closely resembles the game that we know and love today, but that is perhaps only because we are at a closer point in time on its evolutionary journey. The public school system in England is where most historians pick up the story, and as the game increased in popularity in the public schools, others started to create their own sets of rules, Rugby School being one to document theirs in 1845. Others followed suit, Harrow and Shrewsbury amongst them, and whilst setting their own rules was fine when the games were being played 'in-house', taking the game further afield became problematic.

Through all the many differences, there were essentially two underlying codes, 'dribbling' and 'handling' with each school leaning more heavily towards one or the other. It was a common occurrence for some clubs to switch codes from one week to the next depending on the opposition. Even the number of players in a team could be varied. This allowed for a handicap system when one team was known to be stronger than the other.

The basic object of the game was very much like it is today, to set up a situation whereby the ball could be kicked between the goal posts. Depending on the set of rules followed, this was either under or over the crossbar. That however is where the similarities almost end.

The game mainly involved kicking the ball with the feet but it also involved some catching. 'Scrummages' and 'rucks' could take up the majority of the play. A key feature in the English game, as opposed to the Scots, was an offside rule which effectively outlawed passing.

To progress players had to try and break through an opponent's line. Players at the back would try and kick the ball into space for the forwards to rush on to. Some kicked and ran after; others ran with the ball at their feet but once the forwards had the ball they had one thing in mind – to head for goal. The pack of forwards would follow close behind ready to batter through a defence and, should possession be lost, pick up the play and continue the charge. If the ball was moved over the goal line the team could take a kick at goal. A kick from anywhere on the field was known as a field goal.

Matches were decided solely on goals scored, which led to some very unsatisfactory results where a team that had conceded numerous tries (a method of scoring what were considered minor points by running the ball over the opponent's goal line) could win a game by kicking a lucky goal. It also led to results being declared a draw despite one side having scored more tries than the other. If there were no goals, then it was a tie. Most newspaper reports recorded goals, tries and touchdowns - the latter being the number of times a team was forced to touch the ball down behind its own goal line - in order to give a more accurate assessment of matches

Refereeing of the game in the early years was done by the captains of each team, which meant that disputed tries were common. The stronger willed, argumentative players were more likely to be considered for the captaincy. It soon became obvious that the lack of consistency and objectivity was becoming a major obstacle to fair-play and competition.

The one thing to be regretted in football is the want of uniformity of rules. To remedy this a number of associations have been formed, the most prominent of which is the London Association, who solicit the support of clubs to play their rules. An association has also been formed in Sheffield for that and other purposes.

(Sheffield Independent – Tuesday 10th October 1871)

Whereas clubs had once been formed to facilitate private recreational activities, the sport's growing identification with inter-town rivalry meant that by the middle of the Nineteenth century, clubs were being created to represent towns or districts. Therefore, it became important that attempts were made to standardise a set of rules. This ultimately led to the foundation of the Football Association (FA). In 1863, a letter from Ebenezer Morley, the captain of Barnes Football Club in London, appeared in Bell's Life. His letter convinced enough of the leading clubs to meet on the evening of 26th October of that year at the Freemason's Tavern in Great Queen Street, Covent Garden. Morley was elected honorary secretary and Francis Maule Campbell, at only 19 years of age, became the treasurer, a position he already held at Blackheath FC.

Following this first meeting of the embryonic Football Association, Morley set out to draft a set of rules that were enough of a compromise to satisfy the majority of playing clubs. There were broadly two camps with interest in the outcome, the pro-rugby rules lobby favoured a greater blend of handling and kicking than the pro-dribbling game lobby. On 24th November, armed with his draft, which had been predominantly based upon the rugby rules, it asked those present to also consider the Cambridge rules, in which carrying the ball and hacking were absent.

Whilst we know that the Football Association is still going strong today, don't mistake that to mean that their attempts were well received and that their formation was an instant success - far from it. There is an old saying, that "you can't please all the people, all the time" and it was very much the case here.

With the support of J.F. Alcock, captain of the Old Harrovian Forest Football Club, on 1st December 1863 a basic set of rules was drawn up and it was for predominantly a kicking game, with a very limited amount of handling (but still some!), and some of the rougher elements of the sport removed.

At a meeting held a week later, which had been intended to sign off on the rules, those who could not accept those decisions declined to follow. Francis Maule Campbell, speaking on behalf of Blackheath FC was so incensed that he stormed out stating that they would destroy the game of football. Youthful impetuousness maybe, but they, and many others, declined membership of the FA, and would later join the Rugby Football Union upon its formation in 1871.

The published rules from the Football Association can be found elsewhere in this book and you will see that up to law eight there was plenty of common ground with those who favoured rugby. It had still allowed handling of the ball in the rules, and it too included an offside rule which prevented a forward pass from being made at all, forcing the advancement of the ball through dribbling alone. This alone makes the 'football' we know today a world away from the football understood back then and it wasn't until 1867 that the offside rule was altered to allow a player to be onside when at least three of the opposing team are nearer their own goal-line, which allowed the flourishing of a passing game.

Most controversial of all the changes however was that the rules would outlaw 'hacking'. This change alone caused so much of an issue that it almost killed the FA before it had even begun.

"My maxim is hack the ball on when you see it near you, and when you don't, why then hack the fellow next to you!" said one Rugby school boy.

So, what was 'hacking' and why was it so controversial? Its definition is quite simple, but also brutal in an equal measure. Let's not forget that at the time, football was a very physical, often violent and at times dangerous sport. Hacking was the act of stopping a player from dribbling by kicking their shins deliberately to trip them up. Today that would be a clear foul, and more than likely would come with further punishment on top. Back then, it had been accepted as part of the game and the thought of removing it from the game was met with horror in some quarters.

I do uphold hacking because it develops that quality of which every Englishman ought to be most proud – his pluck. I know sir, it is objected that he ought to learn pluck by the use of his fists. I admit the correctness of this objection in theory, but I deny its possibility in practice. We are too phlegmatic a nation to use our firsts for nothing, to fly into a passion without any cause. This cause is supplied in football.

(Bell's Life in London and Sporting Chronicle – Saturday 26th December 1963)

The problem was that rules described a game which was a mongrel, so much of a compromise that it resembled a game that nobody played, and nobody *wanted* to play.

Sporting Life commented in November 1863 *'I do not think the meetings in London are attended by people or clubs of sufficient influence to cause their suggestions to be generally acted upon'.*

The new Football Association was a fragile and unstable organisation, and its rules were so unpopular that in 1867 only six people attended their annual meeting. Even amongst its members and strongest supporters, its rules were frequently ignored or adapted. It is widely regarded as the world's first Football Association but it is difficult to see how that can be justified as a claim. One of the world's oldest football clubs, Sheffield, had introduced a set of rules when they began in 1857 and by the early 1860s there were 14 clubs playing by those rules in the area. The oldest club of any kind was 'The Foot-Ball Club' founded in Edinburgh in 1824.

When the FA was formed there was no geographical remit and far from it being a unifying national organisation with a unifying set of rules, the FA's own Chairman Ebenezer Morley had even asked those present at a meeting in 1867 whether the Association should dissolve itself. Had it not been for the support received from Sheffield FC and a letter of encouragement from the 14 clubs playing under the Sheffield rules, it would likely have disappeared altogether.

The Sheffield rules were notably different in that they had got rid of the offside rule altogether. They had pioneered the use of corners and free kicks. With their encouragement, within a year the FA had been forced into a major revision of its code and had been forced to adopt many of the rules that had made the Sheffield Association all the more popular.

The handling code meanwhile had continued to flourish without a union of rules.

Since the formation of the FA, every year has increased the superiority in point of numbers and popularity of the rugby clubs over those who are subject to the rule of the Association

(Bell's Life in London and Sporting Chronicle)

What came next was somewhat unexpected. In 1870 the first so-called 'international match' was arranged between England and Scotland played under association rules. Strictly speaking it was not an international in the sense to which we are accustomed today which is why many choose not to recognise it as such. For that game both sides were selected by the London based FA, but either way it served its purpose in that people started to realise that it had only been possible due to the standardisation that had taken place.

Rugby therefore decided they had better follow suit.

In December 1870, Edwin H. Ash, the secretary of the Richmond Football Club, wrote a letter to the papers to request that those who play the *'rugby-type game'* should also meet to document a unified set of rules.

The Rugby Football Union was established in January 1871 at a meeting of 32 members in the Pall Mall Restaurant in Haymarket. Of the 32 members present, 21 original clubs enrolled. Those present had a big southern bias, but the outcome was that by March they were able to stage their own international. England faced off against Scotland with several members of the Union committee represented.

The great irony is that with serious injuries frequently reported in the press caused by 'hacking', one of the Union's first acts was to abolish it! The drafting of the rules between January and the start of the season had fallen principally to three men, Algernon Rutter, Edward Holmes and L.J.Maton. That Maton, a renowned rugby player himself, was to break his leg in that period may well have had a big influence on the decision.

With rugby still being played largely in public schools its administrators still regarded Cup competition and professionalism as unnecessary 'evils' and therefore continued in the same 'amateur friendly' manner for some time. In years to come the argument over professionalism was to engulf both codes.

The geographical remit of the FA became clearer when the Scottish Football Association was established in 1873. Wales followed in 1876. The Sheffield Football Association eventually merged its rules with the FA in 1878.

The Southport Gymnasium and Football Club

The development of the town of Southport had been funded primarily by the entrepreneurial activities of local businessmen wanting an idyllic seaside retreat away from the industrial heartlands of Lancashire. With the shifting sands putting paid to any notion of Southport becoming a working port for shipments to Manchester, Southport settled into its title of a classic seaside resort and was able to cash in on the growing trend of sea bathing. Blackpool became the resort for the working class offering cheap thrills and amusements, whilst Southport became a more up-market affair. Its proximity, as a resort, to the more industrialised towns of Liverpool and Manchester saw it grow exponentially at the end of the 19th century and by 1872, when our story really begins, it was thriving. The census taken a year earlier in 1871 had seen a population growth of approximately 8,000 on its previous return in 1861, thanks in part to the boundary extension to take in the area designated for the gas works and the outer districts, and now stood at approximately 18,000. In October the town was granted a royal visit for the laying of the foundation stone of the Cambridge Hall, by H.R.H. the Princess Mary of Cambridge, Duchess of Teck. The Duke of Teck, and many members of parliament were also present.

Southport's people, the 'Sandgrounders', had a noticeably better life expectancy than those in neighbouring towns and this led to the town being seen as something of a 'health resort'. The town's Latin motto, Salus Populi, means 'Health of the People'.

As the 1870s had approached, sport in the town had been exclusively in the domain of the cricketers; organised cricket having first begun in 1859 with the formation of Southport Cricket Club on a ground in York Road near Birkdale station. As cricket grew in popularity over its first decade in the town it was hardly surprising that more clubs should be formed and so it was that 'The Alexandra Cricket Club' was born in 1863. It is through the existence of Alexandra that a football club would be founded nine years later.

It was Doctor George Augustus Coombe who was the real driving force behind the formation of the town's first football club. As the recently appointed (1871) first house surgeon of the Southport Infirmary, he was charged with improving the health of the town's young men. Born at Upwell in Cambridgeshire, the son of R.G.Coombe a surgeon of Burnham, Essex, he was educated privately and trained for medicine at Guy's Hospital, London taking the diplomas of MRCS and LSA in 1870.

The Southport News & Independent was the first newspaper to report the formation of the new club on 27th November 1872.

The Southport Gymnasium and Football Club
This club, which has recently been formed, already numbers a large and influential list of members, and the following gentlemen have kindly commented to act as officers: - the mayor of Southport (S.Swire Esq.), president; W.H.Smith, Esq. (District Bank) vice-president; Henry P. Stephenson Esq. hon-secretary; and Stewart Allen, Esq. hon-treasurer. The Artillery Drill Shed, Part-street, has been fitted up with gymnastic apparatus, and the opening of the gymnasium will take place on Saturday next, the 30th, at half-past seven pm. A field for football has been engaged in Manchester Road, and goal posts have been erected. The want of a gymnasium has long been felt in Southport, and it is hoped that the praiseworthy efforts shown by the promoters (viz, the Alexandra Cricket Club and the Southport Rowing Club) of the present movement will be well supported by the gentry of Southport.

(Southport News & Independent, 27th November 1872)

Although Coombe initially did not take a place on the committee, he was later to become vice president. His absence from the Southport News & Independent report can therefore be explained away but the Southport Visiter was right to offer him credit from the start.

Southport Gymnasium and Football Club
The above club has recently been inaugurated under the most encouraging of circumstances. A gymnasium has been fitted up in Part-street (Artillery Drill Shed) with complete gymnastic apparatus; the chief promoters of this praiseworthy movement are the Alexandra Cricket Club and the Southport Rowing Club; but it is chiefly to the energy shown by Dr. G.A. Coombe of the Southport Infirmary, that the movement has assured tangible aspect. The president of the club is the Mayor of Southport (S.Swire Esq.) and the vice president W.H.Smith Esq. (District Bank); hon. sec., H.P.Stephenson, Esq., and hon. treasurer, S.Allen, Esq. It is hoped that a movement like this, which is calculated to improve the physical development of our young townsmen, will meet with appreciation and support of the gentry of this town. The honorary subscription is 10s 6d, and a donation of £2 2s constitute the donor a life member. Subscriptions or donations received by the hon. treasurer, 2 Hawkshead-street Southport. The club's football ground is adjoining the Alexandra Cricket Club field, Manchester-road, and several matches are arranged for the present season. The gymnasium opens on Saturday evening next.

(Southport Visiter, 29th November 1872)

Samuel Swire, who had been appointed mayor of Southport less than a month earlier, was named club president.

The large field on Manchester Road, which was to become Southport Football Club's first home, was adjacent to the Alexandra Cricket Club, one of the two named organisations known to have given their backing to the venture. It appears that the football club's links with other sports, and cricket in particular, were deep rooted from the very beginning but the story of early sporting clubs in the town is turbulent to say the least and their fortunes are tied heavily to the development of the town itself.

The closest published Ordnance Survey map that we have, surveyed between 1889 and 1890, shows the location of the Alexandra cricket ground as being a large field behind the Hartwood Road area with access off Roe Lane. It is covered today by housing on Melling Road, Irton Road and Grange Avenue. Back then it would have looked very different. Hartwood Road was yet to be built, and when the Southport Cricket Club that had first played in 1859 lost their ground on York Road in around 1864, probably due to the building development in the rapidly expanding Birkdale area, they subsequently re-established themselves in Manchester Road in 1866, next door to the Alexandra Club.

The original Southport cricket club would play on for a further eight years before building again would take over in 1874, and we see the effects of that work on the Ordnance Survey map published in 1894.

There were a phenomenal number of private schools in the Sixties in Southport, most of which played cricket, to the considerable benefit of the local clubs. Chief of these were Sandringham, Southport College, Bickerton House, Sandfield School, Somerville House, Albert House, Royal Balmoral, Sandhurst House and Southport Lodge and from them came plenty of youthful talent. With a wealth of well-educated young Victorian men looking to enjoy some leisure time in the winter, of the two football codes it is no great surprise that when a decision was made to form a football club it was the handling code that was chosen. rugby was clearly the more favoured game nationally, and the only place in the country really bucking the trend was the industrial town of Sheffield.

1894 Ordnance Survey Map - Reproduced with permission of the National Library of Scotland

==*==
1872/73

As the laws of the game had been defined by the Rugby Football Union in July 1871, these will have been the rules first used by Southport Football Club. We believe they took to the field for the first time on Saturday 21st December 1872, away at Seaforth.

Southport Football Club
This club played a match against the Seaforth club on Saturday last at Seaforth. The game was well contested and resulted in a draw, the Southport Club having a few points in their favour. Messrs M. Smith and Chas. Schofield doing good service for Southport, and Messrs Hunter and Hussey for Seaforth.

(Southport Visiter, 24th December 1872)

It is a short report for what turned out to be a pivotal moment in the history of sport in this town, sandwiched incongruously between the news of the Christmas services at St Andrew's Church and the activities of the Young Men's Christian Association, in the middle of the 'local news' column. The original announcement of the formation of the club had included mention of the Gymnasium on Part Street about which there was clearly some enthusiasm, but this is the only time that the word Gymnasium has ever been associated with the club's name. From the report of this first game onwards, it was simply 'Southport Football Club'.

The local press, as well as being a source of evidence for historians, was the primary means of generating publicity for the majority of institutions and organisations before the turn of the 20th century. As a result, it was a crucial component in the development of any sense of communal identity, and its relationship with clubs is of pivotal importance when shaping the attitudes of early supporters. The Athletic News, published in Manchester, had a circulation of close to 200,000 by the mid-1890s, and was an important source of football news. Closer to home the town was serviced by the aforementioned Southport Visiter for more than 20 years before other newspapers appeared, initially as a means of recording all of the visitors to the town's hotels and guest houses.

The earliest sporting contributions to the local press were compiled essentially by enthusiastic amateurs, unpaid by the newspaper. Generally, it was the responsibility of either the honorary secretary or even the team captains to submit a report. As reports became more commonplace, they developed a typical pattern describing the venue, the weather, and the crowd before giving a brief description of the play. If you were lucky, they might tell you who played. Unfortunately for this first fixture we are not so lucky. In all likelihood, the words we read in the Southport Visiter were penned by either R.W.Smith as captain, or Henry Stephenson as honorary secretary, although the copy may well have been edited by the newspaper staff upon submission.

Amongst the men chosen to represent the town's new football club, were many familiar local faces. H.V.Pigot, R.B.Hartley, C.A.Schofield, G.F.Schofield, N.Barron and S.Allen all regularly represented the Alexandra Cricket Club, and whilst the club's first season in existence consisted of only a handful of fixtures, the movement had been established and it was a firm base upon which a legacy could be built.

It was typical at the time for club committees to be made up of playing members. The following were all regulars: N.Barron, F.Gregory, G. Hall, R.B.Hartley, S. Lord, C.A.Schofield, G.F.Schofield, J.Schofield. The important job of captaincy was given to R.W. Smith with P.M. Hunter as deputy. Stewart Allen was named honorary treasurer and Henry P. Stephenson as honorary secretary.

Unlike today, clubs did not necessarily play every Saturday. With organisational difficulties plentiful, and with the threat of poor weather in the winter it is likely that the early seasons were a little more stop-start than we are used to today. There is also the possibility that as recreational sport was relatively new, the press simply chose only to report on fixtures when there was deemed nothing better to write about. We have only been able to identify seven fixtures in the club's first season and from those games they were only able to show one win. Neighbours Ormskirk have the dubious honour of being the first club to fall victim to Southport Football Club, where at Manchester Road they we defeated by two goals, seven tries and six rouges to nothing on 15th March 1873.

The strangers were completely overmatched; in fact they never got a single advantage during the whole time they were playing.

(Southport Visiter, 21st March 1873)

The remaining six games were all more evenly contested, and all resulted in draws meaning that the new club did not taste defeat in its opening season, as far as we can establish. It did however provide plenty of entertainment.

The ground was very wet and muddy, making it extremely hard to run upon, and the numerous "spills" caused great amusement to the lookers on, in consequence of the changed appearances of the players as they rose covered in mud.

(Southport Visiter, 28th January 1873)

As the only club in town, a good transport network is crucial if you're looking to grow, and the development of the rail and tramways coincided with a period of boom for the town. The first sod of the West Lancashire Railway was cut by the club President Samuel Swire in 1873, and the first of Southport's tramways was completed with a line running from Birkdale to Churchtown. In guidebooks produced in later years they would boast that the length of tramway was greater than any other town in the country, in proportion to the population, however at this time the tram system was still growing.

The Crowlands Gas Works situated on Crowland Street opened in July. For many readers the tall towers built on the site many years later would be the first anyone saw of 'home' as they travelled back to Southport. The first rail company to form any type of agreement with the Southport Gas company that operated the works was the Lancashire & Yorkshire Railway, who joined up to the works via the station goods yard at Blowick.

==*==

1873/74

During the summer of 1873, W.H. Smith of the District Bank retired as vice president of Southport Football Club with his place taken by George Coombe, the man credited with the idea of forming the club.

The town's main trades typified the more upper-class nature of the resort, Legal Services, Accountancy, Teaching, Health/Medical and there were still a significant number living off the land and sea. The Southport shrimp is still well loved to this day and the seafront was a busy place. Two and three masted ships were a common sight, along with a multitude of fishing vessels.

With the number of well-educated gentlemen in the town it is perhaps of little surprise that cricket was still the dominant sport. It was however only a summer sport and therefore, particularly for those who boasted a public-school background, rugby football was the obvious winter choice. The rugby season was designed to fill the months without cricket, typically covering October through to March. A full fixture list was created for the 1873/74 season, even if it did take the Visiter until the *end* of October to publish it.

The new season began very well for Southport Football Club, winning their first fixture, against Sandringham School, by one goal and three touch downs.

Their second fixture, scheduled to be against the Claughton club, was postponed. An inauspicious start to the season but this was perhaps an early indication of the fluidity of the clubs and teams at this time. Claughton would later merge with Birkenhead Wanderers to form Birkenhead Park. When Southport resumed for the third scheduled fixture, against Liverpool College, they would win by three goals.

The final record for the season as reported at the club AGM in April was Played 12, Won 7, Lost 1, Drawn 4, the results and line-ups for each of these games are elsewhere in this book. For this record to be accurate however, the first fixture of the season versus Sandringham School must have been considered a pre-season friendly and therefore was not included in this record.

The AGM, which was held at the Victoria Hotel on 15th April, took place with both the club president (Mayor Samuel Swire) and vice-president (Dr. Coombe) 'unavoidably' absent, therefore the duty fell to the previous season's captain, R.W.Smith, and vice-captain, P.M.Hunter, to host proceedings. The meeting was otherwise well attended and after dinner, a toast from the stand-in chair was made of 'Success to the Southport Football Club' and a healthy balance was reported of over £3 (the equivalent of around £350 today). Deputy chair for the evening, Vice-Captain Hunter, went on to say the success had been due to the *'cordial unanimity that prevailed amongst the members'* after which Captain Smith gave thanks to his deputy who had stood in as captain for much of the season due to an unfortunate accident which had prevented him from playing.

(Victoria Hotel, location of the club's very first Annual General Meeting)

Officers for the season were elected with J.C.Irving Esq. added to the vice-presidents alongside Dr. G.A.Coombe. P.M.Hunter was elected as captain, owing to Smith's injury and a new vice-captain, Graceus Hall, appointed to fill his vacant role. George Schofield was noted as the treasurer, in place of Stewart Allen, and the remaining members were fixed as N.Barron, R.B.Hartley, G.Nicholson, Charles Schofield, W.Bromilow, C.E.Hudson, H.V.Pigot and the retiring captain, R.W.Smith.

The meeting concluded after a vote of thanks was given to the officers and committee with the singing of the National Anthem.

Southport Football Club appeared in Charles Alcock's Football Annual for the first time that summer. These football annuals had been published every year since 1868 and included such information as when the club was formed, where the ground is situated, whether they played association or rugby rules, and the colours of the jerseys. They have since become a superb guide for historians.

For the first time, we have an official record of Southport Football Club's membership of the Rugby Football Union and an indication that after their second season Southport considered themselves a club established enough to be included amongst the list of other clubs circulated on an annual basis. Furthermore, the contents of the Annual were submitted by football secretaries themselves and therefore we know them to be the facts as believed by those concerned.

The inclusion also indicated a healthy membership of 76. With a match-day playing squad of either 15 or 20 depending on the opponents, it suggests there were a healthy number of 'supporters' as well as playing members included within that total. Manchester Road is listed as the club's ground and the jersey colours are those that Southport Rugby Football Club still wear to this day - black, red and amber.

Curiously, however, the re-elected Secretary H.P. Stephenson's return for Southport stated their formation year to be 1873 and not 1872! It's easy to see now why identifying the date a club was founded is rarely a simple task.

==*==
1874/75

For a number of years, the Southport Athletic Festival had been staged at the next-door Southport Cricket Club on Manchester Road and it had attracted athletes from far and wide, but the 1874 festival was to be the last held there before building work forced a search for a new venue. There were unprecedented levels of investment in the town in the early 1870s by the town's middle-class elite, and 1874 saw the completion of Cambridge Hall, which had been granted a Royal visit for the laying of its foundation stone three years prior and also the opening of the very grand Winter Gardens and Aquarium.

Whilst ground problems continued to affect Southport Cricket Club, the Alexandra Club's tenure next door continued unblemished. At their Annual General Meeting at the Bold Arms Hotel the Rev. Charles Hesketh had given the club fourteen years' lease of their ground. For Southport Football Club, who shared the ground, this too meant stability.

(A later picture of the Bold Arms Hotel, after its renaming, location of the second club Annual General Meeting)

The new season kicked off on 17th October 1874 with the visit of West Derby. The Southport News & Birkdale Chronicle announced the fixture whilst publishing a full set of scheduled fixtures on the opening day of the season.

We have great pleasure in publishing this list, particularly so, as we notice that the committee has not hesitated to play the strongest and best-known clubs in the county. We cannot do better than wish our local team the same success that they have had during their first two seasons the club has been in existence. As yet they have not met with opponents stronger than themselves, and though this is the first time the club has had the opportunity of playing Liverpool and Manchester, we doubt not that it will be well able to hold its own even against such.

The home matches will be played on the club ground, Manchester-road, and we understand that, owing to the great crush that sometimes took place last year on the ground, and the difficulty of keeping some of the spectators behind the touchlines, admission will probably be by ticket only, that the company may be more select and orderly. The tickets can be had by any of the officers of the club.

(Southport News & Birkdale Chronicle – 17th October 1874)

That the membership had been reported as so healthy, with a surplus in the bank after the season, is even more impressive when set against the context that up until this point no tickets had been sold for games. Interest was so high that effectively they were introduced as a measure of crowd control. With Southport now being a registered member of the RFU, their access to better quality opponents was increasing. With the Lancashire County RFU still not officially formed Manchester Rugby Club had become the de facto county side.

The club's third season began strongly. West Derby were on the end of a bit of a thrashing conceding five goals and a series of minors with no return. Wins quickly followed over United Schools (two goals, one touch down to nil), a combined team of the Bickerton House and Sandringham Schools from Southport, and Bolton (one goal, one touchdown to one touchdown). At this stage the size of teams varied from opponent to opponent, starting the season with a 15 a side game versus West Derby, both Bolton and Free Rangers (Manchester) were a 20 a side affair. The club did not taste defeat until the visit of the Manchester side on 12th December. It was the first time that they had really been tested and they came up short by a goal and four touchdowns to nil.

Shortly before, on November 19th, tragedy had struck for the president of the club, who had also recently been succeeded as Mayor, with the terrible death of his wife. Mrs. Swire was in her bedroom when her nightdress became ignited at an unguarded gas fire, and she died of her injuries.

The return game with Manchester in January also ended in defeat. Draws with Dingle and Wigan followed and in a gesture of thanks to Dr G.A.Coombe he was presented with a chronograph and purse of gold having resigned his post as first house surgeon to the Southport Infirmary in February 1875.

A loss to the Free Wanderers of Manchester continued the sequence of defeats to Manchester clubs but the run was broken by the visit of Pendleton in the middle of March.

The season finished with an exhibition match between Southport and the best of the town's schools, where despite playing with only 12 men, the town's team showed the gulf in class with a comfortable victory. The season's record was Played 15, Won 6, Drew 6 and Lost 3.

==*==
1875/76

Seeing the benefits winter sport could bring, in the summer of 1875 Southport Football Club began to face some local competition as new clubs were formed to play 'the handling code'.

As an indicator of the speed at which the town was growing, the Southport Independent had been issued three times a week for several months when in May it became a daily publication, the Southport Daily News.

Cricket too was still going strong in the town, the Alexandra Club with whom Southport Football Club shared their home, faced competition from the recently formed Birkdale Club. Southport Cricket Club, neighbours to the Alexandra Cricket club until 1874 when they lost their home due to the development of houses and the building of Hartwood Road, reformed playing their first match at a ground near to the cemetery on Scarisbrick New Road. Thomas Blundell Burnett (a name with which we will become very familiar), was noted for his batting, bowling and fielding in their first match back - achieving three wickets, four catches, and being only one of two to notch double figures with the bat.

At the newly relocated Athletic Festival, Southport FC's W.E. Smith drew all the plaudits winning the 100 yards handicap, 440 yards handicap and finishing runner up in the 120 yards handicap. The Southport Visiter reported that loud cheers had erupted from the large crowd that had assembled in the summer of 1875 when he was presented with his prizes. Dr. Coombe spoke to those that had gathered to thank them for their support with the event raising £300.

1875 also saw the opening of the Botanical Gardens with the adjoining museum, built by George Duxfield of the Southport Athletic Society, following a year later.

On 27th August the Southport Visiter noted that at the Christ Church School Sports *'in addition to the contests, games were organised, the inevitable foot-ball was there'*.

'Foot-ball' as a game was becoming popular enough now for shops on Lord Street to advertise footballs for sale in the Southport Visiter.

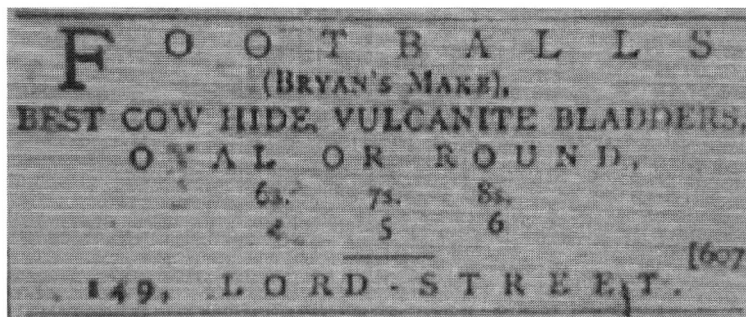

Although 'Foot-ball' was played in the town's schools, Martin Westby's 'England's Oldest Football Clubs' provides an excellent rationale for us to not consider any of them to be part of the history or heritage of the modern-day clubs.

a club has always been defined as an independent entity and these teams were not independent of the educational institutions that created them. Also, schools are also closed to outside members. There is limited potential for an individual school to make a mark in the countywide (and later countrywide) competition for success in football...Surprisingly in spite of those limitations many educational establishments joined the Football Association, some competed successfully in the County challenge cups and indeed one, Oxford University AFC (f.1872), won the FA Cup final outright in 1873/74.

(Martin Westby - England's Oldest Football Clubs)

With increased competition locally Southport struggled to maintain their dominant position. Between December and the end of February 1876, the side tasted nothing but defeat, however the progress that the club had made in its first few years of existence had still meant that it held some sway further afield. Southport were chosen as opponents for a charity match to raise funds for the Manchester Warehousemen and Clerks' School against Manchester. The Athletic News in February commented *'Southport is a junior member of the organisation of which Manchester is the most prominent member in the North of England'.*

The pecuniary results of the recent football match between the Southport and Manchester clubs are gratifying, a sum of £6 10s 6d having been handed over to the treasurer of the Infirmary.

(2nd January 1877, Southport Visiter)

The newly relocated and restarted Southport Cricket Club lasted only one more year. A letter to the Southport Visiter in early January hinted at problems before the club could enter its second season.

TO THE EDITOR OF THE SOUTHPORT VISITER
Dear Sir- There was a cricket club opened, or an old one revived, called the Southport C.C. last summer. There were rules made and passed by a committee, and in one of them it said there should be meetings called at different times, one at the end of the season to show how the club stood as regards the funds, and how the money got was spent. Time keeps going on and still there is no meeting called.
I came to reside here last year, and being a cricketer I joined this club. I paid my subscription, and played about twice, owing to the bad state of the ground. I was told that we were to have a new one, and I also heard it spoke of that were we to have one made for us as if we paid a small sum per year; but alas! I hear nothing of it now. I do not know any of the committee or secretary; but I should like to know who is to blame. If they have too much to do let them give it up. I have no doubt someone else will take it up. I am yours, AN OLD CRICKETER. Part Street, Southport

(Southport Visiter, 4th January 1876)

Whilst a response was offered by Secretary J.B.Jones in the week that followed, suggesting that such a meeting would take place before the first week in February 1876, it did indicate that there had been difficulty in procuring a new ground. We don't know the full reasons why the club folded but this is likely to be a key factor. Their demise also coincided with the loss of prominent player Thomas Blundell Burnett, who a short while later was turning out for the Wynnstay Cricket Club in Ruabon near Wrexham. It was to be the last we would see of him in Southport for four years, and during his time away no further attempt was made to revive the club.

Many of the remaining members of Southport Cricket Club joined Southport Gymnastic Cricket Club, who took over the ground.

==*==
1876/77

In 1876/77, after four years, the fruits of the committee's work were beginning to show. This was a season in which Southport Football Club came of age.

On 30th January 1877 the Southport Visiter commented that *'The Southport Football Club is an exceptionally strong one and includes several well-known athletes'*. It would be difficult to argue with that conclusion. From a schedule of 15 games the club did not taste defeat until Boxing Day, their seventh game, winning the first six. What's more, the goal conceded on that day against Manchester was to be the only goal conceded all season and their only defeat. Only a drawn return fixture against the same side at the end of January spoiled what would otherwise have been a perfect season – their final record was Played 15, Won 13, Drew 1, Lost 1.

As for the 'well known athletes', at the turn of the year the club's stock rose once again as forward G. Schofield became the first Southport player to be selected for the newly formed Lancashire County side when he featured in a drawn game at Whalley Range, Manchester, against Yorkshire. Schofield was to play in several Lancashire County matches and appeared in the Southport team photograph in his county jersey. He also played in the North v South International Trial at Manchester.

The Southport Visiter had always devoted a large section of its publication to listing the number of visitors to the town (and the hotels/establishments where they were lodging), and with the rapid increase in the town's population, fuelled by tourism in the first half of the decade, they had already expanded from a four page to an eight-page publication.

After the heavy investment in the town at the start of the decade the tourist trade was anticipating a boom. Unfounded news, rumoured to have been sponsored by rivals in Blackpool, however, began to filter through of a smallpox epidemic which had kept visitors away for most of 1876, and the effects were still being felt into 1877.

On the 8th March 1877, the Visiter, capitalising on the rising popularity of sporting activities, introduced a new Sports and Pastimes section and almost two years to the date that they had increased to eight pages, they went from two publications a week (Tuesday and Friday) to three (Tuesday, Thursday and Saturday).

The amount of football coverage in local newspapers tells a great deal about the relative importance of the game locally to the Victorian general public. The press was the only medium by which reports on football were transmitted. The public perception of the game, and of a club in particular, was as much shaped by reading newspapers as it was by first-hand experience.

This change of emphasis by the Southport Visiter was a clear recognition that sports were playing an increasingly important part of local life. As the town's premier football club and with a record season under their belts, Southport Football Club could face the future with renewed optimism.

==*==
1877/78

The earliest team photo known to be in existence for Southport Football Club is from the 1877/78 season in which George Schofield is pictured seated in the centre of the photo wearing his Lancashire County jersey. The occasion for the photo being taken is not known, but it could be in celebration of his call-up. As it stands this is the only photo known to exist of the original Southport Football Club.

Back Row (Left to Right): H.Brandon, A.Bean, H.Daly, A.Peck, G.Bromilow, G.Andrew, P.M.Hunter, A.Andrew.
Seated: J.E.Fletcher, G.Nicholson, G.F.Schofield, W.A.Gordon
In Front: F. Dixon, R.B.Hartley, H.G.Stock, C.A.Schofield

The Rugby Football Union continued to revise its rules to improve the game. The scoring mechanism was changed with results now decided by a majority of goals and tries and in some games by a complicated system including 'minors' which were essentially near misses such as touch in goal, dead balls and missed drop goals. Scoring by points had still not become the norm.

One-off annual athletic sports events had continued to attract larger crowds than regular organised football with the below letter showing the general appeal, but by November it had become clear that football was becoming an attraction not just for the more affluent.

Dear Mr Editor – I shall have much pleasure in closing my place of business at one o'clock on Saturday, provided others will do likewise. Don't you think that the mayor would request the tradesmen to close, if asked – I enclose my card, and remain yours truly. – Tradesman

(A letter to the editor of the Southport Visiter on August 16th, 1877)

Southport continued to strengthen and when they faced Manchester, the only side against whom they had failed to win the previous season, their improvement was there for all to see as they won the match by one goal to nil.

The try was entrusted to A. Andrew and though the Manchester umpire said it was a "poster", the referee decided it was a goal. Thus ended the finest match Southport has played with Manchester and the first they have won.

(Southport Visiter, 27th November 1877)

The dispute gave rise to comment on the role of umpires on the game, but more interestingly the effect that betting was beginning to have on football matches.

This most objectionable practice is becoming so very prevalent at local matches that the issues of some games are worth an enormous amount of money to some spectators. Open betting is not so much indulged in a private speculation on the part of the umpires and players, and this may account for the number of disputes which characterise the games of certain clubs in the district. If football is to become a successful winter game, betting umpires ought not to be allowed on any account, as, in consequence of the intricacy of the game, it is in their power to overturn a match at a crucial point when their side is in danger. Some clubs cannot play a single match without dispute, while others are respected in the football world for their fairness and quietness in the progress of the contest and generally the secret of these disputes is the betting nuisance. It is hoped the practice will be discontinued.

The Southport Gymnasium & Football Club

(Southport Visiter, 27th November 1877)

The Sandringham, Dr Lowe's and Mr Ross's schools all now regularly arranged football fixtures and new clubs sprang up in Southport to compete with the original club. Southport Rovers and The Walmers (Birkdale) both became prominent clubs.

From the Southport Gymnasium Cricket Club came another new club, playing a handful of football games in 1876 under the guise of Southport Gymnasium, before a name change in the summer of 1877. They were henceforth to be known as the Southport Wasps. They are recorded in the Southport Visiter on 6th October 1877, playing at the same ground near to the cemetery, against Crosby Football Club.

On Saturday last a match was played between the Southport Wasps and the Crosby Football Clubs. Both clubs mustered strong teams, and the result was a most enjoyable game. The Crosby won the toss, and kicked off in the direction of the Southport goal; some good "scrimmaging" ensued, and a "touch-down" was scored by the local team. When "half time" was called Southport has scored three "tries" and one "touchdown" to nothing. On resuming play Baldwin and Harvey made some brilliant "runs" for the "wasps", which were well backed by the play of the "forwards", and a goal kicked by Baldwin, despite the efforts of Huntingford and Anderton. Play was continued for some time, and the visitors were successful in scoring a "flukey" goal. When time was called the score stood – Southport, one "goal", five tries and two "touchdowns" to Crosby one "goal". Next Saturday the Wasps play at St Helens against the St Helens club, where, we trust, the success that has attended their first venture may be repeated"

(Southport Visiter, 9th October 1877)

Also sharing the same ground in 1877 was the Church of England Temperance Society Cricket Club who had expanded to play football too. Within a year they had changed their name to Southport Olympic.

Elsewhere in the town, in February 1878 the Atkinson Art Gallery opened on Lord Street.

==*==
1878/79

In September 1878 there was something of an 'Indian summer' feel to the weather with temperatures reaching the early 20s. With Southport Football Club, Southport Wasps and Southport Olympic all vying for local honours there were plenty of reasons to be optimistic about the future of the game.

The first meeting between Southport and Southport Wasps came at the end of the first month of the 1878/79 season. Being a match of some local interest, the attendance was good and there was little to suggest that anything out of the ordinary might interrupt the prospect of good seasons for either club.

As large areas of low pressure swept in from the Atlantic during the month of October, possibly linked to the remnants of a hurricane near to Newfoundland, the weather became unsettled. By mid-November temperatures had plummeted, with hard overnight frost, gale force winds and even snow-storms disrupting the playing calendars of many football clubs up and down the country. Across the country November was the start of a run of 15 colder than average months but in the hardy North of England, matches continued wherever possible. At the end of November Southport hosted Manchester once again. The performances of Nicholson and Gordon in the game caught the eye of those who had taken over the County selection duties and following the game they were both selected to play in the Lancashire v Northumberland and Durham game on 30th November. The game, which took place at Manchester's Whalley Range ground attracted 3-4,000 spectators, and resulted in an overwhelming victory for the home County.

As December came the weather worsened still. The consecutive months of December and January both saw sub-zero average temperatures. The next time this was to happen was the big freeze in 1963 when the sea at Southport froze over.

The winter of 1878/79 was the seventh coldest winter on record (records going back to 1659) and from 8th to 26th December there were 19 consecutive days of frost reported in parts of the country. The cold snap continued into the new year and showed little sign of abating.

1879 had an average Central England temperature of around 7 degrees. Put into context most years the Central English temperature is around 10 degrees and even in the coldest of years, 2010 being an example where there were significant periods of snow, this will only dip to around 8 or 9. There hasn't been a single year as cold since. In the aforementioned year of 1963, the average temperature was 8.5 degrees centigrade!

Faced with such inhospitable temperatures, within Southport a committee was formed by the mayor to try and alleviate poverty in the town and £1,500 was raised for clothing, basic food and coal for heat. The Southport Glacarium, the foundation stone of which had been laid back in April 1877 was opened on January 10th, hosting an ice surface 150ft x 50ft for curling and skating. It was just as cold inside, as out!

When I wrote last week there seemed some prospect of football and other kindred sports being resumed and carried on until the end of the season. But our hopes on this head received a shock when it began to freeze again with all its old force and keen-ness, and now we are just as hard frost bound as we have been for the past six or seven weeks.

(Sporting Chronicle, 24th January 1879)

The falling through of the proposed football match between Lancashire and Yorkshire at Whalley Range on Saturday last, was a great disappointment, but it was so evident on Friday that the ground would be in no condition for a Rugby game that it would have been as well to have announced the postponement instead of waiting till the last moment on Saturday morning. Of course whatever hope there had been of a favourable change in the weather was then knocked on the head, and snow and slush reigned supreme. A still greater disappointment to football players is the stop put to the North v South Association match, which was to take place at Sheffield tomorrow (Saturday).

It is very little short of two months since the frost put a stop to football, and the memory of the oldest player fails to recall a parallel case. It does not seem possible that such a state of affairs can last much longer, and there is but one grain of comfort left for the football enthusiast, and that is, his case is no worse than that of either the foxhunter, courses, or steeplechase votary, all of whom who have in like manner, and from a similar cause, found their occupation gone.

(Sporting Chronicle, 25ᵗʰ January 1879)

Fortunately, within a couple of weeks of the report in the Sporting Chronicle there was indeed a break in the weather and on 11ᵗʰ February 1879 the Southport Visiter was finally able to report another game of football when Southport Olympic faced off against their regular opponents Fairfield.

The football match between the Fairfield Wanderers and Southport Olympic (first teams) was decided on the ground of the latter on Saturday last, there being present a large number of spectators, evidently rejoicing at a re-commencement of football after the long spell of frost.

(Southport Visiter, 11ᵗʰ February 1879)

Southport Olympic were one of the fortunate teams whose playing surface benefitted from good drainage. Whilst the temperatures hadn't caused postponements for many clubs, there were still many fixtures called off as the mass thaw had turned their fields into swamps. The North v South match was hastily re-arranged for 17ᵗʰ February at the Kensington Oval, however there was no representation from Southport.

The Southport Visiter reports no further fixtures as having taken place, and we know of only one other scheduled, with Southport Wasps taking on the Rochdale Hornets on the last weekend of the season, 29ᵗʰ March. As a sign of things to come, the Wasps line up was bolstered by a number of prominent players from Southport Football Club

W.A.Gordon, described as a *'cool and safe player'* by the Athletic News, joined up with Lancashire once again in April for the Lancashire v Cheshire match which had been repeatedly postponed. Nicholson, who had been selected for the game against Northumberland in November, had not kept his place.

===*==
1879/80

On the eve of a new football season the Southport Visiter commented that the year of 1879 would long be remembered as the year without any summer. Temperatures hadn't risen over June, July or August as would have been normal, and those months were characterised by low temperatures, frequent and abundant rain and a paucity of sunshine. Only on 16 of the 92 days since the start of June had the temperature reached the average for the time of year.

Given their success only a few years earlier it is probable that had it not been for the harsh winter of 1879 Southport Football Club would have continued to thrive. The quality of the players, with many being selected for representative honours, was such that the side was well respected both locally and further afield. It is difficult to see why they should face such an insurmountable challenge in starting up again, whereas Olympic and the Wasps were still comparatively healthy. Southport Football Club however did not re-emerge after the enforced winter shut-down.

With the original Southport Football Club coming to an untimely end, it appears that Southport Wasps made the decision to drop the 'Wasps' suffix and to continue playing under the name of the once 'famous old club'. When the list of matches was published for the 1879/80 season there was no reference to their former identity, but the club's colours were now listed as blue, white, and red rather than the original black, red and amber. Moving from the previously maligned site close to the Cemetery, they occupied the Manchester Road ground just vacated, however on the published fixture card it was now officially referred to as Roe Lane. The ground had not moved, but the houses on the newly built Hartwood Road backed onto the field and blocked access from Manchester Road.

Any notion that the original side had continued can be dispelled by looking at the names of those involved in games for 'Southport Football Club' before and after the summer. Since the first game in 1872 there had been consistency with a number of prominent members being present season upon season. When 1879 began, all of those familiar faces had gone, replaced with names that had been turning out consistently for Southport Wasps. Of those to make appearances in the 1879 season at least 11 had turned out for Wasps in the preceding two seasons.

The Southport Visiter published a schedule of fixtures on 4th November which showed that three games had been due to take place in October. The Visiter however had chosen not to report on any of them, instead beginning their coverage of the season with the 1st November encounter with the Rochdale Hornets. Southport arrived late having missed the train, and with one man short. Rochdale were the victors by one goal, four tries and six touchdowns to nil.

December brought Breightmet from Bolton over to Manchester Road. The unusually bright weather had brought out a large number of spectators, but they were once again witness to another scoreless effort from Southport. On 5th Dec 1879 the Sporting Chronicle noted that *'Breightmet easily upset the newly-named Southport (late Southport Wasps), by one goal, four tries, and five touchdowns, to nil.'*

To mark a change of guard at the club, a couple of days into the new year a novelty match was arranged pitting past versus present. Once again large numbers came out and a very evenly contested game resulted in a draw, with each side scoring a goal and two tries.

A series of fixtures with Walton were followed by a meeting between what most would consider the two main Southport clubs. In aid of the Band Fund of the 13th L.R.V. Southport faced off with Olympic at the latter's Scarisbrick New Road ground. The Southport Visiter had taken to calling the Southport club 'Alexandra' owing to their links to the Alexandra Cricket Club and on 24th February they reported that the fine weather and the band in attendance had once again brought out a fine crowd. *'Despite the fact that the Alexandra had the sun and wind in their favour – their opponents were too good for them'.*

To close the season, President Lord Skelmersdale invited the club, and Rochdale Hornets in opposition, to a game at his Latham Hall Park home. His Lordship, and members of his family witnessed Rochdale race ahead, winning easily in the end by two goals, three tries and six touchdowns to Southport's nil. After the game both teams were entertained to lunch by Lord Skelmersdale with the health of His Lordship proposed by Captain J.G.Howard.

(Latham Hall and the grounds on which the last fixture was played in 1880)

33

==*==
1880/81

On 25th of August, The Athletic News newspaper reported that 'Southport Football Club will not be continuing for the coming season'. There had been no warning given, and the Southport Visiter, the town's most prominent newspaper, made no comment. Whereas Southport Olympic dutifully published fixtures as normal, Southport Football Club did not. Olympic had become a much stronger outfit, and competition too had come from Southport Hornets. Members of the team moved to their rivals, J.Eastham notably joining Southport Olympic.

Very much like it is today, Southport was a 'retirement' town. It was quite common for energetic youngsters to seek a busier or more bustling commercial town to ply their trade which meant that the resident population was naturally older. In a time where importation of players was frowned upon and 'professionalism' was still some way off, towns relied on their young folk for their sports clubs. This *may* have been a contributory factor in Southport Football Club's demise, however other clubs seemed much better at attracting those few that remained.

Little over a month earlier, in July 1880, the Scarisbrick Trustees had offered the Southport Corporation fifteen acres of land in Scarisbrick New Road, for a park. As the conditions were that an outlay of £15,000 was required the Town Council declined the gift. What might have happened to sport in the town had it been accepted? Would the parks have led to more organised sport, or would it have been supressed? One can only assume that the land in question would be the very same land that Southport Olympic and later Southport Football Club would occupy.

Part II – Switching Code

Burnett's Southport

Whilst the popularity of the rugby game was widespread, the lack of any national competition was a symptom of the troubles that would lie ahead for the sport. In contrast, the introduction of the Challenge Cup by the Football Association in 1871, although a slow burner 'up North', had begun to generate significant interest in the association game by the end of the decade.

In 1880 both Burnley FC and Preston North End FC switched from rugby to association, and it is likely that these are the two clubs referred to by Thomas Hindle, the honorary secretary of the Lancashire Football Association in the 1880 'Football Annual' when he stated:

> *Already I hear of two important Rugby clubs having left their "evil ways" and turned to play the "dribbling game" during the coming season (1880-81), and these will probably be numbered amongst our members next season. These clubs are in different districts and in neither district is the Association game played. This, I think, speaks volumes for the good work the Lancashire Association has done, since its formation, to spread the game. Since the formation of this association in 1878 it has gone on steadily increasing in numbers. At the formation, 22 members signified their willingness to join, and during the season just closed we had 40 clubs on the book, and I have every reason for knowing that we shall have a considerable increase before the coming season arrives.*

Switching codes was a common practice and association football was known to have been played in the town's private schools in the late 1870's (Strathmore House, Duneville and Bickerton House all played under association rules). The two codes shared so many similarities that any two teams that wanted to play each other might agree to play the match by association rules one day and switch to rugby for the return match later in the season. Although over the course of the 1870s and 1880s there would a growing number of rule differences, there were still so many similarities that it would take until 1892, for example, for the Rugby Football Union to *mandate* the use of an oval ball to further cement the distinction.

The census in April 1881 had revealed that the town's population stood at 42,448, a big increase in just 10 years, and in the summer, in very much the same way that the original Southport Cricket Club had faded away to be later revived (in 1875), an attempt was made to bring back the 'original' football club.

What reappeared however for the start of the 1881/82 season was a new club, with new players. The only similarity was the name, Southport Football Club.

A full set of fixtures was scheduled for the new club, and the first of these was played on a glorious sunny day at Bootle on 1st October 1881. The Liverpool Daily Post had made comment in their regular football column, which naturally covered both popular codes, about the prospects of each game for the coming season.

Taking it altogether, the winter pastime shows much vitality; and one thing noticeable is the growing favour of the Association game and the consequent decline of the Rugby game.

(Liverpool Daily Post – Monday 3rd October 1881)

The new season commenced in favourable weather conditions, resulting in large crowds up and down the country. The match between Blackburn Rovers and Bolton Wanderers was attended by 6,000 paying spectators.

With football of any description being popular in the Liverpool District, the same paper naturally covered the game. Southport were looking for a good start to the season but what transpired turned out to be anything but that. To those onlookers, hoping for the sort of form displayed by the old club, they will have been very disappointed. Even those turning out to watch local rivals Southport Olympic who also travelled into Liverpool to face Wavertree, would have come away bruised.

The Rugby game, which finds most favour in this district, had a fair day's out on Saturday, the number of contests being legion. The Bootle Wasps made a shocking example of Southport, who were very light forward, and, with one exception – Melross – rather slow behind. In five minutes from the start the Wasps had gained a couple of tries, which were increased to five before half time, but no goal was kicked. At the finish the Wasps had three goals and eight tries to their credit, whilst their adversaries did not even gain a minor point. There was time - some six or seven years ago – when Southport possessed a team equal to any in the county…Evidently just now – judging from the teams sent over on Saturday – the Southport division are anything but mighty.

(Liverpool Daily Post – Saturday 8th October 1881)

The Athletic News' report of the same game suggested one significant difference. It can't have helped however that Captain William Platt did not turn up until half-time!

Bootle Wasps sat heavily on the Southport, a new organisation which is not without a good player or two in its ranks. Schofield, who played chiefly for the Liverpool Wanderers last year, was in the ranks of the winners, and, as usual, put in good work for his side.

(Athletic News, 5th October 1881)

The Southport Visiter were less critical of their side, commenting that although the team that travelled was light, Bootle were nevertheless a strong side.

SOUTHPORT v BOOTLE WASPS – The opening match of the Southport club was played on Saturday, when a light team journeyed to Bootle, only to suffer defeat at the hands of an exceptionally strong and heavy set of opponents. Another thing that contributed in a great measure to defeat was the fact that only fourteen men mustered during the first half. Play commenced by the visitors kicking off, but the leather was quickly returned, and in a short space of time the result was a try recorded for Bootle. The Southportonians, who, after half-time, had the services of the captain (W.Platt), were still unable to improve matters, and when time was called had put up with a severe defeat. For the visitors, Schofield played remarkably well, and several times carried the applause of the spectators by his fine running. Williams, Forsyth, Garrett, and Henstock also played well for the home club; while Ross, Melross, Jackson, and Sykes played well for the losers, the two former especially making good runs in their attempts to break through. The following were the teams: Southport: T.B.Burnett, full back; A.Ross, J.Melross, and S.Platt, three-quarter; J.B.Richardson, Gaskell, half; W.Platt (Capt.), W.H.Gregory, F.Jackson, F.Hockly, Nelson, J.Sykes, J.R.Topliss, J.Hollis, and W.Hatch, forwards.

The fixture scheduled to take place the following week at Liverpool Old Boys did not happen. One can only speculate as to the reasons, but the evidence is leaning towards an issue with the availability of the Liverpool side rather than that of Southport. What happened instead is perhaps one of the most significant events in the history of sport in Southport.

Thomas Blundell Burnett, named as full back in the side's first game against Bootle Wasps, took the opportunity presented to him by a free weekend to take a team to Burscough for a game of association football. The reports in both the Southport Visiter and Ormskirk Advertiser state it to have resulted in a 3-1 defeat and that *'the names of Southport were not given'* despite listing the Burscough line-up.

Arguments could be made, both for and against, this once forgotten game now being given recognition as the first association game to be played by Southport Football Club. The Southport Visiter refers to the game as being between *'the Burscough club and Mr T.B.Burnett's team'*, but the Ormskirk Advertiser states *'T.B.Burnett's Southport'*. Both state *'the names of Southport were not given'*. The naming of Burnett could lead one to infer that this wasn't an official Southport fixture and that it was a scratch XI put out as an alternative to doing nothing on an afternoon where they had planned to play, but then the Advertiser's record of *'Burnett's Southport'* and *'the names of Southport'* could equally mean the Southport side being captained by Burnett and being representative of the club. Either way, Burnett was clearly favouring the association game and the reason for his choice and the decision to switch will become clearer as you read on.

Thomas Burnett already had plenty of leadership experience by the time he had settled back into Southport upon his return from Wales in 1880. The idea of a selection committee at a football club was still some time off, as was the concept of a Manager as far as we understand it today, and therefore from selecting the team and organising a venue and kick off time, to agreeing a set of rules to play, the captain's role was wide, varied and crucial. Standard practice was that the players involved would generally work out a strategy and tactics for themselves on the pitch, under the direction of the captain. Only the honorary secretary would have a role to rival the importance of the captain, and this was a role requiring a degree of organisation unprecedented for a recreational activity. There is no doubt the organisation of this fixture was down to Burnett.

The rugby fixture one week later against Wavertree on 12th October was often referred to in documented club histories as the final rugby game played by the 'original club' prior to new evidence coming to light more recently. The Athletic News commented that Wavertree were *'weakly represented'* but they still managed to easily overcome the visiting Southport side.

The new Southport Football Club did not make it past the end of the first month, but the Wavertree fixture wasn't their last. Southport played their final rugby game against Bootle on 29th October, fielding two men short and losing by one goal, eight tries and eleven minor points. The Liverpool Daily Post commented that the side was *'weak in numbers, as in talent'.*

The line-up against Bootle was: W.Platt(back); A.J. Ross, H.M Smith, Hodson (¾ backs); Richardson, Gregson (½ backs); S.Platt, Buggins, J.G. Howard, F. Jackson, Hall, T.B. Burnett, P.Edwards (Forwards)

T.R.Barrow and William Rimmer had decided that there was no future in the rugby game at Southport Football Club and had joined Southport Olympic for the visit of Rochdale Hornets instead.

Curiously, there had been no fixture planned against either of the town's other prominent clubs, Southport Hornets or Southport Olympic. One can only speculate that this was because they hadn't considered themselves to be worthy competition.

On 12th November 1881, Southport Football Club made the permanent switch to the dribbling game and a new chapter began for the club.

In the story of Southport Football Club therefore, Thomas Blundell Burnett's role is very significant. He was the instigator of the switch, he was the secretary of the new club, and he was also the captain. He was the pioneer of association football in Southport, of that there is absolutely no doubt. That his role in the history of the sport in this town has been almost forgotten for so long is a shame, but it perhaps says a lot about the man, in that he was quietly efficient, choosing not to boast or brag, but instead to 'get on with it' and to take on any role that would help the club flourish.

Burnett's father Alexander had been a bookkeeper but had passed away when Thomas was just nine years old. Although born in Liverpool, where his father had also originated, he had been christened at Christ Church on Lord Street in Southport and was living with his mother Ellen (nee Blundell) at their home on 99 Railway Street, where at 18 he had been an apprentice coal merchant. It says much for his mother's influence in the absence of a father during his formative years that he adopted her maiden name into his own surname.

Before moving to Ruabon near Wrexham in 1876, he had been involved with Southport Cricket Club and had been noted as a very capable player. Upon his move at the age of 24 he was to captain Wynnstay Cricket Club. His most notable performance as a bowler was a seven wicket haul against Wrexham in June 1876, but he was equally as adept with the bat. He also became a prominent member of their committee, even holding the chair on occasion, saying much of his organisation skills.

In the 1870s the Welsh economy was based around the coal industry almost exclusively. It was from these coal-mining communities that sport in Wales grew. Whilst rugby was the major game of choice for most in Britain, one of the most significant developments from Burnett's short spell in Wales was that he was to turn out for Ruabon for games of association football. To say, however, that he just played would be to under-sell his time with the Ruabon club. He was in fact appointed captain for 1876 and 1877.

Ruabon was a town of industry with a large colliery run by the New British Iron Company. Whilst we do not know for sure, as he listed his previous occupation on the census as Coal Merchant, it is unlikely that Burnett moved to a small village in Wales for anything other than a new job.

On the sporting front, clearly excelling at cricket having also represented Denbighshire, and now also association football, Burnett took part in representative games for North Wales against the mighty Sheffield club. The Wrexham and Denbighshire advertiser noted that *'praise should not be omitted for Burnett, the goalkeeper'.*

The fact that teams could be got together to go such long distances to play matches was in itself sufficient evidence of the popularity of our national winter pastime.

(Wrexham and Denbighshire Advertiser, 26th January 1878)

Despite being an Englishman (born in Liverpool), he was capped once for Wales, in their second ever international against Scotland. These were the days when birth qualification hadn't yet become the rule and the accomplished cricketer, good with his hands, although principally a full-back, volunteered to go in goal. The Wrexham and Denbigh advertiser made the following comment on his performance:

The seemingly weak point in the home team was the goal-keeping; but it must be remembered that that position is a most unenviable one, and the utmost allowance ought to be extended to anyone having the nerve to undertake the guarding of goal in a great match such as that witnessed on Monday.

(Wrexham and Denbighshire Advertiser, 10th March 1877)

Moving back to Southport in the summer of 1880, he became involved with the new Southport Football Club upon its formation in 1881.

When the club turned up with two players short to face Bootle on October 29th, 1881, it would be the last game that the club would play under the handling rules. The next fixture Southport Football Club would play would be on Saturday 12th November, and it would be under association rules against Bootle 'second'.

An Association Club has been started at Southport, and to-day they play their first match, Bootle second team undertaking to put them through their facings.

(Liverpool Daily Post – Saturday 12th November 1881)

A football match, under Association rules, will be played this day, Saturday, between the Southport and Bootle teams. As this is the first match under these rules ever played in Southport it will be an interesting and novel exhibition. Kick off at half-past three.

(Southport Visiter – Saturday 12th November 1881)

The fact that the Liverpool Daily Post and the Southport Visiter were both able to report that the match was intended to go ahead under association rules is evidence enough that it was planned, and that it hadn't been a spur of the moment decision. Finding enough players available on any given Saturday was a common difficulty and there are plenty of examples of teams turning with one or two short due to transport issues, or due to the vagaries of their employment. For example, it was common for clerks to be asked to work Saturdays at short notice.

Whereas Southport Olympic were seemingly able to field two teams most weekends, Southport Football Club could barely scrape together a single XV. This was no ill-thought-out change. Burnett's 'trial' match at the start of October had showed him that were was enough appetite amongst his friends and colleagues to try out the dribbling game but the decision to organise a club fixture had its roots much further back than that.

If we step back four years to 1877 and look at who else was in Ruabon at the same time as Thomas Burnett, we discover a significant name, and a clue to another reason why this may have taken place. There we find the name Robert Edward Lythgoe as the Welsh umpire for Burnett's first appearance for North Wales.

In March 1864 Lythgoe had entered the service of the Shropshire Union Railways and Canal Company and progressed to become Chief Forwarding Clerk where he was placed in charge of all traffic received from Liverpool to be distributed over the whole of the canal system. In 1875 he was transferred as agent at Pontcyslte, near Ruabon, with charge of the Chirk and Llangollen sub agencies. It was there that he became a prominent member of the Ruabon Druids club, and as umpire for the North Wales v Sheffield match he met Thomas Burnett. Lythgoe, although a native of Chester, was, like Burnett, also involved with the early Welsh internationals.

In 1880, at around the same time that Burnett moved back to Southport, Robert Lythgoe moved from Wales to the outskirts of Liverpool to take up the position of chief clerk at Liverpool. Once there he set about the task of forming his own football club. Instead, he was able to persuade Bootle St. John's to become more ambitious and, dropping the 'St John's' suffix, Bootle FC became one of the two significant clubs in the Liverpool district (Everton being the other).

Having played Bootle under rugby rules on the last weekend in October, and having been unable to field a full side, it can't be coincidence that the final rugby side containing Thomas Blundell Burnett met the side organised in chief by Robert Lythgoe and two weeks later returned to play under association rules. The connection between the two gentlemen is the most likely explanation for Burnett to decide to change codes and it is supposed that Lythgoe persuaded him by offering a fixture with his second XI to help get them going. After all, finding 11 men for a Saturday is a lot simpler a challenge than finding 15 and if they were struggling less than a month into the new season, this did not bode well for the remainder.

Burnett presumably asked his team-mates if they were willing to switch and most, but not all, agreed. In fact, only one player had featured in all three games and chose not to play the association game. A.J.Ross instead threw his lot in with Southport Olympic. After the first two games had taken place, perhaps sensing the writing on the wall, T.R. Barrow and William Rimmer had already made the decision to switch across to Olympic. They both featured against Rochdale Hornets on 29th October, therefore missing the final match against Bootle. Perhaps, therefore, these were the two missing men!

There can be no doubt about it. The Association game in Lancashire is becoming more popular every day, and what is more, the clubs in the county palatine are becoming greater experts at the business; and instead of one or two organisations sweeping the board as it were, there are many clubs now pretty nearly all of a level as regards skill and ability in the game.

(Athletic News, 5th October 1881)

The Southport team that took to the field under association rules on 12th November was:

S.Platt (Goal),

B.Pidduck, J.G. Howard (Backs),

P.Edwards, F. Jackson, T.B. Burnett (Capt.) (Halves),

J.R.Topliss, F.Holden (Rights) W.Platt (Centre) J.Melross, J.Sykes (Lefts).

It was a fine day, weather-wise, although the rain which had fallen overnight had made the ground swamp-like in places. The Southport Visiter commented *'that the team will no doubt render a good account of themselves when they get over the difficulty of hands off and forget the rugby rules'*. The comment makes sense when the context is added as to the identities of the first eleven men, our 'originals' or 'founding fathers'. When the club switched codes they hadn't gone out to find 11 new capable footballers, most of those who took to the field were former rugby players. In fact, only F.Holden hadn't turned out under rugby rules in one of the three rugby fixtures played.

Southport v Bootle (2ⁿᵈ) (Association)

This match was played on Saturday last on the home ground, Scarisbrick New Road, in the presence of a fair number of spectators, and after a well contested game resulted in a draw, each side scoring one goal. Bootle, with the wind at their backs, soon made a rush at the home goal, and after three minutes play scored out of a bully. The ball being kicked off Melross made a good run on the left but with no result the ball going behind. Up to half-time the visitors had several corner kicks and put the ball through once but the goal was disallowed, being offside.

On changing ends and with the wind in their favour the home team who were warming to their work and forgetting the Rugby rules, began to have the best of the game and after some good play by Melross and Jackson, the latter shot a capital goal. The Bootle men nettled at this reverse, pulled themselves together and after some capital runs had several corner kicks but without success. The home team again began to have the best of the play, and after a good run and middle by Melross, Platt made a successful shot, which however was disallowed on a plea of offside. Nothing further resulted up to the call of time.

For the home team, Melross, Howard, Edwards and Platt played best and for Bootle, Kennedy, Bradly and Tetley were most conspicuous. This being the first full match under association rules which the Southportonians have played they must be congratulated on the form shown, and when they get over the difficulty of keeping "hands off", they will no doubt render a good account of themselves. They had to pay the penalty for this on Saturday, the visitors securing a great number of free kicks.

(Southport Visiter — 15ᵗʰ November 1881)

The following week the 'new' Southport association club made a trip to Burscough. This too appeared to be Burnett using his contacts, Burscough being the opposition in October when he organised an XI to cover for an otherwise blank weekend. As with his first visit, his new club lost - this time by *'one goal and one disputed goal to nil'* at Burscough.

BURSCOUGH V SOUTHPORT — These Association teams met at Burscough on Saturday last. The home team winning the toss, took choice and goals. Carruthers kicked off for the visiters, and the Burscough forwards taking the ball up, Woodstock put it through the posts a few minutes after the commencement. Nothing more was scored before half-time, although the visitors were hard pressed, and some good shots were prevented from scoring by the excellent goal keeping of Burnett. On change of ends the play on both sides became very fast, Coleman, Woodstock, Stretch, and Thorougood doing good work for the home team, and Melross making some fine runs for the visitors, which were prevented from taking effect chiefly by the excellent play of Stevens at back. The score remained unaltered except a splendid shot by Coleman, which was disputed by the visitors as off side, and a pleasant game ended in favour of Burscough by one goal and one disputed to nil.

(Southport Visiter, 22ⁿᵈ November 1881)

Joining the side for the trip to Burscough was J.Bullock, who had been turning out regularly for Southport Olympic.

In an era when gentlemen players (supposedly) never committed a deliberate foul, the game was effectively run by the captains of the two teams. A referee (a timekeeper really) had only been added to the touchline in 1871 as someone to whom the two captains could appeal if they could not agree.

The term 'one disputed goal' therefore is a product of the game at that time. When the majority of playing fields were not yet marked with lines, with there being no goal-nets and no on-field referee there were often occasions where events were disputed between the two teams and no agreement could be reached. With both sides nominating an umpire to settle disputes in this case it appears that neither the referee, captains nor umpires were clear and therefore the only course of action was to agree that Southport officially lost 1-0.

In 1872 the FA had published an updated set of laws to make it clear that *'a goal shall be won when the ball passes between the goal posts under the tape, not being thrown, knocked on, or carried.'* The new rules clearly distinguished between goalkeepers and other players: *'A player shall not throw the ball nor pass it to another except in the case of the goalkeeper, who shall be allowed to use his hands for the protection of his goal... No player shall carry or knock on the ball; nor shall any player handle the ball under any pretence whatever.'*

Law 8 of the new association rules stated for example that *"The goalkeeper may, within his own half of the field of play, use his hands, but shall not carry the ball."* This invariably led to examples of a goalkeeper bouncing the ball up to the half-way line before launching an attack with a long kick or a good throw, which was perfectly within the letter of the law, though few goalkeepers risked doing it for fear of either leaving their goal unattended or being steam-rollered by an opposing centre-forward.

As the game became more competitive, two umpires, one appointed by each team, replaced the captains' on field adjudication and in 1881 the FA stated that if a player was *"guilty of ungentlemanly behaviour the referee could rule offending players out of play and order them off the ground."*

In their third encounter they faced a team called Blackburn Law who were a noted XI in those days. The Blackburn club displayed superior skill and thrashed Southport 7-0.

BLACKBURN LAW v SOUTHPORT — On the ground of the latter at Southport. Shortly after play commenced repeated shots were made at goal by the visitors, and from their general all round play it could at once be seen that they had the best of the game, as at half-time they had succeeded in scoring five goals in a neat manner to their opponents' nil.
On change of ends the game became of a more even character, and though the home team made repeated runs, they were finally stopped but the determined back of the visitors. Ultimately, at the call of time, the visitors were declared victors by seven goals to nil.

(Blackburn Standard — Saturday 3rd December 1881)

SOUTHPORT v BLACKBURN LAW — *This association match was played on the ground of the former in Scarisbrick New-road, and resulted in an out-and-out victory for the visitors. Immediately after the kick-off the superior skill of the latter in the game was soon manifest, but considering that the "locals" have only played about four games under these rules their display was very creditable but they have not yet got into the way of playing together and keeping "hands off" the ball. The strength of their opponents was clearly manifest from the start, and at the conclusion of the game they were easily defeated, after one of the most friendly matches witnessed in this town. The Southport men played very well considering, especially Parks, who appeared as a "sub". For the winners, Mr Roylance[sic] (the captain) was all there and was well backed up by his comrades, especially the two gentlemen whose names were not given.*

(Southport Visiter, 1ˢᵗ December 1881)

When Preston North End had switched to the dribbling code the previous season, they had been beaten 6-0 by Turton and 16-0 by Blackburn Rovers so large reverses were fairly common for new sides. Disregarding the result, the game was more notable for it being the first time that we come across a man named Ralph Rylance, a solicitor's clerk from Blackburn. The name was to become synonymous with football in Southport as he was to be erroneously credited with much of the pioneering work undertaken by Burnett. It has become a popular misconception in the years that have followed that Rylance was *responsible* for the initial switch in codes and this was a view even reinforced by his own son, Walter, at Southport Football Club's 50th anniversary celebrations in 1931 where he presented a red flag to the club in memory of his father one of the 'original founders' of the club.

The Lancashire Daily Post, Wednesday, August 12, 1931

Less than a month later when Southport invited Burscough back to Scarisbrick New Road, Rylance was lining up for Southport.

46

The Southport and Burscough clubs (Association) played their return match on the ground of the former on Saturday before a considerable number of spectators, amongst them who were several ladies. S.Platt kicked off for the home team against a strong wind; the ball was quickly returned and kept in the centre of the ground, the play being very equal, several good runs being made by the forwards of both teams, Coleman and Smith being most conspicuous. Melross now got possession and ran the ball up on the left wing; the attempt at goal, however, was unsuccessful, the visitors' backs being outside. Baxter took the throw in and placed the ball in the mouth of the Burscough goal, when it went through off one of their own backs. First blood for Southport fifteen minutes from the commencement. Encouraged by this success, the Southportonians began to press the visitors, and good runs were made and several corner kicks were secured; the strong wind, however, prevented any score. Coleman next by a dodgy run took the leather to the home goal and made a good shot but the "reverend" was equal to the occasion, and cleared his charge by fine style. Smith and Platt in the centre were next to the fore, and passing well to the wing, Burnett ran the sphere into the corner and screwed in front of the Burscough goal, and after a slight scrimmage, Bullock administered the final touch, thus securing goal number two for the home team. Up to half-time no other score was made by either side, the ball travelling from one end to the other, play being very fast. On changing ends, and with the wind at their backs, the supporters of the home team looked rather jubilant over the rosy chances of securing more goals, but were doomed to disappointment, the really splendid goal keeping of Reynolds preventing any further score. The visitors, notwithstanding the state of the game, stuck well to their work, some good runs being made by Thorogood, Baldwin, and Coleman. From a long shot by the latter players the Southport colours were lowered for the first time. Although all the home team were confident the ball had actually gone over instead of under the tape, the umpire, however, allowed the score. The Southport men, nettled by the reverse, played up more determingly, and for the rest of the game kept up a continual attack on the Burscough citadel, but were very wild in their shooting, which in a great measure is accounted for by them having to run across a lot of ice near the goal. Southport, when time was called, were left winners by two goals to one. For the Burscough team Reynolds, Coleman, and Thorogood were most conspicuous. The winners all worked hard, and it would be invidious to single out anyone in particular, although if anything Smith played the best. Teams: Southport, backs, E.Ramsbottom, A.Irving, C.R.Rylance, and H.Baxter; forwards, J.Melross, J.Bullock, W.Platt, H.A.Smith, J.R.Topliss, T.B.Burnett (Capt.) Goal: Rev. James Hollis.

(Southport Visiter 27th December 1881)

Burnett returned to the position at which he made his only international appearance, in goal. Although Squire Platt had featured in the first game as an association club, he did not make himself available for any other fixtures to our knowledge in this first season, although he would make the position his own in subsequent years. Making his debut for Southport, alongside the aforementioned Ralph Rylance, was Edwin Ramsbottom, a man who would go on to become the first secretary of Southport Central in 1888, seven years later.

Whilst the inclusion of an experienced association player like Rylance clearly had some impact, at this stage his loyalties were still split and he had not yet committed himself to Southport, choosing to continue to turn out for Blackburn Law. He did however note in his diary entry of 31st December 1881 that he had made a subscription payment to the club.

With the first win under their belts on Christmas Eve, Southport turned over the Tradesmen of Southport in another festive fixture by seven goals to nil. Rylance was on the scoresheet for the first time, but he was overshadowed by Melross and Burnett who both netted twice. Smith and Platt notched one each to round off the scoring. Absent for the short trip to Croston which ended in a 2-4 reverse, also over the Christmas period, Rylance returned for the visit of Liverpool Excelsior on 7th January and again found himself on the scoresheet in another 7-0 win. Melross and Burnett however both notched another two each, as did Colman.

With impressive victories to report on, the prominent Sports Newspaper the Athletic News announced the formation of a new club a few days later.

An Association football club has been started in Southport under the title of the "Southport Football Club," and, from what I hear, the game is likely to become popular there.

(Athletic News, Wednesday 11th January 1882)

Performances were improving rapidly, and Tranmere Rovers were beaten twice, both times 3-0.

Tranmere Rovers v Southport (Association) - The return match between the above clubs took place at Southport on Saturday, and after a well contested game the Southport repeated their previous victory by scoring three goals (one disputed) to none. Teams – Southport: Goal, E.H Hollis; backs, J.B. Richardson, W.Kay, R.L.Rylance and B.Pidduck; forwards, J.Melross, H.A. Smith, A. Briggs, J.T. Woodhead, JH Stone and T.B. Burnett (Capt.). Tranmere Rovers: Goal, C.Rogers; backs, McClean, R. Conway, J. Routledge, and T. Fisher; forwards, W.H. Routledge, J.Bird (Capt.), Roscoe, Edwards, W. Roberts, and Davies.

(Liverpool Mercury – 24th January 1882)

Rylance turned out for his old club, as captain, at the end of January in the reverse fixture in Blackburn and the result was little better for Southport. Although the visitors lasted half an hour without conceding, they went in one goal down at the break. Unfortunately, five goals followed in the second half and all without reply. The Blackburn Standard however were very complimentary.

The Southportonians played a very fast game, but could not manage to score …. Melross, Smith, Ellis, and Richardson played very fast for the Southport team, and considering they have up to this season played Rugby rules, bid well to make good Associationists. At the termination of a very pleasant game the home team were declared victors by six goals to nil.

(Blackburn Standard, 4th February 1882)

With the exception of 'Law', the majority of Southport's opponents in the early years hailed from the Liverpool district. Travel needed careful coordination and if the opponent was too far away this could present significant problems. It was not uncommon for games to be reduced in length due to fading daylight and the late arrival of the opposition. These challenges made it even more difficult to establish football as a successful spectator sport.

Whilst the Athletic News had noticed the fledgling club, comparatively little interest was shown within Southport itself. The Southport Visiter's reporting of football was hit and miss, a reflection of the attitude of most towards the sport in general, rather than a specific reaction from the town's oldest newspaper. Whilst some fixtures were given prominence in a 'Football' column, others were either relegated to a small paragraph buried in the 'Local News' column or were not reported at all.

C.B. Fry an Oxford Blue commented on both codes in the popular 'Badminton Magazine' a little later, in 1895:

> *A more interesting question than that of the respective dangers of Rugby and Association is that of their relative merits as games. It is a significant fact that they do not thrive well side by side. Except in very large towns, the two games do not flourish together. Even at Universities, the interest in 'Soccer' is nearly swamped by that in 'Rugger'. If the two teams are playing simultaneously in the parks at Oxford, some thousands watch the one game, while two men, five boys, and a nursemaid lend the countenance to the other.*

Whilst Southport had its problems, they were not unique.

At the start of May the new club held its first Annual General Meeting at Scarisbrick New Road. As an enticement for new members, the meeting was arranged as the official opening of lawn tennis courts which had been laid out by the club. The local news column in the Visiter appealed for anyone *'desirous of joining the society'* to send their names and particulars to Thomas Burnett at the Arlington Chambers on Lord Street.

Elsewhere in town, in March, George Augustus Coombe Esq, the man behind the formation of the original club, adopted a change of name by deed poll to 'Pilkington', at the request of his father-in-law, James Pilkington, the former MP for Blackburn.

Competition

The Southport Athletic Society had moved to a new ground on Sussex Road for their 13th annual athletic sports meeting in June 1882. The large grandstand erected for the event could safely house 2,000 spectators and stood 95 feet in length. The Society began to advertise almost immediately that they would be prepared to receive proposals from secretaries of cricket, lawn tennis, football, and other clubs, for the use of the ground, which was described as within easy distance of the town and properly enclosed.

Whereas the 1881/82 season had been made up of friendlies between effectively unaffiliated teams, encouraged by the success of their first season, Southport affiliated to both the Lancashire and English Football Associations. In 1872 there had been just 61 members of the Football Association, but ten years later this number had risen to 170.

At the start of the new season the Courier newspaper in Liverpool commented that the association game was beginning to overtake rugby in terms of popularity in the City. The paper also discussed the idea of a confederation of the district's 20 or so clubs and a special committee of club secretaries had gathered in May with a clear goal to organise it. The outcome of these discussions was the formation of the Liverpool & District Football Association and the creation of its own competitions, giving clubs in the district more chance of local success than they could attain in the wider Lancashire or Football Association competitions. The secretary of this new organisation was Bootle's Robert Lythgoe, and given his friendship with Southport's Thomas Burnett it is no surprise that Southport were present at these discussions and became founder members alongside 14 others.

Competitive football was to come to Southport for the first time.

Seeking to emulate the success of the Athletic Society sports events, the club arranged their own athletic sports event in August with the intention that it too would become an annual tradition. Athletic sports events were very popular and attracted supporters from far and wide.

The first annual meeting in connection with the club took place on Saturday, on the ground, Scarisbrick New-road. There was a fairly good attendance, and the meeting was throughout of the

51

most enjoyable character, much interest being evinced in the exhibition football match (Association rules) played at the conclusion of the sports, between picked members of the team. The gathering was organised and carried out by members of the club, and great praise is due to the following gentlemen, who officiated on Saturday:- Judges: Messrs. W.J.Conell, W.Dinwoodie, and T.Fairbrother; starter, Mr J.S.Watson; and timekeeper, Mr C.D.Allen. The course was not of the best description for fast times, but it is intended before the next gathering to make a capital grass course, and keep it in good order. The duties of hon. Sec. devolved upon Mr. Thomas B. Burnett, and a most courteous secretary did he prove. The races throughout were keenly contested, and spectators had no small difficulty in "spotting" the winners.

(Southport Visiter, 8ᵗʰ August 1882)

The events were principally as follows: Half mile bicycle race, 220 yards flat race, half mile tricycle race and one mile bicycle race. There was plenty of interest for the early Southport supporters, with quite a few players taking part in the events. Most notably, J.Sykes and W.Platt from the football club placed first and second respectively in the sprint (220 yards flat race). To round off the day, Burnett had seen the opportunity, not just to swell the club coffers through charging admission, but to use the event as a marketing opportunity by staging an exhibition football match with the two teams both picked from members of the club.

The club had secured the old Southport Olympic ground at Scarisbrick New Road and arranged some attractive fixtures for the season.

Commencing with the dribbling game, I am glad to notice the introduction of the Association rules into the majority of the schools in this neighbourhood, and I cannot see any reason why some of them should not, by assiduous practice aspire to county form. The premier club of this district has, I believe, joined both the Lancashire and English Associations, and entered the competitions for the magnificent challenge cups offered by those organisations, and I would strongly impress on other local clubs the advisability of joining one or both associations. The Southport have been fortunate in securing the ground lately belonging to Olympic F.C., situated in Scarisbrick New-road, and have arranged some exceedingly good matches for the ensuing season, home, and home (sic) games having been already entered into with the Bootle, Everton, Wirral, Preston, Liverpool, Birkenhead, Bolton Olympic, and other well-known exponents of the dribbling game. They ought to pull off the majority of their engagements if the members will only go in more for combined play and passing, and indulge in a little less kicking and selfish play. I, however, regret to hear that they will not be enabled to count on the invaluable support of Mr A.Irving as promising a back-player as any in the county, who owing to uncontrollable circumstances, will be obliged to sever his connection with the club at the beginning of the season. There will not be many alterations in last year's team, the only notable one being that Mr T.B.Burnett goes back in Mr. Irving's place – a position which could not be better filled, as he is sure to make his judicious and safe kicking felt in that direction; his confrere has not yet been decided on. The forward team, as at present arranged, will be almost the same as last year's, with the exception of the introduction of the late prominent member of a local club, who has decided this season to cast his lot with Southport. From a general point of view I think the members of the S.A.F.C. have every reason to be satisfied with the position of the club, and every hope and prospect of a successful season.

FORWARD

(Southport Visiter, 19ᵗʰ August 1882)

As no map was created at the time, the exact location of the 'old Olympic ground' is open to interpretation. The 'Football Field' in the Scarisbrick New Road area that is so visible on the 1894 Ordnance Survey map (the first official map produced after 1881) is the location that Olympic had moved *to* and not the ground they had moved *from*. However, from descriptions in match reports we have been able to deduce that it was in fact on a large plot of land opposite the entrance to Chambers Road, roughly where Westmoreland Road runs today, with space enough for multiple pitches. On one side of the field were the back gardens of the few houses that existed on Ash Street. The proximity of those gardens to the football field is known only from a diary entry made by Ralph Rylance in 1883 when he recorded that the ball had been kicked into a neighbouring back garden, commenting that the resident had made a grab for the ball and headed for cover. He was just entering the house when a member of the team grabbed him and rescued the ball in the nick of time. Had he not done so the game would have had to be abandoned for that was the only ball the club had. Access to the field itself was primarily gained from Scarisbrick New Road, hence its reference as the name of the ground rather than Ash Street, but as the field was not fully enclosed it was not entirely possible to prevent access from elsewhere. This is possibly one of the reasons that Olympic had chosen to move.

Local historian David Walshe has created a map of the area as it would have looked in the early years of the club. Using the 1881 census and the town directories that were published each year, he has been able to ascertain which properties existed, and which were occupied in each of the club's early years. Those houses and gardens that existed in 1881 are indicated as such on his map, and on neighbouring properties are indicated their subsequent years of build. 'U' denotes a property as existing but being unoccupied. The first house on the playing fields side of Ash Street (1881), was named Derwent House on the 1890 town plan and is still there today. The next-door property, built a year later and named Lynwood on the town plan, also still stands, as do houses two, four and six on the opposite side of the road.

To further aid in context, Trap Lane would later be renamed Southbank Road and the dotted line indicates the rough path of Westmoreland Road which had not yet been built but is present by the time the earliest Ordnance Survey map was published in 1894, having been surveyed in 1889/90.

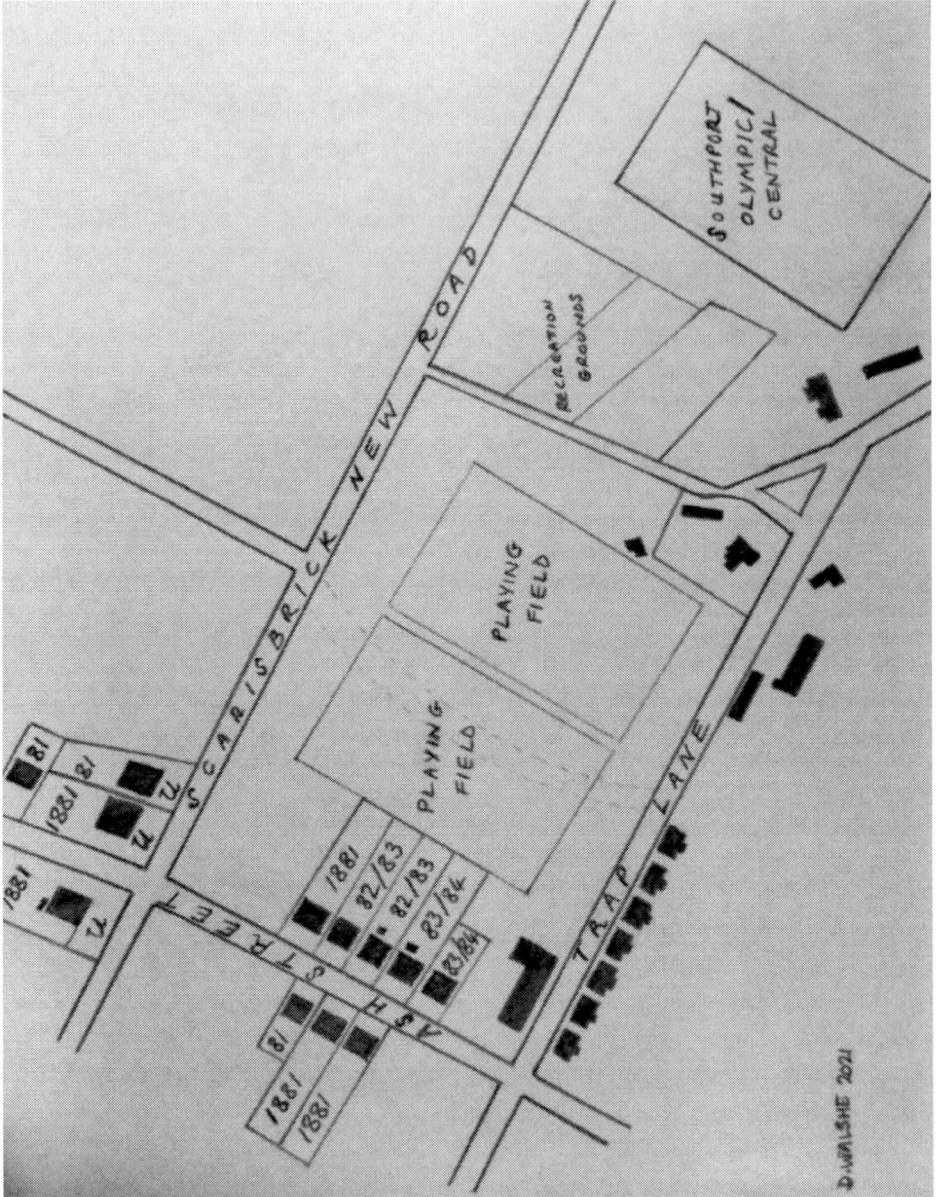

(Map created by David Walshe)

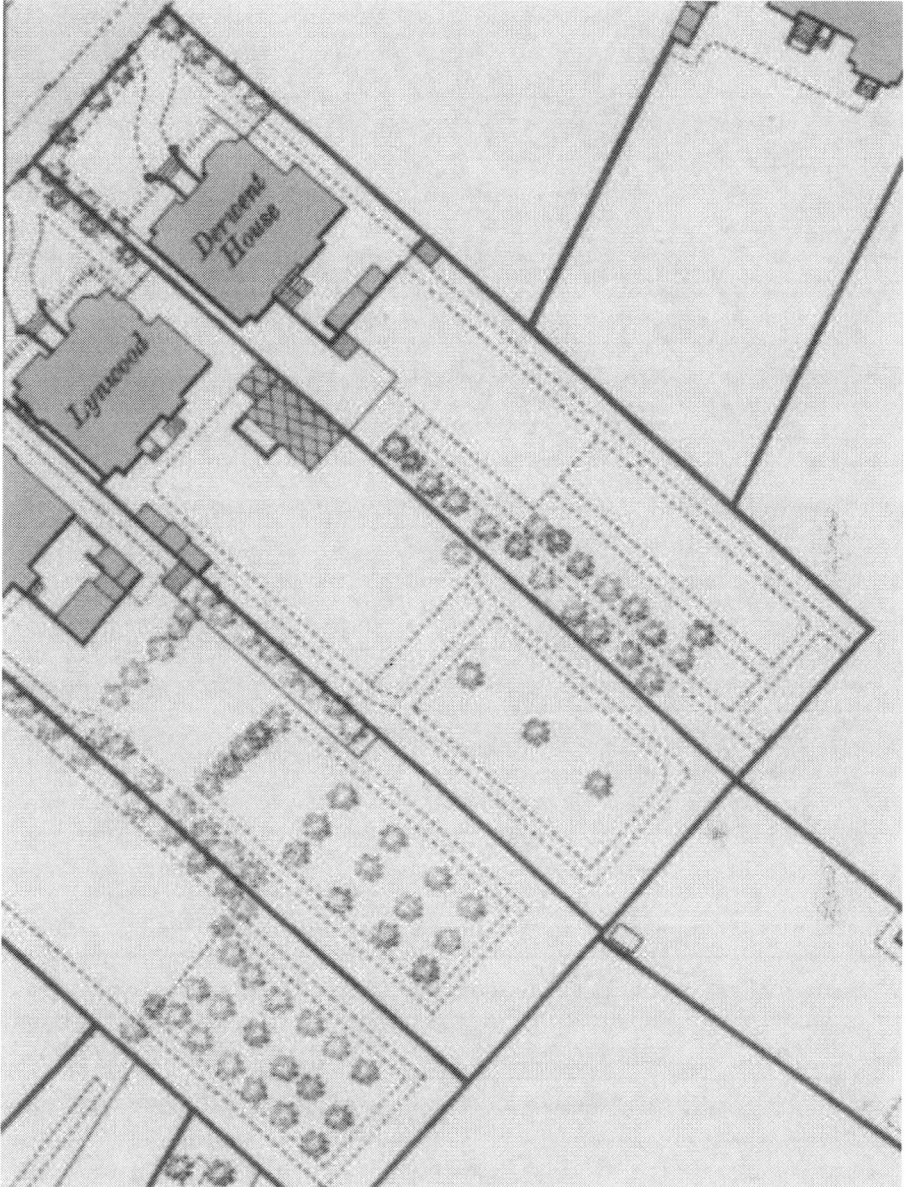

(Derwent House as shown on the Town Plan published in 1890, reproduced with the kind permission of the National Library of Scotland.)

The new football season (1882/83) was preceded by an exhibition match between two of the famous Blackburn clubs – the Rovers and Witton – (although originally arranged as Blackburn Rovers v Blackburn Olympic before Olympic withdrew) as part of the first 'Autumn Festival' of the Athletic Society which took place on August 26th. Adverts were placed in the Visiter to state that *'The Southport Athletic Society are prepared to let large spaces for advertising on their Hoarding, within the Enclosure, on the occasion of their Autumn Festival and Grand Football Match'*. It was a supplementary meeting, established *'with the object of raising funds to pay the cost of enclosing the new ground and laying it out'*. Whilst those objects were not fully met, the advertised football match created some interest. Rovers won by five goals to three and both clubs lived up to their famous names by putting on quite a show. The pitch laid out however was *'too small to give a proper exhibition of the game, and in addition to this, the ground was too lumpy'* (Southport Visiter, 29th August 1882). In goal for Blackburn that day was Herbie Arthur, who would later go on to represent Southport Central.

The season opened for Southport with a handsome 4-0 win over Liverpool Rovers at Scarisbrick New Road at the end of September.

> *This the first Association match of the season in Southport, was played in Scarisbrick New-road on Saturday. The ground was in splendid order, and some fast play was witnessed. The Rovers were over matched, being defeated by four goals to nil, the tackling and kicking of the Southport backs preventing any formidable attack. For the winners, the forwards worked well together, and at times passed cleverly, seeing that this was the first time they had played together. The visiting team turned up short but found a very able substitute in the "Major" from Mobberley. The goals were scored by Briggs, Art Dalby, and J. Coleman (2).*

> *(Southport Visiter, 26th September 1882)*

To regularly participate in football at this time players would need to have had a reasonable income to support what could be described as something of an expensive hobby. We are still several years away from any notion of professionalism even being considered – it wasn't to be legalised for another three years, and it would be a further three after that until it would be a feature in Southport. Not only would they have needed a reasonable income to pay for their travel expenses, but they would also need to have employment that would allow them to have Saturday afternoons off. To effectively raise and manage a team, communication was essential therefore players had to either live near each other, be work colleagues, or know each other through other social organisations. When it came to adding new players to the club, therefore, it was inevitable that more players would switch to association from the town's remaining rugby clubs. A player from the Southport Hornets Rugby Club wrote to the Southport Visiter at the end of August to complain that 'Forward', the anonymous critic who had written the letter of 19th August, had not given his club any mention.

> *…He regrets that the Association Club will not have the invaluable support of Mr A.Irving during the coming season, as he will be "obliged to sever his connection with the club at the beginning of the season." The fact is, Mr. Irving was elected captain of the Southport Hornets – a young club, but one which has some promising players – at their election of officers last May; he*

however, since that time, has decided to go to Australia, and will consequently be unable to play here. Mr Irving was captain of the Hornets for the whole of last season, and played with them the whole of their matches, only playing with the Association Club on two or three Saturdays, when his own club had no match. The impression that "Forward" would give to the public is that Mr Irving had been a regular player with the Association Club, which is a mistake. Why "Forward" snubs the Hornets is not perceptible, and is, as I presume from the tone of his letter unkind, seeing that several Hornets have rendered his club invaluable assistance more than once.

A RUGBY PLAYER

(Southport Visiter, 22nd August 1882)

Irving played only in this opening game of the season, but Dalby was lured over from rugby, later to be joined also by Tom Morris. The line-up, still including three of the originals, was S.Platt (goal), Pidduck, Hands, Briggs, Colman, Alfred Dalby, Arthur Dalby, Calvert, Ambler, Burnett and Irving. Dalby was immediately in the thick of the action with a goal, Briggs, and Colman (two) grabbing the others.

The row over representation in the local press led Reginald Slack, the secretary of Southport Olympic to pen a letter of response to the letters published by 'Forward' and 'Rugby Player'.

Sir – I have read the letters of "Forward", and "Rugby Player", and I am glad the former, as representing the Associationists, has such bright prospects before him, as during last season it must have been annoying in the extreme to find their field entirely vacated when our team commenced action, even if it were only a second team engagement.
Public opinion may alter, the Association enclosure may be well patronised, but I have grave doubts as to its ever providing any great opposition, in this district, to the Rugby game.
The Association Club here is as yet so very young (half a season), that it is premature for anyone to predict what standing it will take in the Dribbling World, but it certainly was making very rapid strides in the right direction at the close of last season. The exodus of spectators when the Rovers and Witton faced each other at the late Athletic Sports, does not point to any increased popularity of the Association game, as if the public will not patronise two such able exponents as the above, the local club can hardly expect a very large attendance of their new field during the coming season.
The Hornets likewise showed greatly improved form, and it is much to be regretted that they should lose the services of their excellent captain, Mr Andrew Irving, whom they very rightly claim as their man alone, and not conjointly with the Dribbling community.
R SLACK, Hon Sec., Olympic F.C.

(Southport Visiter, 9th September 1882)

On 7th October 1882, Southport entertained Liverpool Ramblers in their first ever English Challenge Cup tie (today's F.A. Cup). For such an occasion the club chose an alternative venue and Ramblers were required to change at the Shakespeare Hotel before making the short walk to the Sports Ground at Sussex Road, home of the Athletic Society, where the tie took place. Being fully enclosed with an extensive stand, it presented an opportunity to not only make a little more money, but to showcase the club in a more positive light than might have been the case had they been playing fetch with the neighbours.

The game was watched by 300 spectators according to the Southport Visiter, including many women, and resulted in a 1-1 draw, Ambler scoring for Southport following a neat pass from Arthur Dalby.

SYDNEY v RATHBONE (LIVERPOOL RAMBLERS)

The above match took place at Southport on Saturday, in the presence of 400 or 500 spectators, who evinced the greatest interest in the varying fortunes of a well fought game, the number of ladies who were spectators being an especial and most pleasing feature of the day. The kick off took place at 3 30, and the Ramblers immediately took the ball into the Southport half of the field and for some time closely pressed their opponents, but by a well-concerted rush of Southport, in which Messrs. Colman and Briggs were prominent, a goal was secured. However, after change, the Ramblers, playing admirably, secured a well-earned goal, and thus equalised matters. The rest of the day's play, though the game was well sustained, did not produce any tangible results. The Ramblers backs, Messr's Turner, and Pilkington, deserve especial praise and Messrs. Baxter worked well amongst the forwards. Messrs. Briggs and Colman of the home team forwards, and Mr Barnett, among the backs, also distinguished themselves. The teams were – Southport: W.Platt (goal), T. Barnett and P. Pedcock (backs), K. Rieland and E. Rammsbottom ((½ backs)), Colman, J.Briggs, A. Dalby, C. Hambler, Alfred Daulby, and E..S. Calvert (forwards). Liverpool Ramblers: S. Hornby (goal), Turner and Keyworth (backs), R.M. Pilkington and Heald ((½ backs)), P. Bateson, the brothers Baxter, W. Earls, P. Wilson and W.Croft (forwards). Messrs. Action and Haddon umpires, and Garston referee.

(Liverpool Mercury – 10th October 1882)

It's easy for us to spot the mistakes in the published line-up in the Liverpool Mercury. There is no such player as K. Rieland, that is a mis-transcription of Ralph Rylance, P. Pedcock is Benjamin Pidduck, and Barnett is Thomas Burnett. Hambler, was Ambler and Daulby is Dalby. The Ramblers side was made up of five university men, five old Etonians and one of Errol College.

As for who Sydney and Rathbone are….your guess is as good as mine!

In their first competitive fixture Southport could perhaps have considered themselves unfortunate. Ramblers had made a tactical switch by moving Percy Bateson into the forward line at half time and Louis Hornby, who replaced him between the posts, gave an outstanding display to keep his side in the tie.

When it came, the equaliser for Ramblers must have caught the eye. Harold Baxter, picking up the ball deep in his own half, went on a brilliant solo run. He ran the full length of the field before, with a well-directed shot, he levelled proceedings.

It isn't clear from newspaper reports, but 'H.Baxter' had been a fairly regular feature in the Southport line-up during the club's inaugural season and as it was an amateur sport, still with no concept of player registration, it could well have been the same man representing the Ramblers. Just like Rylance and many others he may have chosen which side he wanted to represent whenever his 'usual' sides met.

The Southport Guardian, a new publication having started in July 1882, did not cover the game at all. In fact, their coverage of sport in general was very hit and miss.

The Southport Visiter reports a match against the Strathmore House School on 14th October 1882 in which Southport were defeated 4-0. This however was in fact the first known game of a second XI. Platt, Hatch and Halsall were noted as playing well for the visitors (Southport), but no line-up is given. The first team took on Bolton Olympic at Scarisbrick New Road on the same day, but the score-line was unfortunately little better at 1-5.

Two weeks after the English Challenge Cup fixture with Ramblers, Southport welcomed the Stacksteads Working Men in the Lancashire Challenge Cup. As a competition that Southport were much more likely to do well in, the Guardian appeared to be more interested and unusually produced a full report.

CHALLENGE CUP COMPETITION – SOUTHPORT v STACKSTEADS
This match was played on Saturday, at Southport. The Southport "Reds" having lost the toss kicked off against a strong breeze, the ball being quickly returned into the Southport quarters, and kept there for some time, the defence of the backs however, being equal to every emergency. The "Reds" now made several attempts to get away, and the left wing taking possession ran the sphere up, and passing well to the centre, Coleman made a splendid screw shot which was wonderfully well stopped by Stacksteads's custodian; still keeping up the pressure the right wing now had a turn, Kay making a long high shot, which beat the goal keeper — first blood for the home team. The visitors now made several determined attempts to score, and worked hard, but without combination, which rendered all their efforts useless, the final shots going in touch, in fact, the "Reds" goal keeper only handled the ball about three times during this half. On changing ends, and with the wind at their backs, the "reds" now pressed the visitors, Briggs and Calvert on the left wing, making some splendid combined runs, from one of which Kay was again successful in scoring. The visitors, still playing hard, made a good run, and shot for goal. Platt, however, was all there, and cleared his goal in good style. The sphere was got away by Calvert, and passing to Briggs another good run was made, Coleman making the final shot, which went across the mouth of goal into touch. On being kicked off Ambler got possession, and passing in front of goal Briggs dashed past the backs and beat the custodian with a capital screw-kick. Stacksteads now broke away and secured a couple of corner kicks, but with no result, the defence of the backs being too good, Rylance and Ramsbottom playing a sterling game at half-back, and Burnett being noticeable for his coolness in averting every dangerous attack. Up to the finish the "Reds" were peppering away at the Stacksteads' goal, only one by Coleman was successful, the goal keeper saving his charge time after time in the most gallant manner. On time being called, the Southport were left easy winners by four goals to nil, thus entitling them to play in the second round of the Lancashire Challenge Cup. Southport Team:- S.Platt (goal), T.B.Burnett (Capt.), R.Pidduck, E.Ramsbottom, and R.L.Rylance (backs),

C.Ambler, J.L.Briggs, C.E.Calvert, T.Coleman, W.J.Kay and J.Melross (forwards). Referee, Mr T.Hindle (Darwen).

(Southport Guardian, 28ᵗʰ October 1882)

This report is the first in which the nickname of 'the Reds' is used in the Southport press, named after the colours in which the side now played. The referee being T. Hindle shows the prestige attached to the competition in local circles, he being the secretary of the Lancashire Football Association. W.Kay, twice a goal scorer in the game, had come into the side in January 1882 after the club had only played a handful of fixtures. It is likely that this is the same W.Kay who would later go onto have considerable influence over the future of the club from a secretarial capacity for Southport Wanderers in 1884.

Before the replay for the English Challenge Cup Southport travelled to Birkenhead but were placed at considerable disadvantage by the ground being covered in long grass and by the home team also wearing the same, scarlet-coloured shirts. The game finished all square at 1-1.

For the replay with Ramblers Southport were able to rely again on the pace and trickery of one of the originals, Josiah Melross. Melross had missed the first tie, being replaced by Calvert, but had returned against Birkenhead *'unexpectedly playing a grand game'*. However, despite his return, their chances were dealt a significant blow by the absence of Platt, the goalkeeper, who missed the train. Thomas Burnett once again deputised in goal, but in the 'boisterous' weather (Sporting Life, 7ᵗʰ Nov 1882), he could do nothing to prevent them from falling to a 4-0 defeat.

The tie for the English Association Cup was played at Aigburth on Saturday. The ground however being heavy militated somewhat against brilliant play. For the Ramblers, Baxter kicked off, the wind against him, and play was confined for some time to centre of the field, but Coleman by a nice run passed to Rylance, who was cleverly stopped by Baxter, the latter taking the ball up to the Southport 25, a shot at goal being safely warded off by Burnett. The Ramblers soon after obtained a corner, Heald making a good shot, but the Southport forwards rushed the ball down to the Liverpool's 25, and a splashing scrimmage ensued in a regular quagmire, F G Heaton clearing the Ramblers quarters. Soon after, in consequence of a foul, Southport had a free kick unpleasantly near the home goal, but the sphere went over the bar. The subsequent play up to half time was slightly in favour of Liverpool but no point was scored. On resuming, the Ramblers forwards, by a nice sweep, threatened the visitor's territory and obtained a corner, but nothing resulting, Rylance sped away, but was cleverly halted by Gladstone, who passed to Heald, who in turn centred to Baxter and the ball was turned over the line. The corner kick was well headed out, but almost immediately another corner fell to Liverpool, and the ball, being well thrown in the goal, was kicked by Baxter from a bully in front of the visitor's posts. Yet another corner fell to Liverpool, and after threatening the Southport goal, the leather was sent off the line to the left of the goal. On kicking out, A Dalby took the ball away and passed to Rylance, who, with Coleman's assistance, pressed the Ramblers quarters. Baxter however, relieved and, after a throw in by Southport, the Ramblers worked down field, but Coleman and Rylance getting possession and working well together were quickly within the Ramblers 25, and a shot at goal was unsuccessful. After the kick out the Ramblers worked with a will and were quickly scrimmaging the ball in front of the Southport posts, Earle putting it through. Again was danger threatened, as the Ramblers, being busy again within the Southport 25, and, by a well directed shot, Baxter again scored: almost immediately after from a corner a fourth goal was kicked by J F Bateson. Southport being defeated at the call of time by four goals to nil.

(Liverpool Daily Post, 4th, November 1882)

LIVERPOOL RAMBLERS *v* SOUTHPORT – *The above clubs met for a second time (having played on Oct 7th and made a tie, one goal each) on Saturday last, at the Ramblers ground, Aigburth, Liverpool. The wind was very high and the ground wet but still some fine play was shown. Southport won the toss, and played with the wind and slight hill in their favour, but failed to score, mainly owing to the good defence of Turner, Heald and Heaton. But when ends were changed at half-time, the Ramblers had it nearly all their own way, and ended winning by four goals to nil. This score should have been larger, but for the very uncertain play of the Ramblers forwards when in front of goal; Baxter scored two, and Earle one, and Dr. Bateson the fourth. Heald's corner kicking and "throwing-in" were very fine, and Baxter, Dr. Bateson, Earle, and Rayner played very well for the Ramblers, while Briggs, Rylance, Burnett, and Coleman played best for Southport. Sides: -Ramblers -F.G. Heaton (goal), G.W. Turner and J. Gladstone (full backs); J. Heald, P. Bateson, and A.M.Midwood ((½ backs)), E. Baxter (centre), Dr. J.F.Bateson and E.V.Rayner (right wing) W.E.Earle and J Acton (left wing). Southport: - T.B.Burnett (goal); B.Pidduck and A.Dalby (full backs); E. Rammsbottom and Rylance ((½ backs)); T. Coleman and Alf. Darby (centres); T. Melross and C. Ambler (right wing), J.Briggs and W. Hatch (left wing). Umpire, Mr R.M.Mortimer; Referee, Mr J. Veitch, Birkenhead.*

(Football – A weekly record of the game, 8th November 1882)

It is from this game where we have the earliest photograph of a Southport association team, presumably taken after the match as Squire Platt, having arrived late and been unable to play is still pictured, but wearing his hat and coat!

Top row: Platt, Hatch, Burnett, Pidduck, Ramsbottom, Rylance.
Front row: Arthur and Alfred Dalby, Cornwall, Ambler, Irving, and Briggs.

Outside of the Lancashire Cup, the form of the Reds was very indifferent. Defeats to Liverpool 'A' (0-1), Bolton Olympic (1-5), Kirkdale St.Mary's (0-7), and United Schools (0-1), the latter being an XI made up of the combined forces of a number of local private schools – Sandringham School, Strathmore House and Bickerton House, were only bettered by a single 1-1 draw at Birkenhead.

The defeat at St Mary's was severe and it was reported that Southport were 'poorly represented', the side being S.Platt, W.Kay, T.B.Burnett, A.Bimpson, W.Platt, E.Ramsbottom, J.Briggs, R.Howard, Arthur Dalby, Halsall and C.Ambler. Whilst they were busy in Liverpool, their respective second strings met at Scarisbrick New Road, with Southport winning by two goals to one where Benjamin Pidduck and Josiah Melross featured in a much stronger performance.

On the day of the fixture with the United Schools, it was reported that a rugby fixture also took place under the Southport name. The report in the Southport Guardian stated that *'this is not the club lately known as the Southport Club, but an old one consisting of members of the Alexandra Cricket Club, who have revived the old club formerly known by the same name.'* There were now two Southport Football Clubs in the town.

The following round of the Lancashire Cup, played in early December at Rishton, turned out to be a thriller. Three changes from the first-round line-up saw Southport adopting the 'six forward game' (a 2-2-6 formation as opposed to the previous favourite 'Pyramid' 2-3-5) with Mellor, Baxter and Hands replacing Southport originals Pidduck, Calvert and Colman, who had been a goal scorer in the previous round. Despite scoring four once again, the defence proved their undoing conceding five in return.

LANCASHIRE CHALLENGE CUP – SOUTHPORT v RISHTON
The second round of the competition for the Lancashire Association Challenge Cup finished on Saturday. These two clubs met at Rishton, and a very good game was played, Southport in the end losing by one goal. Rishton scored five goals to Southport four, but the latter team alleged one of those given to Rishton was the result of a foul, which was not however seen by the umpire. Teams: - Southport S.Platt, goal; W.Kay, H.Baxter, backs; J.B.Hands, R.L.Rylance, (½ backs); J.Melross, E.Ramsbotham, rights, J.J.Briggs, T.Mellor, lefts, C.Ambler, T.B.Burnett (Capt.),centres…. W.Hatch, umpire, Mr Singleton (Darwen), referee.

(Southport Guardian, 16th December 1882)

Out of the cup competitions by the turn of the new year, Southport returned to standard club fixtures making the trip to Bolton Olympic in January. Olympic were an established club and Southport were keen to prove their worth by testing themselves against some of the region's stronger sides. *The Olympic won by three goals to one, and although beaten, the "Reds" are to be congratulated on their play against such an old established club'* remarked the Southport Visiter.

Away at Tranmere at the start of February, Briggs (two), Ambler and Melross secured four goals without reply, and a win over Croston by a solitary Rylance goal came a week later. Against the smaller clubs, Southport were more than a match.

Southport v Croston – Played at Southport on Saturday, in the presence of about 300 spectators. The villagers played on the defensive the whole of the game, the back play of the reds preventing any serious attack, in fact the ball only passed over their lines about four times. Shots innumerable were made at the Croston citadel, but only one, by Rylance, took effect.

(Southport Visiter, 13th February 1883)

In March the Southport Guardian suggested that a match should be held in aid of the Southport Infirmary. Over the coming years this would become a popular annual event, thanks in part due to the efforts of Thomas Burnett, but the scheme was met with a troubled start. A tidy sum, £75, had been raised recently for a similar cause at Swinton, and Southport Olympic had seen the opportunity to reach out to the newly reformed Southport Rugby Club. Despite many members of the reformed club having taken part in amateur dramatic performances for the same charitable purpose, they were disinclined to accept the offer to play rugby. In a letter to the Guardian on 10th March, Olympic Secretary Reginald Slack confirmed a request had been made and even complimented their potential opponents on their recent form, but to no avail.

A defeat to Bootle at the end of March was nothing to be ashamed of, but Southport had given them a fright. Southport came from behind to lead as half time approached before a late equaliser left the scoreline at 2-2. Melross put Southport ahead again after the re-start and all was looking good until Corrie scored a hat-trick for Bootle, the match ending 3-5! The only other reverse in the second half of the season came against St Benedicts, but as Southport continued to find their feet even this was turned around in the reverse fixture, where in the last game of the season Ambler, Melross and Burnett did all the damage as the Reds ran out 5-1 winners.

Elsewhere in the town, ten years on from the first sod being cut by the original club President Samuel Swire, the West Lancashire Railway was completed and rail traffic between Derby Road and Blackburn began. It was a year of many rail improvements for the town, making the visitation of clubs much easier in the process. The Birkdale and Southport Tramway Company would soon follow, opening a line from London Square to Kew Gardens and the Lancashire & Yorkshire Railway opened a new station in St Luke's Road. Within a year the Southport and Cheshire Lines Extension Railway was also to open.

==*==
1883/84

A further unification of association rules across each of the home nations, England, Scotland, Ireland and Wales, led to several rule changes in time for the 1883/84 season.

Although the pitch markings we are so used to today were still another nine years off, a marked or painted touchline was introduced in addition to the flags previously utilised and the option of using tape for a cross-bar was removed, meaning fixed goalposts and crossbars were compulsory for the first time. We know from the report of Southport's second home game, against Burscough on Christmas Eve 1881 that Southport had not used a fixed crossbar to this point. The report from this game clearly indicates that a tape was strung between the two posts, as there was a dispute whether the ball had gone over or under it for Burscough's goal.

There were a number of other changes introduced, bringing the game much closer to the spectacle we enjoy today. These included a rule that the ball had to be kicked forward from the kick-off and the offside rule was adjusted to account for corners. The remaining changes all came in relation to the use of hands, further distancing the association rules from rugby; the throw-in was changed to prevent the taking with one hand, with players now required to throw the ball from above the head using two hands, and the goalkeeper was allowed to take up to two steps while holding the ball. Further standardisation occurred in the way the pitch was laid out.

The limits of the ground shall be, maximum length, 200 yards; minimum length, 100 yards; maximum breadth, 100 yards, minimum breadth, 50 yards. The length and breadth shall be marked off with flags and touch line; and the goals shall be upright posts, 8 yards apart, with a bar across them 8 feet from the ground. The average circumference of the Association ball shall be not less than twenty-seven inches and not more than twenty-eight inches.

The Laws of the Game (1883) by the Football Association

It was to be another ten years before goal nets were to become compulsory, vastly reducing the number of disputes as to whether the ball had crossed the goal-line or passed between the posts.

First published in 1868, The Football Annual was a yearly reference work covering football, rugby and association primarily but also other codes, played in England. It would typically include the laws of the game, which during this period changed frequently, a summary of any major events in the previous season and, crucially for us, a listing of all football clubs in England. It was edited almost exclusively by Charles Alcock, an FA committee member and secretary, the man widely credited as the creator of the English Challenge Cup. In May of each year club secretaries were invited by Alcock to submit their details for inclusion in that year's edition. Southport's first entry in Alcock's Football Annual as an association club came in 1883 with T.B.Burnett listed as honorary secretary operating from 179 Lord Street. The most interesting part of their entry, noting that the submission of information came from Burnett himself, is the formation date of 1881. For those used to seeing that date it perhaps doesn't stand out as unusual in any way, but it importantly confirms that whilst there had been clubs bearing the same name prior to 1881, *this* club did not consider themselves a continuation of any of them. Whilst Southport (Association) Football Club appeared in the Football Annual for the first time, there was no entry for the reborn Southport (Rugby) Football Club.

Meanwhile, having been involved in the second incarnation of the Southport Cricket Club in 1876, Thomas Burnett joined with friends J.Allured and W.Tunstall as one of *'three old Stalwarts'* to make one final attempt to revive the old cricket club in the summer of 1883. The resurrected club chose W.J.Conell, the treasurer of Southport Football Club, as its new captain, and Colonel Edward Fleetwood-Hesketh, the last vice president of the original Southport Football Club, as its new president. Their playing field was slightly further along Scarisbrick New Road on the recreation grounds next door to the new Olympic football ground. The fields are clearly visible on the 1894 map, and in today's context are roughly where Falkland Road and Rutland Road now stand. A pavilion is clearly shown on the 1894 map, however it is not known whether this had been in place in 1883.

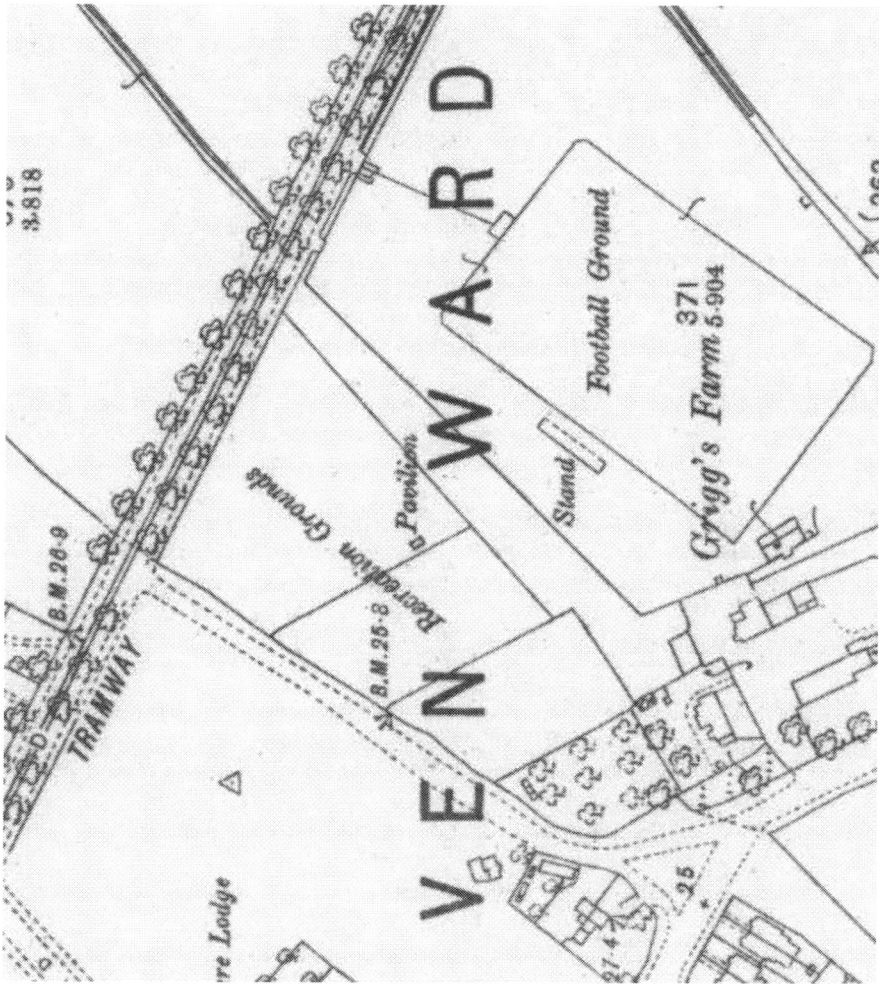

(OS Map 1894 Reproduced with permission from the National Library of Scotland)

The season began in an unusual fashion, when Southport Football Club met Southport Cricket Club for a game with the bat and ball to open their new home. Those aligned with the football club must have been mightily relieved that Burnett chose to play for them as he almost single-handedly took them to a one run win (57 v 56) thanks to a fine personal performance picking up seven wickets!

Before the season was to properly begin, Southport would also face Southport Olympic although this time it was at association football, rather than rugby!

At the club's Annual General Meeting in September, held at the Bold Arms Hotel, Burnett retained the role of honorary secretary, Charles Scarisbrick was re-elected president, W.J.Conell elected treasurer and Ralph Rylance was elected as captain. This was perhaps in recognition that Burnett was needing to share his duties after having worked so hard to establish the club on a firm footing. A full list of fixtures was arranged with teams including Bootle, Everton, Wirral, Liverpool Rovers, Birkenhead and Bolton Olympic.

The 1883/84 season opened on 8th September with a 4-2 win away at Croston. There was remarkable consistency in the Southport team at the time. Squire Platt, Josiah Melross and Thomas Burnett were all still present from the very first XI to turn out at Bootle two years previously, with Ralph Rylance another from the first season now captaining the side alongside Dalby and Briggs, who had been mainstays of the side throughout 1882/83.

The line-up for the game at Croston was: S.Platt, H.Baxter, R.L.Rylance, E. Rammsbottom, J.Melross, P.Mellor, Aughton, R.Whittaker, C. Ambler, T.B.Burnett, E. Martin.

The same line-up, except for Briggs replacing Aughton, visited Everton a week later. Owing to problems with their original Stanley Park home, Everton had been preparing a new private enclosure at Priory Road. However, for their first game of the season, it was not quite ready and they were therefore forced to play on a public surface at nearby Walton Stiles. It's fanciful to suggest that the quality of the surface is really to blame for the 3-0 reversal.

Everton v Southport – Everton began to play off their list of matches on Saturday in a game with Southport. The contest ended in a victory for Everton by three goals to nil. Teams – Everton: Lindsay, goal; Morris and Marriot, backs; Parry and Cartwright, (½ backs); right wing, Williams and Berry; left wing, Richards and Higgins, centre McGill and Pickering. Southport: Platt, goal; Baxter and Whittaker, backs; Ramsbottom and Rylands, (½ backs); right wing, Melross and Martin; left wing, Briggs and Mellor; centre, Burnett-Blundell and Ambler. Referee, D.Lamont

(Liverpool Mercury)

Despite their previous failed attempts to arrange a charitable fixture with the new Southport Rugby Club in aid of the Infirmary, Southport Olympic did finally managed to secure an opponent. Fresh from their pre-season dalliance with the round ball, Olympic and Southport Football Club agreed to repeat the exhibition on New Year's Day 1884, an act for which the Southport Guardian was full of praise and admiration. Whether it was the persistence of Olympic or the ingenuity of Thomas Burnett in reaching out, we do not know but Burnett was clearly taken with the idea and penned a letter to the Manchester Courier in October appealing for other clubs to follow their example.

THE SOUTHPORT CLUB
Hon. Sec., Mr. T.B. Burnett, 25A, London-street, Southport

During the two years that this club has been in existence it has made steady strides in public favour; and as the same team will again do battle this season, it is not unreasonable to expect more will be heard of the club ere long in very aristocratic football company. There is one feature about the arrangements of this club which may well point to a moral to many outside clubs in the county; a day is set apart for a match for the benefit if the infirmary, and, considering the goodness of the cause, there will be, it is hoped, on this occasion, if on no other, so far as spectators are concerned, a bumper. The match is fixed for January 1, and no better start for the New Year could possibly have been imagined.

(Manchester Courier – 22nd October 1883)

As the original Southport Football Club (1872) had been established to promote the wellbeing of the town's people, it was clear that both the new Southport Football Club and Southport Olympic still held those principles dear.

The Reds had once again entered the English Challenge Cup for the 1883/84 season. Drawing Blackburn Rovers at their Leamington Road ground, Rovers won the tie 7-1 but in context, losing to Blackburn was no real disgrace. Their victory over Southport was to be the start of an unbeaten Cup run that saw Blackburn all the way through to 1887 when they finally succumbed to Scottish club Renton (Scottish clubs were at that time invited to take part, very much like English clubs were invited to take part in the Welsh Cup fifty years later). The run spanned 24 rounds, scoring 87 goals and winning the cup three times.

Blackburn Rovers v Southport – As was expected, the Blackburn Rovers had an exceedingly easy task on Saturday in defeating Southport in the first round of the competition for the Football Association Challenge Cup. But the visitors played so well in defence of their goal, and the Rovers were so weak in attack, that the meeting, on the Leamington ground, only resulted in favour of the Rovers by seven goals to none.

(Bolton Evening News - Monday 22 October 1883)

The Blackburn Rovers v Southport encounter for the Association Cup was more of a farce than anything, so far as real good play went; but there was a lot of interest attached to the game, because of the good defence of the visitors in these moments of danger. The goal-keeping and back play for Southport was really surprisingly good, and Platt, Baxter and Burnett came in for a great deal of attention. For the most part, however, they were let off by the Rovers forwards, whose shooting was worse than I have ever seen it before, the spectators lots of times sending up derisive cheers at their poor attempts.
In the field however Rovers displayed fine form, as form goes, against such a team as Southport, though it must be said for the latter that they set themselves well out in the field, and sometimes they even passed with great cleverness. It was short-lived though, but it enabled Forrest to arouse the feelings of the spectators into enthusiasm by his grand kicking at half-back. Lofthouse again played well on the left and the passing of Douglas and Duckworth was very choice. Sowerbutts will make a good centre, if ever the Rovers are in need of a permanent player in that position, and his only fault

69

on Saturday was that of all the other forwards — bad shooting at goal. Instead of winning by seven to nil, the Rovers should have trebled the figure!

(Athletic News - Wednesday 24 October 1883)

English Cup Tie — Blackburn Rovers v Southport — This match was played at Blackburn on Saturday afternoon, but there was no great degree of excitement manifested anent the result, and the Rovers did not achieve such a sensational victory as did Darwen over Bootle the week previous. Play commenced at 20 minutes past three, the Blackburn men having to go against the wind in the first half. Suter soon lowered the Southport colours, whilst Lofthouse kicked a the second, and two more were added before half-time. In the second half Southport held their opponents at bay for nearly half an hour, but at last Avery defeated the visitors' custodian, and finally the Rovers win an interesting game by seven goals to nil. Teams — Rovers: Arthur, goal; Suter and Beverley, backs; McIntyre and Forest, (½ backs); Avery, Douglas, Duckworth, Lofthouse, Strachan and Sowerbutts, forwards. Southport: Platt, goal; Baxter and Burnett, backs; Rylance, Derby, and Ramsbottom, (½ backs); J.Melross, T.Morris, Mellor, Briggs, and Whittaker, forwards.

(Liverpool Mercury — 12th October 1883)

Nobody had given Southport a chance before the tie had taken place, and many had even questioned the cheek of the two-year-old club entering such a prestigious competition. Expecting to lose count of the number of goals that a club like the mighty Blackburn Rovers would put past them however the Reds were not daunted in the slightest and went out in front of fully 1,500 spectators and gave their all. Although the result was a foregone conclusion, even the most ardent of Blackburn followers could not fail to give credit to plucky Southport. Three goals being conceded in the last 10 minutes gives a false impression of the passage of play throughout the game. Great lessons could be learned from witnessing first hand one of the great passing sides in the country and it wouldn't be long before the Rovers would once again visit the seaside town at the request of Captain Ralph Rylance, whose own roots were in Blackburn.

A couple of notable names in the Blackburn XI that day were Joe Sourbutts and Joe Lofthouse who both later made a handful of appearances for Southport Central. Lofthouse went on to play seven times for England whilst with Rovers before arriving at Central.

Where progress in the national competitions remained unrealistic, the Lancashire Cup provided better fayre.

Hurst Park Road were seen off 3-0 in October, Wheelton by four goals to three in December before drawing the 'other' Blackburn giant, English Cup Holders Blackburn Olympic who prevailed 2-0 shortly before Christmas.

The match with Olympic however was more notable for incidents off the field as the following report from the Lancaster Gazette and General Advertiser shows:

ALLEGED THEFTS FROM FOOTBALL PLAYERS.
Henry Aughton, upholsterer, was brought up at Southport, on Monday, on two charges of stealing a silver watch and chain, the property of Robert Coventry, of No. 15 Union-street, and for unlawfully pawning another watch, the property of Paul Moorfield, of Pine-grove, sadler. The prosecutors are members of the Southport Association Football Club, which on Saturday played the Blackburn Olympic in the third round of the season. The teams met at the Shakespeare Hotel in the afternoon, and went to the clubroom of the local gentleman, where they changed their clothing. Coventry put inside his bag his collar and tie, a watch and chain, and 1s 6d. In money, the latter being in his waistcoat pocket. Prisoner was in the room at the time, and Moorfield handed his watch to him to take charge of while he went to play. About half past four they returned to the clubroom, when Coventry found that his bag had been cut open at the side from top to bottom, and his waistcoat was on the floor. His watch and chain had gone, as well as the money. In the afternoon on Saturday, the prisoner pawned the watch belonging to Moorfield at the shop of Mrs. Clara Thompson, Eastbank-street, Southport, which is close by the Shakespeare Hotel. About eight o'clock on the same night he was arrested in the refreshment rooms at the Southport Railway Station, at which time he was in an intoxicated state. When he was searched, Coventry's watch was found in his possession, and also a pawnticket for another watch. The bags of the Blackburn men were also cut open, and money extracted from all of them. The prisoner was remanded until Wednesday for the appearance of the Blackburn men in court.

(The Lancaster Gazette and General Advertiser for Lancashire, Westmorland and Yorkshire — 29th December 1883)

Southport's old foes Liverpool Ramblers put paid to any success in the other local competition, the Liverpool Challenge Cup, with a 4-2 reversal at Scarisbrick New Road at the end of November 1883. Six of the same XI to have fallen to the Ramblers the previous year lined up for Southport; Baxter, Rylance, Melross, Briggs, Dalby and Burnett, but the previous year's beaten finalists (Ramblers having succumbed to Bootle in the final) were too strong for the Reds.

SOUTHPORT v LIVERPOOL RAMBLERS – This match – one of the first ties of the Liverpool and District Cup competition – was played at Southport on Saturday. The Ramblers had whipped up a strong team, whilst Southport were deprived of the services of Ramsbottom, their half-back. During the first half Southport had somewhat the best of the play, and succeeded in scoring a goal. On changing ends, the Ramblers invaded the home quarters, and matters were equalised owing to one of the Southport (½ backs) playing the ball through his own posts. This had a demoralising effect upon Southport and three more goals were quickly added to the Ramblers score. Subsequently Southport, by the aid of Mellor, gained a further point and the game terminated in favour of the Ramblers by four goals to two. Teams — Southport: S.Platt, goal; H.Baxter and T.Blundell, backs; R.L.Rylance, W.Whittaker, and A.B.Dalby, (½ backs); T.Morris, J.Melross, J.L.Briggs, P.Mellor and E.Martin, forwards. Liverpool Ramblers: H.A.Bailey, goal; G.W.Turner and J.B.Ismay, backs; A.R.Midwood, H.W. Bewley and J.Head, (½ backs); W.Rayner, R.Winter, G.Smith, H.S.Brown, and A.B.Pritt, forwards.

(Liverpool Mercury – 26th November 1883)

71

Having won the toss Rylance elected to play with the wind to his back, and at the break Southport were leading 1-0. After the re-start Southport managed to keep the Ramblers at bay for some time, only an unfortunate own goal letting them back into the game. The equaliser knocked the Reds out of their stride and three more goals were scored in rapid succession – all of which could have been prevented. Picking themselves up for the final ten minutes Mellor managed to pull a goal back for the home side but it wasn't enough.

Meanwhile, the first annual meeting of the reborn Southport Cricket Club took place at the end of November and showed the venture to have been an encouraging success. A first team record of nine wins, eight defeats, three draws and a small credit balance after all expenses paid. Burnett was of course top run scorer for the season! His closest rival was fully 74 runs behind.

In December talk turned to the invitation that Ralph Rylance had extended to his Blackburn counterpart after their earlier encounter in the English Cup.

Southport v Blackburn Rovers
This match, which has been the sole topic of conversation amongst football players during the last week, was played on Thursday afternoon; and although the weather was very unfavourable, the fame of the "Rovers" club drew together about 500 spectators, who seemed to thoroughly enjoy the brilliant dribbling and dodging of Jemmy Brown, the well-known international centre-forward, the splendid bending and kicking of Suter, and the smart tackling of Forrest, one of the cleverest half-backs in England, and who, it is expected, will don the international cap this season. The Rovers, winning the toss, chose the Southbank-road goal, and having a strong wind at their backs kept up a continual fusillade on the Southport citadel during the whole of the first half, but owing to the excellent goalkeeping of Platt and the capital tackling and kicking of the Southport backs they were only able to score once, and this might have been saved if Platt had not slipped down. At times the Southport forwards, headed by Morris and Melross, broke away, but were unable to break through the defence of Suter and Forrest, although once a clever shot by Morris almost scored, but Arthur was on the alert, and banged the ball out of danger. On changing ends, and with the wind at their backs, the "Reds" now began to have a look in, Morris and Melross making several dashing runs, but were unable to score, Suter playing in the most determined style; Arthur clearing his goal in good form whenever pressed. The Rovers' forwards played better against the strong wind than with it, Brown, Lofthouse, and Sourbutts making lots of clever dribbles, but in every case the final shot was unsuccessful, Brown in particular having very hard lines. When time was called the home team had lost the match by one goal to nil, a result which to them is very satisfactory, seeing the formidable opponents they had played against."
"After the match the teams sat down to a substantial tea, served in capital style by "mine host" Nixon, of the Shakespeare Hotel. Mr Rylance occupied the seat of honour, and had for vice Mr Arthur. After all had cried "Hold, enough!" the remainder of the evening was devoted to song and sentiment, the success of both clubs being drunk with enthusiasm such as only footballers know, the visiters giving their entertainers a specimen of how musical honours should be rendered. The proceedings terminated at sufficient time to allow of the Blackburn men walking leisurely to the station, their departure being witnessed by their Southport friends.

Competition

(Southport Visiter, 18th December 1883)

The absence of Burnett and Platt from the Southport side that faced Levenshulme on the last Saturday of the year can be explained by their inclusion in the Liverpool and District side once again, in a representative game against Denbighshire at Wrexham. Wrexham was an area familiar to Burnett who only a handful of years earlier had been included in a North Wales representative side in Denbighshire against Sheffield. The Liverpool side however was unable to draw on some of the strongest players from the district, notably those representing the Liverpool Ramblers and Bootle, due to commitments elsewhere and the side fell to a 6-0 defeat.

For Southport, their selection problems were made worse by an administrative mix up which saw Rylance, Baxter, Briggs and C.Morris also fail to show, with their places taken by second team men. It's difficult to understand how the captain of the team could miss any fixture given the importance of the role but this did not prevent the Reds from putting on a fine display and sending their Manchester opponents home with a defeat to mull over. Tom Morris and Josiah Melross notched goals one and two, with J.R.Hatch grabbing a third shortly before the interval. After the re-start Morris completed his hat-trick as the Reds finished up 5-0 winners. Rylance's absence was perhaps an indicator that his interests lay increasingly elsewhere.

On 2nd February 1884, the Southport Visiter reported that a special meeting had been called for the new Southport Cricket Club, with matters to discuss of the greatest importance. Preliminary conversations centred on a suggestion by the Southport Athletic Society that the Cricket Club should join forces with them. This was followed up with a meeting of the Athletic Society at the Royal Hotel on 21st March where formal discussions took place regarding the formation of cricket, bicycle, tricycle and football clubs under the Athletic Society banner. Whilst it was the cricket club that had been directly approached, it is worthy of note that there were members of the football club amongst their number.

Southport's biggest win to date was recorded on 23rd February 1884 when Croston visited Scarisbrick New Road. Tom Morris helped himself to five, Percy Mellor grabbed a hat-trick, J.J.Briggs two and Burnett one as Croston were thumped 11-1. The result was followed up a week later by a 4-1 win over a representative team dubbed the 'best of the district', Tom's younger brother Charley grabbing a couple.

One of the results of the season came in the middle of March, holding the mighty Everton to a 2-2 draw at their new home of Priory Road. Curiously the previous fixture, a 1-3 defeat at Liverpool Ramblers, had been the last fixture in which Captain Ralph Rylance would take part. For the draw with Everton the captaincy was taken over by A.B.Dalby. We now know from the report of a Liverpool Chancery Court case in November 1884, in which Rylance had been accused of forcibly taking an elderly lady 'of unsound mind' away from her home in Blackburn to marry his brother-in-law, that Rylance had in fact gone to America. The court transcript reported that Rylance was not present to defend his case.

The Liverpool & District FA representative side faced North Wales in April at Bangor, winning 5-0. A number of Southport men were once again included in the line-up. Ramsbottom stepped in due to the unavailability of Lindsay of Everton, and the successful forward pairing of Mellor and Morris had finally taken the eye of the selectors. With a goal scoring record of nearly a goal a game for Morris it's not difficult to see why.

On Thursday 8th May 1884 the Southport Visiter reported on the Southport Olympic AGM which had taken place two days previously.

It was proposed and carried by a large majority, that the club play next season under both the Rugby and Association rules.

(Southport Visiter, 8th May 1884)

It was a vote and decision that would have major repercussions for years to come and on 3rd July, a further meeting was held at the Shakespeare Hotel for the express purpose of considering the formation of a Southport Olympic football club under association rules. On the 8th July, the Annual General Meetings for Southport Football Club and Southport Olympic both took place, the former at the Bold Arms, and the latter at Mr Monk's rooms on London street. The Olympic committee wanted it to be formally recorded and *'distinctly understood that whilst wishing the new organisation (Olympic F.C. Association Rules) every success, there is no connection between it and the original Olympic Football Club, which will of course, continue playing on its old field under Rugby Union Rules.'* The first practice night for the new organisation was fixed for 22nd July at 8pm.

==*==

1884/85

Athleticism had become idealised as a noble cause in Southport, and it was not simply for recreation that it was heralded. It was seen as an expression of civic pride, a means of raising funds for charity and as unifying force for the people of the town.

The Southport Athletic Society could trace their origins back even further than the original Southport Football Club (Rugby) of 1872. It had led a nomadic existence during its first decade, moving from Birkdale where the first annual athletics event had started, to Manchester Road as neighbours of the Alexandra Cricket Club (and Southport Football Club), and then on to Cemetery Road after losing their Manchester Road ground to the advancing builders in 1874.

The first annual festival of this society was held on Saturday afternoon last, on the Palace Hotel grounds in Weld Road, Birkdale, and the inaugural gathering has fully justified the expectations of those who predicted success to the society. Considering that muscular development has for many years past formed part of the school training of all youth, and that athletic sports have now become a popular national institution, it is rather surprising that Southport should have remained so long in the background in this respect, as the events of Saturday amply prove that they are thoroughly appreciated.

The day being remarkably fine, a large number of persons assembled to witness the sports, and the grandstand, which extended along one side of the ground, was filled with spectators; the fair sex, whose presence on such occasions never fails to stimulate competitors to do their utmost to win their smiles, and throws a peculiar charm over these sports, being unusually well represented. There was also a large crowd round the course, and great interest appeared to be manifested in the various contests. The number present amounted to about 4000.

(Southport Independent and Ormskirk Chronicle, 10th August 1870)

The Athletic Society went on to play a very significant role in the formation of the Amateur Athletic Association, the creation of which was a turning-point in the development of the sport of athletics nationally. Peter Lovesey writes in his centenary history of the AAA in 1980: *'A vital part of the agreement that sealed the foundation of the AAA was the commitment to the Championships rotating between the South, Midlands and North'.*

On June 15, 1879, the Southport Athletic Society, after completing another successful athletics festival during the day, hosted a tea at the Prince of Wales Hotel and proposed *"to take into consideration the desirability of forming a Northern Amateur Championship Meeting"*. The annual championships held in Fulham until this point were invariably won by 'gentleman' amateurs from Oxford or Cambridge Universities very much in the same way that 'gentlemen' had dominated the early years of football.

In August of the same year, 13 northern athletic clubs constituted themselves as the Northern Counties Athletic Association, later to be known as the North of England Amateur Athletic Association. It is today the oldest athletic association in the world having been reconstituted as Northern Athletics in 2006. Without the Southport Athletic Society, it may never have existed at all. The first joint secretaries of the Northern Counties Athletic Association were George Duxfield and Thomas Fairbrother, who were both members of the Southport Athletic Society and Duxfield himself went on to become president of Northern Counties and a vice president of the AAAs of England.

The Northern Counties decided to hold an annual championship, as proposed by the Southport Athletic Society, and the first championships were held on Southport Athletic Society's ground in 1880.

Due to the poor quality of the track at their previous home on Cemetery Road, the Athletic Society had made an ambitious move to relocate to a new home in the summer of 1882 having secured a large plot of land from the Scarisbrick Trustees on Sussex Road. Their new home was over eight acres in size. There they laid an excellent cinder path, exactly a quarter of a mile in circumference, and along the straight of the running track they erected an open grandstand, which was fully 95 yards long and cost over £500 (£65,000 in today's money) - a sizeable expense.

The ground was officially opened on June 10th 1882 for the 13th Annual Athletics Festival and W.Crabtree the Borough Surveyor placed an announcement in the Southport Visiter on the day of the event that having carefully examined the grandstand it was an uncovered structure safe for 2,000 occupants. It was a significant building! The Botanic Gardens Museum that had opened in 1876, was designed by the local architects Mellor & Sutton of London Street but it had been built by George Duxfield of Duxfield Brothers, Southport. It is extremely likely that the construction of the grandstand at Sussex Road would too have been completed by Duxfield due to his very close ties with the Athletic Society.

In time for the 1884/85 football season, the desire of the Southport Athletic Society to start football, cricket, bicycling and tricycling sections had been realised. At Southport Football Club's 1884 AGM held at the Bold Arms Hotel on 8th July there was a statement from the Chairman Mr E.Ramsbottom, to the effect that the club had become merged with the Athletic Society. This entailed an increased subscription payment of a further 3 shillings from the usual 7s 6d, taking it to 10s 6d, but it was pointed out that the arrangement would effect a considerable saving to the members of the club, as in future the whole of the travelling expenses of the members would be paid by the club.

It was unanimously decided to change the red jersey hitherto worn for a red and white striped flannel shirt. A tender had been offered by Mr. Trounson, Lord-street (a member of the club), and accepted, to make these shirts at a uniform price of 10s 6d each, which was considerably lower than the prices submitted by Liverpool firms.

It was decided to start practice at once, and until the new ground in Sussex road be ready, it would take place in the Circus Field, Eastbank street, every Tuesday evening, at 7-15, when it is hoped that every member will endeavour to be present.

The resignation of Mr. T.B.Burnett of the hon. secretaryship of the club, which he has held for so long a period and filled with so much credit, was received and accepted with regret. After the usual vote of thanks to the chairman, the meeting terminated

(Southport Visiter 10ᵗʰ July 1884).

As part of the merger Thomas Burnett joined the committee of the Athletic Society and handed over the secretarial duties to fellow Athletic Society member Richard William Thornton Hatch, a prominent Freemason and the eldest son of Alderman Hatch.

Under the banner of the Society the football club still operated to the outside world as an independent entity, as did the cricket club which too had published its fixtures back in April, but their new home offered the highest standard of local sporting facilities resulting from their many years of success.

The move to Sussex Road for the Athletic Club had come at some considerable expense and therefore it made perfect sense that the planned hosting of football fixtures from the stadium might be a way to recoup some of the costs.

The sports ground had been used for many football matches prior to the arrival of the football club in 1884, including the exhibition match between Witton and Rovers staged on the ground shortly after its opening in 1882. It had been believed that this match was the catalyst for the club to seek affiliation with the Football Association, but we know from contemporary reports that affiliation had already been sought prior to the exhibition match taking place.

The Athletic Festival held in the summer of 1884, attracted a huge attendance, estimated to be more than 5,000 strong, and over £215 was taken at the pay-gates which had been installed at the entrance to the fully enclosed ground.

(OS Map 1894 Reproduced with permission by National Library of Scotland)

With the growth of football, it's not difficult to see why such an arrangement might be made between two of the town's biggest sporting entities. More and more land in the town was being given over to the builders and the shared use of a facility such as the Sports Ground made perfect sense. At the request of the Athletic Society, the committee of the football club took over the responsibility for maintenance of the ground and in return they could have use of it rent free. It was an arrangement that seemed to suit all parties and the football club entered the 1884/85 season with optimism and high hopes.

For the opening month of the new season Thomas Burnett was otherwise occupied on the cricket field. He would return to the football pitch when the cricket season ended. After the early exit of Captain Ralph Rylance in March, before the season had even finished, Dalby's temporary captaincy was made permanent.

To those interested in the football game, we would again draw their attention to the fact that our local association exponents, who have this season been amalgamated with the Athletic Society, open their season this afternoon on the Sports ground in Sussex-road, when they meet the Stoke-on-Trent club. Included in the team are several players who have done service for their county. The following local players will don the red and white jersey: - Team: S.Platt, goal; Baxter and Critchley, backs; Ramsbotham, Dalby (Capt.), and Johnson, half backs; Morris, Melross, Briggs, Mellor, and Bailey, forwards. Kick off at 3-30. Trains run every few minutes from Chapel street station. Subscribers to the Athletic Society will be admitted to the ground and stand free of charges; and we hope that the general public will lend their patronage to the society, and attend at Sussex-road grounds whenever a match is down for decision

(Southport Visiter, 6th September 1884)

If a large gate had been anticipated for the first fixture at Sussex Road, the weather put paid to that and the Athletic News commented that '*matters, as a consequence, [were] rendered very unpleasant*'.

Owing to the inclement weather, it was decided that play would be restricted to two periods of just 20 minutes. Having lost the toss, and with it the choice of ends, Dalby kicked off for Southport at 3:30pm. The hundred or so souls that had braved the weather were treated to a fine, even game, and witnessed the visiting captain, Joshua, wearing his England international jersey for the occasion. The goals conceded in the 2-0 defeat were said to be unfortunate, the first being allowed by the referee when the Southport backs had all but stopped play believing there had been a handball. The second resulted from a speculative long shot which had caught Platt stranded off his line and unable to get back in time.

The number of local clubs increased dramatically and in the two years following its formation in 1882, membership of the Liverpool & District FA had trebled. From the annual charitable fixture that had taken place so successfully in January 1884 sprang the Southport Football Association a body formed by the secretaries of several local clubs whose principal aim was to organise the Southport Charity Cup, giving local sides regular competitive football. Eleven different Southport sides would enter for its first season.

Southport's next fixture was against one of these new sides, Southport Wednesday, and it was an early chance for them to exert their local dominance. The 4-0 win was more flattering for Wednesday than it was for Southport, such was their superiority.

The Southport Guardian's brief report gives us the first opportunity to see the new nickname of 'the Stripes', adopted following their change from plain red, to red and white striped flannel jerseys.

SOUTHPORT v SOUTHPORT WEDNESDAY
The above local clubs met on the Sussex-road ground, in the presence of a goodly number of spectators. Play commenced at 3:30 by Briggs kicking off for the "stripes," the ball being quickly worked down into the Wednesday quarters, where it remained for the greater part of the afternoon. The result at the finish was Southport four goals to "Wednesday" nil, which certainly would have been increased but for the splendid defences of Blundell, Behum and Holden.

(Southport Guardian, 20th September 1884)

Another local side to emerge at this time was Southport Wanderers, a new club who had been based initially on Portland Street before moving shortly afterwards to the Scarisbrick New Road home vacated by Southport Football Club. Although unreported in the local press, their first game, wearing red and black jerseys, took place on the same day, Saturday 13th September 1884, against Halliwell (of Bolton).

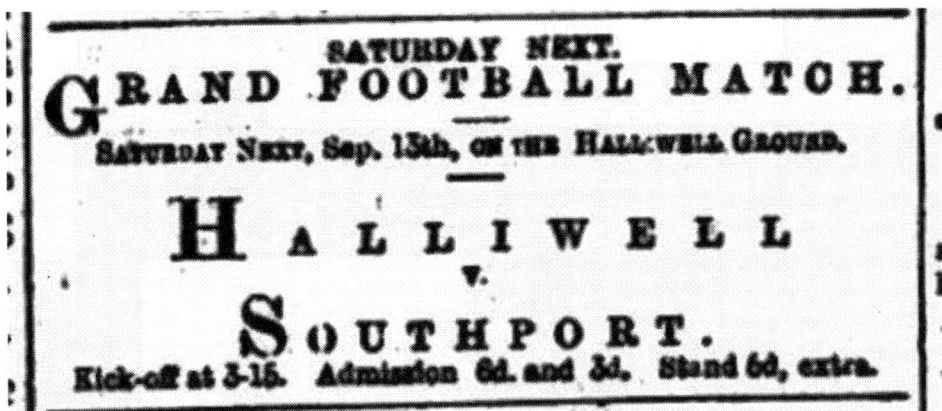

SATURDAY NEXT.
GRAND FOOTBALL MATCH.
Saturday Next, Sep. 13th, on the Halliwell Ground.
HALLIWELL
v.
SOUTHPORT.
Kick-off at 3-15. Admission 6d. and 3d. Stand 6d. extra.

(Bolton Evening News, 11th September 1884)

Although they were a distinctly different club to the original Southport Football Club, the advertisement for the game in the Bolton Evening News goes some way to explain why there was much confusion in the sporting press. Whether this had been a deliberate tactic to capitalise on the popularity and success of the original association club in the local area is unclear. It's also unclear whether Halliwell themselves believed that they had arranged a fixture with the original Southport association club.

HALLIWELL v SOUTHPORT
Halliwell opened their season on Saturday, a team representing Southport being their opponents. The visitors won the toss and played with a strong wind at their backs, but after a temporary visit to the Halliwell quarters the ball settled down in the Southport half and there it remained, with very few exceptions up to half-time, when Halliwell by some splendid all-round play had obtained eight goals, besides having one disallowed. On resuming the bombardment still continued, and they added another dozen to their total, winning by 20 goals to nil, a score which would have been greatly increased but for the grand defence of Parks, one of the Southport backs. The goals were scored by Scobie (7), Ross (5), Kay (3), Hamilton (2), Crossley, Dobson and Black (one each). Details about such a one-sided game would of course of superfluous. Halliwell: Bateson, goal; Pettigrew and Bone, backs; Dobson and Crossley, (½ backs); Haslam, Kay, Hamilton, Black, Ross and Scobie, forwards. Southport: Kay, goal; Parks and Griffiths, backs; Traveloras, Tattersall, and Haslehurst, (½ backs); Morris, Walmsley, McIntyre, Farrer and Martin, forwards. Referee, J.J. Bentley.

(Bolton Evening News, 15ᵗʰ September 1884)

There is no evidence that Wanderers themselves were upset about the confusion, and the lack of a report for the fixture in the Southport press is a sign that they felt it served them well to have the result of their initial foray remain out of the public eye. For the local press, it was usually the duty of the secretary or captain of each club to submit match reports, so the omission was most likely deliberate. The Athletic News however did not appear to be under any illusions as to the identity of the visitors and they were less than complimentary.

A remarkably one-sided match took place on the Halliwell ground on Saturday, when Halliwell played their first match of the season. Their opponents were the new-formed Southport Wanderers club, who sent a weak team, in fact so weak that they were beaten by twenty goals to none, eight being scored in the first half and the remaining dozen in the second half. Scobie kicked no fewer than seven, and Ross four. Black, Pettigrew, Done, and Scobie, four new Scotchmen, and Hasla, (late of Eagley) each made their debut for the winners.

(Athletic News, Saturday 13th September 1884)

Southport Football Club were clearly concerned at the case of mistaken identity. With the score line of this game being a 20-0 defeat they acted quickly to set the record straight!

A letter printed in the Liverpool Mercury on Tuesday 16th September, written by Richard Hatch, the new secretary of Southport Football Club, revealed their concerns.

TWO RICHMONDS IN THE FIELD
To the Editors of the Liverpool Mercury
Gentlemen – I find a football match, "Southport v Halliwell", played at Bolton on Saturday, reported in your issue of to-day, the latter winning by 20 goals to nil. As this is calculated to do the Southport Club much unnecessary damage on the football arena, I beg to say that the Southport first team played a home match on that day, winning by 4 goals to nil, against a scratch team of

Southport District. I understand that the team beaten by the "Halliwell" was the first team of a new Southport club, called "The Southport Wanderers". – Yours, &c.
R.W.T Hatch, Hon. Sec. Southport Association Football Club.
37, London Street, Southport, Sept 15, 1884.

The Athletic News, who notably hadn't made the error themselves, also sought to clarify for anyone in doubt.

The "one-sided" match at Halliwell on Saturday last, as reported in several papers, is now explainable, as it was not the Southport club that Halliwell met and defeated by 20 goals to nil, but simply an eleven of "novices" who know very little of the game, and who style themselves Southport Wanderers. The various reports must have some-what nettled the Southport team, who, I see, gave Stoke a good game the week previous, only being defeated by two goals. I am pleased to make this known to my readers, as it is no small matter to be termed the second club in a match of this description.

(Athletic News)

Even the Manchester Courier and Guardian were forced into publishing a correction contending that they had originally reported it as Southport due to the information having been received from previously reliable sources.

Football – A correspondent writes:- Referring to your issue of Monday, I note an account of a football match, Southport v Halliwell. This should be "Southport Wanderers" – a totally different organisation in every respect." (the information was supplied by Messrs. Lever and Shaw, of Blackburn, of whose accuracy we had no reason to entertain any doubt.)

The Bolton Evening News, who may have been the offending party, realised their mistake also.

If the number of goals scored is any criterion Halliwell may well be said to have commenced their season well. Their opponents were not a bright lot, but it would appear that the Halliwell forwards know how to get goals, for it is not often we see twenty scored in one afternoon. The visitors were advertised as Southport, but from what I hear it is not the Southport club but Southport Wanderers. Large as the total appears it would have been doubled but for the defence of Parks, one of their backs. One can hardly judge of the Halliwell players by seeing them perform against such a poor lot, but they worked well together, and they are certainly a great improvement on last year's team.

(Bolton Evening News, 15th September 1884)

Wanderers were in fact the club that had been first discussed by members of Southport Olympic Rugby Club back in May, and subsequently agreed at their July AGM. Since the original rugby club's demise Olympic had for many years held the honour of being the town's 'premier' proponents of the oval ball game. The club was large and well run, with many members clearly fond of ball games of all kinds, as evidenced by their fulfilment of the charitable association fixture with Southport at the turn of the year. In time, the Visiter would comment favourably on the formation of the new club:

> *With the addition of several of our local Association lights, it promises to have a brilliant future, and to be one of the strongest organisations Southport has yet had to uphold the Association game. The purpose of the committee is to make the club eligible to all, and for that purpose a small entrance fee of 2s. 6d. is only charged. The committee trust to be able to work the club by the additional number of members the small fee will induce to join. The club now numbering some 150 members, have secured the first field on Scarisbrick New-road, and trust to be generously supported by the public for the coming season.*

(Southport Visiter, 1st November 1884)

For the sake of clarity, as the future of both of these clubs is important to us, from here I will often refer to Southport Wanderers as 'Wanderers' or 'the Wanderers Club' and Southport Football Club as just 'Southport'.

Listed in the line-up for the first Wanderers fixture is Kay. We believe this to be the same William Kay to have played briefly for Southport, but who by this time had switched across to their local rivals where alongside his playing duties he also fulfilled the role of secretary.

The draw for the first round of the Lancashire Cup gave Southport a home tie with Horwich at the end of September 1884. Around 400 came in through the gate, the Southport Guardian reporting that *'a good half of which were of the fair sex'*. The gate was still nowhere near the size of those who gathered there for the athletics and would barely fill a quarter of the grandstand had they all chosen to sit (which they obviously did not). The key advantage of the Sports Ground however was that they all had to enter via the pay-gates.

> *The local captain having won the toss, Bailey kicked off for the visitors, the ball being worked pretty well in the stripes' territory, but was quickly returned by some smart play on Dalby's part, he, on many occasions, relieving his side from the pressure of the opponents. A fine scrimmage was held in front of the visitors' goal, the result being a goal earned in fine style, and being put in off Morris. The ball was again started from the centre, and some clever play by Bailey and Callender for the visitors brought the ball in front of the home goal; and, after several shots being repelled by the backs, Ramsbotham comfortably misjudged the ball, the consequence being a goal for the visitors. The next feature in the game was one of Melross' usual brilliant runs, who, in conjunction with Morris, ran the ball well up the field, the latter player centering, Briggs administered the final touch in a somewhat masterly fashion. Nothing of importance occurred until half-time, the visitors showing a want of "form". Southport had far the better of the latter half, and Dalby from half-back put in a most clever goal, Bailey (Southport) taking charge of the goal-keeper. This was the last point scored by either team and a pleasant game resulted in favour of Southport by three goals to one.*

(Southport Guardian, 27th September 1884)

The result would set up a mouth-watering tie in the second round with the mighty Preston North End in November.

After defeat to Liverpool club Stanley on 4th October, Southport were beaten by Accrington in the English Challenge Cup a week later.

Despite fielding the same XI that had so convincingly defeated Horwich, the game ended in a 3-0 defeat for the Stripes. However, luck was to be on Southport's side as Accrington were disqualified from the competition for fielding an ineligible player and Southport were reinstated.

Whilst Southport were being turned over on the road at Accrington in the Cup, closer to home Wanderers hosted the Lancashire & Yorkshire Railway team, and ended with a greatly improved result of one goal each (with one further disputed goal from L&YR). Other local fixtures followed for the new Wanderers club, visiting Bickerton House school for a game of 10 a side which ended in a narrow defeat (1-2), and Southport Wednesday over whom they claimed their first victory (2-1). Although no full line-ups were given in newspaper reports, in the Southport Wednesday line-up were Melross, Burnett, Baxter and Ramsbottom suggesting that this was an off-shoot of Southport, where matches were, as the name suggests, played on a Wednesday.

When the time came for the second round of the Lancashire Cup, clearly expecting little by way of competition from Southport, North End only sent their reserve side. Southport however had other plans. Thomas Burnett made his first appearance of the season, and the Stripes caused something of a sensation by winning 1-0, Captain Dalby scoring the goal just four minutes from time.

SOUTHPORT V PRESTON NORTH END – The latter sent their second team to represent them in this tie at Southport yesterday, and, contrary to expectation, were beaten by a goal. The home team won the toss, and played with the wind at their backs during the first half. The visitors were pressed from the start, and their goalkeeper had to save several shots. After Melross had sent in a capital shot, which was well stopped by the North End goalkeeper, the visitors assumed the offensive, and had hard lines in not scoring. The home team backs defended in good style, and half time was called, neither side up to then having scored. On restarting the North-enders pressed their opponents; but Platt defended his charge well, and after a time the Southport man raced up the field with the ball, but were unable to score til just before the call of time, when Dalby having the ball passed to him by Briggs, kicked a goal, this being the only point in the game. Southport team: S.Platt, goal; Blundell and Baxter, backs; Critchley, Johnson, and Stewart, (½ backs); Morris, Melross, Briggs, Bailey, and Dalby (Capt.). Referee: Mr Gregson, Blackburn.

(Liverpool Mercury – 3rd November 1884)

ASSOCIATION – LANCASHIRE CHALLENGE CUP – Southport v Preston North End

These clubs met on the Sports Ground on Saturday afternoon last to try conclusions of the second round of the above cup competition before a good number of spectators, who from their manner appeared to appreciate the play of both teams. Dalby, having won the toss, elected to defend the railway goal, with the wind at his back. Dempsey kicked off, when Melross and Morris got possession and ran the ball down, nothing resulting, the shot going wide. Smalley got away, but Johnson soon stopped his progress; the home forwards now took up the offensive, but were unable to score, Smalley clearing his charge in fine form. Gillespie and Bolton now broke away and the home goal looked in danger, but the defence was too good. Some give and take play now took place, when half time arrived, with the score nil. On Briggs restarting the ball it was thought that North End would completely run away with the home team; these fears proved groundless, as the stripes were now playing a splendid combined game, the forwards making some good runs, but owing to the strong wind blowing, the visitors began to press the home team. Gillespie and Smalley being most conspicuous, but Platt cleared his goal in brilliant style. Briggs and Bailey now made a run, but Woodrough stopped them and the ball was returned into mid-field. Again the home goal was threatened, the ball hitting the post twice in quick succession. Morris and Melross took the ball down the right, making a long shot; Dalby rushed up, put the ball through amidst the greatest excitement of the spectators, four minutes before the call of time. No further scores taking place, the stripes became the winners by one goal to nil, after a hard fought and exciting game. Teams: Southport: Platt, goal; Burnett and Baxter, backs; Critchley, Ramsbotham, and Johnson, (½ backs); Morris, Melross, Dalby (Capt.), Briggs, and Bailey forwards. North-end: Smalley, goal; Livesey and Woodrough, backs; Brown, Kilner and Eastham, (½ backs); Lamb, Smalley, Dempsey, Gillespie, and Bolton, forwards. Referee, Mr R.P.Gregson, Lancashire Association.

(Southport Guardian, 8th November 1884)

It was said that the Preston players were ashamed to go home after their shock defeat.

After the great victory over Preston in the Lancashire Challenge Cup, Southport faced local opposition in the Liverpool Cup. It was to be the first time that they would face High Park, a club with whom they would go on to develop quite a rivalry over the next decade. In the end it was a comfortable 4-1 victory for the Stripes, but the signs were there that High Park could yet turn into a local force.

Meanwhile in local politics, George Pilkington (previously Coombe) was elected Mayor of Southport on 10th November 1884. Although not a Sandgrounder, he was a popular and well-liked character. When Southport became a Parliamentary constituency in its own right, he was elected as the town's very first MP.

Southport faltered on the road in Aigburth against Liverpool Ramblers on 15th November but were soon back in English Challenge Cup action for the visit of Low Moor from Clitheroe a week later.

ENGLISH CUP COMPETITION (2nd ROUND).

SOUTHPORT v LOW MOOR (CLITHEROE)

These clubs met on Saturday last in the above competition, on the ground of the former. The home captain having lost the toss the visitors elected to defend the railway goal. Dalby kicked off, and Wrigley obtained possession, he, in conjunction with his partner made a good run down the left. Bailey, however, soon stopped progress. The visitors, however, began to press the home backs, and sent in several shots which had every appearance of taking effect; but Platt saved his charge in due form – a proceeding which he kept up throughout the afternoon. Melross and Morris now got away, the latter passing to Mellor, whose shot at goal went wide. The game at this point was very fast, neither side having much advantage until Mellor, getting possession, crossed the ball to Melross, who took it down and made a splendid shot at goal. Briggs rushing up in the nick of time, succeeded in beating the goalkeeper, and amidst ringing cheers from the spectators, first blood was gained for Southport. On re-starting the forwards of both teams were conspicuous for their play, each goal being in turn attacked. Mellor again came to the fore, and, with a smart shot, notched the second goal for Southport. Nothing further of importance took place until half-time was called; the score being Southport two goals, Low moor nil. On re-starting neither side showed to any advantage until Morris's centring, one of the visitor's backs put the ball through his own goal. Nettled by the score against them Low Moor re-arranged their team – the change having a good effect. The forwards making things lively for Platt, but the Southport custodians were all there, stopping the shots in fine style. A shot from the wing was now sent in, which took effect, but was disallowed on the plea of offside. The home team soon afterwards also had a goal disallowed on the same plea. Wigley obtaining possession of the ball took it down the left, and Baxter gave a corner from which the visitors scored. No further score being made up to the call of time Southport became the winners of a really splendid game by three goals to one. The local team were never seen to better advantage than during this game, every man playing in fine form in a most unselfish style. The three "M's", Melross, Morris and Mellor, with Bailey, were repeatedly cheered for the tact displayed, while Platt, though at times kept busily at work, was never caught napping. Ramsbotham early on in the second half, was almost placed hors de combat, but not withstanding this he struggled gamely to the end, and several times removed the leather from a dangerous quarter. Baxter was also in form, and kicked with great judgement. The visitors played well to a man, and in a great measure owe their defeat to the fact that the local forwards were too fast for them.

(Southport Guardian, 29th November 1884)

The opening months of the season could be considered a roaring success for Southport. Progression took place in all three competitions, the Lancashire, Liverpool and English Challenge Cups, and with notable victories over new local clubs Wednesday and High Park, Southport were fast gaining a good reputation.

Over in Scarisbrick New Road, Wanderers on the other hand were working very hard to rebuild theirs after such a poor start at Halliwell. Whilst Southport were occupied with High Park, Wanderers welcomed the visit of the 'A' team from Liverpool giants Everton. In front of a fair number of spectators, they gained another victory by two goals to one.

With increased local interest in the association game, on the 27th November 1884 a meeting was held at the Albert Hotel with a view to forming a Charity Cup competition for

Southport and district. Southport Wanderers were the first club to moot such a competition and Mr Emison from the Wanderers was voted to chair the initial discussions.

There was a large attendance of members of the various clubs in the town who play the Association game, viz., Southport Wanderers, Crescent, High Park, Lancashire and Yorkshire Railway, Christ Church, Birkdale Amateurs, Crossens, and Banks. Mr T.Fairbrother and Mr. Stewart, of the Southport Athletic Club, were also present. Mr. Emison, of the Wanderers' club, was voted to the chair, and Mr R.E.Dickenson, who had been acting as secretary pro tem., read a letter received from Mr R.W.T. Hatch of the Southport Club, regretting his inability to attend the meeting, and assuring the promoters that the idea of establishing a Charity Cup had his hearty support., and at the same time promising to give all the assistance in his power to the movement. The meeting then proceeded to the appointment of officers, Mr. R.E.Dickenson being unanimously elected hon. Sec., and Mr A.Rammsbottom the hon. treasurer. The question of a Charity Cup was freely discussed, the representatives from the various clubs expressing their views as to the lines upon which the undertaking should be worked. The following resolutions were then agreed to :- "That the competition be confined to the above nine clubs. That the committee consist of one member from each club, the secretary and the treasurer, and Messrs. Fairbrother, Stewart and another. That each club send the name of its representative to the secretary on or before the 4th December next. That the entrance fee be 5s. each club. That the question of rules be left to the committee. That the question of ground for playing the ties as to the first round be left to the clubs who are drawn together; the subsequent grounds to be at the discretion of the committee. That the secretary of each club be supplied with a book to collect subscriptions". The following subscriptions were promised during the evening: - Mr Fairbrother, 10s 6d; Mr Stewart, 10s 6d; Mr Emison, 10s 6d; Mr Ramsbottom, 10s 6d; Mr R.W.T.Hatch, 10s 6d; Mr Fairweather, 10s 6d; and the Hon. secretary, 10s 6d. It was stated during the evening that His Worship the Mayor had expressed himself favourable to the scheme, and promised his support. A very hearty vote of thanks was accorded to Mr. Ramsbottom (Wanderers F.C.) for the admirable way in which he had carried out all the preliminary arrangements for the meeting. After the usual vote of thanks to the chairman, the meeting was brought to a close.

(Southport Visiter, 29th November 1884)

Although exits from the remaining cups would come for Southport before the year was out, from the more established clubs of Darwen and Everton, the defeats were only by a single goal.

Wanderers, meanwhile, were still making positive strides. Not many months had passed, and it was clear that support was beginning to grow. Two hundred witnessed their match with Southport Crescent on 9th December even with the great counter attraction in Blackburn between Blackburn Rovers and Blackburn Olympic which had even taken the fancy of five of the Wanderers regular starting 11. In all likelihood, their policy of inclusion for all was assisted by low gate prices, and by the fact that the Scarisbrick New Road ground, unlike the rival Sports Ground, was not fully enclosed and therefore it was relatively easy to take in the game for free by avoiding any pay-gates on the main road.

The County selectors had been present at Southport's game against Preston earlier in the season and had singled out Squire Platt, the Southport goalkeeper, to represent Lancashire against Hallamshire at Sheffield. The Southport Visiter commented (13th December 1884) that *'All followers of the dribbling game in the town will rejoice at this appreciation of local talent, especially those who have had the pleasure of witnessing the good play Platt has shown this season'*.

Whilst Wanderers were making light work of Crossens 5-0, a scoreline big enough for the Southport Guardian to notice Wanderers for the first time, Lancashire came away from Sheffield 4-3 winners on Platt's County debut. Featuring in the same side was Kenny Davenport who would join Southport Central in years to come.

Minus their famous goalkeeper, Southport disposed of Blackburn club Mellor Vale 3-1, Johhny Mayall deputising between the posts.

With the great form shown by the side, particularly in the first half of the year, Southport approached the new year with cautious optimism.

Wanderers in turn kicked off 1885 in style with a well-attended New Year's ball hosted by Mr Valentine at the Portland Hall, whilst later in the day Southport met High Park at Sussex Road. Southport were without their influential Captain Dalby for the clash, but an able substitute was found in Mr Chadwick, master of the Sandringham School, and the Stripes fought out a 2-2 draw. T. Wright, of the Wanderers club, refereed the contest.

On the first Saturday of the year Farington visited Wanderers at Scarisbrick New Road, and the home side neatly dispatched them with a 2-0 win.

For Southport, drawn in the English Challenge Cup third round to face Church (who themselves had progressed thanks to narrow victories over Hurst and South Shore), the first meaningful result of the year came as a complete shock. The Stripes fell to a 10-0 defeat, their biggest to date in any competition, and still the biggest defeat in the English Cup to date for any side representing Southport. Church progressed to the sixth round, disposing of Darwen in the fourth round, receiving a bye in the fifth before eventually losing to the Old Carthusians, winners of the Cup four years previously.

A week later Southport salvaged a little pride with a creditable 1-1 draw at Sheffield, which was notable for being the first time in which there had been any collaboration between Southport and Wanderers. With Southport still missing Dalby, but also without Briggs and Melross, Wanderers had offered the services of J.Parks who played a sterling game at full back.

After facing the local sides of Southport Crescent and Lancashire & Yorkshire Railway, Wanderers had arranged for Preston Zingari to visit Scarisbrick New Road on 31st January. It was a 2-0 defeat for Wanderers but many of the locals had chosen to attend the counter attraction at Sussex Road instead. The Sports Ground was the venue of the first-round fixture of the new Southport Charity Cup competition between Southport and the Lancashire & Yorkshire Railway, with the proceeds of the match being handed over to the Southport

Infirmary. It was a bright sunny day, and fortunately the patronage was good as Southport progressed to the next round without much difficulty.

Blackburn Nomads visited Southport with five Blackburn Rovers players amongst their ranks for an exhibition in the middle of February. Despite the lofty opposition Southport won 6-0.

Wanderers decided to test themselves against the town's original football club for the first time at the end of February. In 'boisterous weather' a gate of only 150 witnessed two local sides battling gale force winds at Sussex Road. The result, a 2-0 win for Southport, had no real significance at the time other than local bragging rights but the game was quite evenly matched.

In March, Southport disposed of the Birkdale Amateurs in the next round of the Charity Cup to set up a clash with Christ Church. Cup fever was now running high in the town, and the committee had found prime space in the window of Mr Viner's shop on Lord Street to display the cup and medals. At 24 inches high, including its ebony stand, with a football engraved on its front, the cup was an impressive sight. A richly chased scroll, with laurel and oak leaves and acorns, surrounded the centre, and finished with the Southport arms and a ribbon with the legend 'Salus Populi'. Space on the back was reserved for the names of the winning teams – and clubs were desperate to be first!

Whilst Southport faced Christ Church on one side of the draw, Crescent met High Park on the other, to determine who would face off in the first final in May. That honour would fall to Southport and Crescent.

Meanwhile, Southport Cricket Club had also arranged their opening fixture of the season to take place on April 11th, 1885, but even they were caught up in the excitement, cancelling the match so that they did not detract from the attendance at the football game, and so that they could attend it themselves. Such was the interest, the Southport Guardian had published a rare front-page announcement for the fixture.

**GRAND FOOTBALL MATCH
THIS DAY.**

FINAL TIE for the CHARITY CUP.
On SUSSEX-ROAD GROUND.

Kick off Three o'clock.

Under the patronage and presence of His
WORSHIP the MAYOR, who will kick off,
and after the match present the cup and medals to
the winning team.

Admission, 3d.; Grand Stand, 3d. extra.

THE CHARITY CUP FOOTBALL COMPETITION
FINAL TIE

*The last scene in this competition was played on Saturday last, and resulted in a victory for the
"Stripes", who, to the astonishment of the numerous spectators, defeated their opponents — the
Crescent — by no less than five goals to nil. The weather was very threatening, yet notwithstanding
this a good gate turned out to watch the game. The sympathies of a large number of the 1200
spectators were unmistakably on the side of the losers, and at times the outbursts of feeling were of a
pronounced description, occasionally making the position of the referee anything but a happy one.
His Worship the Mayor accompanied by the Mayoress on their arrival on the ground received a
hearty welcome. Shortly after the advertised time for commencing hostilities, Dalby led his men on to
the field, and was well received. When the Crescent put in an appearance cheering was very hearty,
and though they were rather on the small side it was pretty evident Halsall's men would render a
good account of themselves. Dalby having won the toss decided to defend the Sussex road goal, Platt,
of course, being custodian, whilst Dawson took charge of the railway citadel. Southport, for about
the first twenty minutes' play were minus the service of Percy Mellor and were consequently at a
disadvantage. They however, held their own, and directly after his Worship had set the ball in
motion hostilities were carried into the Crescent camp. It was not allowed to remain there long for
the juveniles, by a series of really pretty passing, worked the leather towards the Sussex road goal,
only, however to be returned. The game was somewhat hotly contested, but the Stripes, having been
strengthened by the absentee, Percy, began to show advantage, and from a corner, negotiated in
beautiful style by T Morris, the late arrival succeeded in notching first blood for his side. There was
a cry of offside, but the plea was disallowed, and rightly so too. Soon after this a rather strong inside
was kept up in the vicinity of the Crescent goal, and ultimately T. Morris succeeded in scoring point
No 2. The claim was disputed by Crescent, whose objection was supported by the frantic cries of a
large number of spectators. The ground of the objectors having been stated to the referee, that
gentlemen decided against them, which gave rise to considerable unseemly behaviour. The decision,
however, was a correct one as the claim for offside was made for the wrong man. The registering of*

this goal somewhat dumped the energies of the youngsters, and up to the call of half time they lacked the dash and spirit which had characterised their previous efforts. After a brief rest play was resumed, the "Stripes" being two goals to the good. The game at the start was very fast, and the Crescent soon after gave evidence of tiring. However they fought manfully, but to no purpose, as Melross, after a few minutes' play, landed the third goal. The fourth point was scored by Burnett, who had greatly amused the spectators by his somewhat stiff style of play. The fifth and last goal was landed by T.Morris from a marvellous screw from the Blowick side of the ground, and shortly after the whistle sounded. The play all through was the best that had been witnessed in a charity cup tie, and of the winners Morris, Melross, Dalby, Griffiths, Johnson, Mellor and Briggs were most prominent. For the losers, the brothers Rimmer, Bryers, the brothers Morris, Liptrot and W.Halsall were best. Dawson, in goal, saved his charges several times in marvellous fashion, and Platt, when called upon, proved himself all there. The following were the teams: - Southfort: S.Platt, goal; H.Baxter and Griffiths, backs; Bailey, A.B.Dalby (Capt.), and Johnson, half backs; T.Morris, J.Melross, T.B.Burnett, Briggs and Mellor, forwards. Crescent: Dawson, goal; W.Rimmer and R.Rimmer, backs; Liptrot, Sharrock and W.Morris, half backs; R.Halsall, W.Halsall, C.Morris, A.Bryers and J.Leadbetter, forwards.

Immediately on the conclusion of the play the spectators rushed to the grand stand where his worship supported by a large and influential gathering, including among others Col. Hesketh, J.P., waited to distribute the cup and medals.

The MAYOR said – It is my pleasing duty to present to the winning team today a medal each to commemorate the plucky and successful manner in which they have worked their way through the various clubs they have had to compete with, and finally by this afternoon's crowning effort established themselves in the proud position of holders for the season of the Southport Charity Cup. (Cheers.) The good old game of football is one which finds special favour in my eyes, providing as it does every requisite for vigorous and healthy exercise and calling into play all those physical qualities which we as English men hold most dear. (Cheers.) I do not know any game which so thoroughly tests the skill, strength, pluck, and endurance of a man as football; and many of our heroes who have lately laid down their lives for their country on the battlefields of Soudan, first attracted the attention of their comrades by the display of those qualities on the mimic battlefield of the school football ground., which afterwards gained for them immortal distinction in the stern contests for their country's honour (Cheers.) It is said by the timid that it is a dangerous game, and that the players are very liable to accident. If I know my countrymen rightly, it is that very spice of danger, which lends a charm to the game itself – (hear, hear) — and I don't think the most timorous would counsel our young men to avoid a physical contest for fear they should be hurt. But granted that it is not desirable that we have our bones broken or our eyes blacked, I doubt very much whether the percentage of accidents is greatly at football than any other manly exercise, such as riding, driving, shooting, swimming, skating, etc (cheers). Then, what are we to do? If we go into the street we are liable to trip on a piece of orange peel; if we cross the street we may be knocked down by a passing cab. Mark Twain, after summing up on the percentage of risks from travelling by rail, going to tea and other causes, remarked that the most dangerous place to go was undoubtedly bed, because so many people met with their death there. (Laughter.) I am quite sure a man will be better able to stand the rough, hard knocks he is sure to receive if he is to make for himself any position in the world by pluckily and good humouredly giving and taking them on the football field. (cheers.) But whilst congratulating the winning team, we must not forget their plucky opponents. I have only today learned that both teams practically belong to one club, and as it is very evident that the losers are younger and smaller men, our sympathies naturally go with them as the weaker team.

(Applause.) They have played a very hard and plucky game, and next year I trust they will be able to reverse the result. (Applause.) This series of matches has been organised and played for the benefit of our local Infirmary; and I am glad to hear that the result is likely to be a substantial donation to that very deserving institution. (cheers.) It will possibly be more acceptable to the winners to receive their medals from the hands of the Mayoress than from mine. I will therefore with your permission ask her to perform that pleasing duty. (Cheers)
After the presentation of the cup and medals.

(Southport Visiter, 14th April 1885)

With victory in the Charity Cup, Southport confirmed their place as the 'premier club' in the town. Of the 30 matches played, 17 were won, 10 lost and 3 drawn, scoring 89 goals and conceding 40. (The Football Annual entry of 1885 actually notes P30 W16, D4, L10, GF90, A42 but the evidence contradicts those statistics).

(The final team photograph known to have been taken of Southport's first association football club – taken after the Charity Cup final in 1885.)

Top Row (L to R): J.H. Johnson, H.Baxter, J.H. Griffiths, J.Bailey, T.B.Burnett, R.W.T. Hatch (referee)
Bottom Row: T.Morris, J.Melross, A.B.Dalby, S.O.Platt, P.Mellor, J.J.Briggs

Whilst football had originally been started in the town as a means to fill the winter months where cricket was not played, there was growing recognition of the sports appeal to non-cricketers, and therefore it became commonplace for small-sided tournaments to take place at the end of the season to keep interest for such members. Southport were invited to take part in such a competition in Liverpool by the old friend of Thomas Burnett, Robert Lythgoe.

NOVEL FOOTBALL CONTEST IN LIVERPOOL – On Saturday evening, an interesting contest, under Association rules, took place at the Liverpool Gymnasium, before a large company of spectators. The "field of play" was 28 yards in length by about 10 yards, and seven teams of four players each entered the lists, as follows: -Everton, Everton B, Bootle, Bootle B, Southport, Stanley and Liverpool Gymnasium. The Liverpool Ramblers entered, but did not compete. Mr R.E. Lythgoe, honorary secretary of the Liverpool and District Association, was referee, and the awards were as follow: - Gymnasium beat Everton B, 1 goal to nil; Southport beat Bootle, 1 goal to nil; Everton beat Bootle B; Stanley beat Gymnasium, 1 goal to nil. The semi-final and final ties will be played off at the Gymnasium this evening, when his Worship the Mayor of Liverpool will present the district cup and medals to Earlestown and Everton, winners and runners-up during the past season.

(Liverpool Mercury – 4th May 1885)

In Southport, Wanderers and High Park both staged six-a-side tournaments of their own, 18 clubs being said to have entered the competition arranged by High Park. The field was 80 by 30 yards and the teams played 15 minutes each way.

Not content with raising £30 for the Infirmary, the season concluded with a match between the winners of the Southport Charity Cup. The two teams lined up mas follows:

Southport: Mayall, (Goal); Baxter, Griffiths, (backs); Bailey, Platt, Johnson (½ backs); Melross, Dalby, Morris (Capt.), Mellor, Hodge, (forwards).

Southport & District: Moorhead (Wanderers), (Goal); J.Parks (Wanderers), Cadwell (High Park), (backs); Sellers(Wanderers), H.Shaw (High Park), J.Liptrot (Crescent), (½ backs); Dutton (Christ Church), Halsall (High Park), Hazlehurst (High Park), Hoban (High Park), Hill (High Park), (forwards).

The Athletic Society, with whom the club had partnered, was also thriving. With the annual Amateur Athletics Association Championships now being rotated between the South, Midlands and the North, Sussex Road was chosen as the first Northern venue.

The first annual AGM for Southport Wanderers was held on 27th April at Mr Scarlett's Rooms on Chapel Street. It was attended by over 40 members. The committee, despite all of the expenditure associated with establishing a brand-new club were able to look back on the season with a balance still in hand. Having steered the new club through its first season as captain, W.Kay stepped down from his duties and was afforded a vote of thanks from all those present. Subscriptions were fixed again at just 2s 6d, with a view to establishing Wanderers as the representative town's club.

The Railway Hotel, with Mather's adjoined Sales room on Chapel Street, opposite Corporation Street.

The Premier Club

Southport announced a series of ambitious fixtures for the coming 1885/86 season; Port Vale, winners of the North Staffordshire Charity Cup, Earlestown, winners of the Liverpool and District Cup and Newton Heath, runners up in the Manchester and District Cup were all scheduled alongside fixtures with Everton and some of the more prominent local clubs.

On 15th August the Southport Guardian reported that *'Not only should the first object of a club be to encourage football playing, but it is only through a good second or training team that the strength of the first be maintained. We trust the club will, so far as possible, take its recruits solely from the second team'*. Burnett for the most part withdrew from the field though he was to make the occasional first team appearance, but he reprised his role on the committee by overseeing second team commitments and assisting Richard Hatch, who, although appointed to the post of honorary secretary as part of the tie-in with the Athletic Society, appeared to want a less prominent role. In a bid to compete for members with the other clubs in the town, subscriptions were slashed to five shillings. Fixtures were arranged with the second strings of Everton, Earlestown, Stanley and others, alongside matches against the local schools and junior sides such as Sandringham School and Holy Trinity.

Many of the players involved with Southport and Wanderers opened the season on 29th August 1885 by representing Southport & District against High Park on the latter's Devonshire Road ground. The team selected to represent the District was as follows: Muirhead (Wanderers), goal; H.Baxter (Southport), Griffiths (Southport), backs; Bailey (Southport), Sellars (Wanderers), Liptrot (Crescent), half-backs; W.Halsall (Crescent), R.Blackledge (Crescent), P.Mellor (Southport), Dutton (Christ Church), T.Morris (Southport). On the day, Liptrot was unavailable with his place taken by Wainwright of the same club, Crescent. Southport Captain Tom Morris claimed a hat-trick, and Christ Church's Dicky Dutton one more as the District overcame High Park by 4 goals to 1. Thomas Burnett acted as umpire for the District team.

The season would open officially for Southport with the visit of Turton. Association football in Lancashire in the 1880s had been born essentially from two clubs, Darwen (founded 1870) and Turton (1871). Turton, just north of Bolton, was established by the Key family, who had made a fortune pioneering innovations in the flax-spinning industry. Although many years had passed since they had been at the peak of their influence, they still carried with them a recognised name and therefore to open the season with a win over their illustrious opponents gave Southport much hope.

A Capital match is expected as the visitors have a good team and are the oldest Association club in Lancashire

(Southport Visiter, 5th September 1885)

As the season began only Josiah Melross remained of the originals, in a side containing several newcomers. He had spent much of the summer engaged successfully in athletic meetings across the region, however, and was therefore unable to play in the opening fixture. Barely a week before the season began, he had picked up a handsome marble timepiece valued at five guineas as his prize having won the 100 yards handicap at Hoo Green sports. Beating a field of 43 through the heats, he overcame a seven yard head start given to a rival competitor in the final, H.Howarth from Middleton, to win by a clear yard.

The line-up for Southport was far from being at its strongest, missing the aforementioned Melross, but also Captain Dalby and the erstwhile goalkeeping talents of Squire Platt. Johnny Mayall stood in for Platt, and gave a good account of himself, the captaincy fell to Tom Morris. The line-up was: J.Mayall, H.Baxter, J.Griffiths, J.Briggs, P.Mellor, C.Morris, W.Hodge, T.Morris, A.Bailey, J.Johnson, J.Halsall.

SOUTHPORT v TURTON — The opening game was played at Southport on Saturday afternoon, and resulted in a win for Southport by 3 goals to 1. The home team won the toss and played with a strong wind at their backs. They had the best of the game, but were only able to score once during the first half, Hodge adding the final touch, Bentley scoring a goal for Turton by a beautiful shot. Changing ends and with the wind against them, the seasiders played a capital passing game, and scored two more goals.

(Liverpool Mercury - 7th September 1885)

Despite some erratic shooting, a feature of the side throughout much of the previous season, the report above suggests that Southport were very good value for their 3-1 victory. Having won the toss Morris chose ends rather than take the kick off, and therefore placed Turton at an immediate disadvantage shooting towards the railway goal with the sun and wind in their faces. Southport's first goal, by Hodge, came after a period of extended pressure and the cheers from those assembled were of relief that the ball had finally gone between the posts. Turton equalised before half time and it was expected that they would step up a gear in the second half with the wind in their favour. Southport, however, had other ideas. Charlie Morris and Percy Mellor added to Southport's total in a half that could have seen even more had it not been for the goalkeeping heroics of the visiting custodian J.J. Greenhalgh.

The public will be pleased to know that several important improvements have been made to the ground for the comfort of spectators, notably boarding round the portion of the grandstand, which is now a capital protection against the weather.

(Southport Visiter, 8ᵗʰ September 1885)

On the same day that Southport faced Turton, Wanderers' final preparation for their season-proper, was a peculiar one. Having arranged to kick off against the new Blowick club, only six men showed. Five from the committee had to step in to make up the numbers and the game ended in a 2-2 draw.

The Liverpool Challenge Cup had given the Stripes a first round draw away at Burscough for the Stripes, and with Melross returning to the side at the expense of Halsall, another 3-1 win was achieved. Bolton Wanderers reserves meanwhile visited Scarisbrick New Road to face the Wanderers. By the end of the game Bolton had registered no less than 16 goals, a further four disallowed, whilst the locals could not even register a single point. Wanderers had put together a side with which they were increasingly confident of being able to steal away the Cup from their friendly rivals at Sussex Road, importing players from Preston to assist, but with no other first team playing in the town, a good number of spectators witnessed a complete capitulation, and the overwhelming conclusion was that they should leave matters in the hands of the locals.

Whilst professionalism in Lancashire had effectively been given the green light by the Lancashire Football Association that summer, it was with the caveat that all professionals needed to be registered with the local and national Football Associations. Furthermore, they were only permitted to play for one club in a season (1ˢᵗ September – 30ᵗʰ April). In Scotland the FA had made the decision not to allow clubs to play against any team containing professionals, which for clubs like Blackburn Rovers and Preston North End caused quite a problem. Both clubs regularly travelled north of the border for fixtures and, faced with such a restriction, Preston took the decision to cancel their plans to face the Scottish giants Queen's Park. Blackburn Rovers, however, agreed to make alternative arrangements rather than forfeit the chance to play at Hampden Park. Rovers arranged for a team consisting solely of amateurs to travel to Glasgow under their name, whilst their professionals took on rivals Blackburn Olympic nearer to home.

Whilst it's true that interest in football had now grown in Southport to the extent that big games in nearby towns such as Preston or Blackburn would often draw spectators away from local matches, the Hampden fixture piqued interests for an entirely different reason as Southport's Tom Morris and A.Bailey were called upon to assist the handful of amateurs that were in the Blackburn ranks.

Considerable excitement was caused on Wednesday night amongst the local football community when the fact became known that T.Morris and A.Bailey of the Southport Football Club, had been asked by the Blackburn Rovers to play for them in their great match at Glasgow this afternoon against the Queen's Park, the crack Scottish Club. The stubbornness of the Scottish

Football Association with regards to the professional question nearly caused the match to drop through, but the Rovers, in order not to disappoint their doughty cup opponents, determined to get together a strong amateur team, this being the cause of our two well-known players being asked. Quite a little crowd of footballers assembled on Friday morning at the West Lancashire Station to see Morris and Bailey off, and hearty wishes of success were freely expressed.

(Southport Visiter, 19th September 1885)

Queen's Park at this time had been regular entrants into the FA Cup and had built quite a rivalry with Blackburn after contesting two finals with them. Of course, neither Morris nor Bailey wanted to pass up the chance to be involved in such a fixture, even if it was to be without some of the Rovers' strongest men. It was a team dubbed *'more Lancashire than Rovers'* by the Glasgow press, which is even more curious as neither Morris nor Bailey held any county honours. How they had been chosen for selection is a bit of a mystery. Tommy Morris did rather well in the 7-1 win in Glasgow, as it happens, and many suggested a county invitation may actually be on the cards if he kept up his form.

Back home, with the enforced absences of several key men, Morris and Bailey amongst them, results took a bit of a nose-dive and threatened to derail Southport's season before it had ever really begun. The game against High Park marked a turning point.

HIGH PARK v SOUTHPORT

The premier club journeyed to High Park to play their fixture with the villagers last Saturday. There was a large turnout of spectators who had the pleasure of seeing a good match. H.Baxter won the toss and chose to play with the wind at their backs. Tasker kicked off, and it was soon apparent that the game was to be a fast one. Southport rushed the ball up to the Park's quarters, but Barton caught them up, returning the ball with a high kick. Hoban and Hill getting possession ran up the length of the field and shot, but it went behind the line. Southport now pressed the High Parkers, putting in some shots which Spencer fisted out in grand style; but from a corner nicely put in Southport drew first blood. This reverse roused the High Parkers, who began to show some really grand play, their dribbling and passing fairly bothering the premier club. Hoban getting the ball passed it to centre, Haslehurst passing again to Hill, the little left winger made the game even at half time. After a short rest play was resumed, Southport rushing off with the ball, but Cadwell and partner were all there. High Park now pressed their opponents, three corners following in succession; but owing to the high wind Singleton put all three behind. Not to be denied, they still kept the ball in Southport's quarters, Baxter and Griffiths defending well, but at last the winning point was gained by High Park, amidst the shouts of delight from their friends and supporters. Southport now playing desperately, at times introducing the elements of roughness into their play, but High Park were in no ways disconcerted, playing a safe defensive game to the finish, ultimately defeating the premier club by two goals to one. For the winners, Spencer in goal played a splendid game. The coolness and ease with which he got away the shots of his opponents was very much admired. Cadwell and Barton played a good game, the latter improving every match. The way Jos. was bottled up by the 'little un' was a caution. The half backs also did a big share of the work while the five forwards compared favourably with their doughty opponents. For the losers, Briggs,

Baxter, and Griffith played a good defence game; but the forwards were disappointing, playing too selfish a game and with a great want of combination.

(Southport Guardian, 26th September 1885)

The match was not the first time the two clubs had met, that event having taken place little under a year earlier when Southport had progressed at the expense of 'the Parkites' in the Liverpool Challenge Cup, but this was the first match on High Park soil, and the first time the town's original club had failed to beat another local club. The Southport Guardian had become accustomed to referring to them as the 'premier club' and, to the casual reader, most would not question the use of the term. After all, until this point no other local side had yet disposed of the Reds or the Stripes as they were now known and therefore the claim had some merit on the field. They had seen off all competition and even had the trophy to prove it, which had been presented to them by the Mayor.

It was common for reports in those days to have been written and submitted to the newspaper by the home club and therefore the frequent use of the 'premier club' adage in this respect could have been intended by High Park to emphasise the magnitude of their achievement in beating the reigning Charity Cup holders.

The Southport Guardian's brand new 'Our Athletic Column', included in their first Wednesday issue of the following week, is as interesting as the report of the game itself in that it is the first time the club's 'premier' tag is called into question. It features the below comment from an un-named contributor, whose resentment at being seen as second-best is obvious.

Several football players have sent in opinions which, for the present, we shall publish with but slight comment of our own. "A member of an ambitious Southport club" sends us word that he decidedly objects to the continual hoisting up of the Southport Club's colours by describing that club with painful iteration as the "premier club". He thinks the "premier" might be dropped for about a fortnight, just as an acknowledgement of the fact that other clubs are making a try for the club this season. Our friend of the "ambitious club" should allow a little more for the pride which each man ought to feel in the process of and position of his own team, but we believe his hint is fairly intended, and it may prove useful generally

(Southport Guardian, 30th September 1885)

The anonymous source of this comment may have come from High Park, who certainly fell into the category of 'ambitious club', but I think it is unlikely. The term 'premier club' gives greater emphasis to the size and magnitude of their victory so I doubt that they would object to it. The author suspects that the quip may have come from those involved with Southport Wanderers who were showing significant strides in the 12 months since their formation. Their ambition became clearer still when, on 23rd September, members of the Wanderers and another local club, Southport Crescent, had met to thrash out terms of an amalgamation of both clubs. As Crescent were the previous season's beaten Charity Cup finalists, as a combined force they were gearing up to make a strong run for the Cup.

Another incident of note reported in the same column shows how much the Cup had captured the imagination of the local youngsters.

An old Football Player writes:- I don't at all believe that the football 'craze' does any good to the game, but mischief decidedly. Football has its proper place, and suffers if it takes too much attention at times when a match is not being played or a club meeting held. The extent, however to which football is agitating the juvenile mind alone may be guessed when I relate a literally true incident that came under my notice in Sussex-road the other day. Several respected householders were rung-up before seven o'clock with the intention that they were 'particularly wanted'. On coming sleepily downstairs, they found a juvenile of ten summer waiting with a collection sheet, and smiling inviting their subscriptions to a club which he and his little friends were forming with the ambition about winning a cup.

(Southport Guardian, 30ᵗʰ September 1885)

Preston's Fishwick Ramblers were just about the strongest side to have yet visited the town when they arrived at the end of September 1885 to play Southport and the game elicited many loud cheers and much excitement, even if it was for the play of the visitors rather than the home side as they ran out 7-0 winners. Two days later and the visit of Sheffield brought with it the third defeat on the trot - a fact that wasn't lost on those who bore witness. It must be said, however, that up to this point the Stripes had not been able to turn out their strongest XI in any of the first month's fixtures. T.Wright and J.B.Richardson made their debuts against Sheffield, and even Burnett had to dust off his boots to ensure the fixture went ahead. When Percy Mellor and Josiah Melross then went on to pick up injuries in the game, the crisis deepened.

The weakness of the Southport team appeared in the mean tearing about the field, and not playing the scientific game or each man keeping his own position and not over-running too far that of his comrades....The dash and go of the Southport men is a quality they must not lose, but they really must "drill" more, and let discretion conquer their impetuosity, so as to conserve their energies. In home matches they always have the better chance, in a more special sense, than is common with more methodical playing clubs, but if they ever are to meet such clubs as Sheffield, Queen's Park, the Blackburn Rovers, the Blackburn Olympic or the Preston North End, on equal terms, they must reserve their strength for operations over a more limited area and depend more upon each other. Each man must feel that where he ends his run and passes another man will take up and each must be prepared to follow on with a good run at his own point and carry up the ball until a shot for goal may be made for himself, if a forward, or by the forward to whom he passes.

(Southport Guardian, 30ᵗʰ September 1885)

Whilst Southport were in the middle of a selection crisis, on 29th September the now newly merged Wanderers and Crescent clubs, under the name of Wanderers, held their first

General Meeting. J.G, Emmison took the chair and congratulated the two clubs on forming what was sure to be a successful new club being able to draw on the combined strength of the two sides.

By this uniting of the two clubs the playing strength has been considerably increased, and he had little hesitation in prophesying a successful season. The good feeling that existed amongst the members argued well for this result, and he had not the least doubt that by attending to practice and when at play each man playing unselfishly the club would before long take the leading position amongst the local clubs.

(Southport Visiter, 1st October 1885)

Without their key men, Southport travelled to another of the great Lancashire clubs, Darwen, for the Lancashire Cup at the start of October. In recent weeks Darwen too had been struggling for form, not having won a game so far - therefore Southport hoped that the Cup would give them an opportunity to turn around their fortunes, even if they were facing one of the most famous clubs in the North of England.

A lot can be said for the benefit of home advantage, and Darwen's heavy ground certainly gave them that. After taking the express train to Bolton, and a half hour wait for the same to Darwen, upon arrival the Southport players found their way on foot to the finely laid out ground with large grandstand, changing in the room on the top side of the refreshment pavilion as the large enthusiastic crowd filed in.

It was a late kick off with Southport eventually taking the field at 4.43, Darwen following behind them a full ten minutes later in blue and white stripes to Southport's red and white. The first fifteen minutes were fairly even and cries of 'Well played, Southport' could be heard according to the reports. Then the first goal went in for the home side, a smart shot through a scrimmage of players and bouncing in off the legs of Baxter. It was to be the first of many as Southport left the field at half time 4-0 down.

After the break and with a light breeze in their favour, Southport appeared to have improved, notching a goal quickly after the resumption of play through a Charles Morris header from his brother Tom's centre. It was, however, to be the only bright spot of the game. Darwen quickly scored again. And again. And again…. Thankfully they stopped at 12!

Burnett had returned to the position of umpire for the game, whilst Richardson and Wright had both kept their places in the absence of the injured duo. Platt returned in goal but could not stop the onslaught.

The critics were quick to pounce again and the Southport Guardian happy to publish their comments.

An 'Old Football Player' who acts as a kind of mentor to the Southport Club, writes :- I wish to impress upon each member of the Southport team the necessity of trusting more in playing the passing game than the long kicking often indulged in, as it is evident…that a long kick (unless a shot at goal, or from the backs to the forward line) is as likely to land the ball at the foot of an opponent as to one of the home side; whereas a pass from one player to another gives a far better opportunity of eluding the opposing players.

(Southport Guardian, 14th October 1885)

The following week, although Southport led Astley 2-0 at half time, they were beaten 3-2 in an English Challenge Cup-tie. The negativity surrounding the club had now reached fever pitch and everyone seemed to offer an opinion.

After the unbroken series of reverses this afternoon the Southport team has experienced this season, speculation was rife on Saturday afternoon at the Sussex-road ground, as to whether they would be able to take down the Bridgeites. On the stand side the spectators were not so confident as to the result, as rumours where astir that the visitors said they were going to win by ten goals to none. However, that did not disturb our local men much, for they were determined on – if not beating them well – at least giving them as good a game as possible. Rumours were afloat early on that Buttery had arrived, but anyone who had met the man mentioned by "An Old Footballer" would at once have seen the two were not identical. The visitors were a very even lot, rather light, but speedy, and throughout the game played a fair gentlemanly game. There was almost an entire absence of that roughness sometimes seen at these encounters, charging being little indulged in, although one portion of the spectators shouted loudly to their particular favourites to "take the man". The old fault, noticed before on the local players' part, was again present – want of organisation. Is it not possible to keep your own positions Southport? The visitors I think gave you a lesson in this. Seldom did you see them in a cluster, racing the ball from right to left, but they kept more to their own positions in the field. Unless our local men get over this habit, they will never play a winning game. The Southport players, individually, are a finer and speedier lot of men, but the fatal indulgence I have mentioned frustrates all the endeavours of individual players to score.

(Southport Guardian, 14th October 1885)

Questions were asked in the Athletic News as to whether Astley had in fact fielded an ineligible player in Buttery, but no appeal resulted. The two-goal advantage had only been surrendered in the face of very strong winds and it was an unfortunate handball by Briggs in the final minutes, which gave the 'Bridgeites' a free kick in a dangerous position from which they scored their winner. Southport were defeated after a gallant fight but in light of the recent heavy reverses, there were still some positive signs.

Fortunes did change, and they started with a 4-1 win over Southport Wanderers on 17th October. It was to be the first of five fixtures between the two clubs over the course of the season.

SOUTHPORT v WANDERERS

Teams- Southport: S.Platt, goal; H.Baxter and Griffiths, backs; Bailey, Briggs and Johnson, (½ backs); T.Morris and J.Melross, right wing; C.Morris, centre; Mellor and Richardson, left wing; Umpire, Mr.Hatch

Wanderers: W.Kay, goal; Parks (Capt.) and Berry, backs; Sellars, Liptrot and Sharrock, (½ backs); R.Halsall and W.Halsall, right wing; E.Stead, centre; Leadbetter and T.Lea, left wing; umpire, Mr. J.E.Emmison; refer Mr. Whittaker.

The tram car stops opposite the Wanderers' ground. Wish there was a tram-line when we have to go to Sussex-road. Time for leisurely survey of the field, the start being postponed for 15 minutes. Field suggests captain Mayne Reid's "rolling prairie" after a steam-roller had passed once over. It is level in so far as the hollows are not noticeable. Still it is dry, being sandy, like all Southport grounds. Must go further inland for the quagmire, or to play on the side of the "broo". No dressing-room on field, so players balance on a plank, called, by courtesy, a grand stand, and adjust boot-laces. Wanderers' committee wise to not run into debt. One supporter comes up with a sovereign towards a dressing tent, and a fair "gate" is being taken — Southport to divide the gate but not the sovereign. Think a few of the Wanderers might be more smart in their dress. Wonder why Baxter of the Southport is "got up" to resemble in body a magnified Wasp. Hope Squire Platt has put on his woolen jersey underneath his stripes, for the wind whistles between the goal posts. Fix ourselves on the grand stand, and mighty glad the vanished fog has not let the rain down. No cover anywhere at a Southport football match. Ladies plucky.

(Southport Guardian, 21ˢᵗ October 1885)

The game offered much excitement and at times the front row of spectators got so close to the pitch that they impinged on play, those at the back losing their view almost entirely. Others climbed the walls and mounted the fences of the neighbouring Ash Street houses much to the chagrin of the owners. The report also confirms that at this time, none of the grandstands within the town had any cover, which explains why the weather had such an impact upon attendances. The report also shows that Wanderers were not a club flush with money, and the bare essentials were all that were available to those who came to visit them at Scarisbrick New Road.

The brothers Morris, Tom and Charlie, both scored two apiece and the overall play from Southport was a vast improvement. The difference was in the quality of finishing, the Wanderers forwards not able to deliver as clinically as their counterparts, but they showed the makings of a good team.

It was a happy thought when it was found that both the Southport and Wanderers first teams were without a fixture last Saturday to arrange a match to be played on the Scarisbrick New-road ground. The friendly rivalry which has existed between these clubs has done much towards improving the quality of the play, and there were not a few people who, since the amalgamation of the Crescent with the Wanderers, had come to the conclusion that the claim of the "Stripes" to the distinctive title of "premier" club had departed. As the result showed, however, the Sussex-road men were the best at the finish.

(Southport Visiter, 24ᵗʰ October 1885)

The Visiter also suggested that more of the crowd should have *'sought fit to avail themselves of three coppers'* and therefore contributed to the expenses incurred in arranging the match, rather than seeking any means possible to avoid parting with their money. It was to become a common complaint with the Visiter repeating the suggestion in January.

The field will be canvassed, and it is hoped that the contingent who throng outside the field will to-day put their hands in their pockets and part with the small sum of three pence and witness the match in comfort.

(Southport Visiter, Saturday, 16th January 1886)

The publication of the 'Southport Football Handbook' by Messrs. A Ramsbottom and Sons of Eastbank Street at the end of October 1885 showed how popular the sport was becoming. It included the cup draws and fixture lists of all of the local clubs, and over the course of the season there would be displays of the various different club jerseys and the medals for the winners and runners up of the Charity Cup competition in their shop window.

After the victory over Wanderers, Southport returned to Sussex Road for a Liverpool Cup tie with Burscough. Having crashed out of the other two competitions early, there was hope that this one would help them to rescue their season. Mellor reported ill on the morning of the game, his place being taken by Hodge in an otherwise unchanged line-up. The weather was appalling, and the strong winds put many off attending, the pay gates and grandstand being decidedly quieter than expected. Calls for a roof to be added to the grandstand were growing.

The match itself was hardly noteworthy other than for the wind assisted winning goal, a high kick from Melross which sailed over the Burscough goalkeeper Georgeson and between the posts.

Wanderers meanwhile had a much more attractive tie, as they travelled to Everton's latest home, Anfield Road, in the same competition.

EVERTON v SOUTHPORT WANDERERS – This game was played at Anfield-road on Saturday, in the presence of a goodly number of spectators, and resulted in a victory for the home players by 3 goals to 1. The wanderers kicked off, but were quickly driven back on the defensive, Richard, Gurley, and Farmer each putting in capital runs; and the latter gave the visitors' goalkeeper a warm handful. Then the Wanderers surprised everyone by dashing away, and, after some capital passing, scored first, amidst some cheering. The home players then worked hard, but were weak in front of goal; and then the Wanderers centre effected a pretty run down, but kicked wide. The game was pretty even up to half-time, the result then being in favour of Southport Wanderers by 1 to 0. The visitors at once became aggressive, but Everton returning found plenty of work for the opposing backs. Dobson placing the ball well in the Wanderers' goal, Richards quickly shot it through amidst cheers. Immediately after, the ball was again scrimmaged through the same goal, although the visitors were by no means satisfied with the point. Everton now pressed strongly, and from a corner well placed by Corey, Farmer rushed through a third point for his side. The game continued in favour of Everton and Corey again shot through, the point being disallowed.

(Liverpool Mercury – Monday 26th October 1885)

As Everton had been runners-up to Earlestown in the final of the competition only a few months earlier, very little chance had been afforded to Wanderers, but the home side did not pick up the easy victory that had anticipated. Wanderers were in fact cheered all the way to the dressing room for the manner in which they had put up a fight in a 1-3 defeat.

At the start of November, a re-match had been arranged with the United Schools of Southport but with their opponents withdrawing, a last-minute fixture with Liverpool Cambrian was arranged in its place, resulting in another 3-1 win the Stripes. Criticism had been levelled at the club that the reason for the original postponement had actually been the inability of Southport to raise a team and the absence of a number of the regulars from the line-up against Cambrian suggests this may have been the case. The surprise inclusion of a couple of Wanderers players in the line-up for the game hints, however, at a growing affinity between the two clubs and perhaps the relationship building skills of members of the committee, and in particular Thomas Burnett.

With Mellor, C.Morris and Wright failing to show for the hastily arranged game, Sellars, Leadbetter and Lea from the Wanderers stepped in, all three playing well - Lea even laid on the third goal with a smart pass for Tommy Morris to finish.

Although three back-to-back wins were welcome, the underlying issues in the Southport team still remained and a mid-week conference was arranged for the members to gather to discuss their shortcomings. Commentary on what is now commonly referred to as the 'sweeper-keeper' style of Squire Platt was common.

Allow me a word re your criticism of Squire Platt, the Southport goalkeeper. If you agree to describe Platt as 'occasionally' nomadic, I can coincide with you, but I object to 'essentially'. I cry against Platt going out so far for this reason. He is, deservedly, a popular player, and when he is half across the field, the backs leave kicks to him which they ought to take in combination, or which the wings and centre ought not to have allowed to pass. This taking of another player's kicks is, speaking in a football sense, unpardonable in the goalkeeper, for no other player can fill his place. Therefore I endorse your remarks, save the one word already specified, which, however, may not deserve the importance that has been attached to it in this communication, and by other outsiders.

('An Old Football Player', Southport Guardian, 11th November 1885)

Against the backdrop of such discussions Southport had to pick themselves up for a visit to Everton, the biggest of all of the clubs in the district. The Cambrian fixture had been briefly in doubt, given the torrential downpours before kick-off, and although there had been a brief cessation during the game, the rains had continued for much of the following week. Southport arrived late and the game was reduced to two halves of 35 minutes each as a consequence. Mayall, the stand-in goalkeeper in the absence of Platt, was kept busy, and were it not for him and the backs, Baxter in particular, the scoreline might have been a lot higher than the 3-0 reversal that transpired. Until close to the finish there had only been one goal difference in the tie. In comparison to the experienced Everton side, the Southport team was full of youthful exuberance, but little in the way of tactical nous was shown.

Southport Wanderers visited Sussex Road for a quick return fixture the following week. Although Platt was able to return to the Southport side in goal, the Stripes were still noticeably weakened by the absences of Baxter, Mellor and Richardson giving Wanderers hope that they could lower their local rivals' colours. The bitter Southport cross winds put paid to any hopes of a high gate. Another late start also meant both sides were more than happy to accept a compromise of half an hour each way.

In the first match Southport scored 4 to 1. Taking Southport all in all, we have never seen them to better advantage. The ball was less often out than usual, the goalkeeper stood his ground without a single excursion, Mayall kept his own side as back capitally and Griffiths never missed any of his few chances. The centre play was good, and the forward play showed marked advance in combination.....Judging the Wanderers by their former match with Southport — we have never seen them in any other occasion — our opinion is that they are improving at such a rate as to promise very well indeed for the future.

(Southport Guardian, 18th November 1885)

The result finished 3-1 to the Stripes and although local dominance was in the process of being restored for Southport, opponents from further afield were still proving too much for a team lacking in experienced on-field leadership. Johnson joined the side who were without Platt once again for the visit to Stanley in Liverpool. Mayall dropped from the back line to take up position between the posts once more, but the Visiter reported that the cry was 'Platt, you're wanted' as the side shipped five in his absence, with only one in reply.

In truth, the game had been closer than the score-line suggested. At halftime Southport were only 2-0 down and Bailey had restored some hope with a quick goal after the restart. It wasn't until the very end that Stanley scored three times in quick succession. What the score-line doesn't reveal is that Melross had unfortunately picked up another injury and the majority of the game was played with just 10 men. It was a long time before the concept of substitutions was to be introduced, of course.

Outside of the county cup competitions, Wanderers still often struggled to arrange suitably competitive fixtures with clubs from outside of the town. A match had been arranged with the Preston association club. However, upon learning of their demise, Wanderers reached out to Wigan who were happy to oblige. On their arrival at Scarisbrick New Road, they were disappointed to learn that the visiting XI was comprised of more second team men than first. The Southport Guardian reported that it was against a side made up of only half of the Wigan first XI – although it concluded that it must have been the lesser half.

The Southport Guardian report doesn't add a great deal to the description of the game but does add some comment regarding the comforts of the ground – or lack of them.

Fortunately, the small wicket by which the Wanderer's ground is accessible from Scarisbrick New Road is not a type of the "gates" which gather on the grand stand, which, by the way is a cost thing for the feet, but lifts one up into the cutting wind. Hence, instead of hearing cries of "Go it, Wanderers!" "Play Up, Wigan!" the spectators were singing out "Isn't it cold?" "What a lot of starvation for three pence!" and so on. The veterans complained the least and the young men monopolised the growling.

(Southport Guardian, 25th November 1885)

Wanderers continued their good run of form by defeating neighbours Burscough by three goals to one on 28th November. The Stripes of Southport took their defeat to Wanderers on the chin, and in good spirits welcomed Liverpool Ramblers to Sussex Road. No goals were scored by either team in what the Southport Guardian described as *'one of the least spectated games seen there for some time'* but the Visiter pointed out that this was perhaps more likely the fault of the ground in so much as it was more conducive to sailing than football, such were the size of the puddles sat on the playing surface. Had the club any kind of working relationship with the Athletic Society, on whose ground they were playing, one might have expected a concerted effort to be made in terms of remedying what was becoming a common problem. Tensions appeared to be growing between the two parties.

As December approached the town was gripped by election fever with the opportunity to select the first Member of Parliament for the Southport Division of Lancashire. The Visiter commented that in such times of political excitement it was inevitable that other activities in the town would take more of a back seat. The election itself saw George Pilkington elected as the town's first MP. He was the president of Southport Wanderers and was certainly a friend of the game in general as his speech at the presentation ceremony of the Charity Cup in May had shown.

Southport had meanwhile engaged the services of John Unwin, the town's Mayor, as president for the forthcoming year. He wrote to the Visiter to mark his acceptance of the position on 12th December. Whilst the election was ongoing there had been calls in the town to make use of vacant land on the foreshore and suggestions that it should be put to better use as an athletics field that could also be used by the town's various sports clubs, football and cricket included. Wanderers still officially occupied two fields, Portland Street and Scarisbrick New Road, and there were many others in use throughout the town, so it was not for lack of available space that it was being suggested. It was instead for the development potential it had as an attraction. In much the same way that the Sports Ground on Sussex Road had been developed to cater for large events, it had been part of the pre-election discussion, championed by the Mayor, that the foreshore should have a similar attraction. For those in charge of Sussex Road, it would be difficult to support such a proposal if it might remove the possibility of being able to hire out their own ground. There was a much greater call from them for the tram companies to remember where the Blowick area is and extend their lines accordingly to Sussex Road. The Lancashire & Yorkshire railway station at St Luke's remained the closest but this still presented patrons with a considerable walk.

The Liverpool Challenge Cup threw up the next big challenge for Southport by producing a draw with another big Liverpool club, our old friends Bootle.

Let this be said of the Southport Club, that they don't growl when they lose. The placidity with which they can stand even a succession of defeats would raise the envy of a stoic.
Southport have failed to get into the second round for the Liverpool Cup, and this is what a supporter of the Sandgrounders tells us –
"Baxter and Briggs did well, but the rest of the team would have been improved by six new players, or by new form on the part of six old ones."
The referee (Mr. Gregson of Blackburn) said – "I saw the Southport team when they first began to play three years ago. In this match against Bootle they played as they did then. Let us, however, beg of the other local teams not to count on the cup until they have won it. Southport always play best at the end of a match, and they have something in reserve for the end of the season, if they don't wait too long before pulling themselves together."

(Southport Guardian, 16th December 1885)

The Southport Visiter were a little more forceful in their criticism of the 5-0 defeat to Bootle and noted that *These defeats are becoming too frequent to be pleasant, and a big effort should be made to score a success, else the title of "premier" club will have to be foregone'.* They appealed to 'Mr Secretary Burnett' for some fresh blood indicating that Burnett had taken over more of Richard Hatch's duties.

Wanderers faced another big local club, High Park, on 12th December where a large crowd assembled on the Scarisbrick New Road ground to witness a 2-1 victory for the home team.

By Christmas, and particularly as the worst of the weather was setting in, the issue of poor gates was really starting to cause problems for Southport. The Guardian had made frequent comments about the difficulty with which the Sussex Road ground could be accessed by public transport in comparison to some of the other local clubs, particularly those with fields on Scarisbrick New Road. Teams travelling from a distance rightly expected their fair share of the gate receipts to cover their expenses, but when the gate was paltry in the first place, it left Southport with little or nothing else.

On 19th December the Visiter upped the ante and openly addressed the rumours swirling around the town.

There are all kinds of rumours in this town about Football. The "premier" club it is said is going to the dogs, and that within the next few weeks the place that knows it today will know it no more for ever. Well we have all heard this kind of thing before, but it has all proved to be rumour, nothing but rumour. It is only fair to say with this regard to this the latest rumour respecting the decline of the "Stripes" that Baxter, the redoubtable full back, has thrown in his lot with the

Wanderers, and that his withdrawal from the "Stripes" has been followed not only by one or two players but also by an old supporter of the "Stripes", and one that in days past has discharged the duties of secretary.

(Southport Visiter, 12th December 1885)

It was not for the first time, as the report suggests, that questions had been asked about the viability of being able to sustain two big local clubs. The Visiter had openly questioned back in October whether there was merit in considering an amalgamation in order to ensure that the town could field a team capable of challenging any club in the land. The club's off-field strength was being called into question in much the same way that its on field strength had been in the early part of the season. It perhaps comes as little surprise that talk in the town was rife as to the future of the club.

Southport wants a strong football club, a club with first and second teams able to meet all comers, a representative club, in brief worthy of the high name of the borough. The Southport club needs fresh blood, but there is no one other local club strong enough to supersede them. The Wanderers run the Stripes hard, but do not place them second. High Park, which also puts Southport on their mettle and has beaten them, represent a district, and has a territorial title of its own. What is to be done? If not too daring a proposal, we would venture to suggest that High Park be left to develop its powers and that Southport and the Wanderers unite. Southport would gain some of the players they lack, and the Wanderers could secure a name which they deserve to share. Bold as the idea seems, it is likely to be very seriously discussed and may be carried into effect.
Birkdale might, also, well consider whether some amalgamation scheme is not feasible.
We advocate no changes, however, until all the cup ties have been decided.

(Southport Guardian, 23rd December 1885)

The idea to merge the two clubs together had some merit. In fact, Burnett had already reached out for help in fulfilling the hastily arranged fixture with Liverpool Cambrian earlier in the season. There was already a working relationship. The interesting aspect is that whilst the club had started the season with the intention of running a second string, there is little evidence to suggest that the experiment went very well. There are very few second team reports published in the local papers at all. Despite wanting to use the team to support the first team in providing players, they could not do so when they had found themselves short for the fixture with Cambrian. Financially too the move to the Sports Ground was not paying off in the way that the club had hoped it would. Encouraged by the large attendances the athletics events always attracted, there had been optimism that the crowds would come, but they did not. Gates were dwindling and with it too were any hopes of a profit.

The original football club, formed to play rugby in 1872, had been formed as the Southport Gymnasium and Football Club, but the gymnasium, housed in the old artillery drill shed on Part Street, was so separate from the field on Alexandra Road on which the football was played that after the initial opening of the gym, nothing further was said about its links with football and the two entities became entirely independent. Here, 14 years later the idea was once again being floated that there should be a club combining cricket, football and a gymnasium. It had been the Athletic Society's intention to implement this idea, but those who had chosen to take them up on it weren't seeing the benefits that had been sold to them. The idea had already been floated that Southport and the Wanderers could merge, with each able to profit from the other's strengths, but now consideration was being given to a shared set of resources, with all the practical and financial benefits that implied.

This hadn't been the first time that a combined XI had been suggested with a view to producing a more competitive Southport team. When the Southport Guardian had introduced their Athletic Column in October 1885, locals began to submit letters to the editor. One such letter had suggested a team could have been selected from Southport and High Park.

"A Man of North Meols" writes: - 'I would like to suggest to the committee of the Southport Club the advisability of arranging a week-day match with one of our champion clubs, say Preston North End, or Blackburn Rovers. As we have no opportunity of seeing clubs of such calibre without going some distance out of Southport, I think if such a match could be arranged a goodly number of people would be induced to attend it. Could not a team be chosen from Southport and High Park Clubs which would play a good game? Besides, our local players would be sure to learn a good deal from such a visit, as the magnificent passing and dodging of the forwards of the Preston and Blackburn Clubs are something to be remembered

(Southport Guardian, 7th October 1885)

Given the rivalry between Southport and High Park it is hard to imagine either club would have been willing to enter into such an arrangement and have to concede that any players from the rival club were better than their own.

All that said, had gates been stronger and the Southport club healthier, would any such discussion had been held at all? The Visiter succinctly outlined the case for combining resources:

As things are at present we have the Southport, the Wanderers, High Park, Christ Church, Old Boys, and until recently the Crescent, besides a long list of "small fry", each of whom has its gusts of followers probably playing their first team matches at home on the same day. What is the result? The public are divided as to choice of match, and the consequence is that the number of spectators are so few that the money taken for admission does not nearly cover the expenses incurred in advertising, and the committee have hard work to keep their clubs out of debt.

(Southport Visiter, 26th December 1885)

It would have been a more optimistic outlook had the gate receipts from the Christmas Day fixture with High Park gone into the club coffers. Unfortunately for Southport, however, that this was a charitable fixture in favour of the Infirmary and from this match the club received not a penny. A thousand people gathered for the game, which was the largest attendance seen on the ground for some time.

Southport once again struggled to field a full team of their own and had to rely on the good will of the Christ Church club in allowing Hesketh to cover for absentees as a guest. Platt was again conspicuous by his absence, as were Harry Baxter and Tom Morris. All in all, the result at least restored some pride, falling in favour of Southport by a single, Charley Morris goal to nil. The gate was boosted by the last-minute arrival of a large number of spectators who had trudged across from the late cancellation of Southport Wanderers' planned fixture with the Blackburn and District side who had failed to show.

The following day Southport met Wigan, and thankfully there was a spill over effect on the gate from the previous day. Once again, however, Southport found themselves short of players. Platt, it turned out, had been unwell, Griffiths had hurt his ankle, and Baxter had, as reported by the Visiter, decided to turn out for the Wanderers! (Who incidentally played and beat Burscough in front of another large crowd at Scarisbrick New Road). Thankfully the Wigan side that turned up was decidedly weaker than expected and they were easily turned over. Southport finished the game very much like their old selves with a 6-1 win, sending home happy those who had paid for the privilege.

On 29th December the Visiter's football column led with the headline 'The Rumoured Secessions from the Stripes'. Whilst confirming that Baxter had indeed joined Wanderers, we are told that Platt had never had the intention of deserting the Stripes and he denied emphatically that he had ever sought admittance to the 'Red and Blacks'. This at least restored some confidence that the club would at least complete its fixtures.

Wanderers saw out 1885 with a hard fought 3-2 win over Burscough and started the new year with the visit of Halliwell, the same club whom they had faced in their first ever fixture less than 2 years previously. Unlike on that occasion, where they suffered a rather humiliating defeat, the new year began with a well contested draw. Included in the Wanderers line-up was James Farrar who had just returned for the holidays on conclusion of his professional studies in Edinburgh. He would become one of the few players to remain involved in the coming years and would eventually be included in the earliest Southport Central teams in 1888.

Making the short trip over to Devonshire Road a few days later, however, Wanderers came crashing back down to earth. High Park registered three goals each side of half time without reply and completely outplayed the visitors. William Kay was missing from his usual place in goal, and indecision by his replacement Dunkerley cost them.

On New Year's Day, Newton Heath, runners up in the Manchester and District Charity Cup, travelled to the Sports Ground to take on the Stripes of Southport. This was a much-heralded fixtures and there had been an expectation that Newton Heath's arrival would generate great interest. More out of necessity than desire, the now 33-year-old Thomas Burnett returned to the side for the first time since September's opener against Sheffield, but less than a quarter of the gate that had assembled there for the visit of High Park a week earlier witnessed a good 2-1 win. Some estimates were that there were only just over 100 present to witness it.

The Southport forwards played up better than usual. Newton Heath came with four successive victories and a "prophesy" of winning yesterday. Southport in lowering their colours achieve their third victory running, and are, to the satisfaction of many local admirers of the game, solidifying their strength, and regaining a position from which it must be the effort of other Southport clubs to dislodge them or fail gloriously in trying.

(Southport Guardian, 2nd January 1886)

Southport appeared to have turned the corner on the field and made it two out of two in a week when they defeated Liverpool Ramblers on their own ground 2-0.

Mellor Vale withdrew from their prior arrangement with Southport due to a heavy frost making travelling conditions treacherous. This gave Southport a free weekend to prepare for their next encounter with Wanderers. Wanderers chose to do the same, sending their second string to Banks for a cup tie which they won 5-2.

Baxter's recent sojourn with the Wanderers was, he insisted, a well-intended device to stir up Southport. His return coincided with the improvement in fortunes of the side now starting to attract the nickname of 'the Sandgrounders' so if that was genuinely the case, it appeared to have worked. The temporary transferring or loaning of players from one local club to another was becoming more frequent, although those terms should not be applied in the modern sense as no players were actually under contract. A more accurate reflection of the practice would be to say that players made the occasional guest appearances for other clubs, and that their usual club did not necessarily have to consent to it. Against High Park, Southport had utilised the services of Richard 'Dicky' Dutton of the Christ Church club. He was a much sought after, quality, player, and much criticism was heaped on the club and player via letters in the newspapers. Borrowing players for the odd game was seen as a good way to keep up cordial relations between clubs, but when the player does not go back, it was viewed as akin to poaching, and very much frowned upon. The system of players being cup-tied did not yet exist, but there was an unwritten rule in effect across much of football that if a player had represented one club in a competition, then he should not represent another. In the case of Dutton, his friends made the argument that his inclusion in the Southport side for any cup competitions should not be called into question as at the point of transfer the cup games were still three months away and why should a player not be allowed to transfer in order to test himself against a higher standard of opposition?

The debate rumbled on for weeks but whilst this was going on, Southport had another match with Wanderers to contend with. The irony was that Wanderers themselves fielded two guest players in the game, Liptrot and Stead both missing out. Those players came from further afield rather than another local side - Gorst and Townley 'guesting' from Blackburn Swifts. They had originally arranged for two men from Preston North End who withdrew late. Townley was to return to play as a guest for Southport Central a few years later but he much more famously lifted the English Cup with Blackburn Rovers in 1890 and 1891. At the end of his playing career, he became a coach and was a pioneer of the game in Germany, coaching the mighty Bayern Munich, and also had a four-month spell as coach of the Netherlands national team which included participating in the 1924 Olympics in Paris.

The question as to why the Wanderers' second team hadn't been drawn upon to replace first team absentees came down to their desire not to upset a team doing so well in the new Southport Junior Cup competition that had been introduced to give the youngsters in the second XI's something to compete for.

Southport themselves had also brought in extra help. Riley of the Post Office was brought in at the back, although his performance hardly justified his inclusion, and former Captain Dalby returned. Melross and Johnson both took to the field with ankle strapping, Griffiths still absent through his ankle dislocation. Baxter avoided the game through illness which seemed rather convenient for a man whose loyalties had been recently called into question. Even with deputies, Southport still kicked off with only 10 men as Briggs, who had missed the train from Liverpool, arrived late. Southport's second team drew with Old Boys in the Junior Cup, and it's assumed that the same principle was applied as the Wanderers, not wanting to disrupt their chances.

A side choosing to supplement their usual line-up with 'outsiders' would under normal circumstances have struggled to justify any bragging. However, in this case, with both sides choosing the same approach, and with this simply being a friendly encounter and not a cup game, Southport had no problem in congratulating Wanderers upon their victory.

Considering the manner of previous victories for Southport, the result may have been a surprise on the back of an up-turn in form. Wanderers raced into a two-goal lead within the first 10 minutes assisted by a strong wind as Southport struggled to make any headway. They added another before the break. Southport pulled a goal back midway through the second half through Percy Mellor and the same player again took advantage of the weather to bring the score to 3-2. The Guardian commented that *'The wind spoilt accurate play, but the match was full of healthy excitement, and good humour prevailed, both among players and spectators.'*

The debate about guest players rumbled on and the Southport Guardian columnist added weight to the notion that borrowings should be made from other local clubs, as Southport had done. They published comment from an 'athletic contemporary' the following week: *'However unwilling we may be to admit it, no person of experience can dispute it. Association Football, instead of being a game of honest, healthy rivalry is now a big fight for existence, and it is no longer played in Lancashire with the manly spirit which won for it thousands of admirers. The importation of Scotchmen has given birth to a very bad feeling, which bursts out under the slightest provocation, and unless there is a very radical altercation, Association football will die of starvation'.*

Up until this point, debates over the rights and wrongs of professionalism had not reached Southport. Instead, a series of healthy local rivalries had developed, interspersed with fixtures with clubs further afield in which the town's men could be suitably tested. The biggest challenge facing clubs in the area was in finding facilities able to accommodate those willing to pay to watch them.

Whilst the first XI of Southport entertained Wanderers in January 1886, the second team faced the Southport Old Boys, where the Southport Visiter commented that *"Stripes' were a nondescript set as far as uniforms went. There were all kinds of jerseys in the team, red, black and white, yellow and black (zebra style as we have heard it described) plus others, and it was a puzzle to onlookers to know "who was who"…There was some amusement caused by one of the losers appearing in the first half clad in a waterproof cape, which somewhat interfered with his action.*

(Southport Visiter, 23rd January 1886)

The cold weather continued for weeks, and heavy snow spoiled the Wanderers fixture with New Springs on 23rd January. A moderate gate witnessed Wanderers eke out a 1-0 win in slippery conditions.

The return trip to Newton Heath for Southport at the end of January was severely lacking in terms of an exhibition. On a quagmire of a pitch, the two teams agreed to play just twenty minutes each way. Southport travelled with four short of their normal contingent, Platt, Morris, Baxter and Briggs all absent, but Dutton from Christ Church was still involved. The pitch was so poor in fact that when the first goal was scored, the stand-in goalkeeper Sykes could not even use his feet as they had sunk so deeply into the mud. The final score line of 4-0 to Newton Heath was not an outcome to be concerned about given the conditions.

In the week following the game, clearly irked by the criticism levelled at the club concerning their guest player Dutton, Captain Tom Morris wrote a letter to the Guardian outlining the circumstances that led to him being approached on Christmas Eve to play in the game against High Park. Knowing that he himself would be unavailable he approached Dutton at his home and asked him to take his place and that no financial reward of any kind had been offered. Those circumstances were disputed by the Christ Church club with allegations of inducement through the payment of expenses though this seems unlikely given the club's financial circumstances.

A goalless draw with Eccles and a defeat in Preston at Fishwick Ramblers followed for Southport and Wanderers took on the Blackburn Swifts earning a creditable 1-1 draw, before the two sides were due to face off against each other again at Sussex Road on the last Saturday of February.

While on the grumbling and fault-finding we must give our friends the "stripes" a gentle dressing down. We should like to know who is responsible for the sending in the reports of matches. They come to hand very sporadically and often require looking up. This is not as it used to be, and, let us hope those whose function it is to look after reports will not neglect their work. And there is another thing that seems to trouble the multitude, who frequently want to know how it is the Sussex-road club always go away from home minus the pick of their first team. There is and has been considerable talk of late with respect to this matter, many of the supporters contending that it is just the old cry over again of cricket, you can get a good team out at home, but then "the players" prefer, to put it mildly, to abstain from long or even short journeys. This is a kind of thing that is not very creditable, and it is to be hoped, and we trust cricketers will excuse the remark here, that during the coming season we shall not have to report that "in the return match so-and-so was poorly represented". By-the-bye another pertinent query has been put with respect to the Southport Club, vis, whether "the second has gone prospecting". This we are unable to answer, but if our enquiring friend would look over last Saturday's team more than one or two second men were fighting against the Ramblers

(Southport Visiter, 20th February 1886)

The responsibility to send in reports, and the responsibility for the co-ordination and organisation of fixtures is a duty normally undertaken by the honorary secretary with the support of the captain. For the first couple of years both of those duties were ably fulfilled by Thomas Burnett. There had been no complaints raised publicly about a lack of information being provided but the game hadn't been nearly as popular as it was now becoming. Burnett had begun to hand over his duties from the summer of 1883, with the captaincy firstly being held for part of the season by Ralph Rylance, and later by Dalby and then Morris. The move to Sussex Road and the merger with the Athletic Society provided a new secretary in Richard Hatch but even then after just one season Burnett had felt compelled to try and help out once again. Burnett had been the one constant presence at the club since day one but even he was now clearly struggling to keep everything ticking over in the face of increasing demands.

With the inconsistent form of Southport, and the previous reversal still a recent memory, Wanderers were considered favourites by some for the first time when they next clashed. The form book in that respect however was well and truly thrown out of the window. Baxter returned to the Southport side following injury and Dutton rewarded his temporary new team by putting the home side ahead within five minutes of the kick-off. Percy Mellor then grabbed a hat-trick as the Stripes ran rings around the Wanderers. Wanderers, in fairness, were without their usual custodian, William Kay, but on their day, Southport were just too strong. The result, at 4-0, was a little flattering nonetheless with two of the four goals being disputed for offside, and Haslehurst for Wanderers missed an easy chance that could have made the score line 2-1. Unusually, however, Wanderers did not take the defeat in their normal sportsmanlike manner, and their persistent bickering with the referee, Mr Gregson from Blackburn, was so bad that it caused spectators to write and complain to the Southport Visiter. Off the field, with membership growing, Wanderers were showing themselves to be a very capable outfit, on the field they were still clearly lacking.

The Wanderers second team faced Churchtown Congregationals in the Final of the newly introduced Junior Charity Cup on 6th March 1886. Snow still lay on the playing surface of the Sports Ground, the default venue for any large sporting event in Southport at the time, making it difficult for the youngsters to really show off their skills. It was a difficult one too for the casual supporter, with both sides taking to the field in black and red stripes. Farrar stood out for the Wanderers, not just because of his undoubted ability, but because his Jersey was decidedly paler than anyone else's on the field! He had received a telegram asking if he would return from Edinburgh to take the place of Wardley in the final, and I'm sure he was glad that he acquiesced. Wanderers were good value for their victory and were proud first holders of the trophy after a resounding 3-0 win. Having met each other only two weeks previously, resulting in an even 1-1 draw, a large number of spectators had gathered in anticipation of another close game. The Southport Infirmary stood to benefit with over £12 collected at the gate. The silver cup and medals for both teams were presented by the Mayor.

Whilst in local circles Southport Football Club were still showing themselves to be the dominant force in the senior ranks, in comparison to some of the bigger clubs in the area there were major signs of weakness. Even the Cricket and Football Field publication was beginning to pick up on the town representative's shortcomings.

Southport is very much deteriorated from the club which, with a slice of luck, ran so far into the Lancashire Cup competition last season. On Saturday the Bootle A team was entrusted with the fixture at Southport and proved capable of holding their own, each side scoring a goal after an uninteresting game. Morris played very finely for Southport as he invariably does, but the two Bs are evidently an anachronism in the team.

(Cricket and Football field – 20th March 1886)

The Bootle result, albeit a draw, was against their 'A' team and therefore should have been better.

The "Stripes", we understand, had on Saturday a set to with Bootle, on the Sussex-road ground, the outcome, so rumour says, being a draw — a result which it is stated was due to the wonderful play of the visitor's custodian. Another rumour has it that Southport had a palpable goal given against them. We did not see the match, and therefore cannot say how this may be for truth. Someone in connection with the Sussex-road club seems to have had a lazy fit on this week, we should think, as we did not receive a report of last weeks' proceedings. How's this Mr secretary or captain? The public like to know that the original Association team are still in existence, and also what they are doing.

(Southport Visiter - 20th March 1886)

Against Everton the following week, although a win may have been beyond their reach, the 8-2 defeat they actually suffered was hardly the preparation they were looking for as a warmup to the first round of the Charity Cup.

Everton induced Southport to play their return fixture at Anfield-road, and a capital attendance was attracted to the ground. In future, I fancy Southport's "drawing" power will not prove so powerful, for they are certainly not a club of the calibre to give Everton a stretching.

(Cricket and Football Field – Saturday 27th March 1886)

At the end of March, thoughts at last turned to the senior Charity Cup and for the first-time teams from outside of the town had been asked to enter. So it was therefore, that

Southport drew Burscough in the first round. The heavy snow which covered Southport the previous week for the junior competition had now receded, but the neutral Devonshire Road ground of High Park at which Southport and Burscough were playing remained heavy. The only detraction from a strong gate was High Park's own Charity Cup tie with Skelmersdale United, held at Sussex Road (half of which was still under water), but the Infirmary stood to benefit well either way.

Burscough appeared without three key men, and had elected not to include Baldwin, captain of the Wigan team, who had been a regular feature for them of late, instead choosing to rely on their usual men. Southport welcomed back Baxter, but Griffiths was only able to spectate with his ankle deemed not yet strong enough to stand the rigours of a match, and particularly one in such heavy conditions.

Southport won the toss, and resolved to play with the wind, which blew strongly and in gusts across the ground diagonally, not directly towards the Burscough goal. Burscough were in high favour with many of the spectators, and at first they seemed to have the pull, despite the wind. Baxter, however, checked his first flush of eagerness with a big kick, and the Burscough custodian had to hand out the leather. Southport, also, got a corner, and the Burscough back saved well, leading to the cry, often during the first half, of "Well done, Boscar". The fortune of war changed rapidly, for the next moment the Southport "Scot" had his own goal to save. Back to the "Boscar" end the ball travelled, and the citadel was within an inch of the capture. The Southport forwards kept warm, and after a short tussle, Dutton spied a weak point in Burscough's tough armour, and took advantage at the right moment. Southport 1. This was rather a surprise for some of the spectators, and "later on" there was a great surprise in store. Nearly all through accurate kicking was out of the question, the wind taking a delight in carrying the ball out of play., and hither and thither to the confusion of the forwards of both sides. No more score was made during the first half, during which the Southport backs, neither of them in form, required frequent support. Half a dozen times the ball got near the mouth of the Burscough goal, but Georgeson saved splendidly, his defence being a rare treat. The Southport goalkeeper had so little to do that he wandered very far down the field. Some capital runs, however, were made by Burscough, and they were expected to perform feats of scoring in the second half, with the wind partly at their backs. After change of ends, the wind blew harder than ever, and the play increased in vigour, and became very exciting. Realising the danger of their position, Southport played like giants refreshed, and seemed likely to do better against the wind than with its aid. The play of Briggs during the second half especially, was simply splendid. He was a host in himself. Bailey, who had played a consistently good game all through – save that we did not admire a throw in of his which led to hands for Southport – worked with a will, and the brothers Morris' as usual, kept the ball with speed and skill. Dutton showed greater readiness in shooting, and was again and again appealed to by the spectators, with whom he seemed a prime favourite, to raise the Southport score. Burscough were clearly being overplayed, and it was rash on the part of one of their swiftest men to run right across the High Park practice ground whenever the wind carried the call to that extent. The same player showed a lack of energy on the field proper, and well he might after such unnecessary journeys. It seemed impossible for Southport to score, so impregnable was the Burscough fortress. After half an hour's fruitless play, Southport fell off for a moment, and the ball was carried to their end of the field, winding up with a high-kick which landed at the bottom right hand post, and to everybody's astonishment went through. Southport 1

Burscough 1. The Southport goalkeeper evidently expected to save with his hands up to his face, and the ball descended so rapidly and at so acute an angle, that it passed his knees without an obstacle to its erratic course. There was about a quarter of an hour left, and the excitement grew intense. Both teams struggled gamely, and though there was some rather rough play, of which Burscough got the worst, it was borne in good part. The Southport backs rallied somewhat, and delivered some useful kicks. Burscough, though hard pressed, prevented scoring, and a most interesting match ended in a draw, so that the tie will have to be played off on another ground, probably that of the Southport Wanderers. Of the Southport men not already mentioned, Mellor, who did some very useful work, and Mayall, who played am average game, merit notice. The goalkeeper had an idle-time, thanks largely to the noble efforts of Briggs, who deserves to bare his palm. For Burscough, Georgeson, in goal, excelled himself; and R.W.Bridge proved a very powerful back. Pilkington threw himself again and again into the thick of the fight, though he was ill, and would have retired at half-time but for the critical stage of the game. The rest of the Burscough men, with barely an exception ran well and passed cleverly, their weakness being in dribbling, at which the Southport men made rings round some of the Burscough team in the centre of the field.

(Southport Guardian, 31ˢᵗ March 1886)

The draw having already been made before the replay meant that should they progress the teams knew they would have a bye in the second round and in the semi-final, would be facing the winners of the second round 'derby' between Christ Church and High Park. The replay with Burscough was fixed for 10ᵗʰ April at the Scarisbrick New Road ground of Southport Wanderers.

In the intervening week Southport maintained their match fitness by inviting Liverpool club Stanley to Sussex Road. Stanley having double booked, were only able to send a weakened team and Southport built confidence with an easy 2-0 win. The return and inclusion of Josiah Melross after a long lay-off through injury was a good sign for the upcoming replay. Such was the state of the pitch after all the snow had melted, that the Charity Committee switched the second-round ties to other venues to allow it to dry out.

The much-anticipated replay was described as an 'eye-opener'. Southport's hard luck in front of goal and the resilience of the Burscough defence deserted both, as the Sandgrounders romped to a 7-0 victory. The ability to draw a crowd for such an occasion must have been frustrating for Southport. Had they been able to do so for ordinary fixtures, they perhaps would not have been in the financial difficulties they were in. In all likelihood, the large gate at Scarisbrick New Road were hoping to see an upset, but in this they will have been disappointed. The score line was flattering if truth be told, there were disputes over two goals with claims for offside waved away and two would, these days, have sat before the dubious goals panel and possibly not be given as goals. For large portions of the game, it was evenly contested. Southport were without Griffiths (still), Baxter and Mellor whereas Burscough were able to field a full strength XI. After an end-to-end start, however, a fortunate Tom Morris goal galvanised the Stripes and quite disoriented Burscough who thereafter struggled to recover. It was a bright sunny day, and losing the ball in the sun a free kick had been given for handball. Morris scored straight from the freekick. Brother Charlie was the pick of the forwards claiming a hat-trick, his first a shot through a crowd of players with the goalkeeper,

Georgeson, completely unsighted. Charlie Morris claimed the third goal, Dutton the fourth and Josiah Melross drove the ball off the post and in for the fifth. There was a stoppage in play shortly afterwards which gave all of the players a chance to rest. Unusually the ball was burst and with no other in the ground, a cab was called and was driven into town and back again to fetch another. The break gave Burscough chance to regroup and after the restart the play was much more even, and the Stripes were not as urgent in their play. Two more goals ended the half, Morris completing his hat-trick and Melross with the last.

Having received a bye through the first round of the Senior competition, the two clubs represented in the final of the Junior competition were drawn together once again in the semi-final. This time the Congregationals of Churchtown were more of a match for the Wanderers and the tie resulted in a 1-1 draw at Churchtown's Mill Lane ground.

In order to keep up the practice for their important semi-final against Christ Church, Southport arranged a friendly with Liverpool Ramblers, to take place at the Wanderers' ground with their own being used for Wanderers' replayed tie with the Churchtown Congregationals, and were happy to come away with a 2-0 win. Wanderers, with a known bye through the semi-final stage, booked their place in the final with a 4-2 win in front of around 500 excited spectators.

For the easter Holidays, Wanderers arranged a number of fixtures from which, despite the potential of a cup final to contend between the two clubs, growing collaboration could be seen. With sizeable crowds expected from which both clubs would hope to benefit, the venue for their latest encounter was set as Sussex Road, where entry could more easily be policed with it being fully enclosed. For the visit of Stoke Swifts brothers Tom and Charlie Morris would also assist the Wanderers.

Southport followed their warm-up victory over Liverpool Ramblers with a sterner contest against High Park on Good Friday, but the result was the same.

May Day came, and so too did the semi-final of the cup, Christ Church having booked their place opposite Southport by disposing of High Park 2-0.

SENIOR CUP COMPETITION
SEMI-FINAL TIE
SOUTHPORT v CHRIST CHURCH
The Southport Football Club, the holders of the Southport Senior Football Charity Challenge Cup, on Saturday met the Christ church, in the semi-final tie, on the Wanderers' ground. The commencement of play was postponed until after the May-Day procession, and a good gate resulted. The match was under the patronage of the Mayor (Mr. John Unwin), and Dr. Pilkington, M.P. Partisans of Christ Church were very strongly represented, and wore neat cards in their hats with the legend: - "Play up Churchites, play up". Southport had no such encouragement. Christ Church took advantage of what wind there was, which blew obliquely across the ground, and Briggs kicked off. The ball went out almost directly. Briggs threw in, and the Christ church backs returned well. After this the ball was capitally run up to the Southport end, and Christ Church had a fruitless corner, Southport gaining a goal kick. One of Baxter's huge returns was the next

feature, and Will Morris kicked right across the Christ Church goal mouth. A moment later Burnett had to fist out, and great excitement was raised as the Southport goal was again menaced, but danger was averted and Will Morris gave a useful kick. Still the excitement grew, as the Southport goal again appeared in jeopardy, and Burnett once more used his hands effectually. Briggs took the ball to the other end, and Bailey had a corner kick, which for once he misplaced. Again, the ball travelled towards Burnett, and Baxter sent it skywards. The Christ Church captain had here to cry out "Not so many together", and the Southport captain might have used the same direction occasionally, neither side being distinguished for distributing the men to the best advantage. Bryers, a very useful player, took a corner for Christ Church and placed it nicely, but the leather was ousted. When the Christ Church goal was attacked Hesketh kicked out grandly, and a well directed corner from Tom Morris just passed the post. Halsall kicked out well, but the ball being returned, Hesketh made a remarkably vigorous sortie, rolling both the Southport captain and Dutton into the dust. As a result of the confusion caused, some player kicked so wildly that the ball went out of sight, and was returned by the Southport Cricket Club, not being available for their match. It was high time for the hunted leather to pass to the place of repose behind the goal posts, and sure enough at this stage Christ Church scored amid loud hurrahs. Chris Church 1, Southport 0. The ball was neatly put through in a scrimmage. Change of ends followed immediately, and in five minutes the Southport captain took a corner, but the ball glanced off his foot and Christ Church gained a goal kick. The Southport men quickly worked up the leather again, and Dutton adroitly put it through. One all. The excitement grew again, and stout-lunged supporters of the Christ church team called out loudly "Take that stand-up collar out of these fellows". If anything the evenness of the game increased as the second half proceeded. Christ Church gained a goal kick and foul. Briggs was distinguished for a bit of tenacious play near the Christ Church citadel, and Baxter for some strong returns. In a scrimmage near the Christ Church posts, the ball went through. Southport 2, Christ Church 1. A dispute resulted, some claiming off-side, and others that the ball did not pass through. Christ Church seemed inclined to retire, and the spectators crowded onto the field. Better counsels, however, prevailed, the referee's decision was accepted, and the ten minutes remaining played out. No further score resulted. Mayall it should be remarked, was kicked early in the game, and could do little running. Both sides lacked good passing play and Southport certainly played below their average form, and did badly at corners. Brilliant play occurred on both sides, and Christ Church certainly proved worthy antagonists for the cup holders, who have now to contend with the Wanderers (whose 2ⁿᵈ hold the Junior Cup) for the possession of the trophy.

(Southport Guardian, 5ᵗʰ May 1886)

There was some talk of protest about Southport's second goal. It was claimed that the ball never went through the posts and struck the Southport captain's hand. The dispute even went so far as to sit in front of the Charity Cup Committee. The referee's decision however was upheld. Christ Church had asked for the game to be replayed but the committee thought it unnecessary as it had not been the deciding goal of the game.

The most notable fixture of the year was the Charity Cup Final on 8th May 1886. Of those representing Southport only brothers Charlie and Willy Morris remained from the previous season's final, where they had lined up in opposition. For Wanderers, however, having absorbed the Southport Crescent club earlier in the season, four of their XI had experience of playing in the final from the previous year when Crescent had been beaten finalists, namely

Halsall, Leadbetter, Liptrot and W.Rimmer. That said, their passage to the final had been decidedly easier having only had to dispatch of the Churchtown Congregationals, a side their second team had already defeated. Against that good fortune however was the loss of Aitken and Kay, presumably through commitments as there had been no mention of injury, whose experienced heads they sorely missed.

CHARITY CUP FINAL TIE. WANDERERS v SOUTHPORT – The football season proper closes this afternoon, when the Wanderers will contest with Southport (the holders) for possession of the cup. The match takes place on the Sport ground, Sussex-road, and his Worship the Mayor (Mr. J.Unwin) will kick–off at 4-30, and afterwards present the cup to the winning team. His worship will be supported by Colonel Hesketh, J.P, Mr. J.H.Ellis (town clerk), the Infirmary Committee, members of the Corporation, and other influential gentlemen. A most exciting game is looked forward to, and it is hoped that the gate will be the "best on record", as the proceeds go to the Infirmary.

(Southport Visiter - 8th May 1886)

SOUTHPORT CHARITY CUP – FINAL TIE
WANDERERS v SOUTHPORT
PRESENTATION OF THE CUP BY HIS WORSHIP THE MAYOR.
Saturday last saw the close of the football season of 1885-86, when the Wanderers and Southport met on the Sport' Ground to struggle for the silver trophy – last season Southport and the Crescent were left to contend for the cup, Southport eventually winning easily by five goals to none, thus becoming first holders. This year the Wanderers have been exceedingly lucky in the draws, in the first round drawn against their second team, who, of course, scratched; the second round they had a bye, and next were drawn against the Churchtown Congos, whom they defeated by four goals to two – thus running into the final tie, whilst Southport, in the first round were drawn against Burscough; and after a hard game, the result was a draw. On re-playing the match, Southport ran out winners by seven goals to none. In the second round a bye, and afterwards had to meet Christ Church, whom they defeated by two goals to one, the latter match putting them into the final. Among footballers the match has been the principal topic of conversation during the past week, and there were not a few who thought (after Southport's poor display against Christ Church) that the Wanderers would just about win. Southport played their second team, Burnett playing in goal, vice Platt. The Wanderers had whipped up a strong team, having the assistance of Farmer and Griffiths, Parkes keeping goal. Unfortunately for the Infirmary, the gate suffered owing to the miserable weather, rain falling at the time for commencement. Punctually at 4-30 both teams appeared on the field, the following opposing one another : - Wanderers: Goal, Parkes; backs, Rimmer and Griffiths; (½ backs); Sellars, Farrar and Liptrot; forwards, Leadbetter, Halsall, Haslehurst, T.Lea and H.Lea. Southport: Goal, Burnett; backs, Baxter and Mayall; (½ backs); Bailey, Briggs and Johnson; forwards, Dutton, W.Morris, T.Morris, P.Mellor and Chas. Morris. Umpires, Messrs. Jolley and Allsop. Referee, Mr Whalley. At 4-35 the Mayor kicked off amidst loud cheers. Both teams quickly got to work, and play was even for a time. Willy Morris ran down the right; Griffiths cleared with a big kick. Briggs was cheered for a fine piece of play, robbing three of his opponents in clever style. T.Lea obtained possession and raced down the field, his final shot going behind. Farrar had the first shot at the Southport goal; Burnett kicking out and giving a

corner, Baxter got in a fine kick. Hands given to Wanderers off T.Morris, Liptrot shooting over the line. Haslehurst essayed a shot, but Baxter easily cleared. C.Morris went down the field, Sellars kicking out. Mellor sent in a beautiful centre from the left, Parkes saving in a wonderful manner. A fierce scrimmage ensued right in front of the Wanderers' goal; Farrar getting the ball away. Bailey got off, but shot behind. Mellor and T. and C.Morris were cheered for some pretty passing. Mellor again put in a splendid centre, and Southport all but scored. Wanderers had a chance, Baxter amusing the spectators by the way in which he cleared. T.Morris made a good attempt, Griffiths getting the ball out of danger. T.Morris got another grand shot in, but Parkes was wonderfully smart and cleared finely. W.Halsall had a nice chance but kicked out T.Leadbetter got possession, and neatly dodged Bailey. Baxter, however, got the ball away. Parkes ran out with the ball in his hands; Southport claimed, and got a free kick just in front of goal. Ball was headed about, but Liptrot gave a corner. T.Morris put in a good one, and after a hard scrimmage the "stripes" captain shot the first goal for Southport after 25 minutes play, amidst much cheering. The Wanderers were now handicapped, Liptrot hurting his foot and retiring for the rest of the game. Briggs robbed T.Lea, and was cheered for some dashing play, Johnson also getting in some clever high shots. Dutton and W.Morris passed nicely. Charley Morris had an opening, but shot over the bar. Briggs dribbled along the centre, the ball going over the line. W. Lea got away and passed the (½ backs); Baxter kicking out just in time. Farar put the ball in front of Southport goal, Briggs heading out T.Leadbetter and Halsall showed some neat passing, the ball being kicked over. Sellars was cheered for some good heading. Dutton rushed away, but fell when near goal. Half-time was called with the score Southport one, Wanderers none. On re-starting Leadbetter dribbled down, his shot going over the line. T.Morris had a shy, Parkes neatly throwing out. C.Morris then made an attempt, but Parkes was too smart. Some give and take play followed. T.Morris got the ball, and centring well, Mellor dashed the ball through, scoring the second goal ten minutes from the re-start. With two goals against them, and a man short, the Wanderers fell off in their play. Southport pressing hard, Briggs was very busy in the centre, his vigorous heading much admired. T.Morris sent in a hot shot, Parkes saving cleverly. P.Mellor next had a try, but Parkes could not be beat. Bailey, who was playing a good game, dribbled through to Rimmer, who got the ball away. After a tough scrimmage in front, Mellor put the finishing stroke to goal No. 3, loud cheers greeting this success. Johnson sent in a grand high shot. Rimmer clearing, Haslehurst raced down and got past Baxter, finishing up with a wretched shot. T.Morris passed smartly to his brother Willy, and Charley receiving the ball, quickly scored the fourth and last goal. Halsall and Leadbetter got away, and Baxter kicked out. C.Morris put in a fast shot, Griffiths kicking out, Mellor headed neatly to Dutton, whose shot just went over the bar. Mellor next sent in a fast one, Parked fisted out smartly, Southport still pressed, time being called shortly after, leaving Southport (for the second year in succession) winners of the cup by 5 goals to 0. The winners played a good game all round, if we except Mayall, who appeared quite out of form. Burnett in goal had a very easy time, only having one shot to stop all through the game. Baxter played a good, steady game, the three halfs were in capital form, and worked hard all through, whilst P.Mellor, T. and C.Morris were the smartest of the forwards. Coming to the losers, Parkes was the hero of his side, and saved them from a very heavy defeat by his splendid display. Griffiths and Rimmer defended well, whilst Sellars at half played a clinking game, never seeming to tire with his hard exertions, T.Lea, Leadbetter, and Halsall being the pick of the forwards.

At the conclusion of the game, the players and spectators crowded round the space which had been reserved in front of the stand, and here the cup was presented by the Mayor to the winning team.

The MAYOR said - Ladies and gentlemen, and I am glad a few ladies have had the hardihood to venture out this afternoon and grace this meeting with their presence – I have now a very pleasing way to perform, and that is in presenting this very handsome charity cup to the winning team. It is very much to be regretted that the weather has been so unfavourable for this final competition. It is to be regretted on account of the players themselves, who have had so much greater difficulty to contend with owing to the slipperiness of the ground, and it is to be regretted on account of the Infirmary, as I believe that the receipts to-day are only about one-half what they would have been had the weather been finer. But it does not seem to have damped the energies of the players. They have fought a good contest, which has been honourably won and honourably lost. (Cheers.) I think our sympathies are with the losing team, as they have been placed at a disadvantage almost from the beginning, one of their best players unfortunately meeting with an accident. (Cheers.) It must have been great satisfaction to all who have been engaged in this football competition to feel that whilst they are laying up for themselves a store of strength and energy both bodily and mentally, that they are at the same time contributing to supply the same benefit to those who, by misfortune or accident, have been compelled to go to the Infirmary. (Cheers.) That is a most noble institution, and I trust that none of those who are engaged in football may never need the benefit of it. (Applause.) But if they ever do then I will promise, as one of the committee of the Infirmary, that they will meet with the greatest kindness and the best medical and surgical aid (Cheers.) I have now very much pleasure in handing this handsome cup to the captain of the Southport team, who have won it to-day. (Cheers.) I see that the same team won it last year, and I have no doubt that, if through the circumstances that they may not be in such form another year, they will hand it down untarnished to those who may win it next season. (Cheers.)

The Mayor, then, amidst cheers, handed the cup to Mr T.Morris, who said - Mr Mayor, on behalf of our team, and personally, I thank you heartily for coming down to present this cup this afternoon (Cheers). I am sure everyone will agree that we have worked hard for it, and therefore deserve the honour. (Cheers.) I am sure we all agree that it is a great pity the weather has been unfavourable, but perhaps the Infirmary Committee will be satisfied with the funds they will receive. (Hear, hear.)

The MAYOR – I believe they will be very grateful for what they will get (Hear, hear.)

Alderman HACKING said – I am sure you all feel with me that it would be wrong for us to go away without our best thanks to the Mayor for coming here to kick off the ball and present the prizes, having stayed the whole of this afternoon, which has not been very pleasant. We have found him this afternoon, as we always do, ever ready and willing to do any good work the people may require of him, and I hope we shall show our appreciation of his kindness this afternoon by tendering him our best thanks. (Cheers.) I propose a resolution to that effect.

Councillor KILBY said – Ladies and gentlemen, I have very great pleasure, as one of the vice-presidents of the Wanderers' club, in seconding the thanks to the Mayor, I am sorry as he expressed himself to be, there are so few people here to-day, as I think they would have seen a good game. Although our club have had to work for their success. I hope the Wanderers will have more success next time.

The proposition was carried with loud cheers. Three cheers were given for the Wanderers at the request of Mr T.Morris, and the proceedings then concluded.

The teams afterwards dined together at the Railway Hotel, and Mr J.H. Ellis, Town Clerk, afterwards presented the medals to both teams - gold medals to the winners of the cup, and silver ones to the "runners up". The remainder of the evening was spent in a convivial fashion.

(Southport Visiter – Tuesday 11th May 1886)

The miserable weather had contributed to the gate only raising £7 compared to the previous year's £18 but the 4-0 win over the Wanderers helped cement Southport's reputation as the leading club in the town and therefore the town's main representatives in Lancashire football circles. The winners received medals consisting of a gold Maltese cross, the runners-up a shield featuring a lion or football, provided by the local jewellers and displayed since November in the windows of Messrs Ramsbottom and Sons on 70 Eastbank Street.

The season was a mixed bag. Within the town and within the remit of the Southport Football Association, who arranged the Charity Cup, Southport remained the top-dogs. But in wider circles the club had noticeably failed to keep pace with the advancement and development of the game. Against sides that they had previously expected to overcome, they were found wanting.

At least locally, their playing record for the season was one that most clubs would be proud of but that wasn't good enough for a team purporting to represent the town as a whole. That was the bare minimum expected from the club, and the aspirations had been to develop it to be able to compete with some of the bigger Lancashire and Liverpool sides. The move to Sussex Road had not paid off. It was clearly the 'show ground' for the town, but it had been built principally for athletics and did not yet have the infrastructure to support more regular usage. The lack of a tram or local train stop put patrons off attending. Off the field therefore the club was not in a healthy state financially. Having faced increasing competition locally they had reduced their annual subscriptions to five shillings to try and compete. The addition of a second string to help them to develop their own players too was a failure.

After the Charity Cup final success, the original Southport club, as they had become known, played just one further fixture, against Christ Church, as a benefit to Bailey who would shortly head off for a new life in New York. It is also the last known fixture of their opponents prior to the announcement of a name change to Southport Recreation, and it ended in a 2-0 win for the Churchites. Prior to the match, by the hospitality of Mr Crankshaw, a score of members and a few friends from other clubs were entertained to tea at the Bold Arms hotel. Songs were sung by Thomas Burnett and Alfred Ramsbottom. A toast was given to the health of the host, and to Mr Bailey, who it was hoped would one day return.

Throughout the season there had been plenty of discussion about the future of the club, its strengths and its weaknesses, and there had been growing calls for amalgamation with Southport Wanderers, the club whom they defeated in the final. Whilst their ground at Scarisbrick New Road was less developed than Sussex Road, they were on the main tram line, and were enjoying regular healthy gates which all helped to increase the stability and success of their club. It came as a surprise to nobody that the mid-season calls to consider a merger would eventually be tabled for serious discussion. Whether any proposed merged club would be suitably representative was still a matter for debate. Proposals from a Mr. Ellis had already been made that for exhibition purposes a side should be drawn from the best of all of Southport's players, Southport, Wanderers, Christ Church, High Park et al.

That all said, Southport Football Club re-registered with the Lancashire Association for the 1886/87 season, and it was assumed therefore that at least a scratch team would be organised for cup ties. However, no such fixtures were ever arranged meaning that the original Southport Football Club effectively folded.

Mr J.R.Batty, in supporting, observed that the Southport Football Club, having died a natural death, it was expected that many of the players would join the lacrosse club

(Southport Visiter, 26th August 1886)

Present at the above meeting discussing a new lacrosse club were Richard Hatch, the former secretary, Squire Platt, Tom Morris, L.E.Johnson, Mayall, J.H.Johnson, J.Sykes, and Percy Mellor. In time, even Thomas Burnett, the pioneer of association football in the town, switched his loyalties, at least temporarily, to the newly formed Southport Lacrosse Club, along with Josiah Melross, another of the originals.

A New Identity

B y the summer of 1886 Southport Wanderers had become the most serious challenger to Southport Football Club's status as the town's premier club. They were able to field a first and second XI on a regular basis, something that Southport Football Club had tried but struggled to do for much of the year.

The Athletic Society's annual report published a few months earlier had commented that the committee had regretted their *'unfortunate connection with the football club'* which had resulted in the Society incurring a large expenditure on their account of over £88. They had found that the football club simply could not make ends meet and had been relying on the Society to meet their expenses. The Society had even offered the club the opportunity to use the Sussex Road ground rent free for the forthcoming season, if they would cover the liabilities incurred on the previous 1885/86 season, but they simply could not.

There had been no grand announcement concerning the future of Southport Football Club, but it was common knowledge, particularly after having been unceremoniously dumped by the Athletic Society that they had been struggling to support themselves financially.

At the Wanderers AGM in June 1886, at which a representative of the Southport club was also present, they formally invited their ailing rivals to amalgamate. In the history of sport in the town this meeting is one of the most important, so no apologies are made for including here the full reports of the meeting from the Southport Visiter and the Southport Guardian.

The annual meeting of the above club was held last evening in the saleroom connected with the Railway Hotel. Mr J. G. Emmison occupied the chair, and amongst those present were Messrs. W. Emmison, G. Wallwork, B.J.Purser, O. Hopwood, A. Valentine, A. Rammsbottom, G. Edge, F.M.Wood, Leach, W.Kay, R. Aitken, C.Duncan, Milnes, W.Wardley, J.Parker, and others of the club. Mr R. Geeson of the Southport Football Club, was also present.
The chairman first read a letter of apology from Alderman Hacking, who was announced to have taken the chair, but who could not attend through being out of town. He then went on to explain that the total receipts this year amounted to £56, and the expenditure to £60. Though the receipts this year were £13 more than last year, yet last year the expenses were not so heavy, and the club has £3 3s. in hand. The chairman then read out the balance sheet, and explained that the

members of the club would be supplied with printed copies in a short time. Speaking of last year's results he explained that £17 14s had been taken at a benefit draw. Some might suggest that this should have been done this year, but the committee were unanimous opinion that draws were played out. The gate money this year was a considerable increase on last year, the sum taken on the letter-mentioned occasion being £10 16s 3d, and on the former £13 14s (applause).

Mr Horwood moved that the accounts be passed.

Mr Wallwork seconded, and considered that they should congratulate themselves on going through last season in so successful a manner. They had had, he was sure, a good deal to contend with. Considering that they were only about £4 to the bad, they were really and truly in a creditable position. (applause) He thought the time would come when football would be the game of the town. It was now, in a sense, because they could get more spectators than any of the cricket clubs. He expressed the opinion that if they worked hard in the hand next season they would have £10 or £20 on the right side. He suggested that when electing officers for next season they should appoint a finance committee, and that the gentlemen who were elected should try their best to get subscriptions. It was a town's club, and he was satisfied that they could get plenty of subscriptions if they tried. Mr Wallwork then explained the good results which had served to the cricket club in their perseverance in this way. (applause)

The chairman had mentioned the victory of the second team in winning the first Junior Cup in Southport. (applause) He was sure they all ought to feel proud. He hoped that next season the first team would go on in the same way.

The balance-sheet was then carried unanimously.

Mr Valentine proposed that the subscriptions for members be raised from 2s 6d to 3s, and that cards be supplied be supplied free of charge.

Mr R. Aitken seconded, and it was agreed to.

The chairman proposed that Mr W.Kay be elected as secretary, and alluded to a suggestion that had been made that such officer should receive some remuneration. Mr Kay was willing, however, to accept this office independent of payment.

Mr Wallwork — Did you say that he was willing to take the office independent of remuneration? The chairman — Yes.

Mr Wallwork then suggested that the question of appointing him as secretary be put to the meeting without any consideration of money.

It was then proposed, seconded, and carried that Mr. Kay be appointed.

The question of remuneration that next considered, and after some conversation it was decided that Mr Kay would receive a handsome present if next season was a financial success.

Mr Kay, in returning thanks, said he would work as hard as he could to bring the club before the town. He desired that the committee should be composed of non-playing members, and that they should be limited to half-a-dozen and a chairman. He thought that if that were done there would be nothing to prevent the club going ahead, and being the leading club in the town. (applause)

Hr Horwood proposed, and Mr Aitken seconded, that Mr C.Duncan be elected to the office as assistant secretary.

This was agreed to.

Mr Wallwork proposed, and Mr A. Ramsbottom seconded, the appointment of Mr B Purser as treasurer, and this was also agreed to.

Mr Valentine proposed Dr. Pilkington, M.P. as president.

Mr Purser seconded, and it was carried.

It was decided that all honorary members subscribing 10s 6d should be vice-presidents.

Mr Valentine moved that a committee consisting of six and a chairman be elected.
Mr Ramsbottom seconded.
The chairman here explained that the club had lost their old field, but a gentleman had offered them one in Scarisbrick New-road, which could be boarded round, if required, on reasonable terms. He also made a suggestion about the Southport Football Club amalgamating with the Wanderers. Mr Godson was willing to bring the matter officially before his committee.
It was decided to elect a committee that night, and to leave the appointment of captain till a future date.
The following gentlemen were appointed as a committee: - Messrs. J.G. Emmison (chairman), W. Emmison, A. Valentine, J.Parkes, G. Edge, A Rammsbottom, and W. Wardley.
The meeting then terminated with a vote of thanks to the chairman.

(Southport Visiter – 12th June 1886)

SOUTHPORT WANDERERS' FOOTBALL CLUB

Last night, the annual general meeting of the members of the Southport Wanderers' Football Club was held in the Mather's Saleroom, Chapel-street. There was a large attendance. Alderman Hacking, who had been announced to preside, was unable to do so through absence from home, and he sent a letter of apology. Mr J.G.Emmison was called to the chair, and among those present were Messrs. W. Emmison (hon. secretary), C.Duncan (assistant secretary), Purser (hon. treasurer), Kay, Hatton, Valentine, Hopwood, Milnes, Marshall, Parkes, Aitken, Sellars, Leach, Alfred Ramsbottom, Alban Ramsbottom, Edge, Wallwork, E.Carr, W.Tunstall, F.M.Woof, &c.
The CHAIRMAN, after briefly alluding to the beneficial interest which Alderman Hacking has taken in the club, said the Wanderers might congratulate themselves on a successful season. Coming to the accounts, the turnover had been £56, as compared with £38 last year. (Applause.) The expenditure under nearly every head, however had been greater, and the result was a balance of £4 on the wrong side. That small deficit was really due to the unexpected loss on the match against Stoke Swifts. Save for that loss, their income would have met the outlay.
Mr HOPWOOD: I think you have done very well. (Hear, hear.)
The CHAIRMAN (continuing) said last year they received £17 14s as the result of a draw, but believing draws to be played out – (hear. Hear) – they had this year organised a competition which realised £12.
Mr Hopwood again expressed his satisfaction, and added that he was willing to double his subscription. He moved that the accounts be passed.
Mr WALLWORK seconded, and was surprised they had come out so well. The time would soon come, or had come, when football should be deemed the game of the town. Certainly a football match drew a far larger attendance than they could score at a cricket match. He hoped a finance committee would be elected by the Wanderers. The club was now really a town's club, and he was sure a large amount could be collected in honorary subscriptions. The Southport Cricket Club had appointed a finance committee, and its honorary subscriptions amounted to nearly £15.
The CHAIRMAN remarked that the Wanderers had done a great deal towards bringing football forward in Southport; and the Wanderers stood in the proud position of having a second team which had won the first junior cup in the district. (Loud applause.) The Wanderers' 2nd won in a competition with 22 entries, defeated four first teams from other clubs, and scored 17 goals against five. (Applause.) He only hoped the first team would next year go and do likewise. (Hear, hear.)

The accounts were unanimously passed.

On the motion of Mr. VALENTINE, seconded by Mr. AITKEN (captain of the 2ⁿᵈ team), it was agreed, without a dissentient, that the subscriptions for ordinary members be 3s next year instead of 2s 6d.

Dr. Pilkington, M.P. was unanimously re-elected president of the club, and Mr B. Purses hon. treasurer.

After some discussion as to the payment of the secretary and assistant-secretary, Mr. Kay was elected secretary and Mr C.Duncan assistant secretary. Both had commented to take the office altogether apart from payment. It was cordially agreed that if a balance remains at the end of next season the remuneration of the secretaries be sanctioned.

The CHAIRMAN here made the important statement that while their old ground had been given up, the committee had an offer of a new ground in Scarisbrick New-road. The gentleman who offered this field would enclose it to a height of 7ft 6in, all round, and let it to the Wanderers at a reasonable rental. There need thus be no anciety about a ground for next year. (Applause.) He had now to approach a delicate matter. There has been a talk of the members of the Southport Club throwing in their lot with the Wanderers and Mr. Gosson, of the Southport committee, was present that evening to hear what was proposed. Well, he thought the best attitude for the Wanderers was to hold out the hand of invitation. They must respect the dignity of the premier club, and be prepared for amalgamation or combination, or whatever scheme, if any, might be proposed for the good of football. (Hear, hear)

After Mr. Gosson had briefly explained his view of the present position.

It was resolved to appoint a committee of seven, and to defer the election of chairman until the result of a letter of invitation to the Southport Club was known. It was also resolved not to appoint captains until a future meeting, and the majority seemed to favour the practice of the Blackburn Rovers, who do not select captains until the commencement of the season.

Nine names were submitted for the committee, and the ballot resulted in the elections of Messrs. J.G.Emmison, Valentine, Edge, W.Emmison, Parkes, Wardley and Alfred Ramsbottom.

A vote of thanks to the chairman concluded a very business-like meeting

(Southport Guardian, 12ᵗʰ June 1886)

The meeting confirmed the re-election of Dr. George Pilkington as the president of Southport Wanderers, the man who had originally been behind the formation of Southport (Rugby) Football Club in 1872, and now serving as MP for the town. That Wanderers had been able to call on his support as club president for a second time, shows just how highly the club were regarded. Of all those members present, he surely would have been amongst the most vociferous supporters of the proposed amalgamation.

There had been growing unity between the two clubs over the second half of the previous season and a joint venture had even been called for by the Southport Guardian.

The Guardian issued a follow-up editorial comment four days after the historic meeting:

In Saturday's Guardian appeared a report of the Southport Wanderers Football Club annual meeting. The two chief points were the promise of a good enclosed ground in Scarisbrick New-road,

*and proposed amalgamation, combination, friendly jointure, or working union with the Southport
Football Club, the men of the neat striped jerseys. Instead of one member of the Southport
Committee being present as a deputation, it is a pity all were not there. They would have found the
friendliest of greetings, the kindest consideration for their position, and a manifest desire to make all
things pleasant or rather continue pleasant, for the existing feeling seems deprived of all past
jealousies. A cordial letter of invitation was ordered to be addressed to the Southport Committee,
and the issue is awaited with a good deal of interest. It is fraught with important results to
Southport football, the "town's game", as it has been called, in the future. The ambitious hope
expressed by Mr Ellis when the challenge cup was presented may not be so far from realisation as
some people thought. If there was one borough in Lancashire which ought to send out the premier
county team, a bona fide local team, of course, surely that borough is named Southport.
Stature in the Southport Town Council has happily nothing to do with the championship of athletic
sports. Councillor Kilby defended the Southport Athletic Society when he thought it was being
attacked, and Alderman Hacking is the most regular figure when the Wanderers are in the field.*

(Southport Guardian, 16th June 1886)

Beaten by Southport in the 1885/86 semi-final, Christ Church too had a change of
identity. After briefly floating the idea of calling themselves Southport Athletic, and even
going so far as to announce it, they finally settled on Southport Recreation.

*A general meeting of the above club was held last week, a goodly number of players being present,
for the purpose of electing officers for the coming season and bringing the present one to a close. The
past season has been a most successful season, as the club has played thirty matches, twenty of which
have been won, five lost, and five drawn, scoring no less than seventy-four goals against thirty-seven.
Only in two matches have they failed to score. In the Liverpool and District they defeated Bootle
Wanderers by two goals to one, and in the second sound they made a draw with Earlestown
Wanderers – one goal each – and finally they were defeated by the latter club by seven to one. In the
Southport Charity Cup they made a draw with the Roamers of none each, and then defeated them
by seven to none. In the second round they beat High Park by two goals to none; whilst in the semi-
final they were defeated by Southport by two to one. The election of the officers resulted as follows: -
First team captain, R. Dutton; sub-captain, A. Bryers; second team captain, H. Sutton; sub-
captain, P.Rimmer; secretary, G.W.Hesketh, 64, Tulketh-street; assistant-secretary, A.Bryers;
treasurer, Mr. H. T.G. Beckett. It was also decided to change the name from Christ Church
Football Club to Southport Recreation Football Club. Financially the club stands a little to the
good, while the club numbers of thirty-six playing members. They intend to turn out three teams
next season.*

(Southport Visiter, 8th June 1886)

On 31st August 1886, Southport Wanderers called a General Meeting which took place at
the Railway Hotel. There was a large attendance. Mr J.G.Emmison took the chair. Fixtures
were announced against Loveclough, Peel Bank Rovers and Everton. Tom Halliwell was
appointed captain of the second team, with Alfred Halsall vice-captain but the there was a
motion to delay the decision over the captaincy of the first team. There is no specific record

in the local press of a formal acceptance of the proposal to amalgamate from the committee of Southport Football Club, but it was notable that by the date of this meeting Mellor, W.Morris, Platt and Johnson had all already joined Wanderers indicating that there had been an acceptance that the original club would not be continuing under its own steam. Therefore, the reason for the motion for Southport Wanderers to delay the appointment of a first team captain was that it was still felt that both Tom Morris and Mr Briggs, two of the most senior of Southport's players, might also be induced to join them, and in such case, it was agreed that one of them should be offered the captaincy.

Southport Wanderers, now also including members of the original club, moved to a new ground in Scarisbrick New Road for the 1886-87 season. The Southport Visiter commented that although the ground was a little hard and uneven it was of ample size, enclosed to a height of seven foot six inches and big enough to accommodate three matches at once. A covered grandstand, to seat 140 spectators, and a dressing tent were provided. Three cows which grazed on the field were ushered behind the grandstand during matches. It was conveniently situated on the left-hand side of Scarisbrick New Road opposite to the Olympic field. Wanderers, having previously taken a field further up Scarisbrick New Road, knew that it was on the public tram line and therefore easily accessible. Their previous home had not been fully enclosed, and being completely open on three sides, there had been many occasions where the attendance did not marry with the paid gate, as spectators avoided the pay booths by sneaking in. This new enclosed home would fully prevent that.

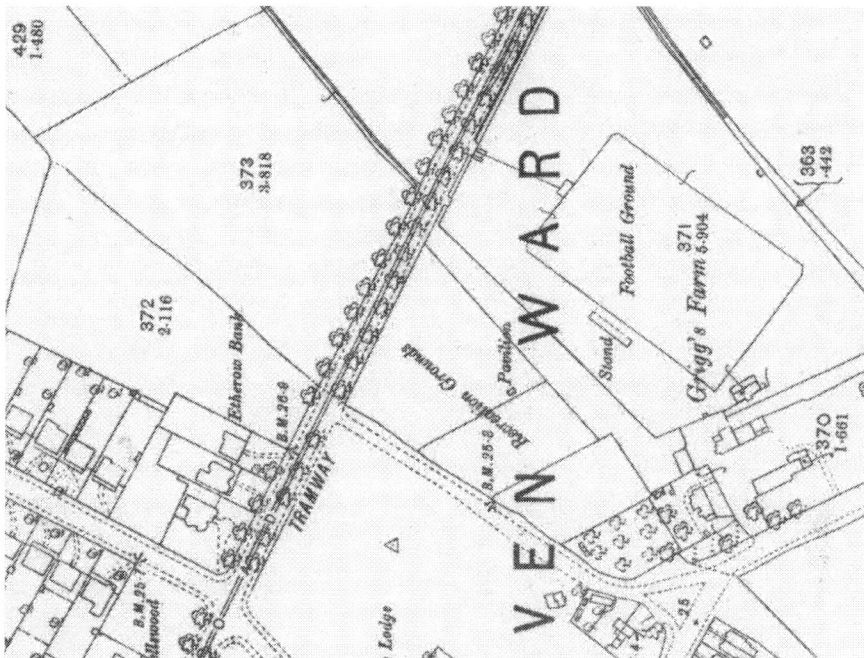

OS Map 1894 Reproduced with permission from the National Library of Scotland. The Football Ground visible is the Olympic field.

The season started brightly with the visit of Antley (of Accrington), who were promptly disposed of 4-0. Mellor wasted no time settling in with a hat-trick on his debut.

WANDERERS v ANTLEY (ACCRINGTON)
The opening game of the Wanderers took place on their new ground in Scarisbrick New Road, on Saturday last, before a moderate attendance of spectators. The home team have been greatly strengthened by members of the late Southport, who chiefly added to the victory of the locals, by four goals to nil. Mellow and W.Morris worked energetically throughout the whole game, and Lea and Kerr proved to be of great service in the front rank. Sellars, Johnson and Hindley were three safe (½ backs); whilst Parks, in the rear, showed some of his old form, and was ably assisted by Griffith. S.Platt had not much to do, but what was required from him he did in his well-known cool manner. The visitors goal-keeper, no doubt, was the saviour of his side repelling shot after shot in a marvellous way. Sellars won the toss and shortly after four, Ashworth kicked off, the locals defencing the Kew goal. Hands, off Morris, for the visitors was soon claimed, but Sellars relieved, and the game proceeded in midfield, when Mellor receiving, put in a well directed shot, which Thornton cleared. A corner for the locals was now given by Wilkinson, Johnson taking the kick, and after a terrific scrimmage the ball was well put away. An occasional visit to Platt was taken up by the visitors forwards, but the backs returned, and the locals got another corner which Morris took and put in a beauty, the ball just hitting the crossbar and dropping over. On the kick out Sudell and Riley raced away down the right, Griffiths concerning a corner, which however was not

utilised. The Wanderers forwards again worked up the field, and by good play, Mellor scored. Afterwards, from a corner kick by Morris, Kerr rushed the ball through the posts, thus scoring No. 1 for the Scarisbrick New-road players. Restarting the locals assisted by a stiff breeze, gained another point, half-time soon after being called with the locals being two goals to the good. On the kick-off Antley, favoured with the wind, made a rush up the field. Johnson saved, and Riley, getting hold for Antley, sent in a ripping shot, which Platt with difficulty cleared. Lea and Kerr were the next to show up and Morris with a long low shot scored again for the winners. Clegg and Hayward got away for the visitors, and were looking dangerous, but Sellars saved with a long kick, and Morris receiving the same promptly kicked the ball through but the goal was disallowed on account of the offside rule. A little give and take play followed now, when Hindley made a pretty good run down the right, and delivered a well aimed shot at the goal, which struck the crossbar and rebounded into play, but Mellor, following up well, placed the leather safely out of the custodian's reach. A few mistakes only remained for play, and no other score being totalled, the Wanderers came out of the struggle victorious as indicated above. Teams: Wanderers: Platt, goal; Parkes and Griffiths, backs; Sellars, Johnson and Hindley, (½ backs); Mellor, W.Morris, J. Kerr, T.H.Lea and C. Riley forwards. Antley: Thornton, goal; Wilkinson and Barrett, backs; Ainsworth, Howarth and Whittaker, (½ backs); W.T. Riley, Sudell, Ashworth, Heyward and Clegg, forwards.

(Southport Visiter, Tuesday 21ˢᵗ September 1886)

Four days later, as the Wanderers' second string, the Junior Cup holders, travelled to Skelmersdale, the first XI's of the two clubs met at Scarisbrick New Road. On a drizzly day a most unpleasant game was played in front of a very small number of spectators. Characterised by bickering and squabbling between the teams, it wasn't long before even the referee got caught up in the bad atmosphere. With the Wanderers leading 2-1, Skelmersdale United's team walked off the field after disagreeing with the referee's decision and Wanderers claimed the match.

Before going any further we should just like to say a word to some of the Wanderers' players, who seemed to be too fond of arguing. If any dispute arise let the two captains settle the same. It is of no use the whole of the team talking; it only wastes time and has no good effect.

(Southport Visiter, 2ⁿᵈ October 1886)

Lancashire FA still looked upon Southport Wanderers as a separate entity from the original association club and did not afford them the same senior status that the Stripes had earned. They refused them permission to enter the Lancashire Senior Cup in place of the 'premier club' and instead had to settle on a place in the Junior competition. Even the Visiter mourned the loss of the original club.

The season promises to be a busy one. It will, however, take some few weeks for our local teams to get into proper working order. The only regrettable fact in regard to our town's clubs is the break up of the premier club of the town, vis. Southport, who have won the Charity Cup since its institution.

A New Identity

(Southport Visiter, 2nd October 1886)

Frustrated by their perceived poor treatment Wanderers did two things to rectify it.

First, they opted to join the Liverpool & District FA, an organisation that itself had split from the establishment organisation (Lancashire FA) to form as a rival, and of which the original Southport club had been a member. The River Mersey divided the two Victorian counties of Lancashire and Cheshire, Liverpool being on the north bank, in Lancashire.

Secondly, at a General Meeting held in R.V.Mather's Saleroom on 28th September 1886, it was unanimously resolved that in future the newly amalgamated club should drop the Wanderers tag and be called 'Southport Football Club'. The Visiter very casually reported the change on 2nd October when they commented *'Briggs took his place in the team as captain, and under his able guidance the club (who, by-the-bye have changed their name to that of Southport, and also taken the old club's colours) should give a capital account of themselves'.*

There was still no Tom Morris, even if he could count one of his brothers amongst the now six players to have switched over.

Judging by his actions days later, it is easy to see why Tom had not chosen to join his brother.

To the Editor of the Southport Guardian
It is well known to my friends, though to some people it may be news, that I am of a very moderate and retiring disposition!, and that this rushing into print is quite distasteful to me, but really the announcement that appeared in your Wednesday issue re: the changing of the name and title of the "Wanderers Football Club" to that of Southport raised my ire so considerably that I felt I must conquer my natural diffidence and protest against such an unusual action. And I feel it to be my duty to inform the friends and supporters of the red, the old "Southport club" and also all who are interested in the game of football that I along with many others consider that the Wanderers have taken a great liberty. I did hear a rumour at the end of last week that a proposal to change the name of the club would be brought before the General Meeting that was held last Tuesday evening but I did not think that the underwritten but perfectly understood law of courtesy in these matters would surely prevent the members from accepting any such proposal though now, judging from their actions, it is evident that they know nothing of such a law. You may be aware sir – "though I say it as shouldn't" – that the players of the real Southport club had a very good name in the Liverpool district and elsewhere for their speed and smartness on the field, and also for the agreeable manner in which they contested the game they were engaged in. the club also gained for itself the title of the premier club of the town by winning the Charity Cup for two years in succession and now it has died a "natural death" but I hold that the right to the old name did not expire at the same time. The Wanderers must have an immense admiration for the name which we bore as they have taken the first opportunity of adopting it. Perhaps they have the idea that by doing so, they also step into the position which the old club held. It is quite a mistaken idea and I do not think that they have such an admiration for the old club, that they might have some regard for the feelings of the old members and rescind the resolution passed at the meeting and then still struggle to bring fame and

glory the honoured name and title with which they have all along been associated viz, that of
Southport Wanderers F.C.
Yours very truly
T.Morris
Late captain of the late Southport Association F.C. 19 Sefton Street, Oct 1ˢᵗ 1886

Morris had instead opted to join the newly formed Lacrosse club. One day after penning the above letter he made his debut.

T.Morris, late of the Southport Football Club, particularly distinguished himself by his capital passing, and put in some really good work. We have no doubt he will win as great distinction at lacrosse as he has done at football.

(Southport Visiter, 5ᵗʰ October 1886)

The Junior Cup gave the newly renamed club the opportunity to show off their combined talents. Bolton Rovers, winners of the Bolton and District Junior Cup, came with a good reputation and large numbers gathered to welcome them, including many of the old club's supporters. Josiah Melross, a prominent local athlete and one of the founding fathers of the club returned to the right wing, six years on from his first appearance.

The match was played on the Southport Club's new ground, Scarisbrick New-road, and when the Rovers drew up in a wagonette about four o'clock a large number of supporters had assembled in the field to witness the play, amongst whom could easily be recognised not a few of the old club's supporters. No time was lost in making a commencement, and Briggs having lost the spin of the coin, the home team had to play the first half with the sun in their eyes. The visitors at once went off with great dash and determination, and it was seen that they would make a blood bid for victory. The right wing couple were very active, and after some pretty passing on their part, Platt was soon called upon to throw out a stinger from the Rovers' centre. The home forwards went down the field, and Mellor, receiving the ball from the right wing, had a good chance of scoring, but missed his opportunity. Not to be denied, the men from Bolton still played up hard, and were soon rewarded, the left wing outside scoring the first goal for the visitors. The home backs were kept busy repelling the smart attacks of the visitors' forwards, who shortly added goal No. 2 to their score. Platt being right away from his goal when the shot went through. Surely such an experienced goalkeeper as he should know it is not the game to be roving away from his post. If he had been in place no doubt the goal would have been saved. Shortly afterwards Sellars, who had been playing a good hard game, was unfortunate enough to get his knee twisted, and had to leave the field. He came on afterwards, but was of little use for the rest of the game. At half-time the rovers were two goals to the home team nil. On re-starting, the "Stripes" cheered on by their supporters, did their utmost to score, and after a time were rewarded, getting a free kick near goal. Briggs neatly put the ball to W.Morris, who defeated the Bolton custodian, scoring the first goal for the home tea. This success roused them to further efforts, and Melross all but scored with a good long shot, the ball just skimming the bar. The Rovers after this pressed the home team, Platt being cheered his goal. Not to be denied, the Bolton men kept up the pressure, and added another goal to the score, the game ending in a victory for the Rovers by three goals to one. The winners kept up their reputation, and were a smart team. The backs kicked well, and very seldom made a mistake, whilst the forwards were a clever lot, passing and kicking in a way that fairly nonplussed the home team, whose forwards should certainly take a lesson from their display. The home backs played well, Cookson again showing what a good back he will make, Griffiths being a decided improvement on his previous displays. The (½ backs) worked well, Briggs especially putting in a wonderful amount of hard work, whilst the forwards were again weak, not showing the slightest combination, Lea and Hindlay in particular being very selfish.

(Southport Visiter, 2nd October 1886)

In local circles, the primary competition for the amalgamated club were High Park and the newly renamed Southport Recreation who appeared to be in a strong position:

The Recreation Club appears to be in a very flourishing condition, as on Saturday last the turn three teams out. Dutton, who played with Southport last year, has gone back to his old club. They have erected a smart-looking tent on their field, and have it painted with the clubs colours. The players are in high spirits, and are eagerly waiting for the Charity Cup competition.

(Southport Visiter, 2nd October 1886).

Haydock were the next to visit Scarisbrick New Road in the Liverpool and District Cup. Sellars was missing with an ankle sprain from an otherwise strong XI that also included Baxter, the well-regarded full back from the old Southport club. Early pressure nearly resulted in a goal from Briggs whose effort skimmed the bar, but shortly afterwards they got their just rewards. The setback galvanised Haydock but they were fortunate to have equalised when an apparently accidental hand ball in front of goal had resulted in a free kick, from which the ball deflected off one of the Stripes to draw the visitors level. A misunderstanding during the second half gave Haydock the lead. With five minutes remaining some unnecessary rough play from one of the visiting forwards resulted in a player being ordered off the field of play, but with so little time remaining, Southport were unable to take advantage, losing by two goals to one.

In December disaster struck off the coast at Southport when a ship called the 'Mexico' ran aground. In horrendous weather 27 lifeboat men from Southport and St Annes, tragically lost their lives attempting to rescue the crew. The season's Charity Cup competition therefore took on added meaning, raising money for a replacement lifeboat and for the families of the town's deceased heroes.

With the mood understandably low in the town at the turn of the year, the proprietor of the Railway Hotel on Chapel Street, Mr R.V.Mather, recognising the role that football was now beginning to play, tried to raise spirits by laying on a substantial dinner and an evening's entertainment for around 60 local footballers. The entertainment was principally provided by the players themselves, with Squire Platt, William Kay and Bob Aitken amongst them, although in some quarters the gesture seemed to cause unintended offense. The invitation hadn't been extended to every club in the town, and Southport Recreation appeared most upset that they had been passed over. Indeed, only Hesketh, the goalkeeper, had managed to gain admittance, and for a club whose second string had already reached the final of the local Junior Cup they perhaps had reason to feel aggrieved.

Southport's second team, affectionately known as 'the Pippins', although still the reigning junior cup holders had failed to reach the local final for a second year. Instead, Recreation's opponents were High Park, although Southport were making great progress in the Liverpool and District Junior Cup, beating Liverpool club Cunard in the first round, 4-0.

Four days later and High Park showed that perhaps Recreation still had some way to go to be considered a premier club in their own right as they thrashed them 10-0 in the final.

The Southport first team had no fixtures throughout most of January 1887 and were well rested by the time they donned their jerseys once more for a 4-1 win over Burscough on 22nd of the month. A charitable fixture had been arranged before that for a team representing Southport and District against an equivalent from Wallasey. The omission of Southport left half-back Tom Sellars from the advertised selection however raised eyebrows, and the Southport Visiter were forced to print a letter from the redoubtable anonymous critic 'FORWARD' questioning the decision.

I have been informed from an official source that the team selected to represent Southport does not include the genial left half-back Sellars, and I should think I am one out of many who regret this, for as a player in his position in the football field, it must be admitted by all followers of the Association game that he has no equal in the district, and how on earth the Southport Charity Cup Committee could have overlooked this I am at a loss to understand. Yours & c., FORWARD

(Southport Visiter, 25th January 1887)

The above letter, and the response from 'CHURCHTOWN' a week later gives us a good insight into how the selection of the District team was handled. The Southport Charity Cup Committee was made up of prominent members of most of the local clubs and in Churchtown's reply he outlines the results of a vote that took place to decide the player to take the position. The author was clearly defending his own club, as the man to win by six votes to three was W.R.Wright of Churchtown.

The Senior section of the Charity Cup kicked off for Southport on 5th February with a visit to Portland Street, the home of the Southport Old Boys. Unfortunately for the Stripes, their inclusion in the competition lasted just the 90 minutes. Squire Platt was beaten three times with only one in reply. Captain Briggs complained about the goal scored by William Halsall and lodged a protest after the match which was roundly booed by the majority of the 700 supporters who were witness. After the game the victors retired to the George Hotel as guests of Councillor Crankshaw, a staunch supporter of the Old Boys.

The planned District team game against Wallasey included just two from the Stripes, Captain Briggs and forward Percy Mellor. Goalkeeper G.W.Hesketh, Dicky Dutton and Fred

Rimmer represented Recreation. Cadwell, Hill, and the two Tasker brothers came from High Park – the Parkites therefore having the strongest representation. Nicholson (Old Boys) and Wright (Churchtown) made up the XI. Raising funds for the Infirmary, the game took place at Sussex Road with Southport winning by a single scrappy goal to nil.

Southport's second string continued their journey in the Liverpool Junior Cup with St Marys the opposition at Scarisbrick New Road. The form of the Pippins proved a counter attraction to the District game, with a fair number turning out to watch the youngsters put four past the Kirkdale side that had only a few years before been able to beat the original Stripes. Goalkeeper Guest on this occasion probably had the easiest game of his life only having three shots to face in the whole game, and being a match for all of them. Tom Sellars who had missed out on selection for the District, took to the field as referee instead!

Perhaps just to give him something to do, Guest was promoted to the first team the following week for the visit of Oakfield Rovers. Rovers claimed victory with a scrimmaged goal right at the death.

With Guest returning to the second team after just one game, the first team called on 'the old original' as he was dubbed by the Visiter, William Kay. The former secretary kept a clean sheet as Southport beat Liverpool Ramblers 1-0 in Crosby. They will have regretted their early exit from the Cup as the win over Ramblers was the start of an unbeaten run that would see them through to the end of the season in fine form.

Southport at last seem to have got into working order, judging by their display on Saturday last against Lytham. Undoubtedly it was the best game they have played this season, and the spectators certainly had reason to be pleased with the performance of the "Stripes". However, there is still room for improvement in the forward division, and their shooting in front of goal requires a lot more practice...By the way, what becomes of the Southport Committee during the matches, there seems to be about two real "workers", and the rest – well – we suppose "they haven't for a long time now".

(Southport Visiter, 12th March 1887)

Several inches of snow threatened to interrupt the rhythm in March, and I suspect that Liverpool Ramblers had wished they hadn't turned up at all, when the Stripes sent them packing on the wrong end of a 10-0 score line.

Southport now seem to have got two good teams together, and, with a first class working committee, ought now to do well until the end of the season

(Southport Visiter, 19th March 1887)

The second team thought they had progressed into the semi-final of the Liverpool cup with a hard fought 2-1 win against St Peters Swifts, who had until that point been most people's favourites for the trophy. The match had been played at Everton's Anfield Road, such was the interest in the game. St Peters lodged a protest after the game on the inclusion

139

of Farrar on the grounds that, although a regular second team man, he had played in the senior competition. After a thorough examination of the facts, the Liverpool and District Association agreed with St Peters and ordered the game be replayed without Farrar taking part. It was most unfortunate as Farrar had only been included in the offending game at the last minute due to Kay being too ill to take part on the day. The good news to come out of the same meeting however was that J.J.Briggs, the skipper, had been chosen to represent Liverpool County in their match against Cheshire in Manchester.

In preparation for the replayed game, a game of first versus second XI was arranged at Scarisbrick New Road. A fast and exciting game ended in favour of the second team 5-1. Although the firsts were missing Briggs for the reasons given above, it was far from a weakened team that had taken to the field.

Whilst 1,000 witnessed the final of the Southport Charity Cup between High Park and Southport Old Boys, a good number also took advantage of the cheap tickets that had been put on offer to travel to the Police Athletic Ground in Fairfield to cheer on the youngsters in their replayed semi-final.

With cries of 'Play up, Boys!' the Pippins raced into a two goal lead which they carried into half time. Within five minutes of the restart the Swifts had pulled both goals back and were standing on level terms. Soon after and the Swifts took the lead for the first time. 'Little Alf' Halsall, the Southport captain, pulled his men together and switched to a short passing game to outfox their weighty opponents. It worked!

Ding Dong were both teams playing to secure the winning point, but at the call of time neither side had added any further point, the game standing at three all. After a long discussion it was decided to play the extra half-hour, when the wearers of the "black and red" jerseys ran around the Swifts and placed two more goals to their credit, defeating the protestants by five goals to three, that entitling there to enter into the semi-final of the above competition

(Southport Visiter, 26th April 1887)

With the end of the season fast approaching, just one week later, Seacombe St Paul's travelled to Southport for the semi-final of the Liverpool & District Junior Cup, arranged at the neutral High Park's Devonshire Road enclosure. It went off without all the drama of the previous round, an easy 3-0 win in front of a big crowd. This was the first time a team from Southport was to appear in a final of any competition containing non-Southport clubs. Earlestown awaited the winners…and it was back to Anfield Road!

What price Southport now for the cup!

(Southport Visiter, 17th May 1887)

When the big day came, they were good value for any money that had been placed, and won the town's first regional honour by lifting the Liverpool and District Junior Cup. The youngsters' overall record was a marvellous one, Played 27, Won 23, Drawn 3 and Lost 1, scoring 112 goals and conceding 21. They had won five matches on route to the final and collected the trophy in front of 3,000 spectators!

The victorious Southport team, who wore the red and black jerseys that once belonged to Southport Wanderers, journeyed from the ground to Exchange Station in wagonettes amid the tooting of horns and blowing of bugles of between 100 and 150 supporters. When the train arrived back at Chapel Street Station 500 people heartily welcomed the winners. The captain, Alfred Halsall was carried shoulder high to the Railway Hotel, the club headquarters.

As the season officially closed, the Annual Meeting of the club was held at Mr Mather's Sale Room next to the Railway Hotel on 13th July. Citing difficulties faced at the start of the season, presumably as the original Wanderers club adjusted to its new merged status, Mr J.G.Emmison in the chair, gave praise to the second team for their achievements. The balance sheet for the season showed a loss of £9, with £10 carried over from the previous year, with much of that attributed to the rail fares paid by the second team in the Liverpool Cup. Indeed, this had been made worse by having to travel back for the replayed game as a consequence of the protest. The club had also purchased new jerseys for the season, with the second string taking the original red and black. Where the jerseys from the original club had gone is anyone's guess, but combined with Tom Morris' earlier letter of protest about the adoption of the name Southport Football Club, it does suggest that the merger hadn't been as amicable as one might have thought. A new committee was appointed for the season of E.Ramsbottom, B.Purser, Milnes, Valentine, J.G.Emmison, Dawhurst, Bulock, Edge, Watson, R.Gosson, Lea, A.Ramsbottom, Wardley, Sellars, Griffiths, Smith, Kay, Taylor, Andrews, Halsall, Hesketh, Liptrot, Shell, and Duncan. Mr Purser was re-elected treasurer, and Kay and Duncan were re-elected secretaries.

==*==
1887/88

Despite their regional success, the Athletic News continued to see Southport Football Club as one of the 'junior clubs' in the area. Perhaps this wasn't surprising given the growth of professionalism in the North. Little Southport was being left behind.

The 1887/88 season started early with a fixture on 18th August in aid of the Ratepayers Association. The Charity Cup committee had once again selected a team to represent the Southport District, but this time it was to face the Stripes, which therefore limited the availability of players to represent the District.

Making a surprise return in the line-up of the District team was Tom Morris. Having originally started out with Southport Crescent in 1882/83, he had joined the original Southport Football Club in 1883/84 becoming a popular player and a prolific goal scorer. He was the captain when he last featured for the Stripes, in the Charity Cup Final against Southport Wanderers in May 1886, in what turned out to be the old club's final game. He refused to join Wanderers alongside some of his former teammates when the original club ceased to function and instead joined the Lacrosse team along with William Platt and Thomas Burnett.

As an acknowledgement of the perceived strength of the Stripes, the District side was supplemented with a number of well-known guests from Blackburn Rovers, Blackburn Olympic and Everton. With their assistance the District team came out 5-3 winners.

After the original club's severance of ties with the Athletic Society and their ultimate demise, the Sports Ground on Sussex Road had laid unoccupied for most of the season. It was still used heavily for athletic events and for Charity Cup matches, but always as a neutral venue with no side calling it their regular home. Southport Recreation changed all of that at the end of August.

> *It is not generally known that the Recreation Football Club have secured the Sports Ground, Sussex-road, for the forthcoming season. Such, however, is the case, and it is pretty evident that they mean business. In our opinion they could not have found a ground better adapted to the requirements of football, as the fact of the old Southport Club — which was the premier football organisation of the town and district — occupying it for so long a period fully testifying. The majority of the football fraternity in Southport seem to be under the impression that the members of the above club have disbanded owing to the resignation of several of its members. All who entertain such an absurd idea are grievously mistaken, for in reality it is in a very flourishing condition, and bids fair even more successful in the coming season than it ever has been before.*

(Southport Visiter, 27th August 1887)

Despite the grand announcement, there may have been more to the rumours than the editor of the Visiter gave credit for. Whilst results were favourable, Recreation struggled to put out their strongest XI for weeks.

Whilst Recreation and the Southport Old Boys had kicked off their seasons on 10th September, Southport Football Club were facing problems of their own making.

There seems to be a sort of split amongst the players in the Southport camp, re the advisability of playing men from out of town, in other words professionals.

(Southport Visiter, 20th September 1887)

Southport Captain J.J.Briggs was making a stand against the decision of the committee to bring in two new men from Blackburn, Akeroyd (often mis-spelt Ackroyd in the local press) and Whittaker.

With Briggs refusing to play, both Akeroyd and Whittaker were included in the line-up that faced Birkenhead Argyle on 24th September. The side was also made up of half a dozen of the previous season's Liverpool Junior Cup winning side, with several prominent first teamers standing by their captain in protest. Whittaker had in fact already played in the game against the District as one of Southport's men, even though the opposition had featured others from the famous Blackburn clubs. It was the arrival of Akeroyd, however, that appeared to cause the most upset. With the benefit of hindsight and knowing that Akeroyd would later go on to captain Southport Central, it is clear he must have been a strong character and that Briggs could easily have felt that his position in the team, as leader, was threatened.

After the form that the side had shown at the end of the previous season, there weren't many who saw the need to strengthen the team at all, let alone with outside talent. Given the split, the Visiter argued that it would be a wiser course for the committee to agree to only play locals and not risk losing some of the most influential members of the team by bringing in guests. With Briggs refusing to play, a meeting was scheduled to discuss the situation on Monday 26th September at the Railway Hotel on Chapel Street.

The argument of the protestors was made easier by the performance of Whittaker in the game, missing a *'ridiculously easy goal'* and who *'seemed to play only for the gallery and consequently did not come off'*. At the clear the air meeting it was decided by a large majority to discontinue the use of the Blackburn men and play nothing but local talent. Briggs was immediately reinstated for the visit of Liverpool Ramblers and set a good example by his performance. The local men won 3-2.

When Southport faced Bromborough Pool on 8th October, there were changes once more to the team. With Southport not publishing the line-up in advance, as was the usual practice, there was much speculation amongst local supporters as to why. The reason however wasn't down to foreign talent but it was that Southport Recreation's difficulties in fielding an XI of any strength had finally got the better of them and the Stripes had reached out to them offering to amalgamate the clubs together after their 3-0 win over Croston. Five of the XI that therefore took to the field at the Mills Recreation ground in New Ferry were former Recreation men; Pasquill, Sutton, Rimmer, Blackledge and Bryers.

A general meeting of the various football clubs in the area took place on 12th October with a remit to elect a committee for the Southport Charity Cup. The chair of Southport Football Club, Mr J.G.Emmison led the meeting where it was decided that there should be no more than one elected member from each club. That said, Mr Gosson, also of Southport Football Club, was chosen as secretary after Dan Ashton stood down from the position due to business engagements. Also to join the committee were a number of men with no affiliation to any club but with an interest in football. Councillor Crankshaw and Mr T.J.Dewhurst were appointed, and were joined by R.W.T.Hatch and H.Baxter, the latter two who both had a history with the original Southport club.

Not two weeks later, Baxter was back in a striped jersey.

With the well-established Christ Church-cum-Recreation now firmly part of the Southport Football Club ranks, the club was able to field three teams most weeks. Players from the old Recreation first XI were generally split between the first and second team, with the effect that it allowed Southport to field an additional 'Reserve' team with players shuffling down the pecking order accordingly. Whilst Briggs had seen off the challenge of the foreign talent, he hadn't bargained for having to make room for an influx of new players from Southport Recreation and he was moved out to the right wing with Rimmer taking his usual place at half back.

Briggs seemed rather at sea, but no doubt will improve as he gets used to his new position.

(Southport Visiter, 12th November 1887)

There were wrinkles to shake out still as form fluctuated across each of the teams. A comfortable win one week could be followed by a drubbing the next. As a method of trying to sort out the 'men from the boys', an inter-club game was organised between the second team and the reserves. The match also gave the selectors for the Junior Cup team the opportunity to see the areas that needed to be strengthened if the club were to follow up their regional honours by picking up the coveted trophy nearer to home. The Southport Visiter reported that shortly after the game took place, every local club planning to enter a team into the Junior Cup had been asked to submit the names of those who it considered first team men. The named individuals would then be considered ineligible to compete in the junior competition. For Southport, those selected were as follows: Tynsley, Aitken, G.Halsall, Sellars, Briggs, Pasquall, Blackledge, F.Rimmer, T.Lea, T.H.Lea, Bryers.

Whilst the club were confident in naming a first XI, it was rare that away from home all were available. It appeared to be an all too familiar story that whenever travelling the firsts had to be supplemented by the seconds. Therefore, it meant that the second team became almost as experienced as the first, and the reserves – effectively the third team in all but name – played like there was always an opportunity likely to present itself.

When the Junior Cup started at the end of November, the seconds, the *'wearers of the black and red'*, which were the colours originally worn by Southport Wanderers after the first team had chosen to retain the red and white stripes of the original Southport club, dispatched

Ormskirk Wanderers 2-0. With the weather putting paid to any pretty football, the Visiter gave some sage advice to players entering the field in such conditions.

It might well be just advisable here to warn football players as to the foolishness of leaving the coats &c., lying about the field during the progress of the matches, as we have received a letter from one of the Ormskirk Wanderers players informing us that his pockets were rifled during the competition last Saturday; so players beware.

(Southport Visiter, 3rd December 1887)

The *'Montpellier of the North'*, Southport, faced the *'Brighton of the North'* and Fylde Cup winners, Blackpool, mid-December. Whilst the result was a 2-2 draw rather than the win they felt they deserved, there was much worse to reflect on as Captain Briggs picked up a nasty knock that threatened to rule him out for the rest of the season. He did return, but not for two whole months. It was a loss that was keenly felt as the Stripes went on a winless run stretching through to the start of February, starting with rivals High Park! The second team maintained their form despite losing men to the first team and progressed once again in the cup, defeating the Lancashire & Yorkshire Railway Second XI 3-1.

The Christmas fixture was against the Southport Old Boys and the committee should have been asking Santa for some new equipment.

The game was brought to an abrupt conclusion by a couple of balls bursting when about 20 minutes time had to be played…In the second half, after Southport had registered a goal, the ball burst, and another being supplied, the home team had hard lines on many an occasion. The second ball, however, shared the same fate as the last, and the match could not be concluded.

(Southport Visiter, 27th December 1887)

Tom Morris made his second football appearance of the season in the New Year's Eve fixture against Churchtown. There was still no explanation as to his sudden change of heart after having been so angry when Wanderers effectively absorbed the original club that he had held so dear. His lack of match practice was very telling, however, and he was a shadow of his former self. The fixture took place unusually on the Cricket Field owned by a Mr Dewhurst, who served as the vice chair of the Southport Charity Cup Committee, and ended all square at 1-1.

As the season progressed into 1888, Southport were to find themselves playing against a number of old faces who had since moved onto other clubs. Melross was still as fit and strong as ever and regularly turning out for Birkdale alongside Dalby, but the biggest surprise of all came when an announcement was made in the Southport Visiter at the end of February about a new team being formed…the Old Southportonions!

A team of old Southport players have entered for the Charity Cup competition, and under the wing of Messrs. Ramsbottom, Hatch, and Burnett, who, we believe, are the principal movers in the matter, promise to make a bold bid for the Cup. In the first round they are drawn against Birkdale, and the "old have beens" are confident of entering the second round. We are also led to believe that it will be the means of a new club being formed for next season and Southport may yet boast a good club, as was the case some two or three years ago. The old Southport men will be chosen from the following: - Platt, Burnett, Mellor, Hodge, Chadwick, Heald, T.Morris, C.Morris, Johnson, Mayall, Ramsbottom, Rylance, &c.

(*Southport Visiter, 18th February 1888*)

The Old Southportonions had arranged for their first fixture to be on 18th February, a week before the Cup began, against the 'new' Southport Football Club. When it came to the day however, only three players turned up to play in the snow, Platt, Johnson and Hodge. It was hardly the sort of start a side would want if they were to make a credible run at the Cup. With supporters having turned up expectantly to see the Old versus New spectacle, a hastily arranged game was made instead between the three old guard, some of the committee and members of the new Stripes. Briggs and Kay, as previous members of the old club, and now captain and secretary of the new club, joined their three old comrades as the scratch side battled hard in a 3-2 defeat.

The Stripes would begin their Charity Cup campaign by facing the Southport Old Boys, once again on the Cricket field whilst the Old Southportonions had been drawn to face Birkdale. The Southportonions had kept their line-up close to their chest in the week before the game, perhaps thinking that the element of surprise would give them an advantage. The line-up was: S.Platt (Goal), J.Griffiths, E.Ramsbottom, J.H.Johnson, W.Morris, J.Parks, R.Roberts, W.Robinson, J.Gibson, W.Hodge, P.Mellor, E.Melross. With the counter attraction of the Southport v Old Boys game being played at the same time, only about a dozen had bothered to turn up to watch.

Although there had obviously been enough of the old players keen on the idea of one final 'hurrah', there must have been a number of them who subsequently changed their minds. In the end, they had to supplement the line-up with Roberts, Robinson, Gibson, and E.Melross, none of whom had ever represented Southport before. E.Melross we assume to be a relative of Josiah…who was lining up in opposition for Birkdale, who incidentally won the game 2-0. It was the only match the Old Southportonions would ever play. The surprise omission really was Tom Morris. Of all the old players, he probably had the most to prove. After his performance against Churchtown at New Year, he had returned to the Lacrosse field with his tail between his legs. From the original announcement, the only aspect to have turned out accurate was that a new club would be formed for the new season, and that Edwin Ramsbottom would be a key driver in its creation.

Over on the cricket field, 300 had assembled to see the outcome of the latest clash between Southport and the Old Boys, sides that were believed to be evenly matched in most quarters. With the kick off delayed due to the late arrival of Briggs, the Southport captain who had only recently returned from injury, the Old Boys captain won the toss and elected to face the wind. After only two minutes Thomas Lea, a player also confusingly known as Thomas Lea-Jones or even Thomas Jones on occasion, punished him for what seemed a rather strange decision. Within half an hour, three more goals had been scored, Lea with another two to complete an early hat-trick, and Briggs from a corner that had been delivered by Forshaw.

After the change of ends Old Boys capitalised on a mis-kick from Aitken who had misjudged the wind, to get an early goal back but with such a deficit already, very few gave them any hope of getting back into the game.

The winners are to be congratulated on their victory, for they played a clinking game all through, the forwards, in the first half, playing a most unselfish game, and to this must be attributed the score.

(Southport Visiter, 3rd March 1888)

The win was marred by an injury to Lea towards the end of the game which had resulted in him having to drop into the back. Whilst not serious, it kept him out for the following few weeks missing games against Everton Reserve and Bolton Reserve.

The second team courted controversy once again in the Junior competition. Facing High Park they had been kept on the field for 45 minutes before the Parkites had turned up, and with the score level at the end of time (1-1), owing to the delay, Southport refused a period of extra time. High Park consequently kicked the ball into the empty net and attempted to claim the match. The Charity Committee had none of it and ordered the game to be replayed.

With a dose of revenge in mind, for the replay High Park were made to wait for Southport, although only for 25 minutes this time. The tactic did not work, however, and High Park raised their game to dump the Pippins out 4-1. High Park went on to beat the Southport Old Boys 7-1 in the final, to retain the cup.

With the Junior Competition finished for another year, attention turned again to the seniors, and Southport and High Park were to meet again, this time in the semi-final.

On 14th April, in fine spring weather, 500 assembled at the Sports Ground. As was usual, the match kicked off well past its advertised 3pm time, but this time because the referee had failed to put in an appearance. High Park took a first half lead to the delight of the majority of the crowd. They made it 2-0 shortly after the restart, but Southport staged an impressive comeback:

High Park supporters jubilant, Southport rather downcast. The "Stripes" had a look in, and Rimmer saved a good shot from Briggs. Still keeping round the High Park posts, Blackledge had a chance, and cleverly put the ball beyond the reach of Rimmer, scoring the first goal for Southport, this success being loudly cheered by the now delighted Southport shouters. Lea got in a splendid overhead shot, which Rimmer smartly saved. Each side played up hard, and both teams having hard lines; Briggs was noticeable for a clever bit of play, the ball was right in front of goal, and finding himself pressed he turned round and back heeled the ball, which almost went through,

Rimmer just scraping the ball round the post on his knees. Southport still had the best of it, and Blackledge missed the easiest chance imaginable. Lea however made amends by scoring a brilliant goal, and equalising the game, amidst a scene of the greatest enthusiasm. With fifteen minutes still to play the excitement was intense, both sides being loudly urged to play up. Encouraged by their success, the Stripes played a dashing game, and made matters warm for the High Parkers, obtaining two corners in quick succession, and from a fierce scrimmage infront of goal Southport rushed the ball through, and took the lead amidst great excitement...The whistle blew for time; Southport amidst great rejoicing and congratulations, leaving the field winners of the best match seen in Southport this season by three goals to two.

(Southport Visiter) 17ᵗʰ April 1888)

With no time to waste, the final, against old rivals Churchtown, was just 10 days later. After such an exciting semi-final it was inevitable that the final would fail to live up to the hype. After drawing 2-2 in a game that the Southport Visiter described as *'one of the slowest and most uninteresting games we have ever witnessed'*, the teams would have to do battle again to get their hands on the prize.

The game, as an exhibition of the Association code, was a failure, but as the match resulted in a draw, the local charities will get the benefit, and no football enthusiast will begrudge having attended.

(Southport Visiter, 28ᵗʰ April 1888)

In the replay 1,000 people crowded in to watch Southport fight back after trailing by three goals to equalise with the last kick of the game. The goal was hotly disputed as the referee added four minutes to compensate for the time lost kicking the ball amongst the spectators. The Charity Cup Committee decided that extra time should be played and when Southport attempted to score a goal and claim the game, they were prevented by a number of Churchtown spectators who invaded the field.

Never in the history of local football has such a scene on a field been witnessed as that of last Saturday on the Sports Ground when Southport and Churchtown met for the second time of asking to decide who should have the honour of holding the Southport Charity Cup for another twelve months. The committee are to be congratulated on their efforts to advertise the match well, and in this they were successful, obtaining the largest gate ever taken in Southport – over 1000 spectators being present – the amount taken bring close on £17. This result is certainly very satisfactory, and no doubt the powers that be in the future will not be afraid of spending a few shillings in advertising, when they find what results from the same.

(Southport Visiter, 5ᵗʰ May 1888)

On 8ᵗʰ May, 1,200 packed into the Sports Ground to witness the third attempt to decide the outcome. Churchtown led into the half time break but Thomas Lea scored after 7 minutes of the second half to level matters. Southport eventually won the final 4-1 with goals from Forshaw and Bryers (two).

After the match the cup was presented, the usual speeches made, and the "Stripes" drove off with the cup, much elated at their victory. Some lively proceedings went on at night, and the winners showed rather questionable taste in driving about the town, displaying the cup and kicking up no end of row. In our opinion the festivities could well have been carried out in a much more respectful manner.

(Southport Visiter, 12ᵗʰ May 1888)

Elsewhere, the original Southport Cricket Club breathed its last when they lost their ground to the inevitable building work. Faced with an uphill battle against the more established and better supported Alexandra and Birkdale clubs there were to be no further attempts to revive the club. Shortly afterwards and, very much like Wanderers had done, the Alexandra club took over the name of Southport Cricket Club and continued playing under this name until 1902 when they amalgamated with Birkdale to form Southport & Birkdale Cricket Club.

The Professional Game

In the summer of 1888, the year the Football League was founded, prominent and influential men within the town felt that Southport needed to pull together a team of a stronger calibre, able to compete at a higher level. There had been discussions three years earlier, in 1885, as to whether the 'premier club' had the strength to adequately represent the town, but professionalism was still banned and the town continued to be gripped by the local Charity Cup, failing to see the potential benefits of taking the sport further afield. After professionalism was legalised, the amalgamations of firstly Crescent with Wanderers in 1885, Wanderers with Southport Football Club in 1886 and then Recreation with Southport Football Club in 1887 were the first steps towards achieving the objective of fielding a more competitive team.

On 22nd May 1888, in what had become a familiar summer event and in what now can clearly be seen as an attempt to form a truly representative side, a team representing 'Southport & District' was put together. Everton visited the Sports Ground but came away 3-0 victors. The line-up for the District representatives was as follows: Tyldesley, (Goal); Baxter, Cookson, (backs); E.Rimmer, Horton, Leadbetter, (½ backs); Graham, Blackledge, T.Lea, Halsall, Bryers, (forwards). Both teams were entertained by Harry Baxter to supper at the Shakespeare Hotel.

On 2nd June the Southport Guardian newspaper revealed that there was a scheme in the town to provide a football club of *'mighty proportions'*. Mr Thomas Hewitt with Mr Wm. Watson and Mr Edwin Ramsbottom initiated the movement with the idea to combine the football players in the town to create one strong team.

There is a scheme a foot in the town to provide for next season a football club of mighty proportions – so far as playing talent is concerned. Several local gentlemen have conceived the idea of raising an importation team which is to play in Southport some of the crack clubs of Lancashire such as Everton, Blackburn Rovers and Darwen etc.
Subscriptions towards the undertaking have been already promised to a fair amount and sometime during the beginning of next week a meeting will be called to work out arrangements. The scheme may be a success but is more likely that subscribes will lose sight of their money. If the undertaking could be managed and the public would support it then we should have the pleasure of seeing weekly

some good matches but we fear that the people of the town would prefer to keep the admission money in their pockets. They usually do.

(Southport Guardian – 2nd June 1888)

The Southport Visiter followed up this report seven days later, making it clear that the club being discussed was in fact a new club.

A NEW FOOTBALL CLUB – A strong movement is on foot to establish in Southport a football club which shall, by engaging the very best men as professionals, carry the name of Southport victoriously over many fields. This scheme is a very desirable one, for so much interest is taken in football at Southport that the town can well afford to maintain a team which shall meet even Preston North End on equal terms, and with such a club we shall have something to look forward to next season. We understand many prominent townsmen are willing to support the new club, and a well-known gentlemen will take the chair at the meeting to be held in Victoria Galleries, Chapel-Street, on Tuesday evening next, at nine o'clock. It is hoped all interested in this matter will endeavour to attend.

(Southport Visiter, 9th June 1888)

The idea met with favour and the initial meeting called to discuss the formation of such a club took place on 12th June. What is clear from these and subsequent reports is that this was not simply a rebranding of the 'best' local side, Charity Cup winners Southport Football Club, as a professional entity. Whilst Southport had attempted to engage two professionals at the start of the previous season, the process had not been without its problems and half the team had threatened to leave. Instead, this was a radically different organisation to anything that came before it - an entirely new club. What wasn't yet clear was where it would leave the other clubs.

The meeting held in the Victoria Galleries, Chapel Street for the purpose of forming a new football club for the town was largely attended and in a great measure enthusiastic. The Town Clerk (J.H. Ellis) presided and made some very sensible suggestions. Mr Watson said it was his wish to see a good eleven in the town. He believed there was clement to work a good team. The object was to raise an eleven so good that it would be considered an honour to play them. They wanted a team to play Darwen and Everton and not only play them but give them a good game and perhaps beat them. Some fresh talent was wanted in the town. He did not know how much they would have to pay the players they imported but he thought he could get them at a very small cost. They would never get people to go to matches now. At present they visited Liverpool and Preston to see a good game but he was of the opinion that spectators would stay in Southport if there was a really good team. These remarks were endorsed by Cllr Griffiths, Mr Geddes and others and it was eventually resolved by a large majority to form a first class team to represent the town of Southport. The meeting agreed to call another meeting to consider the best methods of carrying out the above resolution into effect. A committee was appointed consisting of the secretaries and captains of all the Southport clubs.

(Southport Guardian, 16th June 1888)

(A view of Chapel Street c. 1890. The last of the tall buildings in the row is the Victoria Buildings)

(The Victoria Buildings, c. 1904, pictured right, which still stand today on the corner of chapel street and corporation street, then known as Market Passage. The ground floor is today occupied by a branch of an international bank)

The committee formed to arrange for its official launch was made up of the captains and secretaries of all of the major Southport clubs, which at that time would have consisted of Southport Football Club (née Wanderers), Churchtown, Southport Old Boys, High Park, Lancashire & Yorkshire Railway, Birkdale, High Park Rangers, Southport Ramblers and more besides.

FORMATION OF A NEW CLUB FOR SOUTHPORT
A meeting was held in the Victoria Galleries, Chapel-street, on Tuesday evening last, to decide whether it would be advisable to form a new club in the town.
Mr J.H. Ellis (Town Clerk) occupied the chair, and those present numbered about fifty, amongst them were Councillor Griffiths, Messrs. Geddes, Taylor, Watson, E.Ramsbottom, Hewitt, McGowan, Shell, Carr, Haslehurst, and representatives from the numerous local clubs.
The chairman, in his opening remarks, said the meeting had been called for the purpose of considering whether to form a new club in the town – a club which would be capable of competing with any club in this county. The idea was to weld the clubs together to make a team to advance the reputation of the town. Anything he could suggest to forward the object he would be very happy to do. They had some good footballers amongst them, and if they could get a first class eleven to represent Southport he should be very glad. He hoped those present would take a right view of the matter whether for or against.
Mr Watson said it was his wish to see a good eleven in the town. He believed there was element to work a good team. The object was to raise an eleven so good that it would be considered an honour to play with them. They wanted a team to play Everton or Darwen, and not only play them, but give them a good game, and perhaps beat them. Some fresh talent was wanted in the town. He did not know how much they would have to pay the players they imported, but he thought they could get them at a very small cost. They would never get people to go to the matches they had now, as at present they visited Liverpool and Preston to see a good game; but he was of the opinion the spectators would stay in Southport if there was a really good club in the town.
Councillor Griffiths and Mr Geddes spoke in favour of the scheme, and hoped it would be carried on in a satisfactory manner.
The following resolutions were carried: -
"To form a first-class team to represent Southport"
"That a meeting be held within a week, to consider the best method of carrying the foregoing resolution into effect"
"That a committee be appointed, consisting of the secretary and captains of all the Southport clubs, to report to the future meeting their views on the matter"
The meeting terminated with a vote of thanks to the chairman.

(Southport Visiter, 14th June 1888)

At a second meeting, held at the Railway Hotel a week later, on June 19th, Mr. R.McGowan successfully proposed that the name of the club should be 'Southport Central Association Football Club', in recognition of this being the coming together of clubs in the greater interest of the town. He was once considered a leading light of the Parkites (High Park) and spoke very much in favour of the new club's creation - the other club representatives from High Park were silent. When the proposition to form a committee was put, 11 voted in favour, none against but 19 abstained. Only one person, a Mr Taylor, spoke against the scheme saying he had no confidence in the likelihood of success.

Mr James of Hoghton Street was appointed honorary treasurer and Edwin Ramsbottom secretary. Ramsbottom of course had links back to the original Southport Football Club, with whom he had featured in the very first English Cup game for any side representing the town. As one of the pioneers of early football in Southport, he was now about to play a significant role in the establishment of an entity designed to bring the town together. The prediction earlier in the year that a number of members of the original club, nicknaming themselves the Old Southportonions, might start a new club, appeared to be coming to fruition.

The remainder of the committee was formed as follows: Messrs J.Whittaker, J.H. Ellis, Learoyd, J.Geddes, R.McGowen, D.Ashton, J.Carr, J.Shaw, T.Fairbrother, T.F.Shell, Royle, J.Smith, J.Watson, E.Trounson and Cllr. Griffiths, who acted as chairman.

Amongst those names, Thomas Fairbrother was one of the two key men behind the success of the Southport Athletic Society, alongside George Duxfield. J.S.Watson had for many years held fundraising concerts within the town at Portland Hall. He was a graduate of the London Academy of Music, and had been appointed one of the local examiners to the Royal College of Music.

Also present was John Geddes, a prominent local gentleman who had made his fortune from owning wire manufacturing businesses in both his hometown of Warrington, and also in Manchester. He had moved to Southport in the middle of the decade, living near to the home of the Southport Old Boys in Portland Street, and in 1887 had been the first person to put forward a donation (£1,000) towards the new Infirmary which was eventually built between 1892 and 1895 on Scarisbrick New Road. He was also the chairman of the Botanic Gardens Company and the Southport & Birkdale Provident Society. His name is remembered still today on a stone tablet on the Marshside Fog Bell building, which Geddes himself had rebuilt in brick in 1896 for, as he put it, 'the good object of saving human lives'.

On Tuesday June 26th a gathering took place of gentlemen who had not been invited to attend the initial meeting. Taking place at the Shakespeare Hotel on Lord Street, Mr Joye, a member of the Central committee, attended and was invited to speak. After doing so there was great resolve by those present to attend Central's next meeting.

This took place on the evening of 3rd July under the presidency of J.H.Ellis. An executive committee was formed comprising of Messrs McGowan, Watson, Hewitt, F.Wood, I.Smith, H.Whalley and E.Ramsbottom. A resolution was passed *'that the Executive Committee be requested to organise and canvass for subscriptions necessary to defray expenses of the club during the coming season and that they incur no liability in excess of assets without the authority of a General Committee'*.

Mr Joye proposed, and T.F.Shell seconded that the Ratepayers Association be requested to patronise the club and to subscribe to its funds. The Ratepayers Association donated £5 and 5 shillings. More than £50 was collected altogether.

Southport Central had been born, the town's first professional club, and with it came the inevitable consequence that a number of the amateur teams that had gone before it would begin to fade away. Whilst J.S.Watson had strongly protested at the second meeting that the idea of the new club was not to squash the existing clubs, this is in effect what happened to some of the most prominent. The idea had been to bring all of the existing amateur clubs together to create a strong professional club to represent the town, whilst their own clubs could continue to play locally. Some did for a time at least, High Park and Southport Old Boys perhaps as the highest profile began the 1888 season steadfastly refusing to admit that their club was on any lesser footing than the new organisation. Southport Football Club, the town's Charity Cup winners, however, chose not to.

Since the formation of the original club in 1881 Southport Football Club had seen itself as the town's representative club. As football grew in the town, they clung to their title as the 'premier club' with pride. In their drive for success, their switch to Sussex Road and their unprofitable amalgamation with the Athletic Society ended up creating so many financial problems that they just could not go on. Southport Olympic meanwhile had sought to capitalise on some of the excitement around the association game and had formed Wanderers in 1884, who stepped into the fold when the original club went under. Renaming themselves Southport Football Club they too desired to be the number one act in town. To the credit of both the original club and then Southport Wanderers, in local circles, they were; but on the county stage the growth of professionalism after its legalisation in 1885 had seen the town's teams fall further and further behind. It was inevitable that at some point the question had to be asked – could Southport sustain a professional club of its own?

In 1887, with Akeroyd and Whittaker, the idea to import talent to strengthen the team had been poorly communicated, and poorly executed, but the committee had already seen the writing on the wall and knew the direction the town's game was heading. The second Southport Football Club breathed its last in May 1888, and many of those involved with the club threw themselves into the Central project.

fris is Any nearest.

THE SOUTHPORT CENTRAL F. C. having secured the SPORTS GROUND, the finest enclosed ground in Lancashire, WANT HOME AND HOME MATCHES for next Season with First-class Clubs only.

E. RAMSBOTTOM, Hon. Sec.

2, Southbank-road, Southport.

SOUTHPORT CENTRAL ASSOCIATION FOOTBALL CLUB.

The above Club WANT a few first-class PROFESSIONALS for next season.—Apply, with full particulars (in confidence),

E. RAMSBOTTOM, Hon. Sec.,

2, Southbank-road, Southport.

(Cricket & Football Field – 30th June 1888)

The Sports Ground on Sussex Road, still considered to be the show ground in the town, was rented for the use of the new Southport Central F.C., with a refreshment tent noted as one of its new features. The question was whether the new professional club could bring in the crowds to justify the expenditure of such a ground, where the two previous amateur outfits that had tried to make best use of it, Southport Football Club and Southport Recreation, had already failed to do so.

As preparations for the new season got under way the local press were excited and enthused.

SOUTHPORT CENTRAL FOOTBALL CLUB

We are informed that great activity it being shown by the executive committee of the Central Football Club. Two teams have been chosen. The first team having been selected from some of the best known players in Lancashire, together with the best local talent, should ensure the public an opportunity of witnessing some really good scientific football. The names of the players are: Goal, Tyldesley; backs, Walsh and Aitken; half-backs, Horton, F.Sugg (Capt.), and Ackroyd; forwards, W.Sugg, Lea-Jones, Farrar, Sowerbutts, and Graham. We consider this team will hold its own against most Lancashire clubs. A great feature in the selection of the team is that every man will be eligible to play in both the English and Lancashire Cup competitions. The reserve team, which will be known as the Southport Swifts, is under the captaincy of F.Rimmer, and is strong enough to meet any team which was previously represented Southport. The ground in Sussex-road has been overhauled and relaid where necessary. The first match will take place on the Sports

Ground on Srptember 1st. Liverpool Stanley being the opposing team. Season tickets are now being prepared, and those gentlemen who have given their names as members would help the committee by taking up their tickets as soon as possible. Applications should be made to the secretary, Mr.E.Ramsbottom. A general committee meeting will be held in the course of a few days, when the executive will give a full report of the steps already taken to secure a successful season.

(Southport Visiter, 18th August 1888)

The Southport Central is going ahead and mean to have a good team, though if it is to be a costly one it will not pay in aristocratic Southport. Duncan, of Halliwell, and Sourbutts, of the Rovers, are two of the new hands, and all round the team is pretty strong, but it will take them more than the next season to get out of the Juniors.

(Athletic News – Tuesday 28 August 1888)

At a meeting held on 29th August, Mr. J.Watson explaining the objectives of the club, predicting that it was likely to place Southport in the front rank of football with the anticipation of bringing increased crowds of visitors to the town and it was confirmed that 'foreign talent' would be encouraged by paying players for their services.

SOUTHPORT
The establishment of a football club composed very largely of professional players has infused a wonderful amount of life and vigour into the chief of local clubs. Nearly all of them have gone on the same tack, and instead of only having one or two professionals the paid players are going to overshadow the amateurs. The spectators will no doubt enjoy the change, as it will mean better play that before; but, from a purely athletic point of view, the change is not a desirable one, inasmuch as young players will not have the same opportunities as hitherto of taking prominent places, fewer amateurs will be engaged, and the game will become simply a series of speculative exhibitions. Another point about the coming season is not altogether desirable, and that is the length of the lists of fixtures, which extend in some cases from September to May. Nine months of football leaves only three for cricket, and on account of the overlapping it is certain that the best players will not be available at the commencement or at the close of the season. This is a matter which ought to be better arranged than it is.

(Lancashire Evening Post – 30th August 1888)

A list of all football club secretaries was published in the Athletic News, dated 11th September 1888. Whilst Edwin Ramsbottom was confirmed as acting secretary operating from 2 Southbank Road, it is interesting to note that Crescent, High Park and Old Boys are all still listed as distinct clubs operating in the town, showing that whilst many had voted in favour of the formation of the Central club, when it came to the crunch, not everyone was happy to let their old clubs be absorbed or replaced by the new entity as Southport Football Club had chosen to do. Despite having vociferously supported the motion, High Park were to surprise everyone by choosing to continue on their own.

Many of the gentlemen who served on the Charity Cup Committee were the same gentlemen who had been involved with the birth of Central. The Cup had been a vital component in the sport's growth in popularity which had eventually led to the need to form the town's first professional club, Southport Central, and it had also been an essential fundraising tool for local charities, principally the Infirmary. With the birth of the professional club meaning that the number of local clubs had reduced, it became necessary to revise the structure of the still locally revered competition. It would later be proposed at October's Charity Cup Committee meeting that the competition should adopt the rules of the East Lancashire and Bolton and District Charity Cup Associations and invite only four clubs to compete for the senior competition. These clubs would be paired up as deemed appropriate by the committee to secure the healthiest competition. The hope would be that the reduced number of fixtures would bring with it reduced expenses, something key now that clubs were paying players, but at the same time increase interest, leading to larger attendances. High Park and Churchtown had chosen to boycott the meeting altogether. For the Junior Cup, rules were tweaked to prevent any professionals or members that played beyond the first round of the senior cup from being involved.

The Southport Central first team would consist regularly of four local and seven imported professional players with a strong East Lancashire element including Walsh and Akeroyd from Blackburn Olympic, Mullins and Duncan from Halliwell and Joe Sowerbutts from Blackburn Rovers. Akeroyd had made one appearance for Southport Football Club at the start of the previous season, where his inclusion had caused Captain Briggs to protest about the use of imported players. Secretary Edwin Ramsbottom of course was involved with the very first Southport Football Club and could be considered now as one of the pioneers of football in the town.

On 1st September a large crowd assembled for the visit of Stanley, a Liverpool club.

The football season is once more upon us, and last Saturday most of the teams in Southport donned their armour and prepared themselves for the hard work of the winter. The match of the most importance in Southport was that between Southport Central and Stanley, one of the leading organisations in the Liverpool district. The first team of the Southport club, as most people interested in football are already aware, is composed of professional players with the exception of five local men, vs. Lea-Jones, R.Aitken, F.Horton, J.Farrar and Tyldesley, so that with such a team football enthusiasts may reasonably expect great things this season. The Sports Ground in Sussex-road, has been engaged for the use of the new club, and a better field could not have been chosen in Southport, not only for the accommodation of spectators but also for the use of the players, asa level ground renders the play much more accurate, and helps the man considerably. Much has been done towards improving the ground, and there is every prospect of the club having a successful season.

(Southport Visiter, 4th September 1888)

Reports vary as to the attendance, accurate figures not being counted, but estimates anywhere from 500-700 were given, considerably more than would normally be achieved by one of the amateur clubs in the town - with the exception of course of the large cup games that always attracted interest. Central started on the back foot as one of the new men, Sowerbutts, had not arrived in time for kick off. For any sceptics of the professional project this will have given them all the ammunition needed, but it must be remembered that this was hardly uncommon and there are examples littered throughout the previous seven years of football in the town of games being played with understrength sides for either part, or all, of the game. Sowerbutts did eventually turn up after around 20 minutes.

The play was even for most of the game, and despite their initial numerical disadvantage and facing the wind in the first half, Central had kept Stanley at bay for half an hour. After this Stanley were credited with their first goal, local man Lewis Tyldesley in goal unable to reach a high shot. Keeping up the pressure Stanley scored twice more before half time was called, but the score line had hardly reflected the effort expended by the new outfit. In the second half, both sides scored one each, but Duncan and Lea(-Jones) both came close and could feel particularly unfortunate at not having scored themselves. In the 4-1 defeat, Southport's solitary goal was scored by Farrar, another local man – the same Farrar to have been the subject of controversy in the Junior Cup a couple of years previously. The Liverpool Mercury credited the goal to the stand-in Captain Akeroyd, however we will defer to the Southport Visiter for a more accurate report on the goalscorer.

The game was contested in midfield for time, until Farrar, obtaining possession, ran the ball through the visitors' posts.

(Southport Visiter, 4th September 1888)

The committee men present will have been very satisfied that despite the result, they had seen enough to give them the confidence that they had assembled a side of some merit.

STANLEY v SOUTHPORT CENTRAL

Played at the Southport Sports Ground on Saturday. About 500 spectators greeted the first appearance of the new Southport club, the introduction of the professional element being favourably received. The dress of the central, white and navy blue is neat, and befits a "maritime borough" as Southport loves to be called. Over the breast pockets of the white jersey is embroidered in colours the Southport arms and the motto "Salus Populi". On the grand stand were many ladies, including the Mayoress (Mrs E.J.Rimmer). Members of the Ratepayers Association, who have subscribed £5 5s to the club gave their patronage and the mimic warfare was waged to the martial strains of Herr de Mersy's Band. Stanley won the toss and played with a light wind. Their goal was the first beseigned, but Richmond, who defended grandly throughout, averted the danger, and Stanley became the aggressors. Tyldesley, a fine custodian, eventually saving with his hands, and Aitken, with the first of a series of long kicks, repulsing a renewed assault. Southport ran the ball the other end, but missed a good chance; indeed, their forwards were too eager and so unused to each other's play, that once, when the Stanley's goal was undefended, the ball went over the bar. After about half an hour's pretty even play, Stanley showed their superior attack and had registered three goals at the call of half time. On resuming the wind freshened a little, and a slight shower fell. Southport had soon again to defend, and Stanley scored for the fourth and last time. Several corners were conceded to Southport, and on the whole the ball was neatly centred, but nothing was ever attained. Once, however, Southport showed both brilliant and effective play from goal to goal. Aitken, by a beautiful return, sent the ball into mid-field. Ackroyd (who acts as captain until Frank Sugg can join) dribbled onwards, and Graham "took" the only Stanleyites who looked dangerous leaving Ackroyd to send the ball flying through the posts. Southport's first and only score evoked hearty recognition. For the rest of the game Southport pressed, and twice sent the ball just past the post and once an inch over the bar, but in the end the score still stood Stanley 4, Southport 1. Of the players not already mentioned, Horton and Sourbutts for Southport and Jones for Stanley were the most prominent, but every man on the field worked hard, and the return match (Dec 1, at Liverpool), when both clubs are in full practice will be interesting. Teams – Stanley: Roberts, goal; Richmond and W.Wilson, backs; Roberts, Martin and J. Wilson, (½ backs); Cowden, Threlfall, Jones, Brown and Millington, forwards; umpire, Mr R.J.Ross. Central: Tyldesley, goal; Walsh and Aitken, backs; Taylor, Ackroyd and Horton, (½ backs); Graham, Sourbutts, Farrer, Lea Jones, and Duncan, forwards; umpire, Mr McGowan. Referee, Mr R.J.Gosson.

(Liverpool Mercury, 3ʳᵈ September 1888)

Here in the Liverpool Mercury the report confirms that Central were a new club, as did the Southport Visiter, who referred to them for a number of weeks as 'the new organisation'. The most interesting part of the report however is in the description of the playing kit. This too was clearly designed to mark a distinction from anything that came before it. Gone was the familiar red of the original Southport, or the stripes or hoops of Wanderers, to be replaced by clean white and navy blue. The jersey also included use of the town's original crest which showed a lifeboat on the waves of the sea above the motto 'Salus Populi'. When the County Borough of Southport was much later established in 1923 and this authorised coat was changed to include a lymphad rather than a lifeboat, permission was given for the rugby club to use the crest, but they would not grant the same permission to the association club.

Southport Central had not a very auspicious opening, for Stanley defeated them by four goals to one, after having had by far the best of the game. By far the best forward on the field was R. Jones, who played a grand game. J. Wilson, Marin, an W. Wilson were the best of the defenders. Sowerbutts and Duncan were the pick of the Central, and Ackroyd at half-back did well, but the Stanley combination was too much for them.

(Athletic News, 4ᵗʰ September 1888)

After their poor opening result, all eyes were on the following week's fixture as Central turned their attention to local side the Southport Old Boys, one of the teams who had chosen not to form part of the professional project. Given their stance to remain independent, a healthy rivalry had been created between the two clubs. There's no obvious evidence of any bad blood between Old Boys and Central but this wasn't to be the only local rivalry that would play out across Central's first season in existence. Adding to the attraction of the tie was news that the Liverpool and District Association had made their draws for the Senior and Junior Cup competitions. Central were placed into the Senior section with a home draw against Whiston. Old Boys had to settle for the Junior competition, and a draw against Earlestown Reserve, alongside Churchtown, who received a bye through the first round.

After Central's opening game defeat, the followers of the Old Boys had every reason to be confident that their side would at least match, and perhaps even better their new opponents. Old Boys, although choosing to remain independent, had instead engaged a team consisting mainly of professional players themselves.

Thomas Lea headed the first goal for Central after 15 minutes, and then followed up with another shortly after. Duncan hit the post with an overhead kick and Graham followed up the rebound to notch the third goal. One minute after the restart Graham grabbed his second and Central were by this time out of sight. The visitors made strenuous efforts to score but the Central defence were just too strong for them.

Southport Central defeated what many people consider their great rivals in Southport - the Old Boys — by six goals to nil, a victory decisive enough. The central team will be bad to beat when they get going.

(Athletic News 11th September 1888)

It was to be little over a month between kicking a ball for the first time against Stanley in a standard club fixture and the first competitive match, with the start of the English Challenge Cup. Having beaten St Helens and Chorley convincingly, scoring 15 goals and only conceding five in the process, Southport entered the Cup in a rich vein of form.

Not everyone was pleased however with the free-flowing goals. The leading local newspaper suggested that the new club were playing against teams unable to provide strong opposition.

Why on earth don't the Central get some one to play with? It can't be that they are so very clever, and can knock any club out of time. The fact is that the energetic secretary has been arranging with teams which he knew for certainty would have no chance with his own. Perhaps he is under the impression, like a good many more are, that no matter what kind of a team the opposing club possesses if the locals are on the winning side the gates are sure to increase. This is a mistake, as the spectators get just as tired of witnessing a one-sided match, even if their pets are always on the winning side, as they do when they are continually seeing them defeated.

(Southport Visiter, 6th October 1888)

Drawn away at Bacup against Irwell Springs, the fledgling club's first away game, it was an exciting match. Leaving the Lancashire & Yorkshire station at 11:30, a large number of locals joined the team on their travels.

A HARD GAME AT BACUP
Suitable football weather prevailed at Broadclough when the Alpine Club opposed Southport Central in the encounter for the English Cup. Dyson is still absent as a matter of course, his recovery from the injured leg at the Manchester Infirmary being very slow. "Boy" Sykes makes a

rather good substitute, whilst Bob Dyson improves with practice. Though the loss of Cooke (now of Rossendale) is greatly felt by the Springs Club, yet Hird does his duty in a commendable manner. Southport were well represented, and the game throughout was of an exciting character. At the end of ninety minutes the game was – Southport, three goals; Springs, three goals. Extra time was played, when Southport added two more goals and Springs one. The Southport men were in splendid form, as, in fact, both sides were. Hird, Billy Haworth, and Little Thompson for the Springs played an excellent game. The visitors' goalkeeper had some hard shots to fist out. There was a large attendance, no small number hailing from Southport.

(Athletic News, 9th October 1888)

Irwell Springs had a good reputation which meant that the Sandgrounders (now the predominant nickname of the new organisation) travelled without any great expectation. Upon arriving at the ground, they were dismayed to find it in such wretched condition. The club had attempted to induce Springs into switching the tie, offering to share gate receipts evenly plus travel expenses but it had been refused. If Irwell Springs' reputation was a well-earned one, the poor surface acted as a leveller, as a hard-fought battle ensued which required an additional period of 30 minutes extra time to settle. The only goal scorer known from the reports published was Thomas Lea who had grabbed Southport's first of five.

Winning 5-4 after extra time Central were beginning to show signs of being a decent side.

Lewis Tyldesley, in goal for Central on that day recalled later that the crowd had become frustrated with the form of Harry Baxter and that he raised their indignation further by kicking the ball clean out of the ground.

Brave Central! You came out of the ordeal exceedingly well on Saturday last, and deserve to be congratulated. We have pleasure in doing so. Irwell Springs had a very good reputation. You had just the opposite in East Lancashire, at all events, but by the brilliant game you played in the first round of the English Cup, you have made for yourselves a name, and we have great confidence that you will keep it. The ground was not suitable to your tastes — we mean to your feet — but, notwithstanding this fact, you gained a victory by five goals to four. Irwell Springs were astonished. We were astonished. The spectators were astonished, and we believe you were astonished yourselves. At the conclusion of the match all the Southportonions were jubilant, and we are given to understand that the energetic secretary was so delighted that he ran a hundred yards in even time.

(Southport Visiter, 13th October 1888)

Whilst they met the challenge of 'Springs' in the English Challenge Cup, the second-string side were forced to face off with Whiston at Sussex Road in the Liverpool Challenge Cup. This should have been a first team fixture and it is disappointing that no concession had been given for the Liverpool Cup tie to have been played on a different date. Southport Central's second string, the Swifts, whilst being predominantly the same set of players to have played as 'Southport Football Club' the year previous, were not up to the standard required to be able to compete successfully at county level, which is one of the primary reasons why Central had been formed in the first place. The Swifts were overcome 1-3.

A week later, Haydock St James were to be the new club's first opponents in the Lancashire Junior Cup. In front of a good attendance at Sussex Road, a first half brace from Taylor set Central on the way as they cruised to a 4-1 win.

Meanwhile, rivalry between the remaining local clubs and Central was growing. After Central had progressed in back-to-back competitive matches an anonymous local correspondent informed Haydock that Central had played an ineligible player. An inquiry found that there was no truth in the allegation, but it typified the ill feeling that existed.

On 20th October a return match with Stanley showed the progress being made on the field.

Stanley went to Southport to open the new ground of the Central, and were beaten rather unexpectedly. They easily defeated the same team at the commencement of the season, but they were on this occasion without the services of Jones, who on the former visit of Stanley to Southport played very brilliantly, and this might to some extent account for the difference in the result.

(Athletic News, 23rd October 1888)

At Southport, before nearly 1000 spectators. Stanley kicked off, and the ball was immediately taken into the visitors quarters, Taylor, by a grand shot scoring for the home team. Some give and take play followed, and ultimately from a scrimmage in front of goal Lea and Jones forced the leather through, thus registering the second point for the Central. Nothing further occurred and at half time the score stood – Southport 2, Stanley 0.
Result – Southport Central 3 – 0

(Lancashire Evening Post, 20th October 1888)

In their first season Southport Central had often experienced difficulty in arranging fixtures and when they applied for matches some clubs treated them rather curtly. Lytham simply wrote on the memorandum bearing Central's application 'We do not know this club!' and returned it to their secretary.

When it came to their opponents in the second round of the Challenge Cup, South Shore, they too did not quite know what to expect but the locals were enthused by the success of the new club and wanted to do all they could to support them. One such supporter, the self-titled 'Inflated Sphere', wrote to the Southport Visiter to implore the local steamboat companies to lay on transport for fans by boat to Blackpool for the upcoming second round tie.

ENGLISH CUP TIES – SECOND ROUND
SOUTH SHORE ON THE JOB

South Shore were not particularly well acquainted with the Southport Central until last Saturday, and were somewhat doubtful about the result, as the professional team were somewhat mysterious in the matter of its composition. However, events proved that the Shore men had no cause for alarm, as the Central players, although good, were not clever enough for South Shore, who scored in a minute after the start – thanks to Dick Elston. This was equalised by Joe Sourbutts, the old Rover, and Shaw, the Central full-back, put No. 2 through his own goal. In the latter half, South Shore played a great game, Walsh, Cookson, Halliwell, and Parkinson all getting goals. Finally, South Shore came through by seven goals to the Central one. Shaw, Ackroyd, Sourbutts, Duncan, and Taylor were the best men in the Central team.

(Athletic News, 30th October 1988)

SOUTH SHORE v SOUTHPORT
At South Shore.
The professional combination met with a good reception. Mr Sam Ormerod (Accrington) was the referee. South Shore appeared with their full strength for the first time this season. Cookson kicked off, and a throw-in followed to Southport. Dick Elston, after a beautiful dribble, scored the first goal for Shore. Tyldesley fisted out shots from Elston and Parkinson. Dakin was hurt, but the game proceeded. A corner came to the Central, and then Cookson almost scored. Sourbutts afterwards equalised. The Southport men were pressing with the wind. A free-kick to the Shore in the Central goal was very dangerous. A minute later South Shore got a second goal, and at half time led by 2 to 1.
On Resuming, play became exciting, as Cookson and Parkinson each missed chances. Cookson added a third with a long shot, and Halliwell a fourth. Three more goals were scored in rapid succession, one being a remarkable shot by the South Shore captain. The ball was sent up to the goal and diverted to the left, where Elston, who had his back to goal, kicked the ball over his head, and the leather falling from a considerable height, went through the centre of the goal, amid loud cheers.
Result – Southport Shore 7, Southport Central 1.

(Lancashire Evening Post – 27th October 1888)

Despite being soundly beaten, and in front of roughly 200 supporters who travelled from Southport, the club took their defeat well and Blackpool entertained both teams and the referee, to tea at the Palatine Hotel, Blackpool, after the game. What the reports from these two regional titles don't tell you is that Southport were handicapped by the absence of Blenkhorn who had missed his train and by consequence had to play with 10 men.

The score does not by any means represent the true state of the game, and except on very few occasions during the first half the ball was continually within shooting distance of the Shore goal, and the Central were unlucky in not scoring at least four or five times.

(Southport Visiter, 30th October 1888)

The Swifts once again had to deputise in place of the first team for the scheduled visit of Fishwick Ramblers and although losing 1-3, came out of the game with a great deal of credit. The inclusion of new signing Park, another import, gave the Swifts a much-needed boost. Central were by now fielding three teams, just as Southport Football Club had done the previous season. According to the advertisement placed in the Cricket & Football Field on 17th November by Secretary R.Aitken, the Swifts was *composed of last year's Southport 1st team*, and much of last year's seconds had now become a third string.

Central progressed further in the Lancashire Cup at the start of November with a 5-3 win over Bootle Wanderers. Robert Lythgoe, the old friend of Thomas Burnett was the referee. It was to be the last game played in goal by Lewis Tyldesley before Central strengthened with the new signing of goalkeeper Ingram who subsequently kept a clean sheet on his debut.

Central had been formed with the goal of giving a team from Southport a better chance of competing with the bigger clubs in the country. At the end of November came Central's first real opportunity to test whether the plan had worked. When Blackburn Olympic visited, the first Lancashire club to have won the English Cup in 1883, most expected Central to be beaten, however few expected Central to fare as well as they did.

The match terminated in a victory for the Central by two goals to one. It would be invidious to specifically compliment any member of the Central, as the combined team gave the most correct exhibition that has ever been witnessed at Southport, and the spectators thoroughly appreciated their splendid efforts to score against the wind. The Olympic forwards exhibited some good passing, and had it not been for the good display of their backs, the home team would have scored a more substantial victory.

(Southport Visiter, 20th November 1888)

The Football League had been formed as the world's first association football league in the summer of 1888 by the leading clubs of the Midlands and the North. The driving force behind the new organisation had been Aston Villa Chairman William McGregor who had stipulated a rule that each town could only have one entrant into the League. He had chosen Blackburn Rovers rather than Olympic, and they were still reeling from the decision. They were struggling to compete with Rovers on and off the field and the Olympic that existed in November 1888 was a far cry from the side that had won the English Cup five years earlier.

In December the Athletic News commented *that football is looking up in the pleasant sea port whose only defect is being without the sea*. It was a realistic assessment of the 22 games Central played before the turn of the year as they claimed a creditable record of 14 wins, two draws, and six defeats all told.

The New Year however did not start well at all!

A great deal of excitement had been building over the Christmas period at the prospect of the scheduled clash between Central and the Parkites of High Park at Sussex Road on New Year's Day. The gate of 2,000 was the largest yet recorded for an ordinary club fixture. In answer to the Visiter's open question of *'Which is the best local football club'* Central did themselves no favours by having to play the first 10 minutes of the game with just seven men as four were late to arrive. Whilst it did not materially affect the score line, no goals having been scored during that period, that was more likely to have been due to the dense fog that had descended onto the ground rather than Central's robust defensive play. By the time the absentees arrived the fog was beginning to lift and unfortunately supporters could see what would transpire much more clearly.

As far as the scoring had gone, High Park had led at half time 2-1 before the professionals had come back to take a 3-2 lead. As the second half neared its conclusion however the Parkites firstly equalised and then snatched it at the death, deservedly beating Central 4-3.

High Park drew all the plaudits and cheer after cheer went up from the High Park players at the full-time whistle.

The shock result took Central out of their stride and the bragging rights were with the club who resided a stones' throw away, on Devonshire Road.

Any hopes of bouncing back quickly were dashed when Central met Fleetwood Rangers four days later in the fourth round of the Lancashire Junior Cup. Missing four of their regulars, Duncan, Mullin, Blenkhorn and Ingram, all of whom were ineligible under the Lancashire rules, they crashed to a 0-2 defeat. It was a poor opening week of the year and Central needed a reaction. Fearful of losing their reputation, Central knew that improvements were necessary and unless they were to turn on the style, they would start to lose support.

Next up were the famous Blackburn club, Witton, who had last visited Southport back in 1882 for an exhibition match against Rovers. The establishment of a professional club in the town six years later was precisely so that they could compete with clubs of this stature, but here, the omens weren't good. Witton had already disposed of Central's English Cup opponents South Shore, something Central had been unable to do themselves, and Central were missing one of their best players, Joe Sowerbutts, the former Blackburn Rovers forward, through injury. A third defeat on the spin was unthinkable.

Central had to turn to newcomer Heslop to fill in. Although trailing at the interval it was the newcomer that they had to thank for pulling them level, running the ball through the posts in the second half. The performance against Witton was more than encouraging and a draw would be seen as very creditable. It could have been better still – the returning 'Geordie' Duncan was convinced that he had given Central the lead with a shot that many people thought had gone through the posts. Still in the era before goal nets were added to avoid disputes, the referee however gave the visitors the benefit of the doubt and the result stood at one goal apiece.

The game of association football was still in its infancy and rules and regulations were changing from year to year to counter the disputes that regularly occurred. This wasn't to be the last time that Central were to be on the wrong end of a referee's judgement that season.

Scarcely more than three weeks after their painful defeat by High Park on New Year's Day, Central had a chance to put things right against their local rivals. This time it was in aid of the local charities and for the Charity Cup, a competition that had been established off the back of the annual charitable fixture for the Infirmary that had been part the ethos of the first Southport (Association) Football Club.

Although a new club in every sense, Central had been formed ultimately from the amalgamation of various smaller clubs, Southport Football Club, Southport Wanderers and Christ Church/Southport Recreation, and it wouldn't be long before Old Boys too would throw in their lot with the Central club. However High Park remained defiant rivals.

Whilst originally drawn to play the tie at Sussex Road due to the quality of the facilities on offer to the patrons, the Parkites refused on the grounds that it would give an unfair advantage. Agreement was at first reached to play it at a neutral venue with Portland Street, home of the Southport Old Boys, suggested. However, it was the Central players who, mindful of the purpose of the competition being to raise money for charity, conceded any advantage and offered to switch the tie to the better enclosed Devonshire Road home of their opponents. High Park's stubborn stance had done them no favours with the local press.

The Central players said as the High Park ground was better enclosed than the Old Boys they would be willing, so that the charities would not suffer, to encounter them on their own field. This shows that they have every confidence in themselves, and after the stubbornness the Parkites have shown in the matter, I sincerely hope that the Sussex-road players will prove victorious.

(Southport Visiter -19th January 1889)

Central's brave offer certainly helped the gate, as the largest crowd ever assembled in Southport to that point of 2,500 paid to watch the two teams battle it out to a 1-1 draw. Central's chances hadn't been helped by the enforced absence of their Captain Walter Akeroyd who had become injured in the Witton game, and Blenkhorn who had business matters to attend to. When Hill gave the home side the lead mid-way through the first half the Southport Visiter remarked *'the shouts and cheers that followed the goal must have been heard miles away'*. Taylor equalised but Central had to thank Ingram whose brilliant goalkeeping had kept them in the game.

At a meeting of the Charity Cup Committee in the week that followed it was unanimously agreed that the replay should be fixed for the following week, 26th January. The representatives of the High Park club in attendance, however, requested that the tie should be postponed owing to the absence of a couple of their players who would be unable to take part in the match (Fairhurst and Caldwell were injured). The irony had been lost on them that their request was being made even though Central had not only been willing to switch the tie to Devonshire Road, giving High Park a huge advantage in the first tie, but Central had played without fuss, with two of their most influential men missing. Their cynical request was dismissed after a brief discussion.

Sensationally, High Park refused to accept the decision as fair and scratched from the competition altogether, giving Southport a walk over. High Park were not prepared to field a weakened side even if Infirmary funds suffered.

Members of Central's management committee came forward and generously volunteered to play another match for the benefit of the various institutions who would have otherwise lost out. To them, the cause was of greater importance than the result and the Charity Cup committee gladly accepted. Negotiations subsequently took place which saw a visit from Blackpool.

A bitter argument subsequently broke out between fans of the local rivals via correspondence in the Southport Visiter. High Park's supporters claimed they had been harshly treated and refused to accept that comparisons could be drawn to the first encounter where Central had been short of men, instead taking cheap shots by labelling them a mongrel 'Churchite-cum-Recreation-plus-Central' club. It was clear that the Visiter had no sympathies for High Park and the dogmatic and inflexible stance they had taken.

SOUTHPORT CENTRAL AND BLACKPOOL PLAY FOR CHARITY
Southport Central should have met High Park in the Southport Charity Cup competition, but the High Park committee scratched at the last moment, as they had some of their team indisposed, thinking that this would considerably lessen their changes against Central. The charity committee approached Blackpool, and Alderman Bickerstaffe, the president of the Blackpool club, at once consented for the team to visit Southport, so that the charities would not suffer, the kindness of the Blackpool people being highly appreciated by the Southport and district charity committee. Both teams were well represented, and a grand game ended in a draw of two goals each. Grand indignation is felt in Southport at the action of the High Park committee, the general opinion being that they have behaved in a very childish manner, especially as the proceeds of the competition go to the local charities.

(Athletic News — 28th January 1889)

The Blackpool gate wasn't on the scale that a replay would have been, but it had been the best that could have been arranged in the time allowed. Before the replay date had been agreed, Central had been scheduled to play against Fishwick Ramblers but Blackpool, as holders of the Lancashire Junior Cup and Fylde Cup, were a bigger draw.

Kicking into the wind, Central fell behind almost straight away, Ingram unable to stop a shot from Shaw. Mullin equalised for Central, but it was Blackpool who went in ahead at the break, getting the better of the exchanges and making Ingram work hard for his money. With the wind at their backs in the second half Central found their feet and Hothersall equalised again with a long-range shot. The match finished all square.

Undefeated in three after their shock defeats in the first week of January, Central returned to winning ways with a visit to a Chorley side that had been greatly strengthened in the weeks since their first encounter. Whilst not as decisive as the 6-0 victory they had originally gained, Central again kept a clean sheet in a 2-0 win.

Hindley were next to visit Sussex Road in an ill-tempered affair. Hindley had been one of the few teams to beat Central in the first half of the season, but the Visiter remarked that *'it is a great measure that their victory was due to horseplay more than scientific football. Last Saturday one of the team who has earned for himself the title of "Pet" (we believe it is the same who struck Mullin at Hindley), again wanted to show himself as a pugilist. We hope the Central committee will call the attention of the Association to this gentleman's (?) conduct"* (Southport Visiter, 12th February 1889).

As a mark of respect, the Central players wore crepe bandages, the equivalent of today's black arm bands, in memory of a popular former player Robert Pasquill who had passed away after a short illness less than a week before. First connected with Southport Recreation he had later found himself part of the first XI of the amalgamated club. He signed on with Central upon their formation, was a regular for the Swifts, and played when required for the first team. His last appearance for Central had been in the Lancashire Cup victory over Bootle Wanderers in November.

In a fairly even match Taylor and Graham proved the difference as Central beat Hindley 2-1.

With the High Park dispute behind them thoughts turned to the Charity Cup Final where Central were to meet Churchtown.

CENTRAL v CHURCHTOWN

These clubs met for the first time on Saturday last on the Sports Ground in the final tie for the Charity Cup. Notwithstanding the fact that the day was a bitterly cold one about 1000 spectators, including a good sprinkling of the fair sex, braved the elements to witness the encounter. In the previous round Churchtown, after a stubbornly contested match, defeated the Old Boys by one goal to nil, and the Central were awarded a walk-over owing to the High Park refusing to come up to the scratch after a drawn game of one goal each had been played between those clubs on the Devonshire Road ground. The match did not create much enthusiasm in football circles, as it was the general opinion that Central would win easily, the only question being by how many goals. Provision to the commencement the band of the 3rd. V.B. King's (Liverpool) Regiment, under the commandship of Mr Rimmer, played several selections. Ackroyd won the toss, and decided to defend the Railway goal. Mr J.H.Ellis (the Town Clerk) kicked off for Churchtown, when Hodgkinson returned, and the home forwards getting possession, dribbled smartly down the field, and in less than a minute Mullin had placed a goal to the credit of his side. Hewitt again started, passing to Wright, who made a good run up the wing at the conclusion of which he centred, giving Thornton a chance, but he failed to utilise it. The momentary invasion was followed by Lea-Jones, who neatly evaded Sumner, after which, by a good kick he sent the ball to midfield, where hostilities were carried on for a brief period. The home forwards eventually broke away, and gained a foothold in the visiting quarters, where an opportunity was presented to Duncan, but his shot went wide of the mark. From the goal kick Hobson secured, and made a speedy run up the left wing, until he was robbed by Hodgkinson who kicked to the centre. Johnson however returned, and Hodgkinson missing his kick, nearly let Hewitt in, that player being robbed at a critical moment by Shaw, who relieved the tension. Horton at this point was noticeable by a tricky run, but he was pulled up by Johnson, who again sent the ball well in the Central quarters, and Hobson getting possession, finished a dodgy run by easily beating Ingram, a feat that was duly recognised. Taylor started from the centre, and immediately Graham forced Williamson to concede a corner, which was well placed by Lea-Jones, but Gee was successful in repelling the shot. A determined run was then made by the Churchtown forwards, Wright being soon to advantage. Hewitt then secured the sphere, and sent in a shot which called upon Ingram. From this point until the conclusion of the first half the play was of a pretty even nature, both ends being alternatively visited, but no additional goals were scored, and the teams ended on level terms. After a brief rest Taylor recommenced, and it was at once apparent that the home team meant business, for in less time that it takes to describe, the forwards dribbled down the field, and Taylor sent in a shot which Gee failed to negotiate. After Hewitt had kicked off, the home forwards were soon making tracks for the visitors citadel, and Duncan, Hotherwell and Mullin, in a short space of time, all had shots at Gee, but he succeeded in repelling them in great style. The fusillade was, however, still kept up, the backs having their abilities well tested, but the Central were unable to break the defence. The Churchtown forwards then made a determined attempt to get down the field but the play of Hodgkinson and Shaw was too reliable to allow much encroachment, and the attack on the visitors citadel was renewed with vigour. A perfect fusillade was kept up, during which Graham and Duncan succeeded in upsetting Gee. Afterwards the home team continued to press, but Gee was always to the task, and, as no other points were added, the Central claimed the victory by four goals to one. The following were the teams: - Central: Ingram, goal; Shaw and Hodgkinson, backs; Lea-Jones, Ackroyd (Capt.) and Horton, (½ backs); Duncan, Graham, Mullin, Hothersall and Taylor, forwards. Churchtown: J.Gee, goal; Williamson and Johnson, backs; Wright, Sumner and Cadwell, (½ backs); Carter, Gee, Thornton, Hobson and Hewitt, forwards. Umpires, Messrs. R McGown and R. Bushell. Referee, Mr. Sam Ormerod.

PRESENTATION OF THE CUP AND MEDALS

At the conclusion of the match the cup and medals were presented by the Town Clerk to the successful tea. Mr. A. Rammsbottom called upon Mr J.H.Ellis, who said he had very great pleasure in performing such a duty which is usually fulfilled by the Mayor or the borough, and he was sure they would join with him in the expression of regret that the Mayor was unable to present that afternoon. He was sure his Worship would have liked very much to have been with them, not only to support the good old English game of football by his presence, but to show his sympathy with the Infirmary and other local charities (Applause). The spectators had witnessed a very pleasant and, on the whole, and evenly contested game, and he thought most of them would be of the opinion that the best team had won. (Applause). If he might be allowed to criticise the play of both teams, it would be in the direction that there should be more play upon the ball and less upon the man. (Hear. Hear.) It would be more pleasant for the spectators, and better for the tempers of the men. (Hear. Hear.) But, of course, it took a little time to seguine that in new clubs. They should take a model from the great club, the Preston North End. The game of that club they would find was upon the ball. He did not mean to say that they could not play roughly if they were put to it, but they did not like to play roughly. The Central team had only been started this season, and he hoped that the desire of those who helped in its formation – and he might say he had a hand in it – would be fulfilled before long, and that was that it should be a team not only capable of meeting and beating the best local club, but of meeting and beating the best clubs in the country. (Loud applause). He then handed the cup to Mr Ackroyd, the captain of the Central team.

Mr Ackroyd, in acknowledging the trophy, said he was very much obliged to the Town Clerk for the kind remarks he had made in respect to the Central team. They would be always glad to compete for the Cup, and in any way help the local charities. He was sorry that they had not had

the pleasure of beating all the clubs that had entered, but he hoped next season they would beat
High Park (Laughter and Applause).
The Town Clerk then handed the medals to the members of the Central team.
Councillor Griffiths, in moving a vote of thanks to the Town Clark, said Mr. Ellis was a keen
sportsman, and took and interest to all kinds of games. In fact he was a good man at all kinds of
work, and there were few men more esteemed and respected in the borough than he was. (Applause).
He endorsed the Town Clarks remarks regarding Football, and supplement them with the advice to
the Central tam - shoot hard, and low, and often (Applause).
The Rev. C. Hesketh Knowlys, president of the Churchtown club, in appending to the motion, said
it was a great thing to know how to take a good kicking., and he would assure them that the
Churchtown men would show that they know how, and that next year they would do their best to
beat the Central team. (Applause).
The vote was carried with enthusiasm, after which the Town Clark kindly returned thanks.
Hearty cheers were then given for the Churchtown team, and for the band for their services.

(Southport Visiter – 5ᵗʰ March 1889)

Edwin Ramsbottom's tenure as honorary secretary came to a premature end in March. There was no reason given for his sudden departure however, the Southport Visiter confirmed on 16ᵗʰ March 1889 that all future correspondence should be addressed to Thomas Frederick Shell. He was to handle affairs until the appointment of J.G.Johnson at the end of the season.

After success in the Charity Cup, Central's form fluctuated as they saw out their first season. Akeroyd, the Central captain, almost withdrew his men after half an hour in a match against Heywood in March due to a perception of bias by the referee, but they continued to play and were beaten 3-0. In the return game the entire Heywood team left the field disputing Central's goal scored by Horton. Southport, although trailing 2-1, claimed the match. There was clearly a growing body of evidence to support the need for improvements in player discipline and the officiating of matches.

Southport Central met Heywood Central at Southport. Against the strong wind the homesters
found it difficult to make progress, and play generally was in their half, but Watson and Weir
several times tested the Heywood defence. Kenyon, however, scored, and from a corner the visitors
added a second. After change of ends the home team attacked and obtained a goal. The visitors
hotly disputed the point, and on the referee allowing it they left the field – a very childish proceeding.

(Athletic News – 22nd April 1889)

The most significant outcomes of Central's first season were their first Charity Cup success and the impact that the formation of the club had upon local football in general. A new club had been established that could compete with the best clubs in the region. The local press were behind them, some of the town's biggest political names too, and things were looking up.

The event which caused the most excitement in the town during this first season was the visit of Preston North End who had just carried off the League and English Cup double. They came to Southport on 13th May and were given a rapturous welcome on arrival at the railway station. They were driven to the ground behind a marching band. There was a record gate of 3,500 and North End won 4-2 even though Central were re-enforced for the occasion by Forbes, Townley and Southworth of Blackburn Rovers. Townley had previously guested for Southport Wanderers whilst on the books of the Blackburn Swifts.

That they had been able to arrange 40 games for the season was highly creditable. The record for the first season was Played 40 Won 21 Drawn 6 Lost 13.

Part III – Rugby

Southport (Rugby) Football Club

When it became clear that Southport Football Club would not be arranging fixtures for the 1880/81 season, Southport Olympic and Southport Hornets were more than happy to keep the rugby torch burning and fight it out for the title of the town's best rugby club. Southport Hornets, formed in the preceding 1879/1880 season, played at a ground on Green Lane, which later became Wennington Road.

In October 1880, two months after it had been made clear that Southport Football Club would not be playing, Hornets Secretary Fred Sergeant wrote to the Athletic News to advertise that *The Southport Hornets still have many open dates and will be glad to arrange matches with clubs in the neighbourhoods of Bolton, Bury, Manchester and Liverpool – Address Fred Sergeant, Secretary, Devonshire Buildings, Southport' (Athletic News, 13th October 1880)*

An attempt was made to restart Southport Football Club after the absence of one season, but this lasted only 3 games before the team made the permanent switch to the dribbling game, as noted in Part II of this book.

The Lancashire County Rugby Football Union was formed at a meeting held at The Albion Hotel, Manchester on 22nd December 1881, but neither Southport Football Club, nor any other rugby playing club in the town were represented.

As the popularity of the round ball game grew in Southport, a number of Hornets players switched over to play association football for Southport, notably Tom Morris who became captain, and also brothers Arthur and Alfred Dalby.

Andrew Irving, another promising Hornets regular was the subject of correspondence in the Southport Visiter in August 1882 after he too had turned in an appearance for the new association club.

Sir — "Forward", I fear, has taken too much on himself in his remarks on the coming football season, and I should not like the Southport public to be misled in any way. He is evidently a patron of the dribbling game, as he has so much to say about the Association Club which was started here last season, and which he anticipates is going to do great things against such old clubs as they have succeeded in getting fixtures with. Well, I hope they may, as there is plenty of room for both Rugby and Association clubs in Southport. Before "Forward" puts himself before the public as a representative of the Southport football world it would have been better for him to have acquainted himself more fully with the arrangements that have been made for next season. He regrets that the Association Club will not have the invaluable support of Mr A.Irving during the coming season, as he will be "obliged to sever his connection with the club at the beginning of the season." The fact is, Mr. Irving was elected captain of the Southport Hornets — a young club, but one which has some promising players — at their election of officers last May; he however, since that time, has decided to go to Australia, and will consequently be unable to play here. Mr Irving was captain of the Hornets for the whole of last season, and played with them the whole of their matches, only playing with the Association Club on two or three Saturdays, when his own club had no match. The impression that "Forward" would give to the public is that Mr Irving had been a regular player with the Association Club, which is a mistake. Why "Forward" snubs the Hornets is not perceptible, and is, as I presume from the tone of his letter unkind, seeing that several Hornets have rendered his club invaluable assistance more than once. If "Forward" is to be our mouthpiece during the coming season, I may say by all means let him have a knowledge of his facts before he comes before the public again. For instance, he might have interested the public by telling them that Mr N. Howard, one of the best players of the Rugby game in this district has decided to retire from play, and that the rumours which have been errant concerning him lately are all "squashed"; he might have said that the Hornets have taken the first field in Scarisbrick New-road for next season and that the Olympic have taken a field next to the Association Club in the same road; but it is evident that he is only pushing his own club, therefore he should not attempt to review the arrangements of both games for next season. I would advise him in future to save his remarks for his own club, as he will receive no thanks from members of the Rugby game for his remarks in your last issue.
A RUGBY PLAYER

(Southport Visiter, 22nd August 1882)

Hornets themselves lasted only until the end of the 1882/1883 season and after disbanding, many players, notably full back Tom Sellars, joined the Olympic club in time for the start of the 1883/84 season.

In November 1882 another ultimately failed attempt had been made to start a rugby club under the Southport Football Club name. On 21st November the following report was published in the Southport Visiter confirming that the 'old club' had been revived for the third time, albeit with not a single player remaining from the last rugby fixture in October of the previous year.

SOUTHPORT v LITHERLAND — This match was played at Southport on Saturday last, being the first match played since the revival of the once famous Southport club. Southport having lost the toss, kicked off against the wind, and the forwards, following up well, quickly carried the ball over their opponents' goal-line, Woods gaining the first try. Forde took the place, but failed at goal. Litherland dropped out and playing well together took the ball to the Southport end, when Robinson ran in; the kick at goal failed. After a few scrimmages Southport were again driven back, and a Southport forward kicking too hard in the loose, the ball went to Whaley, who made a splendid run dodging all the backs, gained a try between the posts. The kick at goal resulted in a poster. The game was very even for some time, the Southport forwards gradually forcing their opponents back, and H.S.Rheam getting the ball passed to Hall, who ran in close to the touch-line. Litherland objected and Southport gave way, but directly afterwards the ball was well taken through by the Southport forwards. Heywood gaining a try from which Forde kicked a neat goal. Half-time was shortly afterwards called, the ball being well within the Southport twenty-five. Southport, playing with the wind in their favour, penned their opponents for the remainder of the game. Woods, P. Rheam and Bracewell gaining tries, only one of which resulted in a goal. The play of the Southport forwards during the latter half completely non-plussed the Litherland men, and when "no side" was called the score stood as follows: - Southport, two goals and three tries; to Litherland one poster and one try. For the home team Woods and Hall were best behind, and of the forwards Chadwick was most conscious, being well backed up by Munn, Bracewell, and the Rheams. For Litherland, Whaley and Lycett behind. Tarbuck and Robinson forward, were best; Litherland played fourteen men.

Teams — Southport: T.Forde, back; J.Hall, W.Gregory, J. Fairrie, three-quarter backs; W.Woods and W.Clarke, (½ backs); F.Baildon, J.H.Bracewell (Capt.), P.Chadwick, Heywood, J.Moore, D.Munn, A.Peck, H.S.Rheam and P.Rheam, forwards.

(Southport Visiter, 21ˢᵗ November 1882)

A short fixture list was published four days later, indicating that the original intention had been to play Chester on 11th November, but it seems this fixture did not take place. The fixture list did confirm that the club had re-taken the field at Manchester Road and that ambitious rugby fixtures had been arranged with clubs from Manchester and Liverpool.

Fixtures and reports, however, appeared very infrequently in the local press for the new Southport (Rugby) Football Club who were clearly a second-class team compared to their rivals.

With Southport Hornets now gone, and with Southport Football Club playing few games, this left another opening, and the name of Southport Wasps re-emerged at the start of the 1883/84 season.

Neither side were ever considered serious contenders for the title of the town's team. Olympic had picked up the torch and were running with it. All trace of the briefly resuscitated Southport Football Club had once again disappeared by the end of their second season and Wasps only completed two further seasons themselves.

The Olympic Club

The name Southport Olympic is to be found first in 1875 with a rugby fixture taking place against Freshfield College on 26th October. As this was a time before points were the method of determining the victors, it was a drawn game officially due to the lack of goals. The score was deemed to be in favour of Olympic by two byes and 21 touchdowns to nothing. The line-up was: Thompson, Farrow (backs); Hindle (¾ backs); Eastham, Galley (½ backs); Harper (Capt.), Crabtree, Smith. Edwards, Platt, Thomas, Tunstall, Duxfield, Davies, Smith (forwards)

The line-up included many players who would go on to represent other local clubs over the coming seasons. Eastham, Harper and Platt were to join Southport Wasps in 1876, and become staples of the side that became Southport Football Club in 1879. G.H.Thomas would join the original Southport Football Club.

Olympic's second fixture was against a representative team from Bickerton House school. Once again, it was a drawn game, with both sides having scored a goal each, but the result went slightly in favour of Bickerton with two byes and four touchdowns to one bye and two touchdowns.

Other than one further fixture in December, against Freshfield College, (with a draw, which went in favour of Olympic by one touchdown to nil) there appear to have been no further fixtures under the name.

=·=

On 13th April 1877, the Southport Visiter announced that a cricket club linked to Christ Church had *"thrown its doors open to the town'* and had been given the new name of the Church of England Temperance Society Cricket Club. There are some similarities in the lists of members to suggest that they may have been the same entity as the 1875 Southport Olympic, although it is probably unlikely. The Cricket club was based at Scarisbrick New Road.

A football club connected to the Temperance Society was in existence as early as November 1876, although there are no records of fixtures or results published under this name in any of the Southport press until February 1877, most likely because practice games were not deemed worthy of a report. A 'Paper Chase' was held by the Temperance Society club on 25th November from a field adjoining the Cemetery (likely to be some of what is known today as the Portland Street playing fields). A paper chase is an outdoor racing game also known as Hares and Hounds. With one person (or a small number) designated the Hares, and the remainder the Hounds, the Hares set off running leaving a trail of paper behind them (like a scent) for the Hounds to follow. If the Hare makes it to the agreed finish line before the Hounds, who follow after giving a head start, they get to choose the next hare. It was a good-natured game of fun usually played by a big group, showing that the club must have had a healthy membership. Incidentally, cross country runners came to be known as Harriers, after the small hound used to chase genuine hares. The irony is not lost on the author that the Southport Athletic Society later changed their name to Southport Harriers and a very influential Athletic Society member was also a member of the Temperance Society!

Born in Newton le-Willows on 24th October 1850, George Duxfield was a prominent and successful all-round sportsman. A member of the Southport Athletic Society, he would go on to become president of the Northern Counties and a vice president of the Amateur Athletic Association.

On 3rd February 1877, ten men from the Temperance Society organised to play a group of twenty men from St Phillips Choir. An easy win of one goal, three tries and six touchdowns to nothing saw the following men take part. N.Howard (Capt.), F.Mawdsley, H.Thompson, W.H.Ball, G.R.Duxfield, W.Carr, Fletcher, H.Walmesley, T.Molineux and one other unnamed.

George Duxfield - Athletic News, 2nd October 1975

With no further fixtures that we know of played until the new season, matches resumed in the first week of November with a trip to St Thomas's in Preston (another comfortable win of three goals and two touchdowns to nil).

The Temperance Society Football Club's very first Annual Meeting took place on 31st January 1878, 4 days short of a year to the day of the first known match. It was a joint meeting between the cricket and football parts of the club with the chair occupied by Mr L. Conroy, and it took place in St. Andrew's Hall. Mr Duxfield, as secretary, presented his balance sheet from which it appeared that the club was in a very healthy condition, with no debt and a balance in hand. Subscriptions were set on the proposal of J.Allured (treasurer) as 7 shillings 6 pence for cricket members (only), 5 shillings for football members (only) and a combined subscription of 10 shillings for members partaking in both sports.

(St Andrew's Hall, Eastbank Street, prior to demolition in the 1960s)

During this first full season, 10 fixtures were played - 5 Wins, 2 Draws and 3 Defeats – the final game being a win against Preston Athenium on 23rd March.

==*==

1878/79

The official change of name to Southport Olympic by the Temperance Society Club appeared in the Southport Visiter on 30th April 1878, noting that the opening Cricket game of the season for 'The Olympic Club' took place on 27th between two teams selected by the treasurer (Allured) and secretary (Lloyd) at Scarisbrick New Road. It is not known why the name Olympic was chosen. It is only speculation, but one possibility is that early 'Olympic' athletes were known for their strict abstinence from alcohol, a cause which clearly met their own. Olympic was however a fairly common suffix for sporting clubs at the time and there may have been no specific significance.

The cricket season finished at the end of September, and under their new official moniker, Olympic travelled to Rice Lane, Walton on 15th October. It turned out to be an easy victory for Walton with Southport failing to score. Walton racked up a goal, a try, a touch in goal and six touch downs. The first line-up was J.Halsall, B.Slack (backs); R.Fletcher (Capt.), W.H.Ball; H.Walmsley, J.Ellerby; H.Johnson, E.Bridge, J.C.Wright, G.B.Duxfield, C.Andrews, J.H.Hollis, J.Rockliffe, W.H.Carr.

On 2nd November, making the short trip to Litherland, Olympic were evenly matched but came away with their first victory after a try scored by Fletcher was converted by Yates.

The 1878/79 season was marred by an extremely cold winter which saw the suspension of the majority of organised sport up and down the country. The opening of the new

Glacarium on Lord Street where patrons could skate and play curling offered some of the only sporting entertainment. When the thaw began in the middle of February, after over two months, Olympic were the first of the town's three big clubs (Wasps and Southport Football Club being the other two) to resume action.

The football match between the Fairfield Wanderers and Southport Olympic (first teams) was decided on the ground of the latter on Saturday last, there being present a large number of spectators, evidently rejoicing at a re-commencement of football after the long spell of frost.

(Southport Visiter, 11th February 1879)

==*==
1879/80

When the new season began it would have been a surprise to the Olympic committee to learn that they were now considered the leading club in the town with Southport Football Club failing to re-emerge after the harsh winter. Southport Wasps decided to drop the 'Wasps' part of their name to continue the Southport Football Club tradition – and perhaps add to the confusion of historians. Rather than reduce the number of clubs in the town to two however, it remained at three as into the gap stepped the Southport Hornets.

The new season began with a trip to Walton. It was a poor start for Olympic, losing by two touchdowns and three dead balls to four goals, four tries and four touchdowns, having played two men short up to half time and losing another in the second half. The issue of missing men had been down to travel issues which would become a familiar theme over the course of the next decade. It wasn't due to a lack of members. The second XV were able to fulfil a fixture at Scarisbrick New Road showing that the club still had strength in depth and whilst fans of the oval ball game still had a choice of clubs to follow, Olympic were by far the biggest and best supported in the town.

Despite the poor start to the season Olympic recovered well. We have found evidence of 15 fixtures having taken place during the 1879/80 season, most of which were reported in the Southport Visiter. Of particular interest was the fixture at Preston on 8th November where they played off against 'North End'. According to the press *'A large number of spectators seemed to thoroughly appreciate the efforts of both teams'.* Within a year North End would switch to association rules and become one of the most famous football clubs in the land.

In February 1880, in aid of the Band Fund of the 13th Lancashire Rifle Volunteers Olympic faced off against the club now bearing the Southport Football Club name (formerly Wasps) at their Scarisbrick New Road ground. The Southport Visiter had taken to calling Southport 'Alexandra' owing to their links to the Alexandra cricket club and on 24th February they reported the fine weather and the band in attendance had once again brought out a fine crowd. *'Despite the fact that the Alexandra had the sun and wind in their favour – their opponents were too good for them'.* Olympic won comfortably by one goal, one touch in goal and seven touch downs to nil.

The final known record for the season read Played 15, Won 6, Lost 6, Drawn 3

==*==
1880/81

Whereas Southport Olympic dutifully published fixtures as normal for the 1880/81 season, Southport Football Club (formerly Wasps) did not. Olympic had become a much stronger outfit, and competition too had come from Southport Hornets. Over the coming years many of Southport Football Club's players would move across to join one of the town's remaining two clubs, Olympic and Hornets, as would the supporters. Within the year they would be joined by another local team, the High Park Grasshoppers.

Captain Edward Fleetwood Hesketh had consented to be club president for the year, and the Earl of Lathom, the Right Honourable Lord Skelmersdale added some gravitas to the continuity claim by switching his patronage from the now defunct Southport club. It was clear that the town viewed Olympic as the natural successors to the original club.

Rather than opening against Walton as they had for the previous few years, Olympic began with an away visit to Liverpool Resistance in Dingle. Only 11 first team fixtures were reported in the Southport Visiter for the season, suggesting a large number went unreported. From the fixture list published at the start of the season we know of at least 14 others that were planned. The results of the games known suggest that Olympic's form was indifferent, winning as many as they lost, and drawing the rest.

==*==
1881/82

Whilst attempts were made to restart Southport Football Club at the start of the 1881/82 season, they were short lived. It had long been understood that when this club made the permanent switch to play association football in November 1881, those members who did not wish to play the round ball game had switched over to play for Southport Olympic or Southport Hornets at this point. When Southport Olympic took to the field against Aspull on 19th November 1881, however, there were just two former Southport Football Club players in the line-up, A.J.Ross and William Rimmer.

The line-up against Aspull was: A.Wright (back), A.J.Ross, W.H.Ball, H.Aughton (¾ backs); Haslehurst (Capt.), R.Parry, Bridge, Parks, Slack, W.H.Carr, William Rimmer, Robinson, Finney (forwards).

Of the players to have played in those three games for Southport Football Club only three, Ross, Barrow and Rimmer, ever made the switch across to Olympic, and only one had played in all three games, A.J.Ross. Both T.R. Barrow and William Rimmer had already seen the writing on the wall and joined Olympic, featuring in their game against Rochdale Hornets on 29th October, before the final rugby game was played by Southport Football Club.

The reasons more players did not switch to Olympic at this point are perhaps now better understood. Because there had been a period of a year without a Southport Football Club at all, the better players that had once represented the town's original club had already left to find new clubs at the start of the 1880/81 season. This also goes some way to explain why they struggled so badly when they did restart. The best players had all found homes at either Olympic or Southport Hornets already.

Players switching teams in the days before professionalism was far from unusual anyway, and to further emphasise this point Barrow did briefly return to his old side, for an association game on New Year's Day against the Tradesmen of Southport. J.Bullock, also tried his hand at association, turning out in Southport (association) Football Club's defeat at Burscough on 19th November and once more, against Liverpool Excelsior on 7th January 1882, before he returned to Olympic the following week for the visit of Wavertree.

The Southport press, which in 1881 was now solely represented by the Southport Visiter, after the demise of the Liverpool and Southport Daily News, and before the first publication of the Southport Guardian, reported 19 fixtures in total having taken place during the 1881/82 season. Curiously there had not been any plans for Olympic and the restarted Southport Football Club to meet, which considering Olympic had made arrangements with the Hornets, suggested that Olympic did not see the new club as worth the challenge. They were right to be sceptical as after only three games they switched to association football anyway.

Local bragging rights went to Olympic with big wins in both games arranged against the Southport Hornets and of the 19 games played, whilst one result is unknown - against Little Lever on 1st April - there were 6 wins, 5 draws and 7 defeats. Of the draws, one published no score, two were dead heats, one was in favour of Southport and the other in favour of their opponents (bear in mind that a game was still often considered drawn if there were no goals scored, even if one side dominated play and scored more minor points than their opponents).

The final known record of the season: Played 19, Won 6, Drew 5, Lost 7, 1 Unknown

==*==
1882/83

The 1882/83 season began amidst a little controversy as a result of correspondence in the local press. It began with a letter from what is assumed to be a member of Southport (association) Football Club. Whilst the majority of the letter discusses the writer's 'own' club, he made comment on the merits of the rugby game.

With respect to the Rugby game I cannot say — with one exception — that it assumes such a roseate tint as the sister game. The time is not long past when the Southport club was the terror of the Rugby world in the North, and no Lancashire county team was considered perfect unless it included four or five men from Southport — ned tempora mutantor — and now we have only one club in the town with anything like pretensions. I refer to the Olympic, which, after undergoing many vicissitudes, has at length reached a turning point in its career, a result owing in a great measure to the unceasing efforts in their hardworking hon. secretary. From the plucky and hard fought games they gave their opponents, and their improved form towards the close of last season, they have

succeeded in attracting some slight attention in the sphere of the Rugby Union, and have arranged some very good matches with well known Manchester and Liverpool clubs for the ensuing season. In conclusion, I think football enthusiasts in this district will have no cause for complaint, as every half-holiday will witness a good game on one ground or another.
FORWARD

(Southport Visiter, 19th August 1882)

This letter first drew a response from a member of the Southport Hornets club before Reginald Slack, the secretary of Southport Olympic, also sent in a response.

Sir — I have read the letters of "Forward", and "rugby Player", and I am glad the former, as representing the Associonists, has such bright prospects before him, as during last season it must have been annoying in the extreme to find their field entirely vacated when our team commenced action, even if it were only a second team engagement.
Public opinion may alter, the Association enclose may be well patronised, but I have grave doubts as to its ever providing any great opposition, in this district, to the Rugby game.
The Association Club here is as yet so very young (half a season), that it is premature for anyone to predict what standing it will take in the Dribbling World, but it certainly was making very rapid strides in the right direction at the close of last season. The exodus of spectators when the Rovers and Witton faced each other at the late Athletic Sports, does not point to any increased popularity of the Association game, as if the public will not patronise two such able exponents as the above, the local club can hardly expect a very large attendance of their new field during the coming season.
The Hornets likewise showed greatly improved form, and it is much to be regretted that they should lose the services of their excellent captain, Mr Andrew Irving, whom they very rightly claim as their man alone, and not conjointly with the Dribbling community.
R SLACK, Hon Sec., Olympic F.C.

(Southport Visiter, 9th September 1882)

The 1882 season for Olympic officially kicked off with a Married versus Singles game at Scarisbrick New Road on Saturday 16th September. This was a common way of arranging practice and for the 15-a-side game, Haslehurst was named captain of the Married members, and Walter Rimmer (although he never took to the field) the Singles. Olympic had been playing on a pitch slightly further along Scarisbrick New Road than the field they had previously been occupying although there were no reasons given for the change.

A *'first 15 versus the next 20'* was arranged for the following week along with a further fixture versus *'18 of the District'*, although neither Southport newspaper (The Southport Guardian had by now joined the Southport Visiter in regular circulation) reported on either game.

With the intra-club and trial matches out of the way Olympic turned their attention to Little Lever and after a hard-fought game came away victors by two tries (W.H.Ball and Walter Rimmer), and two touchdowns to one try and three dead balls.

In November, yet another attempt was made to start a rugby club under the Southport Football Club name, to give Olympic and Southport Hornets competition once again. The Southport Visiter confirmed that this new club was once again linked to the Alexandra Cricket Club and continued to play at Manchester Road with access now from Roe Lane due to the advancement of building works.

Olympic faced another new club, the Birkdale Free Wanderers, at the end of February and a very large number of spectators turned out to see how the newcomers would fare against a more established side. Birkdale managed to restrict Olympic to only a few minor points before the half time break, but their early exertions caught up with them in the second. Olympic won by one goal, six tries and twelve minor points to one touchdown.

Given the interest that had been shown in this fixture, it is little surprise that Secretary Reginald Slack attempted to engage with the reformed Southport club too on the basis that they might raise a significant sum of money for the infirmary by staging a charity game, The Southport club however, perhaps fearful of the potential outcome, did not want to entertain them.

There is no listing in the 1883 Football Annual for Southport Olympic and no mention of any club from Southport being a member of the Rugby Football Union.

==*==

1883/84

Before the 1883/84 season was to properly begin, Southport Olympic did manage to arrange a fixture with Southport Football Club ...although it was the association club not the rugby club that had shown an interest! According to the Southport Visiter *'Olympic have shown considerable ability at the dribbling game, in addition to their usual mode of playing'*. It is no surprise therefore that the following summer, moves were made amongst members to officially start an association section of the club.

At the September AGM J.Bullock was nominated captain of the first team alongside duties as treasurer, J.A.Cliffe, was elected sub-captain. S.Radcliffe was elected financial secretary and Reginald Slack the corresponding secretary operating out of an office on Shakespeare Street.

With no dressing tent on their Scarisbrick New Road field, which would have been the most common form of changing facilities at amateur sports grounds at this time, dressing rooms were instead made available at the Scarisbrick Hotel on Lord Street.

(The original Scarisbrick Hotel (far right) on Lord Street prior to its demolition in 1889)

Olympic's first fixture of the 1883/84 season was away at St Helens. It was, however, the start of a period of uncertainty caused by the unavailability of their usual members. Only six fit men could be found for the trip to St Helens with a number injured in the pre-season fixtures. St Helens were kind enough to make up a team to make sure the fixture went ahead but ran out easy victors.

When Bootle visited for the first home game of the season, Olympic could only scrape together 11. Walter Rimmer, J.Hoban, Ball, E.Bridge, H.Haslehurst, J.Ellerby, H.Jackson, H.Shaw and James Parkes were all missing leaving those remaining very much a weakened side. A week later, against Rochdale Hornets, they were once again three short, W.H.Ball, Amy Ball and Harry Johnson all missing.

The first win did not come until November when they faced Litherland. Although still unable to field a full-strength team of their own, several of the second team members (who incidentally had had no such difficulties, often travelling with squads of up to 18) had to be called upon to deputise. Olympic won a hard-fought game by one goal, two tries and seven minor points to nil.

Rather than be able to build on the win, Secretary Reginald Slack had cause to write to the Athletic News to complain about the conduct of the Clifton side that visited them on 10th November.

The ball is not dead until it has been touched down by the defending side, or has gone past or against the boundary fence. The Southport Olympic goal was a perfectly fair one if the ball was in motion when it was picked up behind the Clifton line. The Clifton idea of a ball being dead when it has been kicked twice after crossing the line is absurd.

(*Athletic News, November 1883*)

Whilst still unable to raise a regular XV themselves, Olympic did come to the rescue of the association club on 17th November, agreeing to stand in as opponents when the United Schools team that had been scheduled to face them had pulled out.

The strong wind interfered very much with the play, very little science being shown. The Olympians, although new to the Association Rules, played a dashing game and with practice would make a good eleven, Parkes in particular playing a fine back game, and Kay also kept goal remarkably well; in fact, had it not been for their good play, the Southport score could have been much heavier.

(*Southport Visiter, 22nd November 1883*)

With defeats stacking up against Fairfield, Wigan and Runcorn, Secretary Slack persisted with attempts to engage the Southport (rugby) Football Club for a charitable fixture, but without any success. Olympic therefore agreed to repeat the pre-season exhibition against the association club on New Year's Day 1884 instead.

Of the 13 rugby games we have found evidence of in the second half of the season, only two resulted in wins. Eight resulted in defeats and two were tied, with one where the result was not declared. Naturally with the side in poor form crowds varied wildly from game to game, dipping as low as only a couple of hundred at times, which was nevertheless still more than the majority of association games could hope to attract. The larger attendances naturally came when there was the expectation of a good quality game against evenly matched opposition, such as with the visit of Fairfield in March. Having been defeated by them away from home at the back end of the previous year the side had been keen to put matters right, and they did with a win by a goal and a try to nil.

In February Olympic's second team had faced off with the first team of the Southport Wasps. Their subsequent win had proven beyond much doubt that locally, Olympic were the number one side in the area. It was when Olympic travelled to fixtures outside of the town that they had been struggling to find their feet. Whilst gates in the towns they visited were invariably stronger than when at home, that was usually as a result of playing against more established teams.

For a club boasting a healthy membership, it was however worryingly common for matches to be played without all the selected men present. This was made even worse when a reasonable crowd had assembled. As the season reached its conclusion 600 gathered for the visit of Liverpool Gymnasium, and yet Olympic were without five of their strongest in Sellars, Parks, Johnson, Ellerby and McIntyre forcing them to draw from the reserves just to fulfil a fixture. Under those circumstances defeats were an inevitability.

Manchester Butterflies, a scratch team made up of some of the best players in the North once again drew a crowd, but once again Olympic were let down, this time with Johnson, Wright, Rimmer, Lund, Marshall and even Haslehurst, the captain all absent! It was a recurring problem that needed to be addressed if they ever hoped to develop.

On Thursday 8th May 1884 the Southport Visiter reported on the Southport Olympic AGM noting that it had been proposed and carried by a large majority that for the forthcoming season both codes would be played by the Olympic club. This perhaps explained the lacklustre second half of the season, with many of the members being more distracted by the blossoming, simpler, association game. On the 8th July, at a further meeting to discuss the proposal, at Mr Monk's rooms on London Street, the Olympic committee wanted it to be *formally recorded and distinctly understood that whilst wishing the new organisation (Olympic F.C. Association Rules) every success, there is no connection between it and the original Olympic Football Club'.*

Just to complicate matters further, those wishing to play association would eventually split from the Olympic club and turn to the field under the name of Southport Wanderers.

==*==
1884/85

With those players smitten by the round ball game off to set up on their own, Olympic prepared for the 1884/85 season with teams selected by the captain and sub-captain playing a series of inter club friendly games on Wednesday and Saturday afternoons.

The Special General Meeting in July had seen James Halsall appointed captain of the first team alongside George Summers as his deputy, with Paul Moorfield elected captain of the second team. Reginald Slack retained the position of secretary in a committee made up predominantly of playing members. Far from the rumours of Olympic having lost its love of the rugby rules in light of its dalliance with association, a long list of fixtures was presented with 10 higher profile teams prepared to travel to Southport without the expectation of a return game.

The Southport Wasps meanwhile became the second tenants of the Sports Ground over on Sussex Road, alongside Southport Football Club, where the Athletic Society had been making overtures about a single organisation overseeing all of the sporting activities in the town. The Wasps also made the decision to switch to black and amber jerseys. There is nothing to suggest that Southport Olympic were ever approached by the Athletic Society, their membership presumably too strong and the club too healthy to see the need to join forces with anyone else.

As the season began the Southport Guardian remarked that there was a very good attendance for the game against Tyldesley on 13th September, although a number wasn't given, and that evidently, they had *'lost none of their interest in Rugby football'*. Tyldesley's strong team included representation from the Lancashire County side. Despite their best efforts Olympic were unable to prevent them from taking a 2-0 victory back home to Manchester.

The Southport Visiter reported that Olympic's insistence on trying to score tries rather than secure minor points was often their undoing, although performances were generally satisfactory.

There is little doubt that the with the man that captain (J.Halsall) has at his disposal, he will soon be able to regain the good name the Olympic held some two years ago.

(Southport Guardian, 27th September 1884)

Despite the promise shown, the first win did not come until October. Even then, they had to rely on an understrength Widnes Wasps second team to visit Scarisbrick New Road for a score line to be turned in their favour. The Southport Visiter passed comment that they were quite out matched when it came to passing ability, and that were it not for their strength in tackling the reversals would have been heavier still.

Olympic continued to attract good clubs to visit the town, the mighty Wigan amongst them, but it was rare that Southport would come away with anything other than 'credit'.

At the end of November, the club held a well-attended concert for members at the Town Hall. Of those taking part in the performances, singled out for praise was William Kay, a man who had been part of the early Southport Football Club before switching over to join up with Southport Wanderers. With Wanderers being an off-shoot of the Olympic club he must have been amongst friends. He supplied the comedy for the evening but had such a rotten cold, that after the first act, he simply wasn't in a fit state to continue for the second.

With the concert having done so much to lift the spirits, it was perhaps just unfortunate timing that the undefeated Bury Unitarians were due to visit the following Saturday. Whilst the Visiter noted that Bury were second best on the day, true to type they still took the victory back home with them.

In December, Olympic Secretary Reginald Slack was honoured with a place on the committee of the West Lancashire and Border Towns Rugby Union, an organisation representing the interest of Wigan, St Helens, Liverpool Old Boys, Walton, Wavertree, Widnes, Warrington and Southport. He was tasked with helping to draw up a draft set of rules for the fledgling organisation, which said much for the esteem in which he was held by members of the aforementioned clubs.

Whilst this union was being formed, discussions of a much more serious nature were being held by another. The Football Association had met to discuss the growing concern of professionalism in their code, and whether or not legalisation could be considered. Whilst it would be some time before the Rugby Football Union would consider professionalism, the outcome from the discussions held by the Football Association would still have huge repercussions on rugby in Southport over the next 5 years.

Now that the 'associationists' had split from the pack, the remaining club members were left to concentrate on rugby. 1885 began therefore with a draw against Litherland rather than the previous year's high profile Charity association match.

In March the new West Lancashire and Border Towns Union arranged the first of what was intended to be regular representative games against similar unions in other areas. Their first opponents were Liverpool. Played at Runcorn in front of 5,000 spectators, Olympic's J.W.Neville and J.C.Bimpson were both selected, and were on the winning side with a score of two goals, two tries and four minor points to Liverpool's five minors.

The season yielded very few wins once again, and despite plenty of promise and entertainment, Olympic never really got going.

Southport Wasps provided little by way of a counter attraction. The real competition came in the form of the new Charity Cup competition played by the association clubs for which there was plenty of local interest. Southport Wanderers, despite a poor start, were developing a competitive team and were hopeful of one day being able to capture the Cup for themselves.

A minor spat in the press resulted from a game arranged between Wasps and Olympic's second team at the end of April. Although the Wasps had redeemed themselves of their earlier defeat by two tries and two minor points to two minor points, Olympic had fielded Mason of the first team and invited Abrams of the Birkdale Wanderers which had prompted an angry letter to be sent to the Visiter by a supporter.

To the editor of the Southport Visiter

Sir, - I beg to protest against the report furnished to you last Tuesday of the match between the Olympic 2nd and the Wasps. The Olympic have never played the Wasps — at least not this season. A challenge was sent, but the committee would not entertain it, so a member of the Olympic got up a scratch team to play them. I may say that the Olympic 2nd have now challenged the Wasps, and it certainly looks as if they were afraid of defeat, as they have refused to play, although "the gate' was arranged to be given to one of the benevolent institutions of the town. In conclusion, I think it is hardly consistent with the Olympic 2nd teams form, who have beaten most of the crack second teams in Lancashire during the past season, to be beaten by an insignificant club like the Wasps — Yours, &c. A RUGBYITE

(Southport Visiter, 28th April 1885)

To the editor of the Southport Visiter.
Sir, - After thoughts of a fortnight's duration Mr. Slack has condescended to answer my letter. It is all very well for that gentleman to say it was looked upon as the Olympic second. I ask, was it the Olympic or was it a scratch team. As for the members admitting they were beaten on their merits, I distinctly refute the statement, and ask Mr. Slack to mention one that ever said such a thing. This two tries got by the Wasps were both lucky, very lucky indeed, and if the match were again to be played the result would be greatly different. Your correspondent says he has for years been doing all in his power to unite the Rugby players in this district. Then all I can say is that it speaks very little for his capacity in that direction, as any Saturday night after a match the players of the different clubs can be seen wrangling together and discussing their various merits in Chapel-street, greatly to the annoyance of passers-by. Mr. Slack also speaks of the modesty of the Wasps' report; but I may say they have thoroughly blown their own trumpet in the air, named at, as he says their unexpected achievement, and had it not been for their insolence to members of the Olympic, I should never have written the letter complained of. If the Wasps are not afraid of defeat, why do they not accept the challenge of a committeeman (authorised, I believe, by the second team) sent them, and let the receipts be handed over to a benevolent institution, which was often proved charitable to football players in time of need. Hoping they will take the hint — Yours, &c. RUGBYITE

(Southport Visiter 14th May 1885)

The very last we would see of Southport Wasps at all was their entry into the Churchtown six a side association tournament in the weeks that followed. They did not re-emerge for the 1885/86 season.

==*==

1885/86

Olympic started the 1885/86 season with a difficult fixture away at Wigan and were predictably routed by six tries to one.

Although Olympic and Wasps had not merged officially, the second team of the only remaining rugby club in town now accommodated a number of players from the Wasps team of the previous season. In addition to a first XV and second XV playing regular fixtures Olympic were now also able to field a third XV. The match against Wigan had inevitably featured several new members. Freeman, one of the new men pledged to travel from Crosby each week to play for what was now the only rugby club in town. The chief criticism of the performance was that there was too much individual play and it is often the case that a new side takes time to gel together.

Price, a new three quarter back, had moved to the area from the South where, according to the Southport Visiter, he had played with a 'premier' club. His play at times in the second fixture with Haigh (another Wigan side) was described as *'brilliant'* with the Wiganers describing him as the Southport Don-Wauchope (a Scottish rugby International).

Walter Rimmer, appointed captain in the summer to replace James Halsall moved back to half back to accommodate the new signings and this change breathed new life into his game.

It did not take long for the results to pick up. Concluding a run of three games in Wigan, Olympic took on Pagefield winning by three goals, two tries and two minor points. Price excelled again, as did Leadbetter. When Olympic finally returned home, to face Wavertree, their upturn in form continued. A large number had gathered at Scarisbrick New Road eager to see the new side, and they did not disappoint, winning by a try and four minor points to nil.

The Olympic (1ˢᵗ) met Wavertree last Saturday, and again scored another victory by a try and four minors. There was a large gathering on the field, and the spectators were treated to one of the finest exhibitions of the Rugby code ever given in the district.

(Southport Visiter, 10th October 1885)

The Olympic Secretary Reginald Slack had taken to turning out for the second team on occasion, after the strengthening of the first team, but this was starting to lead to problems in reporting on the first team games, it being the principal duty of the secretary. The first warning signs came in October.

The attention of the Olympic secretary is also called to the fact that he did not furnish the report of their Saturday matches. The club this year is exceptionally strong, and doing good work when in the field.

(Southport Visiter, 17th October 1885)

The Southport Guardian introduced a new weekly 'Athletic Column' in October 1885 and had promised a fair hearing to all local sports. Whilst it had been almost exclusively given over to reports from the association game due to its massive growth in popularity, they made credible attempts to persuade those with an affection for the oval ball game to give themselves fair coverage.

The spreading popularity of the Association game is leading to some patrons of Rugby to stand on the defensive. They need not fear. Rugby, properly played, has lasted too long to suffer extinguishing without a great struggle, and it is more than likely the Rugby players will gain considerably in their forward play through Association rivalry. Not many clubs are as strong as Southport Olympic, which can regularly place three teams in the field, and has, we believe, 80 members. Though the Association passing game is certainly attractive to spectators, there were some very big gates at Rugby matches so recently as last Saturday. To some lovers of football the Rugby runs are quite as fine a sight as others think the most superb dribbling.

(Southport Guardian, 21st October 1885)

With no local competition for the rugby game, Olympic were thriving. Secretary Reginald Slack, operating from offices at 19 Shakespeare Street, was running a steady ship. When Manchester Gymnasium visited at the end of October the Guardian heaped praise on the club.

In leaving the Southport club, let me say a word of praise for the captain on his steady play 'on the ball' and keen insight of the game. He is the right man in the right place. The passing of the home team was frequently commented on, and in this they excelled their opponents. I have for many years witnessed some of the best Rugby matches, vis. Swinton, Bradford, Dewsbury, Manchester, Salford, &c., but I never saw the (½ backs) of a club play a more unselfish game, looking to honour the club rather than that of individuals. I'm afraid if I say many more words of praise for the local club they'll think me a flatterer.

(Southport Guardian, 21st October 1885)

Across the board, all three of the Olympic sides were performing well thanks to their newly combined strengths and quality amateur imports. Supporters were even beginning to travel in numbers to watch their side, with a large number of Sandgrounders being part of the 500 crowd at Walton at the end of the month.

The Widnes Star first team will have cause to remember their visit to Southport on Saturday, when they met the second team of the Olympic of that town. A score of five goals, three tries, and three minor points to one minor point is not a bad afternoon's work, and the Southport Olympic club are to be congratulated on having a second team capable of doing such work.

(Football Field, 1ˢᵗ December 1885)

Players were also beginning to build up a reputation for themselves and when Olympic had no fixture due to a cancellation, players often lent a helping hand to other sides, such as Lund and Price assisting the Liverpool Old Boys.

The club had lost none of its strength and held its first annual ball in March under the patronage of George Pilkington the Town's M.P, the man credited with forming the very first football club in the town. The spirit of the original club was now living on through Olympic.

SOUTHPORT OLYMPIC FOOTBALL CLUB.

Under the Patronage of Dr. Pilkington, M.P.

THE FIRST ANNUAL BALL,
In aid of the funds of the Club,
Will be held in

PORTLAND HALL, PORTLAND-STREET,
On Thursday, March 18th.

Tickets :—Double Tickets, 5s. ; Gentlemen's, 3s. 6d. ; Ladies', 2s. 6d.
May be had from Messrs. G. R. Duxfield, 3, Coronation-walk ; C. R. Bell, Tulketh-street and Eastbank-street ; S. Schofield, Chapel-street ; and T. Farrington, London-street.

Southport Visiter – 23ʳᵈ February 1886)

Problems with reporting continued, however, and whilst the Visiter made noble attempts, seldom were Olympic represented in the Southport Guardian from November onwards.

SOUTHPORT v LANCASTER
The following letter has been received in respect to this match: - "I should feel extremely obliged if the secretary of the Olympic or his representatives would send to the papers reports in accordance to

the game as played. The above report in Tuesday's report is, I may say as a spectator and old football player, anything but creditable to the person who wrote it., or it is quite evident that he knows nothing of the game. There are names mentioned who only played moderately, whilst the two best forwards on the field – the late captain (Halsall), who got two tries and one disallowed, and Webster, who got a fine try, are not mentioned at all. I think it is, therefore, nothing but fair that we should let you see that we, the spectators, appreciate good play when we see it, and like to acknowledge it. Hoping that in future you (the secretary) will give better reports of your first team matches and also 'give honour where honour is due' – Yours, &c. FAIR PLAY

(Southport Visiter, 12th November 1885)

It could be argued that Slack had grown tired of the criticism and had simply given up submitting reports of any note. The Southport Visiter made every effort to pass comment on the fortunes of the club week to week, but in terms of reports themselves they were often confined to a handful of lines noting the result. Without the publicity that the local newspapers could provide Olympic were in danger of allowing the association game to take a stranglehold in their absence.

The Southport Guardian made a final desperate attempt to encourage contributions in their column on 17th February *'it's desperate little that is heard of the Olympic in these columns, Rugby! Ahoy!!'*

As members of the West Lancashire and Border Towns Rugby Football Union, Olympic entered the Rugby Union Cup in March. In front of *'undoubtedly the largest assemblage of spectators ever brought together to witness a match in Southport'*, their opponents, Aspull, had brought 300 travelling supporters with them to the third field on Scarisbrick New Road. The gate was estimated to be well over 2,000. Unfortunately for Olympic, despite the form they had shown for much of the season, the visitors were too strong for them and they exited in the first round.

For a later round of the competition Southport's ground was chosen as the venue for the play-off between Warrington and Runcorn who in their first tied game had played in front of 16,000. The Athletic News commented that *'the field they occupy in Scarisbrick New Road is one of the finest in Lancashire for football purposes'.*

Whilst nowhere near this number attended the replay, it goes some way to show that whilst Olympic was a healthy entity within Southport, in comparison to clubs from further field, they were mere minnows.

In an effort to try something different in the summer months, rather turn to Cricket like most football players did, Olympic's members decided to try Rounders. The Southport Guardian confirmed that G.Tomlinson was elected honorary secretary and a new committee formed around him in the new Rounders section of the club. This new development attracted a lot of local interest with practice nights set at Tuesdays and Thursdays and the first match was arranged with Mossley from Sefton Park on Friday morning 23rd April.

197

A game of rounders to the uninitiated, especially if the players be not very expert, looks rather tame, and might even be thought rather undignified by a lover of cricket. But let two good teams be pitted against each other, and then the excitement will grow soon enough, and the game be redeemed from all charge of tameness. Rounders' clubs are remarkably numerous and successful around Liverpool, and why should they not spread to Southport?

(Southport Guardian, 21ˢᵗ April 1886)

The match with Mossley however hardly turned out to be the catalyst that had been hoped for and after a rather crushing defeat available players grew scarce.

The club's AGM was held on 11th May. Reginald Slack was voted to the chair and produced a balance sheet that showed, whilst including a large expenditure for the season, a club in a *'thoroughly solvent'* condition with a small balance in hand. After accepting over 20 new membership applications, the second team Captain Thomas Holder was elected as secretary, therefore taking over the duty of submitting reports from Slack, and for the first time it was decided that the committee should be formed from non-playing members, with eight men selected. H.P.Booth was elected as first team captain, with G.E.Summers as his deputy.

==*==
1886/87

Thomas Holder began his new secretarial duties with the submission of full fixture lists for both the first and second teams to the Southpot Visiter, which they duly printed on 7th September. For the first team, the season would begin with a friendly against the Southport Royal Navy Artillery Volunteers on 11th September, before the season would begin properly with the visit of Pemberton. The second team would begin with a trip to the same opposition.

After the previous season's progress both on and off the field there was great cause for optimism. It took a while to get going, however, with narrow defeats to Pemberton and then Radcliffe.

Possibly due to the vagaries of work arrangements, it was not always possible to put out a full-strength team when travelling to away fixtures and this was indeed the case against Radcliffe when Olympic had been forced to play with just ten men as Lund, Shaw, Oliver, Wright, Marshall and former Secretary Slack were all unable to make the 1:30pm train. This was clearly the main cause of the defeat at Radcliffe but a full-strength side would don the back, red and amber jerseys for the second home game of the season against Litherland, and pick up a win of one goal, four tries and four minors to two minors. With that, they were off and running.

In the week that followed this important first victory of the season, the Rugby Union met in London to discuss a number of rule changes. Firstly, following the move made by the Football Association in the previous year, professionalism was now to be made legal in the rugby game, and a professional would be classed as any player who receives any form of monetary recompense for his time, whether that be for loss of earnings, travel or anything else. It meant that if a committee member was being remunerated for his services, and he also took to the field, then they too would have been classed as a professional. If that change wasn't significant enough, it was decided that matches would now be decided by a majority of points. A goal shall equal three points, and a try one point. When a goal is kicked from a try, only the points from the goal would be recorded. If the number of points were equal or no kicks or tries obtained, the match should be declared a draw. This new scoring system was agreed by 111 votes to 49.

The first match played under the new scoring system was a second team game against Lowe House (St Helens) on Saturday 9th October 1886, with the first team not scheduled for a fixture. Olympic scored 1 try and 4 minors to Lowe House's 4 minors, meaning that Olympic won by 1 point to nil. It is interesting to note that despite the unions attempts to simplify the scoring system, most newspapers reports continued to report scores in the same way that they always had done, on the basis that it gave a better description of the play.

Following a defeat at Tuebrook and subsequent fixtures being cancelled, it took the first team until 30th October to register their first points under the new system. Scoring five tries, two of which were also placed as goals, it gave them a return of 9 points to 0 against Wavertree. This was the first fixture in which, to a man, everyone selected had actually been available to play, including the captain, Booth, who made his first appearance of the season.

The Olympic first team travelled to St Helens on Saturday last to meet the St Helends Recreation. The Olympic, as is usual when making an outward journey, were shorthanded, and, consequently, received the best thrashing they have ever had since their existence as a Rugby club in our midst. The forwards, although they played up manfully, were completely overpowered, and it was in this department that the St Helens men were superior, and through their brilliant display that the score they registered was such a large one. It seems strange that our local Rugby organisation can always muster a strong team at home, and when the club is fully represented they play a capital game; but when they gout of town they are always minu a few of their best forwards. It will be remembered they beat Litherland by a goal and four tries at home, and the Saturday afterwards when playing away they succumbed to a minor club like Tuebrook. Then the following Saturday they succeeded in thrashing Wavertree by two goals and five tries, again at home, and last Saturday, as previously stated, they were beaten by the same amount. However, let us hope that this state of things will be remedied, and that they will be able to muster as strongly out of town as at home, and rise to a crack Lancashire club, which they have every prospect of doing.

(Southport Visiter, 13th November 1886)

Somewhat ironically, following the Visiter's appeal, and after a period of cancelled fixtures, Olympic's next game came at home to Sutton, and owing to a misunderstanding Olympic were only able to field 14 men. Thankfully, those that did turn up were strong enough to record a win of two tries to nil.

On 10th December 1886 disaster struck off the coast of Southport as 27 lifeboatmen lost their lives whilst attempting to rescue the crew from the stranded German vessel 'Mexico'.

The annual Charity Cup arranged for the association clubs in the town took on an added significance, however with Olympic unable to take part being a rugby club, they instead arranged a charitable fixture over Christmas against a town representative side.

Mr Haslehurst, himself once a member of the rugby fraternity, was responsible for selecting the Southport and District representative side and he chose a mixture of association and rugby players from the association clubs of Southport, Southport Old Boys and High Park and also rugby members of Olympic themselves.

As was to be expected, a large crowd assembled for the game but they were witness to a very one sided contest, if you could really call it a contest at all. Olympic were far from at their best but still ran out winners by two goals, one try and ten minors to nil. Unfortunately, despite the charitable intent of the game, the losers took the defeat rather badly and left the field before the game could even be properly concluded. A large sum was nevertheless handed over to the widows and orphans affected by the disaster and the purpose of the match had been fulfilled.

In the new year, a hard frost prevented rugby matches from taking place for a number of weeks. At the start of the season, a new rugby club had been formed in Birkdale, but it was a minor outfit in terms of quality and Southport had not scheduled a fixture against them as a result. However, when Walkden scratched from their commitment, it was deemed preferable to face the new club rather than not have a fixture at all. Therefore, at the end of February Olympic met ·them for the first time. The result was a formality but even with local competition once again available, not even curiosity could draw people away from the counter attraction of the first round of the association Charity Cup. It was a glorious sunny day but it was on Forest Road where the bulk of the spectators could be found as High Park and Southport Recreation played off in the first round.

In March Olympic entered a cup competition organised by the West Lancashire and Border Towns Union. 2,000 spectators gathered in Aspull to witness the encounter. The game was even until the very end when Aspull added a late goal and two tries to their score, thus winning by two goals and two tries, to one goal. Southport had taken with them their largest number of travelling supporters yet seen, on the short trip to Aspull. Their opponents had ben runners up in the competition the previous year but Olympic more than matched them for long periods and it had only been when a player had been forced to withdraw injured that Aspull were able to take a foothold in the game.

The Aspull men acknowledged that the game was of a very even nature and that the score by no means indicated the nature of the play. The opinion of Mr Keen of Broughton, who courteously acted as referee, was that until the Olympic men were disabled, he had never seen a match so keenly fought. So much had been said about the unfairness of the Aspull spectators that the Olympic thought they would not be given the chance to win., but on Saturday last they acted rationally, and every point of good play that was exhibited by both teams was cheered lustily, and when Webster had kicked a magnificent goal from a most difficult place the cheers could be heard miles away.

(Southport Visiter, 12ᵗʰ March 1887)

Aspull went on to lift the West Lancashire Cup and also the Wigan Charity Cup, contesting the latter in front of a crowd of 8,000. Southport were in fact the only side to have registered a major point (a goal) against 'the Aspullites' on route to the West Lancashire Cup.

The story of the season for Southport was that however strong Olympic were to be at home, being beaten only a couple of times, on the road there were persistent selection problems that dogged them throughout. The rise of professionalism, had it been extended to Southport, would have mitigated against this as it was all too often that business reasons were given for the non-appearance of important players.

However successful a club may be with a full team, it cannot compete against powerful opponents without its full complement, and this has been the case with the Olympic throughout the season. Every match they have had to play out of town they have always gone short-handed, and this being the case on Saturday.

(29ᵗʰ March 1887)

After the season had concluded Reginald Slack arranged a match with St Helens and District for the benefit of the Children's Sanitorium. His side was made up mostly of his Olympic teammates whilst the St Helens team was drawn from the military volunteers encamped behind the Cemetery who were members of St Helens, St Helens Recreation, Sutton and Widnes. The win of two tries to nil for Slack's team raised some much-needed funds.

==*==
1887/88

The 1887 Annual General Meeting of Olympic took place on Tuesday 16ᵗʰ August at the Shakespeare Hotel on Scarisbrick New Road. Reginald Slack once again took the chair, but unusually was also elected captain of both the first and second teams. Moorfield was the noted deputy for the first team and Robinson for the second but there was no explanation given as to why such an unusual move was made. Gone too was any reference to Holder as secretary, and the only other major job, the treasurer was given to Rickerby.

Olympic was in danger of becoming a one man show and whilst Reginald Slack had been a figure that had been consistently involved with the club for a number of years, he was the same figure that had been widely criticised so recently over his inability to give the due coverage that the club needed if it was to see off the challenge of the association clubs. From all of the available accounts the previous year the club had been prospering, and it had held a second successful annual fundraising ball at the Portland Hall in January to raise funds. Over the course of the season, however, even the treasurers post would be given over to Slack as Rickerby was unable to continue due to his business taking priority.

The first week of September was spent on the practice field with Slack arranging a fixture against a scratch team of local players. The season kicked off properly with the visit of the West Lancashire Junior Cup holders Widnes St Mary's. This time, Olympic were unable to field their selected side with Lund and Gill absent from the back, and Rickerby, Toole and a number of others missing from the forward line.

The local team did not seem to play with the usual dash for which they were noted last season, and as a consequence their exhibition was anything but good. This in a great measure can be accounted for when it is taken into consideration that the match of last Saturday was the first one in which the team had played together, and it is to be hoped that in their future engagements they will materially improve, and by the end of the season will again stand as a club of note in Rugby cirlces.

(Southport Visiter, 13th September 1887)

The theme of the previous season, with players being unavailable, unfortunately had continued, which made it difficult for the team to build up any kind of rhythm initially. Perhaps it was for this reason that Slack had assumed control, in a desperate attempt to remedy the selection concerns. The Visiter commented that they had often spoken in condemnatory terms of the manner in which the Olympic members turn up when selected to play and the once proud club seemed to be spiralling out of control. 'The Olympic second is going to the dogs' was how their match against junior club Poolstock was reported on 8th October.

After keeping the visiting team and spectators waiting for half an hour, a couple of substitutes had to be chosen. In our opinion, it would be far better if the committee chose players who would play regularly, however incapable theymay be at present, of giving a good exhibition of the Rugby rules, as by constant practice they would be in advance of those who only play one Saturday out of every three.

(Southport Visiter, 8th October 1887)

The team carried on grinding out performances with whomever could make themselves available and eventually their form began to turn. Such was the rarity, however, of victories away from home it was reported with some sarcasm:

It gives us much pleasure to state that the Olympic team won a match away from home on Saturday last. This is an occurrence so rare that the local Rugbyites most certainly have a decided right to crow that they are not dead yet.

(Southport Visiter, 5th November 1887)

In November, however, the first team seemed to turn a corner. Perhaps embarrassed by the publicity, more of the selected men began to make appearances (although there were still a few unable to fulfil their commitments). When Southport faced Walton in mid-November it was their fourth win out of five games, and worthy of note it was the first time that every man chosen for selection had actually played. This must have been the most frustrating aspect of being an Olympic spectator – on their day, they were a match for most sides in the area, but when you turned up on the third field in Scarisbrick New Road, you just did not know what sort of team would emerge in the back, red and amber.

Despite their unpredictability, Olympic were still drawing good crowds, and 700 attended for the visit of Bolton just before Christmas. Bringing their best team Bolton were a big strong side, good in the tight scrimmages but in the loose play Olympic were far superior, winning by a goal to nil, with a try a piece. For their previous encounter Southport had played two men short but once again, when fully represented they showed they were a match for anyone.

The last day of the jubilee year 1887 concluded with a match against the friendly locals Birkdale but the junior side were even more under strength than usual and Olympic recorded one of their biggest ever wins; Five goals, seven tries and six minors to just one minor. It was certainly a good way to end a topsy turvy year.

The first contest of 1888 came at Birkenhead against the Birkenhead Wanderers. Olympic were winners of a well contested game. The improvement since the start of the season was remarkable. Tuebrook, Litherland, Ringley Wigan Old Boys and New Brighton Olympic all tried but failed to get the better of the Olympians and they were in capital form as they headed into the West Lancashire cup game against Wigan.

Last Saturday was the date appointed for the first round of the West Lancashire Cup Competition. The Olympic arrived on Wigan ground in fair time, and were received with loud cheers by about 4000 spectators, who throughout were most impartial, applauding good play on either side. The recent frost and sudden thaw caused the ground to be a perfect quagmire, in many places over the boot tops. From the first it was clear the Sandgrounders would have no chance of displaying their usual tactics, viz. dribbling and wide passes, as the ball was at once sodden and unmanageable.

(Southport Visiter, 6th March 1888)

Wigan won the game three goals, and three tries to nil, as expected, making the most of home advantage but the score by no means reflected the game as for in large parts Olympic held their own and it was one of their best performances.

Between the cup tie and the end of the season, Olympic played very little and bad habits returned with selection often not matching those who played, which had the usual effect on results.

The popularity of the association Charity Cup in Southport had grown exponentially since its introduction a few years previously, and the lack of any rugby cup action in Southport was not doing the sport any favours. Olympic had been unlucky to draw Aspull and Wigan in successive seasons, both away from home and both ties from which they had little chance to progress.

==*==
1888/89

The 1888 Annual General Meeting was held on Tuesday 3rd July, once again at the Shakespeare Hotel. Financially the club was reported to be in good order.

The balance sheet was presented and showed the receipts to be £61 12s. 6d. and the expenditure £40 15s. 3d., leaving a balance in order of £20 16s. 10d. – In moving the adoption of the accounts, the chairman said that eleven years ago the club was £40 in debt, and this year, for the first tie, the balance was on the right side. (Applause)

(Southport Visiter, 5th July 1888)

Slack's reference to *'11 years previous'* would most likely be to the AGM at the end of the 1876/77 season, when the Church of England Temperance Society had decided to start a football section. This suggests that they did not consider that the earlier games played by a team titled Southport Olympic in 1875 were the same club. Taking primary sources as likely to be the most accurate, this is the closest reference we have seen to the formation year of the Olympic club being mentioned.

Reginald Slack was once again in the chair for the meeting, and also re-appointed both secretary, and treasurer. He did however step back from the captaincy and in his place were appointed Lund (first team), and Melrose (second). Those present unanimously carried that Slack should be presented with a gold medal in recognition of his services.

At the first meeting of the West Lancashire Rugby Union in September at which all member clubs were present, Slack persuaded the committee to grant £5 out of the funds of the union to the Southport Infirmary.

The junior Birkdale Rugby club that had briefly existed the previous season fell by the wayside during the summer leaving Olympic once again the sole representative for the district. With the formation of Southport Central, the new professional association club, that summer the number of available games for spectators to patronise naturally reduced.

Southport Central had been a project designed to pool together the resources of many of the clubs in the town to form one 'mighty' club, and they had chosen to move across to the Sports Ground on Sussex Road for their home fixtures. This largely freed up the rugby fraternity to enjoy the spaces on Scarisbrick New Road by themselves but all it served to highlight was that the interest of the locals now lay predominantly on the other side of town.

On 8th September, the first day of the new season, the only rugby game in town was the visit of Gorton to Scarisbrick New Road where, favoured with good weather, Olympic opened the season with a win.

On the road, their first opponents were over in the northern stronghold of rugby, Wigan, where they faced Pemberton.

On Saturday last the Olympic had their first out of town match of the season, and to their credit they took a full team, although not quite as advertised, owing to indisposition of the ir half-backs. Prompt to time Webster led his men into the field amidst loud cheers from the immense gathering, many appearing just as drawn up from the pit, so keen are they in this district to witness games under the handling code of rules.

(Southport Visiter, 25th September 1888)

As was usual for Olympic, although they at least travelled with a full complement of men, they had not been able to field the team as selected and were significantly weakened by the absence of both of their half backs. They were defeated by a goal and a try.

The indifferent form of the side that finished the previous season, rather than that which had contested from November to March, had continued into 1888/89. There were no heavy defeats, but then there were no big wins either. Effectively Olympic were ticking over, drawing games against mostly average sides.

The Olympic on Saturday last ought to have travelled to Birkenhead to meet the Grange club, but owing to an insufficient number of players turning up at the station it was decided to cancel the match. I hope this is the last occasion I shall have to chronicle such a proceeding. The players are a smart lot if they will only put in an appearance, and should render a good account of themselves in the West Lancashire Cup, especially if they should succeed in knocking Wigan out in the first round.

(Southport Visiter, 17th November 1888)

As Olympic had entered 1889, the club was suffering under the weight of association football's popularity. New recruits to the rugby game were scarce, and several prominent members were lured over to play rugby for Wigan, a club still thriving in a still predominantly rugby town.

As had been the case with the association game in the middle of the decade, the focus of each season had turned increasingly towards the cup competitions. Regular fixtures just did not attract the same levels of interest, neither from the supporters or the players. The irregular availability of players had been a major contributory factor for the past couple of seasons.

Reports on regular fixtures had slowly begun to disappear from the newspaper altogether, a tell-tale sign that fixtures were not always being fulfilled. Where they did take place, the reports had been reduced to a handful of lines, hardly something that would pique the interest of the casual supporter, who by contrast could read up to half a page twice a week on the fortunes of the town's professional football club and the still numerous amateur clubs that made up the rest of the town's Saturday afternoon entertainment.

When Olympic played, they showed themselves to be not a bad side, capable of causing an upset, and it was with this in mind that they prepared for the West Lancashire Senior Cup.

Despite their erratic form and obvious problems, they had not yet been relegated to the Junior competition.

For the past two seasons Olympic had been unfortunate to receive difficult draws in the cup. Aspull disposed of Southport en-route to dominantly collecting the trophy in the first year, and then Southport faced Wigan on a mud bath clearly more suited to their more physically imposing opponents, the second year. For the third year running they were drawn away from home, and once again Wigan were to be in the way of a place in the next round.

Olympic's strongest XV always had the ability to make a match out of most games, but knowing the calibre of the sides from Wigan, there were unlikely to be many who would given them any real chance in the cup. However, on the day of the game, when supporters learned that Wigan were without six of their usual players, confidence grew that they might be in for a good game. So it was, therefore, that they set off by train at 3:45, supporters in tow, on Monday 4th March 1888. Southport arrived by 4:30, but in a show of poor gamesmanship were made to wait for almost an hour before the home team entered the field. With the match not kicking off until 5:30 it was no surprise that with ten minutes to go the referee deemed it too dark to continue.

Olympic weren't really at the races, and with Wigan leading by two goals, two tries and three minors to nil, the referee was probably doing Southport a favour by ending the game early. Olympic protested, although quite why they bothered is anyone's guess as they stood little chance of getting back into the game in those final 10 minutes. Their appeal, heard on Wednesday 10th, was upheld however and it was decided that the game should be replayed at Wigan. Rather than accept the decision with good grace, Olympic actually declined the invitation. In a baffling move, they effectively withdrew from the competition altogether, handing a walk over to Wigan. It was a sorry way for any club to exit such a competition. Possibly the only feasible explanation could be that they were unwilling to pay a further set of travelling expenses, when it was plainly obvious what the outcome of the game would be.

Olympic limped through to the end of the season, with nothing to show from their remaining games, looking wounded and out of ideas.

The Closing Ceremony

Olympic had played at a ground on Scarisbrick New Road since their days as the Church of England Temperance Society in 1876. With the town now increasingly preoccupied with the association game and the affairs at Sussex Road, the current home of Southport Central, Olympic were beginning to fade from the public eye.

In the Southport Visiter of 20th July, the editor appealed to them to hold a General Meeting to give an update as to how matters were progressing as there had been nothing said throughout the entire summer.

Taking heed of the advice, on the 16th of August, a *fair number of members* attended the Buffalo Arms on Corporation Street to hear and agree the fixtures for the forthcoming season. Mindful of their selection problems over the previous few years, care was taken to arrange fixtures more local to the town, and to leave out fixtures further afield in the Manchester district. George Pilkington once again consented to act as president and a general appeal for new members was issued.

A committee was elected at a further meeting on Tuesday 10th September and the Visiter defiantly noted that *'The Rugby game is evidently not a thing of the past so far as Southport is concerned, as was expected would be the case this year by a great many. The members of that old combination, the Olympic, are determined that a club of 13 years standing is not to be wiped off the face of the earth by the influx of the Association clubs'*.

The appeal for new members however fell largely on deaf ears.

Whilst a full list of first team fixtures had been published on 14th September in the Visiter, and on the same day the Olympic first team took on Bootle Wasps in the first of their scheduled matches, within two days The Athletic News had already received word that all second team engagements had been shelved.

The Bootle fixture highlighted that not only were numbers so low to necessitate the cancellation of the second team, but only nine men could be found for the first team.

207

On 5th October, Olympic should have faced Birkenhead Wanderers, but the Lancashire Evening Post reported that by that time the side had already folded.

The Athletic News reported *'It appears that the Olympic has now broken up, and, with their demise, the Rugby game is practically extinct in the Southport district.'*

The Southport Visiter, for its part, did not even comment. Instead, what remained of the town's rugby lovers had to be content with a report of Bootle Wasps' game against Waterloo.

Lineage & Formation Dates

I t is only in recent times that the established wisdom regarding the dates of formation of the town's football and rugby clubs has been called into question. At various points in this book, we have dealt with the circumstances that lead us to the point at which we can address each of those challenges head-on and reach an informed conclusion.

1872

The formation date of the original town club has for many years been stated as 29th November 1872. This had been believed to have been the date that both the announcement of the formation of a club was first made and it had also been reported as the date of the first game, against Birkenhead Park. This date must now be challenged. As we know, sport at the end of the nineteenth century was very much a Saturday afternoon experience and 29th November was a Friday. This must immediately ring alarm bells, and so it should.

The date of announcement would be a perfectly reasonable premise on which to select a date, if it was correct. This indeed was the date that the Southport Visiter made an announcement. It may have been the largest and longest-standing local newspaper but the Southport News and Independent had beaten them to the story by 2 days. Neither report actually stated the specific formation date, both just saying *'recently'*. We can be fairly confident it would have been within the previous few days due to the frequency of both newspapers' publication but that still doesn't really help to pin down the official date.

If we are seeking to identify a formal date, a more logical candidate would be 21st December 1872, which is the date that the first reported fixture took place, away at Seaforth. There has been no evidence found of any fixtures taking place before this date, and the aforementioned Birkenhead Park fixture did not take place until January 1873.

It would certainly be reasonable to conclude that the original Southport Football Club was founded in 1872. The only challenge to the club of today using this date is whether that club could be considered the same entity.

Southport Rugby Football Club has celebrated the year 1872 for many years, marking their centenary in 1972 and 150 years of rugby in 2022. It would be sensible to state here that, very much like the approach taken by Southport Football Club, the date they claim as their formation should be seen only as the date on which the first rugby football fixture for 'a rugby club' representing Southport took place because on that there is little argument.

Due to the events that followed for this club, however, it could be argued with some justification that this is not the date the current club was actually founded. Chiefly, it is known that the original club ceased to function in 1879 and Southport Wasps, a previous opponent of theirs, then played under the name for a year before themselves stopping in 1880. An attempt was made to restart the club a year later and whilst that new club did start the season playing rugby, it lasted less than a month before permanently switching to association football.

Putting all that to one side, however, we know with certainty that the current rugby club was once known as Southport Olympic, the decision to drop the Olympic suffix being ratified at the 1913 AGM. Tracing Olympic back from that date leads us to a club formed in 1876 initially as the Church of England Temperance Society.

For Southport (Association) Football Club, the year 1872 must surely now be considered inaccurate. The original rugby club that bore this name was restarted in 1881 and only played three games before deciding to play football.

For rugby, however, the game has continued to be played from 1872 to this day, so that year still holds merit. Southport Olympic inherited many of the supporters, officials and even players when the other amateur clubs did not survive, and they kept the spirit of the rugby game alive in Southport.

1875

We have found evidence of a team entitled Southport Olympic playing a game against Freshfield College, on 22nd October 1875, based at a ground on Scarisbrick New Road. This could be the same entity that later played as the Church of England Temperance Society and who later changed their name to Southport Olympic, but later references by Olympic themselves at Annual General Meetings suggest *they* did not consider these matches to belong to the same club. On that basis, we should discount this.

1876

A football section of the Church of England Temperance Society was noted to have been started in 1876, although no reported fixtures took place with outside clubs until February 1877. In 1878 this same club changed their name to Southport Olympic and played under this name until 1913 before dropping 'Olympic' altogether in favour of 'Southport Rugby Union Football Club'. Whilst there were a couple of short spells, after the period of time covered by this book, in which the playing of rugby is believed to have been briefly paused, it is understood that when restarted, it was the same entity and that therefore it has existed from its formation in 1876 through to the present day. Further evidence to back up the claim for this year comes in the 1888 Annual General Meeting for the Olympic club, where reference is made by the chair and secretary to the club being in a stronger financial position than they had been eleven years previously, which would have been the end of the first season 1876/77. In 1889, whilst in the throes of its death, reference is made to the Olympic club having existed for 13 years…which would make 1876 its natural year of birth, if not its spiritual one.

1881

For today's Southport Football Club, the use of this year is based on the first association football fixture for 'a club representing Southport'. 1881 is proudly displayed on its kit and at the stadium and has consistently been used throughout the club's history with little challenge.

Whenever specific dates are used, the 12th of November 1881 has also been used consistently. This is the date of the first association fixture that was arranged as Southport Football Club. Evidence has now come to light that Thomas Burnett had arranged an earlier association fixture in October, but due to differing reports it is not possible to tell whether this was 'Southport' the club or a scratch XI of his friends from Southport. Whereas one report denotes 'T.B.Burnett's team' another chooses 'T.B.Burnett's Southport'. Furthermore, there is the news publication on 12th November that states that the new association club plays its first game 'today', suggesting that they themselves did not consider the October fixture to be their first.

Even if the method used to determine a formation date was challenged and the date of the decision was used instead, it would still be 1881 as we have seen. After all, the first association club, even though it began by playing rugby, was still formed in time for the 1881 season to start.

The challenge in using 1881 at all is that this club, for all intents and purposes, ceased to function in 1886. Whilst many of the members accepted the invitation of Southport Wanderers to merge with them, and most will have applauded their later renaming back to Southport Football Club, we know that this club ended in 1888 when Southport Central was formed.

1884

This was the year in which Southport Wanderers, the club set up by enthusiastic association lovers that were originally part of the Southport Olympic club, played their first game. They were formed as an entirely separate entity to Southport Football Club as we have seen, and they even became sporting rivals for two seasons. The great irony is that one of the last fixtures fulfilled by the original Southport Football Club was the Southport Charity Cup Final win over Southport Wanderers.

If we were to trace a line of unbroken lineage, you could argue that Southport Wanderers is more of a direct descendent of the football club we have today than the original club, but even this is a stretch.

There is credibility in the notion that rather than merge (which implies an equal partnership), one stronger club absorbed the other, and on that basis the date of formation of the stronger partner – the one that remained standing – would normally be the one that would be used. But they did not do this, and as we rely almost exclusively on the press reports from the time, we must defer to the observed behaviour of what they chose to do.

1886

For clubs who merge today, we are most likely to choose their date of amalgamation. We can cite many widely accepted examples such as Rushden & Diamonds FC born out of an amalgamation in 1992 of Irthlingborough Diamonds (founded 1946) and Rushden Town (founded 1889). The accepted year of formation for this new club was 1992.

For Southport Football Club to follow similar protocol they would have to choose the date upon which it was agreed that Southport Wanderers and the original Southport Football Club merged, in the summer of 1886. A number of players and supporters switched their allegiances over to Wanderers after the infamous AGM, and whilst it would perhaps be much more accurate to say that members of the original Southport Football Club were absorbed by the Wanderers club, the original Southport Football Club did initially register with Lancashire FA for the 1886/87 season. They did not however either arrange or fulfil any fixtures, and by September were considered defunct enough for Wanderers to adopt their name.

We have no evidence to say whether this year of formation for the combined club was ever claimed. In the absence of any evidence therefore we can only assume that it wasn't. The decision to change name after the amalgamation was in order to give the club a status that Wanderers simply would not have overwise had and therefore to use 1886 would not have suited their argument.

1888

Southport Central played its first game against Stanley of Liverpool on 1st September 1888. There is little doubt that the Southport Football Club that exists today is more of a direct descendent of this club than any other that existed in the period of time covered by this book. What makes this date so plausible as an option, is that Southport Central was not merely a continuation of what went before it - this was not simply a rebranding of Southport Football Club as a professional entity. This was a radically different organisation and even the name suggests otherwise.

Those in charge of Southport Football Club, alongside those in charge of many of the other local clubs decided that in the best interests of the town, a new *club of mighty proportions* should be formed and that it should be a professional club, able to compete with the best the country has to offer. It is true that a larger number of committee members and players moved over from Southport Football Club than any other, and that the 1887/88 Southport first team effectively became the reserve string, the Southport Central Swifts, but the club was, as the Southport Visiter repeatedly called them, a *new organisation*.

The first meeting to discuss such a club was reported on 2nd June 1888, and the final of three meetings was on 29th August. It was after this final meeting that you could argue that the club formally existed. But if we are going to choose this year then we should stick to the principle of the first known fixture which was the aforementioned game against Stanley on 1st September.

Prior to the first formal meeting there had been a Southport District team put together to represent the town on a number of occasions. You could argue that this was perhaps more of a forerunner of what was to come than the amateur teams that existed, but it was not Southport Central. The Southport Guardian did acknowledge at various points over its history, and most prominently in 1958 that the club should have been celebrating its 70th birthday that year, pointing out that anything that came before 1888 was wholly amateur. It is said also that upon its 50th year celebrations in 1931, there were letters submitted to the newspapers suggesting that they were in fact 7 years early.

The Conclusion

The conclusion that I have come to after examining all the evidence is that there is nothing inherently wrong in using 1872 and 1881 as the formation dates of the rugby and association football clubs respectively, so long as you are clear what those years really signify.

On 21st December 1872, rugby was played for the first time by a club representing Southport and therefore there is good reason to celebrate it. In truth, we know that whilst this club was first, it was just one amateur outfit amongst many, and the battle for local supremacy led to the survival of the fittest. The emerging club was Southport Olympic, fleetingly a sporting rival of the original club, before inheriting its president, supporters and a number of players when the original club failed to emerge from the most harsh winter on record.

With regards Southport Football Club, 1881 is the year that association football was played for the first time by a club representing Southport. Whether we choose 8th October or 12th November as the date of the first game will now be a matter of debate, however through all the trials and tribulations that followed, this single act was the catalyst for the birth of association football in this town and therefore there is some justification for celebrating it.

However, it must be remembered that prior to 1888 when the first professional football club was formed, the landscape was entirely amateur, clubs came and went with alarming frequency and using 1881 is a bit like claiming an ancestor's birthdate as your own. You may not be the same person, but one would not exist without the other.

Had it not been for George Augustus Coombe (later Pilkington) and the original Southport Football Club's formation in 1872, neither club would have existed today, and had it not been for Thomas Blundell Burnett, then an associated football club would not have been started in 1881 and I wouldn't have just written this book!

Here's to another 150 years!

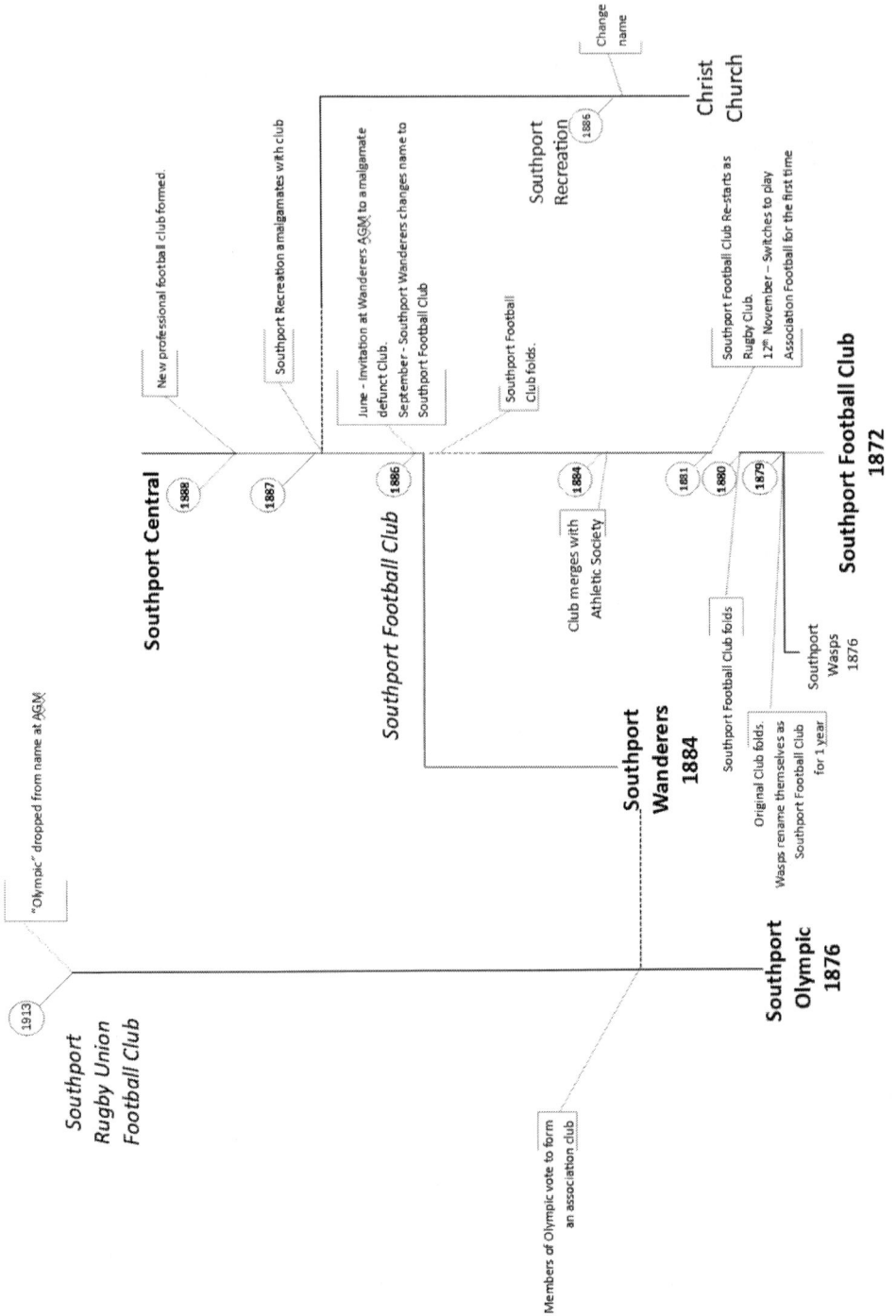

Change name

1886

Christ Church

Southport Recreation

New professional football club formed.

Southport Recreation amalgamates with club

June - Invitation at Wanderers AGM to amalgamate defunct Club.
September - Southport Wanderers changes name to Southport Football Club

Southport Football Club folds.

Southport Football Club Re-starts as Rugby Club.
17th November – Switches to play Association Football for the first time

Southport Central

1888

1887

Southport Football Club 1886

Club merges with Athletic Society

1884

1881

1880

1879

Southport Football Club 1872

Southport Football Club folds

Southport Wasps 1876

Southport Wanderers 1884

Original Club folds.
Wasps rename themselves as Southport Football Club for 1 year

Southport Olympic 1876

Members of Olympic vote to form an association club

Southport Rugby Union Football Club

1913

"Olympic" dropped from name at AGM

Personalities

Samuel Swire

Born: 3rd January 1839 (Ashton Under Lyme)

Died: 9th January 1895 (Southport)

The first president of Southport Football Club was the Mayor of Southport, Samuel Swire.

After retiring as a coal proprietor, he was elected to the Southport Council in 1870. In 1871, he and his wife Elizabeth were living at 180 Lord Street. He represented East Ward in 1872/73 and 1873/74, and was elected an Alderman in 1875 serving until 1885. He served as the Mayor of Southport twice, 1872/73 and 1873/74

The late Mr Swire was justice of the peace for Lancashire, and also for Southport, having been twice Mayor of that borough. He had been a director of several companies, chief amongst which we may mention the Wigan Coal and Iron Company, from the board of management of which he retired only in March last; the Southport Pavilion and Winter Gardens Company Limited; and the Southport Pier Company, of which he had filled the office of chairman. During the time he was Mayor of Southport, the first sod of the West Lancashire Railway was cut by Mrs S. H. Swire, his daughter-in-law. Up to the introduction of Mr Gladstone's Home Rule Bill, in 1886, Mr Swire had been an ardent and prominent Liberal, but with many others he then found himself unable to support the bulk of the Liberal party in their alliance with the Nationalists, and though thereafter her took little part in political life, his sympathies were with the Unionist cause.

(Manchester Courier and Lancashire General Advertiser - 10 January 1895)

Samuel Swire died, aged 81, on 9 January 1895 at Crown House, Southport, Lancashire. He left an estate valued at £86,164, which is the equivalent today of roughly £11.3m.

George Augustus Coombe (later Pilkington)

Born: 27 October 1848

Died: 28 January 1916

Dr. George Augustus Coombe, later Sir George Pilkington was the driving force behind the formation of the club, with the intention of 'improving the physical development of our young townsmen'.

He succeeded Smith to the vice presidency in 1873.

George was born at Upwell, Cambridgeshire, the son of R. G. Coombe a surgeon of Burnham, Essex. He was educated privately and trained for medicine at Guy's Hospital, London and took the diplomas of MRCS and LSA in 1870. He was the first house surgeon of the Southport Infirmary, being appointed in 1871, and retaining the position until 1875 when he engaged in private practice in the town. Upon his departure from the hospital, he was presented with a gold keychain watch and a collection of £100 for his services to the institution and town.

He married Mary Elizabeth Pilkington, daughter of James Pilkington, former MP for Blackburn in 1876 and at his father-in-law's request took that name. He continued to practice in Southport until 1885 in which year he was elected to represent the new constituted Southport division in parliament. He was defeated by George Curzon a year later but was re-elected in 1899.

Twice the Mayor of Southport, firstly in 1884/85 and again in 1891/92, he was a councillor and Alderman on Lancashire County Council, Deputy Lieutenant, J.P. and honorary Colonel of the 3rd Liverpool Volunteer Regiment. He was High Sheriff of Lancashire in 1911.

He was Medical Officer of the North Meols District, Ormskirk Union, Surgeon to the Royal Naval Artillery Volunteers, and Medical Officer to the Southport Convalescent Hospital and the Southport Infirmary.

On 9th December 1886 as local secretary to the Lifeboat Association he rushed from a ball at the town hall to try and join the crew of the Eliza Fernley, but he arrived too late to go to the assistance of the Mexico in what turned out to Britain's worst ever lifeboat disaster.

Pilkington was knighted in 1893.

In 1904/05 he was president of Southport & Birkdale Cricket Club, then of the Rugby Club on two occasions, Southport Central and at some stage also Southport Golf Club (now Hesketh), a Colonel of the local Volunteer Battalion and a member of the Southport Caledonian Curling Club at the Glaciarum on Lord Street which claimed to be Great Britain's first year-round indoor ice rink before it folded.

A Director of the Lancashire & Yorkshire Railway, Sir George resided at Belle Vue, Lord Street West, close to Victoria Park the then home of the rugby club which later became a hotel before being demolished and the site was redeveloped as town houses on Beach Priory Gardens.

He died on 28 January 1916, and Pilkington Road close to the site of the old hospital off Scarisbrick New Road is named after him.

Right Honourable Lord Skelmersdale

Born: 1838, Lathom

Club president 1879/80

Edward Bootle-Wilbraham, 1st Earl of Lathom, known as The Lord Skelmersdale between 1853 and 1880, was a politician. He was a member of every Conservative administration between 1866 and 1898, and notably served three times as Lord Chamberlain of the Household under Lord Salisbury. Having succeeded his grandfather as Baron Skelmersdale in 1853, he was created Earl of Lathom in 1880. In 1892 he was appointed a Knight Grand Cross of the Order of the Bath.

The Lord Skelmersdale was also president of the Southport branch of the Lifeboat Association. The lifeboat always featured prominently in the processions and pageantry which the Victorians loved so much, one such occasion being the re-opening of the Victoria Baths (which the club used as its dressing room in later years) at which his Lordship was noted in the evening for his great gallantry when, 'to make himself agreeable, (he) not only danced with everyone, but every one twice over, as gentlemen were scarce.'

Sir Charles Scarisbrick

Born: 20th April 1839

Died: 15th January 1923

President of Southport (Association) Football Club 1882-83

As a landowner he took a great interest in the development of the Borough. A keen supporter of the Southport Infirmary, through which he became acquainted with George Augustus Coombe (later Pilkington), upon its formation he gifted a sum of £7,000 for the equipping of the children's ward which was subsequently named the 'Bertha Ward' after his wife Bertha Petronella. Shortly after his marriage in 1860 he resided in Germany with his wife, the daughter of Marouard Schoenfeld of Hanau-on-Main and Dusseldorf, during the Prussian War.

In 1885 he was one of 27 founding members of the Southport (later Hesketh) Golf Club, becoming a vice president.

Charles was a director of the Southport Visiter in 1888 and appointed as a County Magistrate in 1890.

He became the Mayor of Southport in 1901, succeeded by his son, and was knighted two years later. He gave great service to the Conservative Party as president of the Southport Divisional Association from his appointment in 1906, the year his son was elected Liberal MP for South Dorset

He was also appointed a Deputy Lieutenant for the County of Lancaster.

Upon his death in January 1923, he was described by Mayor Willet as 'one of the kindest hearted men who ever lived'.

Edward Fleetwood Hesketh JP

Born 1834

Died 18th October 1886

Vice president 1879-80

A captain of the 18th Lancashire Rifle Volunteers at the time of his appointment as vice-president of the club, but a colonel by the time of his passing in 1886 aged 52. Edward Fleetwood Hesketh was the only son of the Rev Charles Fleetwood Hesketh and the last of the line of the male Heskeths. Lord of the manor at Meols Hall, he was educated in Cheltenham and New Oxford, after having been baptised by his own father. He was also a member of the Junior United Services Club, which consisted of the Royal princes, commissioned officers in the armed forces.

Areas of land near the coast around Southport, which included the foreshore, were previously owned by the Hesketh estate. Southport Town Council started to buy up this land in the late 1870s and this continued into the 1900s.

Edward became president of the Southport Golf Club in 1885 and presented the winning medals in the 1886 Charity Cup Final to Southport Football Club just months before his death. The Golf Club was later to be renamed the Hesketh Golf Club in his honour.

At the time of his death, he was unmarried and living at the Rookery.

Stewart Allen

Born: June 1852 (Prescot)

The first honorary treasurer of Southport Football Club, 1872.

The son of Irish wine merchant John Dwyre Allen, himself a well-known member of the Union Club, the family resided a stone's throw from the club's first ground at 2 Hawkshead Street. Stewart was a wine merchant's clerk in the family business.

Stewart Allen was, at just 19 years old, appointed the honorary treasurer of Southport Football Club.

In January 1881 Stewart took part in an amateur dramatic performance alongside W.J. Conell in aid of the Southport Infirmary with a fine performance as 'Old Man'. The family, without Father John, moved to Waterloo Park Crosby but kept their links with the town, taking over the New Inn at Marshside.

Stewart married Margaret Spence Taylor in 1886

William Henry Smith

Born: 1835 (Oakham, Rutland)

The club's first vice president, 1872.

William Smith lived at 147 Leyland Road and was a prominent figure with the District Bank at the time of the club's formation in 1872.

By 1891 he had retired to Bedfordshire with the family.

Henry Phillip Stephenson

Born: October 1849 (Gainsborough)

Died: February 1939 (Vancouver, British Columbia)

The first honorary secretary of Southport Football Club, 1872.

Henry was the son of Taylor Robinson Stephenson, himself born in Gateshead. Used to travelling, with each of his siblings being born in a different location, the Stephensons settled in Southport in the years prior to the club's formation. A 22-year-old broker of stocks and shares, at the club's formation he was living at the family home of Shaftesbury House (31 Church Street) with his father, the Magistrate for the Southport Borough, moving just along the road to number 37 upon marriage to Mary.

After petitioning for Divorce in 1895 he relocated to Hastings with son Edgar and Daughter Nina and new wife Jessie, 23 years his junior, whom he married in 1902.

Henry emigrated to Vancouver, British Columbia, and passed away on 17th February 1939.

Thomas Blundell Burnett

Born: 1ˢᵗ September 1852

Died: 22ⁿᵈ October 1918

Secretary of the original Southport (Association) Football Club upon their establishment in 1881, and captain of the side that took to the field against Bootle 'second' in the first association game ever played by a Southport club, on 12th November 1881.

Born in Liverpool he was baptised on 25th Dec 1852 in Southport's Christ Church.

His father Alexander was a bookkeeper who married Ellen Blundell on 15th Jan 1852.

Alexander died on 10ᵗʰ December 1861 when Thomas was just 9 years old and Ellen remarried on 16th June 1864 to James Turner, in Birkdale.

In 1871 Thomas Blundell Burnett is listed in the census as living with Mother Ellen Turner at 99 Railway Street Southport. He, aged 18, is listed as a Corn Merchant to an apprentice and his mother, a Widower aged only 41 is the Owner of the House.

On 29th June 1875 he is listed as playing for Southport Cricket Club in the 'opening match of this new old club at their ground in the Scarisbrick-road'. Burnett having been noted as achieving 3 wickets, 4 catches and 10 runs (one of only two to reach double figures with the bat).

By June the following year he had moved to Ruabon, a village near Wrexham in North Wales from where he became captain of the Wynnstay Cricket Club. He became part of their committee, even taking the chair at some meetings. Wynnstay had a large colliery run by the New British Iron Co.

In 1876 he also turned out for Ruabon football club and was appointed captain in both 1876 and 1877. Burnett represented North Wales on a number of occasions and on 5th March 1877 he won his one and only international football cap, playing as goalkeeper for Wales in their first ever home international match, losing 2-0 to Scotland. Birth qualification was not introduced until the 1890s.

Burnett remained in the area until 1880 and played a handful of times for Llangollen Cricket Club also.

Moving back to Southport in 1880, he joined Southport Football Club in time for the 1881/82 rugby season. After only one game of rugby, Burnett takes a team across to

Burscough for a game of association football. This trial game was enough to convince Burnett that there was a future for the sport in the town and although briefly returning to rugby, after a couple of heavy defeats he led the switch to the 'round ball game' after one final fixture at Bootle where he met Robert Lythgoe, an influential figure in the Bootle club, and an old acquaintance from Ruabon. Burnett became secretary of the new association club, and captain for its first two seasons of existence.

The Southport News lists him working from 179 Lord Street as a Public Accountant & Auditor, House Estate & Insurance Agent, and Coal Merchant. 'Tradesman's books made up and balanced'. He resided at 5 Leyland Road.

Returning to the cricket field in 1883, he helped to re-form Southport Cricket Club and his efforts in the same year to establish a series of charitable football fixtures in aid of the Infirmary, directly or indirectly led to the establishment of the Southport Charity Cup in 1884. This was a significant development for football in the town. With the exception of the English and County Cups, these were the only competitive fixtures on offer. He remained secretary of the football club until its amalgamation with the Southport Athletic Society in 1884, after which time he joined the Athletic Society committee, before briefly reprising his role to help the club after falling onto hard times in 1886.

Upon the dissolution of the original club Burnett joined a number of players in the formation of the new Lacrosse club, before once again being tempted back as secretary of the newly combined Southport Wanderers/Southport Football Club in 1887. Burnett finally stepped aside upon the formation of the town's first professional club Southport Central in 1888.

In 1887 he had married Jemima Lewis and by the time of the 1891 census they had moved to Queens Avenue in Formby. Clearly a man of means he is noted as a retired accountant at just 38!

Around the turn of the century Burnett and his wife moved to the Grange, Gores Lane in Freshfield, Formby where he remained until his death.

He passed away on 22nd October 1918 at the Cottage Hospital in Buxton aged 66.

His wife (Je)'Mima' Burnett passed away in 1925, aged 78 and they both share the same burial plot in the grounds of St Peter's Church in Formby.

William Platt

Born: 1858 (Southport)

Died: 22/11/1938 (Southport)

Honorary secretary of Southport Football Club (Rugby) 1879/80 Appointed captain of new Southport Football Club (Rugby) for the ill-fated 1881/82 season and original member of the Southport Football Club (Association) team.

A keen and successful sportsman all his life, one of his earliest achievements was on a penny-farthing cycle when he was just 18, winning a trophy in a race at Crewe.

Player and captain for the town's lacrosse club, he also played tennis and won several prizes in rowing and canoeing, and as a swimmer and diver he excelled.

He was a prominent local football player, having played rugby for Corinthians, Wasps and Southport Football Club and was nominated team captain for the 1881 season under the handling code. He remained with Southport after the switch to association football.

At the age of 40 he took up golf and became the captain of the Blundell Golf Club in 1910. He later became part of the council of the Hesketh Golf Club. Secretary also to the Southport Curling Club, he represented the town in contests in Scotland.

Son of Wiganer James Platt, who, although originally a coal merchant and general dealer, was the town's first auctioneer and later chartered accountant, William entered the family business himself when he was a teen and took an active part until shortly before his death.

Honorary club treasurer for Southport Football Club dating back at least to 1879, he remained involved with the club finances up until his death at the age of 80, having taken on the position of honorary auditor of Southport Central.

His father's influence as a Wesleyan preacher saw William continue his involvement with the Church, playing the organ in most churches in the town and singing in many choirs, including the Southport Philharmonic, Southport Carol Society and as a member of the Mornington Road Church Choir.

Politically he was a staunch Conservative but refrained from taking an active role in politics. He did however form and name the County Club and was chairman in 1922. For 60 years he was a very prominent Freemason.

William James B.G. Conell

Born – 1842, Caversham, Oxfordshire

Died – 21st April 1891

Treasurer of Southport Football Club 1883/84

A well-known local journalist, and prominent member of Southport society for nearly 20 years prior to his unexpected death aged just 49, in 1891. His affectionate obituary in the Southport Visiter, described him as a bright, clever and genial man who was regarded with the utmost goodwill and affection.

A resident of Bath Street upon the time of his death, he was a well-travelled man with a good education behind him. Having been brought up in London, he had become friends with none other than Charles Dickens, Artemus Ward and P.T.Barnum such were the literary and entertainment circles that he mixed within. He was also a fluent French speaker and also an actor of considerable ability, having made a living from the stage for a number of years prior to entering the field of journalism. He later became a prominent member of the Southport Amateur Dramatic Society.

His first introduction to the press came whilst in London, penning articles on theatrical productions and he came to the attention of the Southport public when he was promoted to the permanent staff of the Visiter, after becoming a reader and assistant reporter in 1873. That same year he began to pen articles as 'The Sandgrounder', a pseudonym that he used for the remainder of his career. On the departure of the then editor, Mr Conell assumed the responsibility himself and held office for 10 years. Upon leaving his employ at the Visiter, he took over the Southport News, converting it to a bi-weekly under the title of Southport News and West Lancashire Standard. The paper was discontinued after two years in favour of the Southport Standard, and he held the position of editor until his death, passing away peacefully in his sleep on the train home from London.

He was a prominent member of the Southport Athletic Society, regularly acting as judge for the annual sports events. His role as treasurer of the first association club, is a reflection of the many years of good work undertaken for the Ratepayers Association, the Company-house Keepers' Association and the Licensed Victualler's Association for the district.

Upon his passing a large meeting was held to raise funds for his widow, at which he was described as the most popular man in Southport.

William is buried in Duke Street Cemetery.

Richard William Thornton Hatch

Died Oct 1918

Secretary of Southport Football Club 1884/85

Member of the Southport Athletic Society, succeeding Thomas Burnett as secretary of the first Southport Football Club. Oldest son of Alderman Hatch and a prominent Freemason.

Married Sunday School teacher Annie Dewhurst in 1891, daughter of Mr Cornelius Dewhurst owner of the Manor Farm on Southbank Road.

Josiah Melross

Born: 28/01/1864 (Chorlton-cum-Hardy)

Died: Jan-Mar 1951 - (approximate)

Original member of Southport Football Club (Association)

Prior to playing association football he played for Southport Hornets FC. (Rugby) - July 1881.

At just 17 Josiah played for Southport Football Club in the first association game. Combining his sporting excellence with a job as a printer's clerk and later newspaper cashier alongside brother Edwin, he was a prolific local athlete.

After his spell with Southport Football Club, in 1891 he was playing Cricket for Hesketh Park Cricket Club and also taking part in local athletics events.

Josiah was nicknamed 'the flyer' by the Southport Visiter in Feb 1886

Ralph Rylance

Born: 1842 (Prestolee, Bolton)

Died: 30th January 1915 (Southport)

Appointed captain of Southport Football Club in the summer of 1883 having made his debut for the club in January of the previous year.

The third child of Margaret Rylance and James Leather, Ralph was born in 1842 in the small village of Prestolee in Bolton, taking his father's name Leather despite him passing away before he was born.

Ralph (Leather) makes his first appearance on the census records aged 18 at 52 Harwood Street, Blackburn, with his occupation listed as Attorneys Clerk. Two years later, at the end of 1863, Ralph married Margaret Parkinson. They had their first child Mary Ellen in Blackburn in 1864. Her birth was still registered with the surname Leather.

In 1870 their third child, Charles, was born and was registered as Charles Leather Rylance and by the time of the 1871 census the whole family had extended their name to include his mother's Maiden name, Ralph himself becoming Ralph Leather Rylance.

On January 1st, 1881, now a Solicitors Clerk, he registered a provisional specification with the Office of the Commissioners of Patents.

His invention received Provisional Protection only but was for 'Improvements in the formation of floors or surfaces to be used for the purposes of games of football, bowling, lawn-tennis, racquet, croquet, or similar games, and for creases used in the game of cricket'. What he had attempted to patent was the first artificial multi-sport playing surface.

In the 1881 Census, taken in April, Ralph Rylance still lived in Bolton with his Wife Mary and elderly mother Margaret Whalley (maiden name Rylance). His son James Arthur Leather Rylance's birth at the end that year was not registered in Southport and Ralph, still a Solicitors Clerk in Blackburn, played for Blackburn Law against Southport in their third fixture, at the end of November.

Long thought to be the driving force behind the formation of Southport, we now understand Rylance to have played a less significant role, Rylance not making his debut for the Reds until 7th January 1882, two months after their formation, and only making a handful of appearances in the remainder of the 1881/82 season, whilst still turning out on occasion for his original club.

He and wife Margaret went on to have a number of other children, one of whom, Walter, presented Southport Football club with a red flag to celebrate their erroneous 50th anniversary in 1931.

Ralph and family made the permanent move to Southport in the summer of 1882 and he made further appearances for the Reds including in the club's first FA Cup tie at Liverpool Ramblers at the end of the year. In September 1883 he was appointed captain for the 1883/84 season.

Withdrawing from the field in March 1884, however, he made no further appearances for the club, and served no part on any committee.

In November 1884 a report appeared in the Manchester Courier and Lancashire General Advertiser relating to a case being heard at Liverpool Chancery Court in his absence. The charge was that he had forcibly taken an elderly lady 'of unsound mind' away from her home in Blackburn to marry his brother-in-law, 20 years her junior, and to live in the property next door to Rylance on Eastbourne Road in Birkdale. Andrew Parker, a friend of the lady, Isabella Parkinson, had petitioned to prevent Rylance from selling her home in Blackburn worth £6,000. Her family, learning of the marriage, argued that she had not understood that she was married and petitioned to classify her as a lunatic. Pending the outcome of the lunacy proceedings, the judge granted the prevention order. Neither the defendant, Rylance, nor Plaintiff, Miss Parkinson were in attendance as they had both gone to America. This is likely to explain his sudden disappearance from the football field before the end of the season.

Later returning to his home in Eastbourne Road, Birkdale, and now working as an Oakum manufacturer in Liverpool as part of Rylance Medd & Co, he led a management buyout of his business partner John Goldsmith Medd in 1897 and continued to successfully run the business with his sons James and Walter.

Ralph Leather Rylance died on 30th January 1915 aged 73 leaving his estate, worth £9,073 17s 5d to his wife Margaret.

Squire Ogden Platt

Born: 1863 (Oldham)

Died: 26/12/1931 (Southport)

Original member of Southport Football Club (Association)

In 1884 he represented Lancashire County association.

An Auctioneer and member of the Auctioneers and Estate Agents Institute of the UK.

Square Platt, Auctioneer, Valuer, &c., 59 Chapel Street, Southport - Mr .Platt commenced business in Southport in 1884, at 19, London Street, and removed to his present most commodious premises in September 1888. These comprise a handsome suite of offices of two floors. He has an exceedingly extensive connection as a house and property agent, as may easily be seen from the lengthy lists of most eligible properties of all kinds, "for sale" and "to let" at all times displayed in the windows, as well as in the Southport and Birkdale Register, a well-arranged and valuable work issued every month by Mr Platt. His agencies are exceedingly numerous and valuable, He acts for Messrs. Fletcher, Burrows & Co., the well-known colliery proprietors, for Southport and district, and does a considerable business in this line. In insurance matters he is a most active agent, and holds agencies for pretty well every department of insurance business. He acts for the County Fire and the well-known Provident Life, as well as for the National Life, and in addition, he holds agencies for the Imperial Union for Accidents, and for the Edinburgh Employers' Liability office. A special appointment from his Honor the Judge of the Liverpool County Court, under the provisions of the amended "Law of Distress Act" of 1888. Mr Platt also conducts horse sales once a month at the Railway Hotel Mews. He is very much respected throughout the town and district, and , in the conduct of his numerous branches of business, he has managed to make a large circle of friends by whom he is held in the highest esteem. (Southport Trade Directory)

Later became a committee member of Southport Central.

Liberal Councillor 1899 to 1904. Lived at 77 Promenade.

Reginald Slack

Died: January 1930

Secretary, captain and treasurer of Southport Olympic on multiple occasions

Member of the Liverpool Corn trade and resident of Sefton Street, Southport.

For many years a playing member of the Olympic club, during which time he undertook the roles of captain, secretary and treasurer on multiple occasions. An ardent defender of the rugby game during his time with the Olympic club, his drive and enthusiasm for the sport kept the rugby flag flying in the town against increasingly stiff competition from the newer association clubs.

Reginald later became a leading light in the pigeon fancying fraternity where he progressed to become president of the National Homing Union.

Dan Ashton

Born: 3rd April 1856

Died: 14th March 1942

Member of the Southport Charity Cup Committee, and committee member and treasurer of Southport Central Football Club

Born in Bury and brought to Southport by his parents at the age of 8, he originally apprenticed in ironmongery before leaving to join his father's firm, Messrs. William Ashton and Sons Ltd, paper bag manufacturers, stationers, and general printers. He became a prominent local businessman who was highly respected by all who knew him.

A bachelor his whole life, he was keenly interested in the town's football affairs and became a member of the original committee of the Southport Central Football Club. For a number of years he acted as treasurer to the club.

He was also the proprietor of the Southport Journal newspaper until it was taken over by Messrs Robert Johnson and Co Ltd.

A man of a retiring but cheery disposition, he passed away just shy of his 87th birthday.

Thomas Lea (Lea-Jones)

Born: 5ᵗʰ March 1869 (West Derby)

Died: 5ᵗʰ June 1939 (Birkdale)

The first professional player signed by Southport Central, and former player for Southport Wanderers and Southport Football Club.

Tom Lea came to live in Southport as a baby and was the oldest of three boys to have played football for Southport.

Tom and brother Harry together played for Southport Wanderers in 1885 and also the amalgamated Southport Football Club from 1886 to 1888. Whilst representing Southport, he also made the occasional guest appearance for Everton. Tom then became the first professional player to sign for Southport Central in the summer of 1888 and then later rejoined his brother Harry at Accrington before ending his career because of a knee injury in 1895.

Tom was a versatile player, able to change position on the field at ease, often deputising for injured players. He played in every position on the pitch apart from goalkeeper.

He was a life member of the Birkdale Conservative Club, which he joined in 1887 when the club premises were a cottage in Everton Road. Both he, and his brother William, were Town Councillors, Tom being elected to represent the Birkdale East Ward between 1912 and 1918.

Tom's father William had established a shop in Brighton Road Birkdale, which Tom later expanded as he became a wine and spirit merchant. He had been ill for some time prior to his death, aged 70.

The Laws of the Game

Rugby Football Union (1871)

1. A *drop kick*, or *drop*, is made by letting the ball fall from the hands and kicking it the *very instant* it rises.

2. A *place kick*, or *place*, is made by kicking the ball after it has been placed in a nick made in the ground for the purpose of keeping it at rest.

3. A *punt* is made by letting the ball fall from the hands and kicking it *before* it touches the ground.

4. *Each goal* shall be composed of two upright posts, exceeding 11ft in height from the ground, and placed 18ft 6in apart, with a cross bar 10ft from the ground.

5. *A goal* can only be obtained by kicking the ball from the field of play direct (*i.e.*, without touching the dress or person of any player of either side), over the cross bar of the opponent's goal, whether it touch such cross bar or the posts or not; but if the ball goes directly over either of the *goal posts* it is called a *poster*, and is not a goal.

6. A goal may be obtained by any kind of kick except a *punt*.

7. A match shall be decided by a majority of goals only.

8. The ball is dead when it rests absolutely motionless on the ground.

9. A *touch-down* is when a player putting his hand upon the ball on the ground in touch or in goal stops it so that it remains dead or fairly so.

10. A *tackle* is when the holder of the ball is held by one or more players of the opposite side.

11. A *scrummage* takes place when the holder of the ball being in the field of play puts it down on the ground in front of him, and all who have closed round on their respective sides endeavour to push their opponents back, and by kicking the ball to drive it in the direction of the opposite goal-line.

12. A player may take up the ball whenever it is rolling or bounding, except in a scrummage.

13. It is not lawful to take up the ball when dead (except in order to bring it out after it has been touched down in touch or in goal) for any purpose whatever; whenever the ball shall have been so unlawfully taken up, it shall at once be brought back to where it was so taken up, and there put down.

14. In a scrummage it is not lawful to touch the ball with the hand under any circumstances whatever.

15. It is lawful for any player who has the ball to run with it, and if he does so it is called a *run*. If a player runs with the ball until he gets behind his opponent's goal-line and there touches it down, it is called a *run in*.

16. It is lawful to *run* in anywhere across the goal-line.

17. The goal-line is in goal, and the touchline is in touch.

18. In the event of any player holding or running with the ball being tackled and the ball fairly held, he must at once cry *down*, and there put it down.

19. A *maul in goal* is when the holder of the ball is tackled inside goal-line, or being tackled immediately outside is carried or pushed across it, and he or the opposite side, or both, endeavour to touch the ball down. In all cases the ball when so touched down shall belong to the players of the side who first had possession of it before the maul commenced, unless the opposite side have gained entire possession of it.

20. In case of a maul in goal those players only who are touching the ball with their hands when it crosses the goal-line may continue in the maul in goal, and when a player has once released his hold of the ball after it is inside the goal-line he may not again join in the maul, and if he attempts to do so may be dragged out by the opposite side.

But if a player when *running in* is tackled inside the goal-line, then only the player who first tackled him, or if two or more tackle him *simultaneously* they only may join in the maul.

21. *Touch in goal* (see plan).—Immediately the ball, whether in the hands of a player (except for the purpose of a punt-out, see Rule 29) or not, goes into touch in goal it is at once dead and out of the game, and is brought out as provided by Rules 41 and 42.

22. Every player is *on side* but is put *off side* if he enters a scrummage from his opponents' side, or being in a scrummage gets in front of the ball, or when the ball has been kicked, touched, or is being run with by any of his own side behind him (that is, between himself and his own goal-line).

23. Every player when *off side* is out of the game and shall not touch the ball in any case whatever, either in or out of touch or goal, or in any way interrupt or obstruct any player, until he is again *on side*.

24. A player being *off side* is put *on side* when the ball has been run five yards with or kicked by or has touched the dress or person of any player of the opposite side, or when one of his own side has run in front of him either with the ball or having kicked it when behind him.

25. When a player has the ball none of his opponents who at the time are off side may commence or attempt to run, tackle, or otherwise interrupt such player until he has run five yards.

26. *Throwing Back.*—It is lawful for any player who has the ball to throw it back towards his own goal, or to pass it back to any player of his own side, who is at the time behind him in accordance with the rules of *on side*.

27 *Knocking on—i.e.*, deliberately hitting the ball with the hand — and *throwing forward—i.e.*, throwing the ball in the direction of the opponent's goal-line, are not lawful. If the ball be either knocked on or thrown forward, the captain of the opposite side may, unless a fair catch has been made, as provided by the next rule, require to have it brought back to the spot where it was so knocked or throw on, and there *put down*.

28. A *fair catch* is a catch made direct from a kick or a throw forward or a knock on by one of the opposite side, or from a punt out or a punt on (see Rules 29 and 30), provided the catcher makes a mark with his heel at the spot where he has made the catch, and no other of his own side touch the ball. (See Rules 43 and 44.)

29. A *punt out* is a *punt* made after a touch-down by a player from behind his opponents' goal-line, and from touch-in-goal, if necessary, towards his own side, who must stand outside the goal-line and endeavour to make a fair catch, or to get the ball and *run in* or *drop* a goal. (See Rules 49 and 51.)

30. A *punt on* is a punt made in a manner similar to a punt out, and from touch if necessary, by a player who has made a fair catch from a *punt out* or another *punt on*.

31. *Touch* (see plan).— If the ball goes into touch the first player on his side who touches it down must bring it to the spot where it crossed the touch-line, or if a player when running with the ball cross or put any part of either foot across the touch-line he must return with the ball to the spot where the line was so crossed, and thence return it to the field of play in one of the modes provided by the following rule.

32. He must then himself, or by one of his own side, either bound it out in the field of play, and then run with it, kick it, or throw it back to his own side, or (2) throw it out at right angles to the touch-line, or (3) walk out with it at right angles to the touch-line any distance not less than five or more than fifteen yards, and there put it down, first declaring how far he intends to walk out.

33. If two or more players holding the ball are pushed into touch the ball shall belong in touch to the player who first had hold of it when in the field of play and has not released his hold of it.

34. If the ball when thrown out of touch be not thrown out at right angles to the touch-line, the captain of either side may at once claim to have it thrown out again.

35. A catch made when the ball is thrown out of touch is not a *fair catch*.

36. *Kick off* is a place-kick from the centre of the field of play and cannot count as a goal. The opposite side must stand at least ten yards in front of the ball until it has been kicked.

37. The ball shall be *kicked off* at the commencement of the game, after a goal has been obtained.

38. The sides shall change goals as often as and whenever a goal is obtained, unless it has been otherwise agreed by the captains before the commencement of the match.

39. The captains of the respective sides shall toss up before the commencement of the match; the winner of the toss shall have the option of choice of goals or the kick-off.

40. Whenever a goal shall have been obtained the side which has lost the goal shall then kick-off.

41. *Kick-out* is a drop-kick by one of the players of the side which has had to touch the ball down in their own goal, or into whose touch in goal the ball has gone (Rule 21), and is the mode of bringing the ball again into play, and cannot count as a goal.

42. *Kick-out* must be a *drop-kick*, and from not more than twenty-five yards outside the kicker's goal-line; if the ball when kicked out pitch in touch it must be taken back and kicked out again. The kicker's side must be behind the ball when kicked out.

43. A player who has made and claimed a fair catch shall thereupon either take a *drop-kick* or a *punt*, or *place* the ball for a place-kick.

44. After a fair catch has been made the opposite side may come up to the catcher's mark, and (except in cases under Rule 50) the catcher's side retiring, the ball shall be kicked from such mark or from a spot any distance behind it.

45. A player may touch the ball down in his own goal at any time.

46. A side having touched the ball down in their opponents' goal, shall *try at goal* either by a place-kick or a punt out.

47. If a *try at goal* be made by a *place-kick* a player of the side which has touched the ball down shall bring it up to the goal-line (subject to Rule 48) in a straight line from and opposite to the spot where the ball was touched down, and there make a mark on the goal-line, and thence walk straight out with it at right angles to the goal-line such distance as he thinks proper, and there place it for another of his side to kick. The kicker's side must be behind the ball when it is kicked, and the opposite side must remain behind their goal-line until the ball has been placed on the ground. (See Rules 54 and 55.)

48. If the ball has been touched down between the goal-posts, it may be brought out in a straight line from either of such posts, but if brought out from between them the opposite side may charge at once. (See Rule 54.)

49. If the *try at goal* be by a *punt out* (see Rule 29), a player of the side which has touched the ball down shall bring it straight up to the goal-line opposite to the spot where it was touched down, and there make a mark on the goal-line, and then *punt out* from touch in goal,

if necessary, or from any part behind the goal-line not nearer to the goal-post than such mark, beyond which mark it is not lawful for the opposite side, who must keep behind their goal-line, to pass until the ball has been kicked. (See Rules 54 and 55.)

50. If a fair catch be made from a *punt out* or a *punt on*, the catcher may either proceed as provided by Rules 43 and 44, or himself take a *punt on*, in which case the mark made on making the fair catch shall be regarded (for the purpose of determining as well the position of the player who makes the *punt on* as of the other players of both sides) as the mark made on the goal-line in the case of a *punt out*.

51. A catch made in touch from a *punt out* or a *punt on* is not a fair catch. The ball must then be taken or thrown out of touch as provided by Rule 32; but if the catch be made in touch in goal the ball is at once dead, and must be *kicked out* as provided by Rule 21.

52. When the ball has been touched down in the opponents' goal, none of the side in whose goal it has been so touched down shall touch it or in any way displace it or interfere with the player of the other side who may be taking it up or out.

53. The ball is dead whenever a goal has been obtained, but if a *try at goal* be not successful, the kick shall be considered as only an ordinary kick in the course of the game.

54. *Charging* — i.e., rushing forward to kick the ball or tackle a player — is lawful for the opposite side in all cases of a place-kick after a fair catch or upon a *try at goal*, immediately the ball touches or is placed in the ground; and in cases of a drop-kick or punt after a fair catch, as soon as the player having the ball commences to run or offers to kick, or the ball has touched the ground; but he may always draw back, and unless he has dropped the ball or actually touched it with his foot, they must again retire to his mark (see Rule 56). The opposite side in the case of a punt out or a punt on, and the kicker's side in *all* cases, may not charge until the ball has been kicked.

55. If a player having the ball when about to *punt it out* goes outside the goal line, or when about to *punt on* advances nearer to his own goal-line than his mark made on making the fair catch, or if after the ball has been touched down in the opponents' goal or a fair catch has been made, more than one player of the side which has so touched it down or made the fair catch touch the ball before it is again kicked, the opposite side may charge at once.

56. In cases of a fair catch the opposite side may come up to and stand anywhere on or behind a line drawn through the mark made by the player who has made the catch, and parallel to their own goal-line; but in the case of a fair catch from a *punt out* or a *punt on* they may not advance further in the direction of the touch-line nearest to such mark than a line drawn through such mark to their goal-line, and parallel to such touch-line. In all cases (except a punt out and a punt on) the kicker's side must be behind the ball when it is kicked, but may not charge until it has been kicked.

57. No *hacking* or *hacking over* or tripping up shall be allowed under any circumstances.

58. No one wearing projecting nails, iron plates, or gutta percha on any part of his boots or shoes shall be allowed to play in a match.

59. The captains of the respective sides shall be the sole arbiters of all disputes.

The Football Association (1863)

Definition of Terms

A Place Kick - a kick at the ball while it is on the ground, in any position which the kicker may choose to place it.

A Free Kick - the privilege of kicking the ball, without obstruction, in such manner as the kicker may think fit.

A Fair Catch - when the ball is caught, after it has touched the person of an adversary, or has been kicked or knocked on by an adversary, and before it has touched the ground or one of the side catching it; but if the ball is kicked from behind the goal line, a fair catch cannot be made.

Hacking - kicking an adversary.

Tripping - throwing an adversary by the use of the legs.

Knocking On - when a player strikes or propels the ball with his hands, arms, or body without kicking or throwing it.

Holding - includes the obstruction of a player by the hand or any part of the arm below the elbow.

Touch - that part of the field, on either side of the ground, which is beyond the line of flags.

Laws

1. The maximum length of the ground shall be 200 yards, the maximum breadth shall be 100 yards, the length and breadth shall be marked off with flags; and the goal shall be defined by two upright posts, eight yards apart, without any tape or bar across them.

2. A toss for goals shall take place, and the game shall be commenced by a place kick from the centre of the ground by the side losing the toss for goals; the other side shall not approach within 10 yards of the ball until it is kicked off.

3. After a goal is won, the losing side shall be entitled to kick off, and the two sides shall change goals after each goal is won.

4. A goal shall be won when the ball passes between the goal-posts or over the space between the goal-posts (at whatever height), not being thrown, knocked on, or carried.

5. When the ball is in touch, the first player who touches it shall throw it from the point on the boundary line where it left the ground in a direction at right angles with the boundary line, and the ball shall not be in play until it has touched the ground.

6. When a player has kicked the ball, any one of the same side who is nearer to the opponent's goal line is out of play, and may not touch the ball himself, nor in any way whatever prevent any other player from doing so, until he is in play; but no player is out of play when the ball is kicked off from behind the goal line.

7. In case the ball goes behind the goal line, if a player on the side to whom the goal belongs first touches the ball, one of his side shall he entitled to a free kick from the goal line at the point opposite the place where the ball shall be touched. If a player of the opposite side first touches the ball, one of his side shall be entitled to a free kick at the goal only from a point 15 yards outside the goal line, opposite the place where the ball is touched, the opposing side standing within their goal line until he has had his kick.

8. If a player makes a fair catch, he shall be entitled to a free kick, providing he claims it by making a mark with his heel at once; and in order to take such kick he may go back as far as he pleases, and no player on the opposite side shall advance beyond his mark until he has kicked.

9. No player shall run with the ball.

10. Neither tripping nor hacking shall be allowed, and no player shall use his hands to hold or push his adversary.

11. A player shall not be allowed to throw the ball or pass it to another with his hands.

12. No player shall be allowed to take the ball from the ground with his hands under any pretence whatever while it is in play.

13. No player shall be allowed to wear projecting nails, iron plates, or gutta-percha on the soles or heels of his boots.

The Football Association (1881)

Laws of association football, adopted at the February General Meeting of the Football Association, Freemasons' Tavern, London, February 25th, 1881. Effective from the beginning of the 1881-2 season.

Definition of Terms

A Place Kick - a kick at the ball while on the ground, in any position in which the kicker may choose to place it.

Hacking - kicking an adversary intentionally.

Tripping - throwing an adversary by the use of the legs.

Knocking on - when a player strikes or propels the ball with his hands or arms.

Holding - includes the obstruction of a player by the hand or any part of the arm extended from the body.

Touch - that part of the field, on either side of the ground, which is beyond the line of flags.

A Free Kick - a kick at the ball in any way the kicker pleases, when it is lying on the ground; none of the kicker's opponents being allowed within six yards of the ball, but in no case can a player be forced to stand behind his own goal-line.

Handling - playing the ball with the hand or arm.

Dribbling - working the ball along with the feet, pushing it on with a series of gentle kicks, in order to pilot it past opponents towards the desired goal.

Laws

1. The limits of the ground shall be: maximum length, 200 yards; minimum length, 100 yards; maximum breadth, 100 yards, minimum breadth, 50 yards. The length and breadth shall be marked off with flags; and the goals shall be upright posts, 8 yards apart, with a tape or bar across them, 8 feet from the ground.

2. The winners of the toss shall have the option of kick off or choice of goals. The game shall be commenced by a place-kick from the centre of the ground; the other side shall not approach within ten yards of the ball until it is kicked off, nor shall any player on either side pass the centre of the ground in the direction of his opponents' goal until the ball is kicked off.

3. Ends shall only be changed at half-time. After a goal is won the losing side shall kick off, but after the change of ends at half-time the ball shall be kicked off by the opposite side from that which originally did so; and always as provided in Law 2.

4. A goal shall be won when the ball passes between the goal-posts under the tape or bar, not being thrown, knocked on, nor carried. The ball hitting the goal, or boundary posts, or goal bar or tape, and rebounding into play, is considered in play.

5. When the ball is in touch, a player of the opposite side to that which kicked it out shall throw it from the point on the boundary line where it left the ground, in any direction the thrower may choose. The ball must be thrown in at least six yards, and shall be in play when thrown in, but the player throwing it in shall not play it until it has been played by another player.

6. When a player kicks the ball, or it is thrown in out of touch, any one of the same side who at such moment of kicking or throwing is nearer to the opponents' goal line, is out of play, and may not touch the ball himself, nor in any way whatever prevent any other player from doing so until the ball has been played, unless there are at least three of his opponents nearer their own goal line; but no player is out of play when the ball is kicked from the goal line.

7. When the ball is kicked behind the goal-line by one of the opposite side, it shall be kicked off by any one of the players behind whose goal line it went, within six yards of the nearest goal post; but if kicked behind by any one of the side whose goal-line it is, a player of the opposite side shall kick it from within one yard of the nearest corner flag post. In either case no other player shall be allowed within six yards of the ball until it is kicked off.

8. No player shall carry or knock on the ball, and handling the ball under any pretence whatever, shall be prohibited, except in the case of the goal-keeper, who shall be allowed to use his hands in defence of his goal, either by knocking or throwing, but shall not carry the ball. The goal-keeper may be changed during the game, but not more than one player shall act as goal-keeper at the same time, and no second player shall step in and act during any period in which the regular goal-keeper may have vacated his position.

9. Neither tripping nor hacking shall be allowed, and no player shall use his hands to hold or push his adversary, nor charge him from behind. A player with his back towards his opponents' goal cannot claim the privilege of Rule 9 when charged behind.

10. No player shall wear any nails — excepting such as have their heads driven in flush with the leather — iron plates, or gutta-percha, on the soles or heels of his boots, or on his shin guards.

11. In the event of any infringement of Rules 6, 8, or 9, or 14, a free kick shall be forfeited to the opposite side from the spot where the infringement took place.

12. In no case shall a goal be scored from any free kick, nor shall the ball be again played by the kicker until it has been played by another player. The kick off and corner-flag kick shall be free kicks within the meaning of this rule.

13. That in the event of a supposed infringement of Rules 6, 8, 9, 10, or 14, the ball be in play until the decision of the umpire, on his being appealed to, shall have been given.

14. No player shall charge an opponent by leaping upon him.

15. By mutual arrangement of the competing clubs in matches, a referee shall be appointed whose duties will be to decide in all cases of dispute between the umpires; he shall also keep a record of the game, and act as timekeeper, and in the event of ungentlemanly behaviour on the part of any of the contestants, the offender or offenders shall, in the presence of the umpires, be cautioned, and in the case of violent conduct the referee shall have the power to rule the offending player out of play, and to order him off the ground, and transmit his name to the committee of the association under whose rules the game was played, and in whom shall be solely vested the right of accepting an apology.

Results & Statistics - Rugby

Rugby scoring developed significantly over the years, and the point scoring system in place today was not used during the period covering the statistics shown in this book. Goals were the primary method of determining the result, however alongside the result was often a breakdown of the scoring and therefore the score is included here wherever known with the following code used for simplicity. For example, 6G, 2T, 1M would be 6 Goals, 2 Tries and 1 Minor Point. The score of the team for whom the statistics are noted is always shown first. For example, a defeat would be record as 1G v 2G and a win recorded as 2G v 1G regardless of the venue.

G = Goal

T = Try

TD = Touchdown

TIG = Touch in Goal

M = Minor Point

R = Rouge

PO = Punt Out

QW = Quarter Way

The following chapters contain the results and line-ups of all fixtures traceable. Other fixtures may have been arranged but there appears to be no record published in any local newspapers to confirm that they took place

Southport (Rugby) Football Club

1872-73

21/12/1872   Seaforth (Away)   Draw
M.Smith and C.A.Schofield noted in the report. Full Line-Up Not Available.

11/01/1873   Birkenhead (Away)   Draw - No score
Chamberlain, J.Fletcher (full backs); M.Smith, (¾ backs); C.A.Schofield, P.M.Hunter (½ backs); R.W.Smith (Capt.), S.Lord, H.P.Stephenson, J.Schofield, G.F.Schofield, Gregory, Pryce, G.A.Thomson, G.Nicholson, McCulloch, A.Fletcher, Steele, Jones (forwards)

25/01/1873   Claughton (Away)   Draw - 10QW v 2QW.
C.A.Schofield, P.M.Hunter (full backs); R.W.Smith (Capt.) (¾ backs); Hargreaves, Bath (½ backs); S.Lord, Gregory, Pryce, H.P.Stephenson, N.Barron, J.Schofield, S.Allen, G.Nicholson (forwards)

08/02/1873   WIGAN (Home)   Draw - No score
C.A.Schofield, P.M.Hunter (full backs); R.W.Smith (Capt.), A.D.Burnyeat (¾ backs); G.F.Schofield, Batty (½ backs); Gregory, Pryce, N.Barron, J.Schofield, H.P.Stephenson, S.Allen, Magnell, Bracewell (forwards)

15/02/1873   Dingle (Away)   Draw - 1G, 3T v 1G, 1 T
C.A.Schofield, P.M.Hunter (full backs); R.W.Smith (Capt.) (¾ backs); G.F.Schofield, Millington (½ backs); A.D.Burnyeat, Johnson (¼ backs); N.Barron, Gregory, Cox, Ball, Atkinson, Rigg, H.V.Pigot, W.Milner, G.Nicholson, Ray, Cannon, Jenkinson (forwards)

08/03/1873   Wigan (Away)   Draw
C.A.Schofield, P.M.Hunter (Capt.) (full backs); W.Milner, Batty (½ backs); G.F.Schofield, H.V.Pigott (¼ backs); Pryce, Littledale, S.Lord, Gregory, H.V.Pigot, Hussey, Wallace, Bracewell (forwards)

15/03/1873   ORMSKIRK (Home)   Win - 2G, 7T & 6 "Gongs" v 0
A.D.Burnyeat, N.Barron H.V.Pigot, G.F.Schofield, S.Lord, Batty noted in the report. Full Line-Up Not Available.

Only 7 fixtures were found for this first season with a final record of Played 7, Won 1, Drew 6.

1873-74

4/10/1873   SANDRINGHAM SCHOOL (Home)   Won - 1G, 3TD v 0
No Line-Up Available

18/10/1873   Liverpool College (Away) Won - 3G v 0
No Line-Up Available

01/11/1873   BOLTON (Home) Won - 3G, 5TD v 0
P.M.Hunter (Capt.), C.A.Schofield (full backs); W.E.Smith, Musselsini (½ backs); Batty, A.D.Burnyeat, N.Barron, W.Milner (¼ backs); Cannon, Coombe, G.Hall, Hardcastle, H.Greenall, Jones, S.Lord, Pryce, H.V.Pigott, J.Schofield, M.Smith, H.P.Stevenson (forwards)

8/11/1873   DINGLE (Home)   Draw - 2TD, "several" R and a 'kick a poster' v 0
Barrow, Bailey, Burnyeat, Coombe, Greenall, Hall, Hartley, P.M.Hunter, Littledale, Lord, Milner, Mansfield, H.Pigott, Pryce, J.Schofield, C.Schofield, G.Schofield, M.Smith, W.Smith, H.P.Stephenson

29/11/1873   BIRKENHEAD (Home)   Won - 1G v 0
P.M.Hunter, C.Schofield (full backs); Batty, Bromilow, M.Smith (½ backs); Barron, Burnyeat, W.E.Smith, Hartley (¼ backs); Cannon, Hall, Greenall, Littledale, Lord, Mossley, Nicholson, H.Pigott, Pryce, G.Schofield, H.P.Stephenson (forwards)

06/12/1873   OWENS COLLEGE (Home) Draw - 3TD, 1TIG to 0
Barron, Baily, Bromilow, A.D.Burnyeat, Coombe, G.Hall, Hardcastle, Jones, Mossley, G.Nicholson, J.Schofield, C.A.Schofield, Smith, H.P.Stephenson

20/12/1873   Stalybridge (Away)*   Won - 2G, 3T, 2PO, 7TD v 0
*Reported in Field as "Southport Wanderers"
G.Hall (Capt.), A.Andrew, Townsend, G.Nicholson, J.Schofield, S.Andrew, M.Smith, Dorning, J.Andrew, C.A.Schofield, P.M.Hunter, R.B.Hartley, W.Milner

10/01/1874   FREE WANDERERS, MANCHESTER (Home)   Draw - 1TD v 0
A.Andrew, J.Fletcher (full backs); C.A.Schofield, P.M.Hunter (¾ backs); R.B.Hartley, G.F.Schofield (½ backs); R.W.Smith (Capt.), G.Andrew, A.D.Burnyeat, J.Burnyeat, N.Barron, Coombe, G.Nicholson, S.Lord, W.Milner, J.Schofield, M.Smith, H.P.Stephenson (forwards)

17/01/1874   Birkenhead (Away)   Won - 1G, 2QW, 1TIG v 0
Batty, E. Brown, J.Fletcher, P.M.Hunter, C.A.Schofield (backs); R.W.Smith (Capt.), N.Barron, J.Burnyeat, A.D.Burnyeat, Coombe, R.B.Hartley, Hibberd, W.Milner, G.Nicholson, Payne, J.Schofield, M.Smith, H.P.Stephenson (forwards)

24/01/1874   **WIGAN (Home)**   **Draw - 1TD, 1TIG, 8R to 0**
M.Smith, C.A.Schofield, G.F.Schofield, P.M.Hunter, J.Fletcher (backs); R.W.Smith, J.Schofield, G.Hall, Coombe, W.Milner, Pryce, Cannon, R.B.Hartley, Bromilow, H.V.Pigott (forwards)

14/02/1874   **Wigan (Away)**   **Won - 1G, 1T, 2TIG & 4 saves to 0**
A.Andrew, C.A.Schofield (full backs); R.B.Hartley, A.D.Burnyeat (½ backs); G.F.Schofield (¾ backs); R.W.Smith (Capt.), M.Smith, G.Andrew, G.Hall, H.Greenall, W.Milner, W.E.Smith, G.Bromilow, J.Schofield (forwards)

28/02/1874   **West Derby (Away)**   **Won - 1G, 1T, 1PO, 4TD v 2T, 2TD**
Batty, A.D.Burnyeat, J.Fletcher, R.B.Hartley, Wynne (backs); R.W.Smith (Capt.), Barron, Bromilow, Churchward, W.Milner, Pryce, M.Smith, W.E.Smith, H.P.Stephenson, Young (forwards)

7/03/1874   **Dingle (Away)**   **Lost - 2TD, 1TIG v a 1 "disputed" G**
A.D.Burnyeat, Batty, P.M.Hunter, C.A.Schofield, G.F.Schofield, M.Smith (backs); R.W.Smith (Capt.), N.Barron, Bromilow, J.Burnyeat, J.Fletcher, G.Hall, Kewley, Littledale, W.Milner, H.V.Pigot, Pryce, J.Schofield, H.P.Stephenson, G.A.Thomson (forwards)

Final record for the season as reported at the club AGM: Played 12, Won 7, Lost 1, Drawn 4
For this record to be accurate, the first fixture of the season v Sandringham School must have been considered a pre-season friendly.

1874-75

17/10/1874   WEST DERBY (Home)   Won - 5G, Several Minors v 0
P.M.Hunter (Capt.), G.Hall, N.Barron, A.D.Burnyeat, Coombe, W.Bromilow, G.Bromilow, J.Fletcher, R.B.Hartley, H.Greenall, W.Milner, G.Nicholson, H.V.Pigot, Musselbini, G.F.Schofield

24/10/1874   UNITED SCHOOLS (Home)   Won - 2G 1T v 0
No Line-Up Available

31/10/1874   BOLTON (Home)   Won - 1G, 1TD, v 1TD
P.M.Hunter (Capt.), W.Bromilow, R.B.Hartley, J.Brown, E.Brown, C.A.Schofield, A.Andrew (backs); Coombe, G.Hall, G.Andrew, G.Bromilow, G.F.Schofield, P.Greenall, H.Greenall, J.Fletcher, H.V.Pigot, N.Barron, F.Hermon, Smith, H.P.Stephenson (forwards)

07/11/1874   FREE RANGERS, MANCHESTER (Home)   Draw - 1T v 0
E.Brown, A.Andrew, Batty (full backs); E.Brown, F.Herman (¾ backs); R.B.Hartley, N.Barron (¼ backs); P.M.Hunter (Capt.), Coombe, G.Hall, G.Andrew, Bromilow, Pryce, Smith, J.Fletcher, G.Nicholson, G.A.Thomson, Littledale (forwards)

14/11/1874   STALYBRIDGE (Home)   Won - 1G, 3T, 1TIG, 4TD v 0
C.A.Schofield, Hodges (full backs); P.M.Hunter, E.Brown (½ backs); R.B.Hartley, Cox (¼ backs); Batty, Coombe, Bromilow, H.Greenall, P.Greenall, G.F.Schofield, G.Hall, J.Fletcher, N.Barron, Butterworth, H.P.Stephenson

21/11/1874   Wigan (Away)   Draw - 2T, 2R v 4R
C.A.Schofield, E.Brown noted in the report. Full Line-Up Not Available

05/12/1874   DINGLE (Home)   Draw - 1T, 4TD v 0
Batty, E.Brown (full backs); R.B.Hartley, N.Barron (¼ backs); F.Hermon, P.M.Hunter (Capt.), C.A.Schofield (backs); A.Andrew, G.Andrew, Bromilow, Coombe, J.Fletcher, G.Hall, Littledale, Pryce, G.F.Schofield, M.Smith, R.W.Smith, H.P.Stephenson, G.A.Thomson (forwards)

12/12/1874   MANCHESTER (Home)   Lost - 0 v 1G, 4T
No Line-Up Available

09/01/1875   MANCHESTER (Home)   Lost - 1T v 4G, 4T, 9TD
No Line-Up Available

16/01/1875   Birkenhead (Away)   Draw - No score
*No Line-Up Available *16 men v 20*

23/01/1875   Dingle (Away)   Draw – No score given
R.W.Smith (Capt.), Coombe, G.Bromilow, C.Bromilow, N.Barron, Batty, J.Fletcher,
H.Brandon, M.Smith, Schofield, R.B.Hartley, A.D.Burnyeat, Lodge, Mussabini, F.Hermon,
H.Greenall, H.P.Stephenson

13/02/1875   WIGAN (Home)   Draw - 7T, several M to 0
No Line-Up Available

27/02/1875   FREE WANDERERS, MANCHESTER (Home)   Lost - 0 v 1G 1T, 1TIG, 2TD
N.Barron, G.Bromilow, R.B.Hartley, E.Brown, J.Brown (backs); G.Hall, Coombe,
G.F.Schofield, Butler, Squires, Smith, Duff, H.P.Stephenson (forwards).

13/03/1875   PENDLETON, MANCHESTER (Home)   Won - 1G 2T, 3TIG, 2QW v 0
R.B.Hartley, Brown, F.Hermon, P.M.Hunter, Walker (backs); Barrow, G.Bromilow,
Coombe, Atkinson, Moseley, G.Nicholson, W.Milner, G.F.Schofield, Littledale,
G.H.Thomas (forwards)

20/03/1875   UNITED SCHOOLS (Home)   Won - 5G, several T v 0
N.Barron, E.Brown, W.Bromilow, G.Bromilow, Coombe, Fenton, G.Hall, P.M.Hunter,
R.B.Hartley, H.V.Pigot, G.F.Schofield, H.P.Stephenson

15 Played - 6 Won, 6 Drawn, 3 Lost

1875-76

7/12/1875 FREE WANDERERS, MANCHESTER (Home) Lost - 1TIG v 1G 1T, 1TD, 1TIG
J.Schofield, J.Fletcher, P.M.Hunter, Clarke, R.B.Hartley, Littledale, G.F.Schofield (Capt.), P.Greenall, Atkinson, Hargreaves, Venelot, G.Bromilow, W.Bromilow, G.Nicholson, S.Lord

11/12/1875 WEST DERBY (Home) Lost - 0 v 2G, 1 R
No Line-Up available

19/12/1875 MANCHESTER (Home) Lost - 0 v 4T, 1PO and "several" TD
Hunter (Capt.), Bromilow, Schofield, Hargreaves and Lodge noted in the report. Full Line-Up Not Available.

24/12/1875 Manchester (Away) Lost - 0 v 3T, 2PO, "several" TD
No Line-Up Available

19/01/1876 Preston Grasshoppers (Away) Lost - 0 v 1G, 4T, 2PO, 2R
No Line-Up Available

05/02/1876 LIVERPOOL (Home) Lost 0 1T 3TD v 1G 1TD
Batty (full back); J.H.Welsby, Farr (¾ backs); R.B.Hartley, H.G.Stock (½ backs); G.Bromilow, C.Bromilow, J.Fletcher, Townsend, Dorning, Muir, Mossley, Hargreaves, Ashworth, G.F.Schofield (Capt.) (forwards)

19/02/1876 Manchester (Away) Lost - 0 v 1G, 2T, 2TD
G.F.Schofield (Capt.), Newton (full backs); Farr, J.H.Welsby (¾ backs); Cox, R.B.Hartley (½ back); G.Bromilow, J.Fletcher, Hargreaves, G.Andrew, A.Andrew, Townsend, Dorning, Moseley, Garforth (forwards)

26/02/1876 Free Wanderers, Manchester (Away) Won - 1TD, 2T to 0
*Played 1 short
P.M.Hunter (Capt.), Anderson, F.Hermon, R.B.Hartley, H.G.Stock, G.Andrew, M. Andrews, H.Brandon, Bromilow, J.Fletcher, G.F.Schofield, W.Milner, D.Munn, J.Sharp.

1876-77

14/10/1876   West Derby (Away)   **Won - 1G v 1T**
No Line-Up Available

21/10/1876   WATERLOO (Home)   **Won - 2G, 1T v 0**
No Line-Up Available

04/11/1876   Liverpool (Away)   **Won - 4G v 0**
E.Walker, T.Walker (full backs); F.Hermon (Capt.), P.M.Hunter (¾ backs); Stockley,
R.B.Hartley (½ backs); G.Darbyshire, Andrews, J.Fletcher, Schofield, H.Arthur, N.Barron,
G.A.Thomson, H.Brandon, W.H.Edwards (forwards)

02/12/1876   BIRKENHEAD (Home)   **Won - 1G v 0**
P.M.Hunter, W.A.Gordon (full backs); F.Hermon (Capt.), G.Bromilow (¾ backs);
R.B.Hartley, H.A.Dixon (½ backs); J.Fletcher, Atkinson, H.Brandon, G.A.Thomson,
G.H.Thomas, G.Hall, Antler, Maysey, A.N.Other (forwards)

09/12/1876   Rock Ferry (Away)   **Won - 1G, 5T v 1T**
*both teams played short (Rock Ferry 3, Southport 2)
P.M.Hunter (full back); F.Hermon (Capt.); E.Walker (¾ backs); R.B.Hartley, W.H.Edwards
(½ backs); J.Fletcher, Bromilow, N.Barron, G.H.Thomas, Ashworth, Schofield, Bateson,
Charleston (forwards)

16/12/1876   Dingle (Away)   **Won - 3G v 0**
P.M.Hunter, W.A.Gordon (full backs); F.Hermon (Capt.) (¾ backs); A.D.Burnyeat,
H.A.Dixon (½ backs); J.Fletcher, Bromilow, H.Brandon, G.H.Thomas, Bateson, H.V.Pigot,
G.A.Thomson, J.Kenyon, Townsend, Charleston

26/12/1876   MANCHESTER (Home)   **Lost - 0 v 1G**
P.M.Hunter, A.Andrew (full backs); F.Hermon, J.H.Welsby (¾ backs); R.B.Hartley,
H.G.Stock (½ backs); H.Daly, G.Bromilow, J.Fletcher, G.F.Schofield, G.Darbishire,
J.Bateson, H.Arthur, H.Brandon, A.Peck (forwards)

13/01/1877   DINGLE (Home)   **Won - 3G, 2T v 0**
P.M.Hunter, Welsby (full backs); F.Hermon (¾ backs); N.Barron, Dixon (½ backs);
G.Darbyshire, A.Fletcher, G.Bromilow, C.Bromilow, H.V.Pigott, A.Peck, G.A.Thomson,
G.H.Thomas, D.Munn, M.Shepherd (forwards)

20/01/1877   Birkenhead (Away)   **Won - 1G, 5T v 0**
W.A.Gordon, P.M.Hunter, (full backs); F.Hermon, H.Boult, (¾ backs); H.A.Dixon,
R.B.Hartley, (½ backs); C.Bromilow, J.Fletcher, G.H.Thomas, G.A.Thompson, J.H.Welsby,
J.Bateson, Barrow (forwards)

27/01/1877   Manchester (Away)   Draw - 3TD, 1TIG v 1TD

A.Andrew, W.A.Gordon (full backs); P.M.Hunter, F.Hermon (¾ backs); R.B.Hartley,
W.Dixon (½ backs); G.Darybshire, G.Andrew, G.Bromilow, G.A.Thomson, G.H.Thomas,
J.Fletcher, C.Bromilow, W.H.Edwards, A.Peck (forwards)

03/02/1877   ALDERLEY (Home)   Won - 1G, 7T v 0

P.M.Hunter, G.Schofield (full backs); J.H.Welsby, F.Hermon (¾ backs); R.B.Hartley,
H.A.Dixon (½ backs); J.Fletcher, G.Bromilow, A.Peck, N.Barron, H.Daly, H.Brandon,
G.H.Thomas, A.Fletcher, H.Forshaw (forwards)

10/02/1877   Waterloo (Away)   Won - 1G, 1T, 1TD v 0

G.F.Schofield (full backs); P.M.Hunter (Capt.), C.Bromilow (¾ backs); R.B.Hartley,
H.Brandon (½ backs); J.Fletcher, G.A.Thomson, G.Bromilow, N. Barron, G.H.Thomas,
J.Dalglish, Richardson, Ashworth, J.Kenyon (forwards)

17/02/1877   LIVERPOOL (Home)   Won - 1G, 1T(disputed), 2TD v 0

W.A.Gordon, G.F.Schofield (full backs); F.Hermon (Capt.), G.Bromilow (¾ backs);
H.A.Dixon, R.B.Hartley (½ backs); J.Fletcher, G.Andrew, N.Barron, G.A.Thomson,
G.H.Thomas, C.Bromilow, A.Peck, H.Calder, H.Forshaw (forwards)

24/02/1877   WEST DERBY (Home)   Won - 2T, 10TD v 0

W.A.Gordon, A.Andrew (full backs); F.Hermon (Capt.), R.Jones (¾ backs); R.B.Hartley,
H.A.Dixon (½ backs); G.Bromilow, C.Bromilow, J.Fletcher, G.A.Thomson, N.Barron,
G.H.Thomas, H.Daly, A.Peck, R.Parton (forwards)

24/03/1877   FREE WANDERERS, MANCHESTER (Home)   Won - 1T v 0

A.Andrew (full backs); F.Hermon (Capt.), G.Bromilow) (¾ backs); R.B.Hartley, French (½
backs); J.Fletcher, G.Darbyshire, G.F.Schofield, G.H.Thomas, N.Barron, H.Daly,
C.Bromilow, A.Peck (forwards)

15 Played - 13 Won, 1 Draw, 1 Lost
Scored (for) 15 Goals, 26 Tries, 49 Touchdowns
Scored (against), 1 goal, 2 tries, 5 touch downs

1877/78

20/10/1877   Birkenhead Park (Away)   Won - 2T v 0
W.A.Gordon (full backs); J.H.Welsby, F.Hermon (¾ backs); H.A.Dixon, G.Nicholson (½ backs); G.F.Schofield (Capt.), G.Andrew, G.Bromilow, A.Peck, H.Daly, G.H.Thomas, A.Dickson, H.Brandon, G.A.Thomson, A.K.Cannington (forwards)

03/11/1877   LIVERPOOL (Away)   Won - 1G, 2T v 0
W.A.Gordon, G.Nicholson (full backs); F.Hermon, G.H.Stack (¾ backs); R.Hartley, W.A.Dixon (½ backs); G.Schofield (Capt.), G.Bromilow, W.Hunt, H.Daly, H.Brandon, A.Andrews, G.Andrews, A.K.Cannington, H.Forshaw (forwards)

10/11/1877   WEST DERBY (Home)   Won - 1G v 0
C.Baldwin, J.Arthur (full backs); H.G.Stock, G.Nicholson (¾ backs); H.A.Dixon, R.B.Hartley (½ backs); G.F.Schofield (Capt.), G.Bromilow, J.Fletcher, A.Peck, A.Dickson, J.Sharp, H.Daly, M.Sheppard, A.K.Cannington (forwards)

17/11/1877   NEW BRIGHTON (Home)   Won - 4T, 3TD v 0
G.F.Schofield, A.Dickson (full backs); G.Bromilow, C.Baldwin (¾ backs); R.B.Hartley, H.A.Dixon (½ backs); G.Andrew, A.Peck, G.Thomas, H.Daly, S.Russell, M.Sheppard, J.Sharp, Gardiner, H.Wright (forwards)

24/11/1877   MANCHESTER (Home)   Won - 1G v 0
W.A.Gordon, A.Andrew (full backs); F.Hermon, G.Nicholson (¾ backs); H.G.Stock, H.A.Dixon (½ backs); G.F.Schofield, G.Darbishire, Bromilow, G.Andrew, H.Brandon, S.Russell, H.Daly, A.Peck, H.Forshaw (forwards)

05/01/1878   LIVERPOOL (Home)   Draw in favour of Liverpool
Moore, W.A.Gordon (full backs); F.Hermon, Kidson (¾ backs); H.G.Stock, H.A.Dixon (½ backs); Schofield, Andrew, Bromilow, H.Daly, J.Fletcher, A.Peck, Woods, Bury, H.Forshaw (forwards)

12/01/1878   Manchester (Away)   Lost - 0 v 1T
*Southport a man short
W.A.Gordon, A.Moore (full backs); G.Nicholson, G.Bromilow (¾ backs); H.G.Stock, H.A.Dixon (½ backs); G.F.Schofield (Capt.); J.Fletcher, S.Russell, Daly, C.Bromilow, A.Bean, J.Sharp, W.Milner (forwards)

26/01/1878   Preston (Away)   Lost - 0 v 2T
A.C.Dickson, W.A.Gordon (full backs); J.Arkle, G.Nicholson (¾ backs); W.Connington, H.A.Dixon (½ backs); A.Bean, G.Bromilow, H.Daly, J.Fletcher, J.Graham, M.Sheppard, G.Stokes, H.Wright (forwards)

09/02/1878   BIRKENHEAD (Home)   Won - 1T 4TD 1TIG v 0
A.C.Dickson, C.Baldwin (full backs); G.Nicholson, Shaw (¾ backs); H.A.Dixon, H.G.Stock (½ backs); Bromilow, J.Fletcher, H.Brandon, H.Daly, A.Bean, M.Sheppard, Richardson, Petrie, H.Lockhart (forwards)

1878/79

12/10/1878   Liverpool (Away)   Won - 3G,21T,3TD v 1T
Scratch team arranged by G.F.Schofield (Southport) v a Scratch team arranged by W.Edwards (Liverpool)
W.A.Gordon, Heyworth (full backs); Shaw (¾ backs); G.Nicholson, H.A.Dixon (½ backs); H.Forshaw, D.Cameron, S.Allen, H.Daly, J.Walsh, Mason, G.A.Thomson, H. Boult, M.Sheppard, Ross (forwards)

19/10/1878   NEW BRIGHTON (Home)   Won - 3T, 4TD v 0
P.M.Hunter, W.A.Gordon (full backs); G.Nicholson, F.Jones (¾ backs); H.A.Dixon (Capt.), R.A.Percival (½ backs); H.Forshaw, G.Bromilow, G.A.Thomson, J.Walsh, A.K.Cannington, H.Daly, P.Chadwick, M.Sheppard (forwards)

26/10/1878   Southport Wasps (Away)   Won - 3G, 6T, 7TD v 0
A.Crippell, P.Stingles (full backs); G.Nicholson, J.B.Keyworth (¾ backs); H.A.Dixon (Capt.), R.A.Percival (½ backs); Bromilow, D.Cameron, R.Chadwick, Mason, H.B.Bateson, S.Allen, M.Sheppard, Palmer, J.Walsh (forwards)

02/11/1878   Birkenhead Park (Away)   Won - 1G, 1T v 1G
W.A.Gordon, J.B.Keyworth (full backs); G.Nicholson, H.Jones (¾ backs); W.A.Dixon, A.K.Cannington (½ backs); G.Bromilow, D.Cameron, A.Bean, G.A.Thomson, H.Forshaw, H.B.Bateson, H.Lockhart, W.B.Bateson (forwards)

16/11/1878   Free Wanderers Manchester (Away)   Lost - 1T, 2 TD, v 2G, 1T 4TD
W.A.Gordon, C.Cleaver (full backs); G.Nicholson, J.B.Keyworth (¾ backs); H.A.Dixon (Capt.); H.Boult (½ backs); G.Bromilow, A.F.Houlder, H.Daly, A.Bean, R.Chadwick, W.H.Edwards, H.Lockhart, H.B.Bateson, A.D.Burnyeat (forwards)

23/11/1878   MANCHESTER (Home)   Lost - 1T, 2TD v 2G, 1T, 4TD
W.A.Gordon, C.Cleaver (full backs); G.Nicholson, J.B.Keyworth (¾ backs); H.A.Dixon (Capt.), H.Boult (½ backs); G.Bromilow, A.F.Houlder, H.Daly, A.Bean, R.Chadwick, W.H.Edwards, H.Lockheart, W.B.Bateson, A.D.Burnyeat (forwards)

The original Football Club did not re-emerge after the Winter of 1878/79. Southport Wasps chose to play the following season under the name Southport Football Club.

1879/80

*This was Southport Wasps playing under the name of Southport Football Club

01/11/1879   Rochdale Hornets (Away)   Lost - 0 v 1G, 4T, 6TD
*14 men
J.Eastham (full back); J.Saxton, C.Harbey (¾ backs); C.Rigg, H.Braund (½ backs);
J.H.White (Capt.), F.M.Scott, L.Johnson, V.Mart, J.Hollis, B.Marshall, T.Sykes,
H.W.Sheard, J.G.Howard (forwards)

01/12/1879   BREIGHTMET (Home)   Lost - 0 v 1G, 4T, 5TD
H.Lloyd, J. Eastham (full backs); J.Saxton, H.Latimer (¾ backs); C.Rigg, H.Braund (½
backs); J.H.White (Capt.), Howell, L.Johnson, H.Gregory, Chadwick, J.G.Howard,
H.White, Hall, W.Rigg (forwards)

03/01/1880   PAST V PRESENT   Draw - 1G 2T v 1G 2T
No Line-Up available

17/01/1880   Walton (Away)   Lost - 1M v 4G, 2T, 6M
*played 13 men
J.Eastham, Smith (full backs); H.Gregory, Blyth (¾ backs); L.Johnson, Parry (½ backs);
J.G.Howard, Hollis, Platt, T.Sykes, H.White, Cruickshank, A.White (forwards)

07/02/1880   WALTON (Home)   Win - 0 v 1T, 1TIG, 3TD
H.Gregory, L.Johnson, T.Sykes, J.H.White, A.Peck, Scott, Lloyd noted in the report. Full
Line-Up Not Available.

14/02/1880   Walton (Away)   Won - 1T 1TIG 3TD v 0
C.Heap, H.Gregory, L.Johnson, T.Sykes, J.H.White, A.Peck, Scott, Lloyd noted in the
report. Full Line-Up Not Available.

21/02/1880   Southport Olympic (Away)   Lost - 0 v 1G, 1TIG, 7TD
Bromilow (full back); J.Hulse, W.C.Berkely (3/4 backs); J.Hall, T.Sykes (1/2 backs);
A.Greenwood, C.Nicholson, F.Bracewell, B.Bracewell, P.Chadwick, C.W.Brown, W.Platt,
P.Thursby, Hollis, E.Ramsbottom

06/03/1880   BROUGHTON 'A' (Home)   Lost - 0 v 2G, 2T, 1TIG
No Line-Up Available

27/03/1880   Rochdale Hornets (Lathom Hall)   Lost - 0 v 2G, 3T, 6TD
*Invited by Club President Lord Skelmersdale to play at his Lathom Hall residence
F.Curry (full back); J.Saxton, A.B.Schofield (3/4 backs); Gregory, L.E.Johnson (1/2 backs);
Howard (Capt.), Peck, W.Platt, Sheard, Sykes, J.Eastham, E.Wilbraham, Howell
(forwards)

Southport Football Club did not arrange fixtures for 1880-81.

1881/82

01/10/1881   Bootle Wasps (Away)   Lost - 0 v 3G, 8T
T.B.Burnett (full back); A.J.Ross, J.Melross, S.Platt (¾ backs); W.H.Gregory,
J.B.Richardson (½ backs); Gaskell, W.Platt (Capt.), F.Jackson, F.Hockley, Nelson, J.Sykes,
J.R.Topliss, J.H.Hollis, W. Hatch (forwards)
*W.Platt arrived at Half Time

15/10/1881   WAVERTREE (Home)   Lost - 0 v 2T, 7TD, 1T (disputed)
Ball, A.J.Ross, Seddon, J.Melross, Hobson, Barrow, W.Platt (Capt.), J.Sykes, Rimmer,
S.Platt, Pidduck, Topliss, Baxter, Jackson, Robinson

29/10/1881   Bootle (Away)   Lost - 0 v 1G, 8T, 11M
W.Platt (full back); A.J. Ross, H.M.Smith, Hobson (¾ backs); J.B.Richardson, Gregson (½
backs); S.Platt, Buggins, J.G. Howard, F.Jackson, Hall, T.B.Burnett, P.Edwards (forwards)

Fixtures were scheduled as follows but No further Rugby Fixtures were played.

08/10/1881	**LIVERPOOL OLD BOYS (Away)**
05/11/1881	**EVERTON VALLEY (Away)**
12/11/1881	**BOOTLE WASPS (Home)**
19/11/1881	**LIVERPOOL RANGERS (Home)**
24/12/1881	**BOOTLE (Away)**
31/12/1881	**RESISTENCE - LIVERPOOL (Home)**
07/01/1882	**WAVERTREE (Away)**
14/01/1882	**TOXTETH ATHLETIC (Home)**
28/01/1882	**LIVERPOOL OLD BOYS (Home)**
04/02/1882	**TOXTETH ATHLETIC (Away)**
18/02/1882	**LIVERPOOL RANGERS (Away)**
23/02/1882	**EVERTON VALLEY (Home)**
04/03/1882	**WHALLEY RANGE (Away)**
18/03/1882	**RESISTENCE - LIVERPOOL (Away)**
25/03/1882	**WHALLEY RANGE (Home)**
10/04/1882	**ROCHDALE HORNETS 'A'**

261

Southport Wasps (Rugby)

1877/78

6/10/1877   CROSBY (Home)   **Draw - 1G, 5T, 2TD v 1G**
No Line-Up Available

20/10/1877   Bootle Wanderers (Away)   **Lost - Score Unknown**
*13 men.
Hollis; C.Harvey, C.Tuckness (¾ backs); W.Platt, L.E.Johnson (½ backs); J.G.Howard,
W.H.Crabtree, E.S.Harper, Eccles, G.Lloyd, Hudson, R.Dixon, Broome (forwards)

3/11/1877   Preston Ramblers (Away)   **Lost - 1TD v 3T, 4 TD**
No Line-Up Available

10/11/1877   Church of England Temperance FC (Away)   Lost - Score Unknown
J.O.Gatley (full back); C.Harvey, J.Eastham (¾ backs); C.Rigg, C.Tuckness (½ backs);
J.Bargh (Capt.), J.G.Howard, W.H.Crabtree, L.E.Johnson, R.Dixon, W.Platt, R.Segar,
G.M.Smith (forwards)

10/11/1877   Sandringham Schools (Away)   **Lost - 0 v 1G, 2T, 2TD**
No Line-Up Available

24/11/1877   LITHERLAND (Home)   **Won - 0 v 1T,6TD**
No Line-Up Available

8/12/1877   FAIRFIELD (Home)   **Won - 3G 4TD v 1T 1TD**
No Line-Up Available

15/12/1877   EDGREMONT WANDERERS (Home)   **Lost - 2T 6TD 1 TIG v 1G**
No Line-Up Available

12/02/1878   LIVERPOOL WANDERERS (Home)   **Won - 1G, 2TD v 0**
T.Sykes, Shaw (full backs); C.Harvey, Fletcher (¾ backs); L.E.Johnson, W.H.Gregory (½
backs); J.Bargh, J.G.Howard, E.S.Harper, G.Lloyd, W.H.Crabtree, J.Eastham, Roscoe,
Banks, E.Dixon (forwards)

26/02/1878   LITHERLAND (Home)   **Won - 1G, 3T, 6TD, 1TIG, 1DB v 0**
H.Gregory, J.Eastham (full backs); C.T.Baldwin, T.Sykes (¾ backs); Warburton,
W.H.Gregory (½ backs); J.Bargh, J.G.Howard, G.Lloyd, W.H.Crabtree, P.Chadwick,
L.E.Johnson, E.S.Harper, E.Dixon, G.M.Smith (forwards)

05/03/1878   ST HELENS (Home)   **Won - 1G, 1 Poster, 5T,4TD 1TIG v 0**
No Line-Up Available

12/03/1878   PRESTON ROVERS (Home)   Won - 1T, 7TD v 1T
No Line-Up Available

19/03/1878   FAIRFIELD (Home)   Lost - 0 v 1T, 5TD, 1DB
T.Sykes, E.Dickson (full backs); T.Smith, C.Harvey (¾ backs); L.E.Johnson, Finner (½ backs); J.Bargh, G.Howard, W.Platt, G.Lloyd, W.H.Crabtree, E.S.Harper, G.M.Smith, J.Eastham (forwards)

26/03/1878   FAIRFIELD WANDERERS (Home)   Won - 1G v 1TD
Match abandoned at half time due to protest from visiting team
No Line-Up Available

02/04/1878   ROCHDALE HORNETS (Home)   Lost - 1TD v 2G, 4T. 2TD
*No Line-Up Available * 12 Men*

1878/79

05/10/1878   WALTON (Home)   Draw - 1 TD v 2TD
*T.Sykes, C.C.Harvey (full backs); J.Thompson, J.H.Kidson (¾ backs); F.W.Schofield,
L.E.Johnson (½ backs); P.Chadwick, C.Heap, E.Dixon, E.S.Harper, W.Platt, G.Lloyd,
J.Saxton, F.Finney (forwards)*

12/10/1878   Liverpool Wanderers (Away)   Lost - 0 v 1G, 3T
*J.O.Gatley, P.Edwards (full backs); C.E.Thompson, J.Eastham (¾ backs); L.E.Johnson,
H.Thompson (½ backs); J.Howard, E.Dixon, F.Fynney, W.Platt, E.S.Harper, G.M.Smith,
F.H.Dewes (forwards)*

19/10/1878   Preston Rovers (Away)   Lost - 0 v 3T, Several TD
*No Line-Up Available * 4 men short*

26/10/1878   SOUTHPORT (Home)   Lost - 0 v 3G, 6T, 7TD
*J.O.Gatley, C.C.Harvey (full backs); J.Eastham, A.Irving (¾ backs); L.E.Johnson,
W.H.Gregory (½ backs); J.Howard, Bargh, E.Dixon, W.Platt, C.Heap, G.M.Smith,
E.S.Harper, Tuckness, Mayow*

02/11/1878   Rochdale Hornets (Away)   Lost - 0 v 2G, 5T, 6TD
*W.T.Gateley, E.Brunskill (full backs); C.C.Harvey, E.Fynney (¾ backs); L.E.Johnson (Capt.),
T.Smith (½ backs); J.Howard, J.Eastham, W.Platt, E.Dixon, G.M.Smith, G.D.Robinson,
A.Smith, J.Saxton, E.S.Harper (forwards)*

23/11/1878   BLACKBURN (Home)   Won - 1G, 3T, 3DB, 5TD v 0
*T.Sykes (full back); C.E.Thompson, C.C.Harvey (¾ backs); T.Smith, L.E.Johnson (½ backs);
J.Bargh (Capt), J.G.Howard, J.Eastham, G.Lloyd, W.Platt, F.Fynney, G.M.Smith, J.Saxton,
ASmith, H.Smith*

30/11/1878   Broughton (Away)   Lost - 3TD v 1T, 3TD
No Line-up available

29/03/1879   ROCHDALE HORNETS (Home)   Lost - 1DB v 3T, Many M, 1DB
*No-Line Up available. Wasps had the assistance of the "Leading players of the Southport
Club"*

1883/84

24/11/1883   **HIGH PARK GRASSHOPPERS (Home)**
Not Reported

1/12/1883   **Birkdale (Away)**
Not Reported

29/12/1883   **SEAFORTH (Home)**   **Draw**
H.Blundell (full back);C.Blundell, H.Robinson (Capt.), T.Rimmer (¾ backs); Rigby, Oliver (½ backs); A.Corfield, Webster, F.Ball, R.Ball, J.Wright, P.Barton, R.Rimmer, Coventry, V.Flashingram (forwards)

05/01/1884   **BIRKDALE (Home)**   **Lost - 1G, 1TD v 1G,1T,6TD,2DB, 1TIG**
Traveloni, Webster noted in the report. Full Line-Up Not Available.

23/02/1884   **Southport Olympic 2ⁿᵈ (Away)**   **Draw - 1G, 3M v 1G,1T,8M**
R.Ball (full back); H.Robinson (Capt.), P.Barton, W.Wareing (¾ backs); C.Ellis, H.Spencer, (½ backs); J.Wright, J.Binks, W.Rigby, S.Eastham, R.Thompson, J.Gregson, E.Webster, R.Rimmer, H.Blundell (forwards)

15/03/1884   **SOUTHPORT ROVERS (Home)**   **Won - 1G v 0**
*Association Rules
Spender (Goal); H.Robinson, J.Gregson (backs); H.Deacon, W.Wareing, R.Rimmer (half back); Eastham, E.Williamson, Whittaker, J.Binks, J.Traveloni (Capt.)

1884/85

27/09/1884   New Brighton Victoria (Away)   Lost - 0 - 2T,5M
W.Lowe (full back); H.Robinson (Capt.), F.Ball (¾ backs); C.F.Ellis, J.W.Caveny (½ backs); A.Corfield, R.Ball, J.Wright, A.Rimmer, J.Binks, J.Howard, J.Rimmer, V.Rogers, J.Gregson (forwards)

04/10/1884   Litherland (Away)   Draw - 2M v 2M
A.Corfield (back); H.Robinson (Capt), S.G.Oliver, F.Ball (¾ backs); C.F.Ellis, J.W.Caveny (½ backs); R.Ball, J.Rimmer, J.Howard, V.Rogers, A.Rimmer, T.Eastham,W.Ribye, H.Wainwright,J.Hesketh (forwards)

18/10/1884   Edge Hill (Away)   Lost - 3M v 1T,2M
R.Ball (full back); H.Robinson, A.Corfield, F.Bell (¾ backs); J.Atherton, W.Rigby (½ backs); J.Binks, H.Thompson, J.Wright, W.Wareing, J.Rigbye, V.Rogers, J.Gregson, T.Eastham (forwards)

25/10/1884   SEAFORTH (Home)   Won - 1G,4M v 3M
F.Ball (full back); H.Robinson (Capt), W.Hayes, P.Barton (¾ backs); J.W.Caveny, W.Rigbye (½ backs); J.Binks, J.Wright, V.Rogers, R.Ball, R.Thompson, J.Rimmer, J.Gregson, W.Wareing (forwards)

01/11/1884   WIGAN NORTH END (Home)   Draw - 10M v 1TD
F.Ball (full back); H.Robinson (Capt), P.Barton, A.Corfield (¾ backs); J.W.Caveny, W.Rigby (½ backs); R.Binks, J.Wright, V.Rogers, J.Binks, J.Rimmer, J.Howard, A.Rimmer, J.Rigbye, R.Rimmer (forwards)

15/11/1884   Walton A (Away)   Lost - 0 v 2G,2T,17M
W.Wareing (full back); F.Ball, H.Robinson (Capt), W.Holmes (¾ backs); J.W.Caveny, R.Thompson (½ backs); C.F.Ellis, J.Rimmer, J.Howard, R.Ball, J.Binks, A.Sumner, E.Binks, V.Rogers, W.Ashall (forwards)

13/12/1884   LITHERLAND 2ⁿᵈ (Home)   Won - 2T, 6M v 0
F.Ball (full back); H.Robinson (Capt.), R.Blundell, J.Rigbye (¾ backs); W.Rigbye, R.Thompson (½ backs); C.F.Ellis, J.Rimmer, R.Rimmer, J.Howard, J.Binks, V.Rogers, A.rimmer, R.Ball, W.Wareing (forwards)

25/12/1884   BIRKDALE FREE WANDERERS (Home)   Lost - 5M v 1T, 6M
F.Ball (full back); H.Robinson, R.Blundell, Hayes (¾ backs); W.Rigby,R.Thompson (½ backs); A.Courfield, Binks, Wareing, A.Rimmer, Summers, Howard, Rogers, R.Ball, Rigby (forwards)

01/01/1885   CRAWFORD (Home)   Draw - 1T, 4M v 1T, 4M
F.Ball (full back); H.Robinson (Capt.), R.Blundell, W.Brewer (¾ backs); A.Cornfield,
H.Thompson (½ backs); J.Binks, W.Wareing, T.Brown, R.Binks, A.Rimmer, A.Sumner,
R.Rimmer, R.Ball, R.Binks (forwards)

31/01/1885   MR J.W.REID'S TEAM (Home)   Won - 1T, 11M v 1T, 1M
F.Ball (full back); H.Robinson (Capt.), R.Blundell, A.Corfield (¾ backs); W.Rigby,
R.Thompson, (½ backs); J.Binks, R.Ball, J.Howard, J..Rimmer, J.Gregson, W.Wareing,
R.Rimmer, A.Sumner, C.F.Ellis (forwards)

07/02/1885   Birkenhead Rangers (Away)   Draw - 1T, 6M v 1T,6M
F.Ball (full back); H.Robinson (Capt), R.Blundell, A.Corfield (¾ backs); W.Rigby, J.Rigby
(½ backs); R.Ball, J.Wright, A.Rimmer, J.Gregson, J.Rimmer, J.Binks, W.Wareing,
R.Rimmer, C.F.Ellis (forwards)

14/02/1885   Birkdale Free Wanderers (Away)   Draw - 2M v 2M
C.F.Ellis (full back); W.Robinson (Capt.), R.Blundell, A.Corfield (¾ backs); W.Rigby,
J.Rigby (½ backs); R.Ball, J.Leigh, T.Eastham, G.Binks, R.Rimmer, J.Wright, A.Rimmer,
J.Howard, B.Rogers (forwards)

21/02/1885   Pagefield 2nd (Away)   Lost - 0 v 2T
No Line-up available

28/02/1885   HAIGH (Home)   Lost - 2M v 5M
No Line-up available

18/04/1885   Southport Olympic 2nd (Away)   Lost - 2M v 2T, 2M
F.Ball (full back); H.Robinson (Capt), W.Mason, F.Barton (¾ backs); J.Rigby, A.Corfield(½
backs); Bell, Neville, Harrison, Blundell, Mason, Parry, Abrams, Coupar, Gregory
(forwards)

Southport Hornets (Rugby)

1879/80

10/01/1880   Southport Grasshoppers (Away)   Win - 1G, 1TD v 1T, 4TD
H.Aughton, J.Salisbury (full backs); Dickenson (Capt.), Dalby, Sawyer (¾ backs);
H.Roberts, A.Dickinson (½ backs); Robinson, Halsall, Ivy, Grover, Bowman, Holt, Rimmer,
Jervis (forwards)

17/01/1880   BURY (Home)   Won - 3T,4TD v 1T, 1TD
H.Aughton (full back); R.E.Dickinson (Capt.), N.Howard, J.Sawyer (¾ backs); H.Roberts,
A.Dickinson (½ backs); W.Robinson, C.Watt, J.Halsall, W.Glover, J.Jervis, J.Salisbury,
R.S.Ivy (forwards)

07/02/1880   Lancashire Independent College (Away)   Lost - 1TIG, 1 DB v 1G
1"Poster", 4T, 5TD, 5DB
No Line-up given

1880/81

2/10/1880   BOOTLE (Home)   Won - 1G 1T v 3TD
H.Aughton (full back); J.Sawyer, Johnson, Salisbury, (3/4 backs); H.Smith, A.Dickenson. (1/2 backs); W.Robinson (Capt.), Glover, Mills, Tunstall, Thompson, Lodge, Dalby, Melross, Wainwright (forwards)

16/11/1880   ST LUKES (Home)   Won - 2T, 1TIG, 8TD v 0
Tunstall (full back); R.Dickenson, A.Dickenson, Aughton (3/4 backs); Mason, Dalby (1/2 backs); Halsall, Lodge, Boyd, Topliss, Glover, Bowman, Buckley, Jervis, Morris (forwards)

07/12/1880   BURY (Home)   Lost - 1T, 2TD, 1TIG v 2T, 2TD, 1DB
F.Jackson (full back); A.Irving, R.Dickenson, H.A.Smith (3/4 backs); W.Robinson (Capt.), A.Dickenson (1/2 backs); Lodge, Halsall, Glover, Watt, Aughton, Mason, Thomson, Boyd, Topliss (forwards)

12/03/1881   ST NICHOLAS' BLUNDELLSANDS (Home)   Won - 3G,1T,1DB, Several TD v 0
Tunstall, Irving (Capt.), R.Dickinson, Aughton (¾ backs); A. Dickinson, H.Roberts (½ backs); Lodge, Halsall, Thompson, Jervis, Topliss, Melross, C.Bimpson, Bown, Milnes (forwards)

28/03/1881   Walmsley (Away)   Lost - 1T v 2T,4TD, 4 TIG
Tunstall (full back); Chappell, A.Irving (Capt.), R.Dickinson (¾ backs); Aughton, Wright (½ backs); Halsall, Boyd, Thomson, Watt, Hockley, Lawton, Tattersall, Melross, Topliss, Roberts (forwards)

1881/82

01/10/1881   BOOTLE (Away)   **Lost - Score Unknown**
No Line-up available

08/10/1881   WALMERSLEY (Home)   **Lost - 1G, 2T, several M to 0**
*played one man short after half time
A.Dickenson (full back), Ambler, A.Irving (capt), R.E.Dickenson (¾ backs); Ellerby, Milnes
(½ backs); Tunstall, Jervis, Lodge, Thomson, Lloyd, Anderton, Boyd, Holt, Bimpson
(forwards)

29/10/1881   WIDNES WASPS (Home)   **Won - 1G, 2T, 4M to 2TD**
A.Dickenson (full back), A.Irving, A.Dalby, R.E.Dickenson (¾ backs); Milnes, T.Morris (½
backs); Lloyd, Atherton, Thomson, Bimpson, Wignall, Cragg, Salisbury, Bowman
(forwards)

05/11/1881   Liverpool Rangers (Away)   **Lost - 1G, 1 T, 4TD v 1 TD**
A.Irving (Capt.) (full back); A.Dalby, W.Tunstall (¾ backs); S.Cragg, J.Lloyd (½ backs);
W.Anderton, C.Watt, S.Thompson, T.Pidduck, J.Bowman, Cadwell (forwards)

12/11/1881   CRESCENT WANDERERS (Home)   Lost - 2T, 3M v 1TD
R.Milner (full back); A.Irving (Capt.), Arthur Dalby, R.E.Dickenson (¾ backs); J.Lloyd,
Alf.Dalby (½ backs); M Boyd, Bimpson, Tunstall, Thomson, Jervis, Cragg, T.Halsall,
Morris, Bowman (forwards)

19/11/1881   Everton Valley (Away)
Everton Valley did not show, despite Hornets travelling to Stanley Park for the fixture

26/11/1881   ST HELENS RANGERS (Home)   Won - 1T, 1TD, 2DB v 2DB
R.Milnes (full back); A.Irving (Capt.), R.E.Dickenson, Arthur Dalby (¾ backs); J.Lloyd, Alf.
Dalby (½ backs); S.Cragg, W.Anderton, J.Bowman, S.Thomson, C.Bimpson, M.Boyd,
T.Pidduck, W.H.Jervis, G.Lodge (forwards)

29/12/1881   J. G. HOWARD'S SCRATCH TEAM (Home)   Won - 2G, 7T, 9M v 1TD
A.Dickenson (full back); A.Irving (Capt.), Dalby, R.E.Dickenson (¾ backs); Dalby, Morris
(½ backs); Anderton, Lloyd, Jervis, A.Ball, Bimpson, Jones, Thomson, Holland, Fish
(forwards)

31/12/1881   BOOTLE (Home)   **Lost - 1T, 1TD v 1G 1T Several M**
A.Dickenson (full back); A.Irving (Capt.), R.E.Dickenson, A.Ball (¾ backs); A.Dalby,
J.Halsall (½ backs); Anderton, Thomson, Lodge, Cragg, Jervis, Lloyd, J.G.Howard,
Bowman, Bimpson (forwards)

07/01/1882   Widnes Wasps (Away)   Lost - 0 v 3T, 2TD
A.Dickenson (full back); A.Irving (Capt.), A.Dalby, T.Pidduck (¾ backs); J.Lloyd, W.H.Jervis (½ backs); Anderton, Collins, Sellars, Boyd, Jones, Thomson, Ripley, Bowman, Bimpson (forwards)

18/02/1882   HIGHFIELD (Home)   Lost - 1T, 1TD, 1 DB v 1TD, 2 TIG
No Line-up given

22/04/1882   Southport Olympic (Away)   Lost - 0 v 1G, 1T, 8M
Arthur Dalby, Andrew Irving, Alfred Wright, Anderton, Alfred Dalby, T.Sellers noted in the report. Full Line-Up Not Available.

1882/83

28/10/1882   **BOOTLE (Home)**   **Draw - No score given**
Sellars (full back); Hoban, Wignall, T.Rimmer (¾ backs); W.Sykes, Smith, Tasker, Wilgoose, Bimpson, W.Ball, G.Ball, Tunstall, Cadwill (forwards)

25/11/1882   **Tranmere (Away)**   **Draw - 1T, 1TD v 2TD**
T.Sellars (full back); J. Hoban, H.Wignall (¾ backs); S.Cragg, T.Rimmer (½ backs); Tunstall, Singleton, Pidduck (Capt.), W.Sykes, Jones, Cadwell, Bimpson, W.Dickenson, W.Wilgoose (forwards)

10/03/1883   **Formby (Away)**   **Lost - 4Tv 1G 1T**
No line-up available

24/03/1883   **Bury (Away)**   **Lost - 2M v 1G 1T 4M**
No line-up available

Southport (Rugby) Football Club - 2

1882/83

18/11/1882   LITHERLAND (Home)   Result Unknown
T.Forde (full back); J.Hall, W.Gregory, J. Fairrie (¾ backs); W.Woods, W.Clarke (½ backs); F.Baildon, J.H.Bracewell (Capt.), P.Chadwick, Heywood, J.Moore, D.Munn, A.Peck, H.S.Rheam, P.Rheam (forwards)

13/01/1883   Manchester (Away)   Lost - 10Tv 1TD
*14men
T.Forde (full back); H.Wall, J.Fairrie, W.Clarke (¾ backs); J.Woods, Heywood (½ backs); G.Bromilow (Capt.), W.Bromilow, D.Munn, J.Munn, H.S.Rheam, P.Rheam, C.Cannon, J.H.Bracewell (forwards)

03/03/1883   Liverpool (Away)   Lost - 0 v 6G, 1 Poster, 2T
*14men
H.Watson (full back); J.Fairrie, J.Hall, W.Rigg (¾ backs); Heywood, F.E.Bracewell (½ backs); S.Sellars, H.Rheam, N.Rheam, C.Cannon, C.Phillips, T.Forde, J.H.Bracewell (Capt.) (forwards)

31/03/1883   Liverpool (Away)   Lost - 0 v 6G, 1 Poster, 2T
H.Watson (full back); J.Fairrie, J.Hall, W.Rigg (3/4 backs); Heywood, F.E.Bracewell (1/2 backs); S.Sellars, H.Rheam, N.Rheam, C.Cannon, C.Phillips, T.Forde, J.H.Bracewell (Capt.), J.Berwick (forwards)

1883/84

29/09/1883   PRESTON GRASSHOPPERS (Home) Lost - 5G 8T v 0
No Line-Up Available

06/10/1883   Liverpool Gymnasium (Away)   Lost - 1G 2M v 5G 2M
T. Newton (full back); W.J. Rigg, Madge, W.Gregory (3/4 backs); W.Clarke, A. Stelfox
(1/2 backs); H.S.Rheam, W.S.Rheam, T.A.Fords (Capt.), Shorrock, H. Havilar,
W.Robisnon, Heywood, Graham, Cunningham

17/11/1883   Liverpool (Away)   Lost - 1T v 5G
Stelfox (full back); Rigg, J.Hulse, Clarke (3/4 backs); Woods, Heywood (1/2 backs); Fords,
H.S.Rheam, Cumminds, Havilar, W.S.Rheam, Wilson, Formby, Mocatto (forwards)

24/11/1883   SALFORD (Home)   Lost - 4G 8T v 0
No Line-Up Available

08/12/1883   LIVERPOOL GYMNASIUM (Home)   Lost - 1T 1M v 3T 3M
Hornby, Watson (full backs); W.J.Rigg, A.E.Tunstall, J.C.Connolly (3/4 backs); W.Woods,
H.Heywood (1/2 backs); T.A.H.Forde (Capt.), C.Phillips, A.Jepson, J.Dickinson,
P.Chadwick, W.Havilar,H.S.Rheam, W.Gregory, J.Fairrie (forwards)

05/01/1884   New Brighton (Away)   Lost - 0 v 4G, 9T, 5M
*arrived with only 11 men
Connolly (full back); W.Rigg, T.S.Hughes (¾ backs); Heywood, Cox (½ backs); H.S.Rheam
(Capt.), W.S.Rheam, W.Clarke, B.Clarke, Formby, Cummings, McMillan, Cowper
(forwards)

26/01/1884   Liverpool Old Boys (Away)   Lost - 0 v 1G, 3T
Clements (full back); Farris, Sykes (3.4 backs); Heywood, Rigg (1/2 backs); H.S.Rheam
(Capt.), W.Rheam, Cumminga, Thompson, Roberts, Jones, R.Bell (forwards)

Southport Olympic (Rugby)

1875/76

21/10/1875   FRESHFIELD COLLEGE (Home)   Draw - 2 byes, 21TD v 0
Thompson, Farrow (full backs); Hindle (¾ backs); J.Eastham, Galley (½ backs); E.S.Harper (Capt.), Crabtree, Smith, Edwards, Platt, Thomas, Tunstall, G.R.Duxfield, Davies, Smith (forwards)

30/10/1875   Bickerton House (Away)   Draw - 1G. 2 bye, 4TD v 1G, 1 bye, 2TD
No Line-Up Available

11/12/1875   FAIRFIELD   (Home) Draw - 1TD v 0
No Line-Up Available

1876/77

*As the Church of England Temperance Society Football Club

03/02/1877   TWENTY OF ST PHILIPS CHOIR (Home)   Win - 1G 3T 6TD v 0
Played with 10 men
N.Howard (Capt.), F.Mawdsley, H.Thompson, W.H.Ball, G.R.Duxfield, W.Carr, Fletcher, H.Walmesley, T.Molineux and one other unnamed.

1877/88

*As the Church of England Temperance Society Football Club

08/11/1887   St Thomas' Preston (Away)   Win - 3G 2TD v 0
R.Fletcher, J.Shaw (full backs); N.Howard, G.R.Duxfield (¾ backs); W.H.Ball, R.Dickinson;
H.Walmesley, W.H.Carr, H.Richards, C.Mawdesley, R.Culshaw, H.Johnson, W.Marshall,
G.Edge, J.Darbyshire (forwards)

10/11/1887   SOUTHPORT WASPS (Home)   Draw - No Score Known
J.Shaw, R.Fletcher (full backs); N.Howard, H.Thomson (¾ backs); G.R.Duxfield,
J.C.Wright, W.Carr, H.Walmesley, R.Culshaw, H.Richards, H.Johnson, J.Rockcliffe,
G.Edge, E.Roscoe, Thomas Bell (forwards)

8/12/1877   Preston Athenium (Away)   Lost - 0 v 7T 2TD
N.Howard (Capt.), W.Marshall; R.Fletcher, W.H.Bell, G.R.Duxfield, W.H.Carr, E.Roscoe,
H.Johnson, W.Atkins, H.Richards, J.Rockcliffe, J.W.Jones

15/12/1877   Preston Olympic (Away)   - Result Unknown
J.Shaw, R.Fletcher (full backs); W.H.Ball, N.Howard (Capt.), W.H.Smith (¾ backs);
H.Walmesley, A.C.Broome, W.Platt, E.Roscoe, R.Culshaw, H.Richards, W.Marshall,
R.Dickinson, J.Rockcliffe, G.Edge (forwards)

15/01/1878   WATERLOO (Home)   Won - 1G, 5%, 1TIG, 4TD v 0
J.Shaw, W.Marshall (full backs); W.H.Ball, R.Fletcher (¾ backs); N.Howard (Capt.),
H.Walmsley (½ backs); W.Platt, E.roscoe, H.A.Smith, W.Carr, G.R.Duxfield, H.Johnson,
G.Edge (forwards)

26/01/1878   ST THOMAS' PRESTON (Home)   Won - 1G, 6T,1TIG, 10TD v 0
G.Edge, W.Marshall (fullbacks); W.H.Ball, J.Shaw, G.R.Duxfield (¾ backs); N.Howard
(Capt.), H.A.Smith (½ backs); H.Johnson, J.Eastham, H.Richards, W.H.Carr, T.Ball,
J.Darbyshire (forwards)

09/02/1878   SOUTHPORT RANGERS (Home)   Draw - 1T, 5TD v 1T,1TD
G.R.Duxfield, L.Conroy (full backs); W.Marshall, G.Edge, F.Pattison (¾ backs);
H.Walmsley (Capt.), H.A.Smith (½ backs); H.Richards, H.Johnson, F.Mawdsley, T.Ball,
J.Darbyshire, J.Bullock, W.H.Jervis (forwards)

16/02/1878   NORTH END (PRESTON) (Home)   Lost - 1TD v 1G, 2T, 5TD
J.Shaw, G.Edge (full backs); R.Fletcher, W.H.Ball (¾ backs); H.Walmsley (Capt.),
H.A.Smith (½ backs); W.Carr, J.Bargh, H.Richards, G.Lloyd, G.R.Duxfield, J.Eastham,
W.Marshall, H.Johnson, F.Mawdsley (forwards)

23/02/1878   PRESTON OLYMPIC (Home)   Lost - 1DB v 3G, 2T, 6TD
F.Patison, J.Halsall (full backs); W.H.Ball, R.Fletcher, W.Marshall (¾ backs); H.Walsmley (Capt.), H.Richards (½ backs); W.Platt, G.R.Duxfield, H.Johnson, J.Bullock, J.Rockliffe, J.Dunn, S.Radcliffe (forwards)

02/03/1878   Sandringham School (Away)   Won - 1G, 2T5TD, 1DB v 1TD
F.Pattison, G.Edge (full backs); R.Fletcher, W.H.Ball, H.A.Smith (¾ backs); H.Walmsley (Capt.), J.Shaw (½ backs); H.Richards, W.Marshall, W.H.Carr, G.R.Duxfield, F.Mawdsley, H.Johnson, J.Rockliffe, J.Bullock (forwards)

23/03/1878   PRESTON ATHENIUM (Home)   Won - 1T, 2TD v 0
F.Pattisou, G.Edge (full backs); R.Fletcher, W.H.Ball (¾ backs); H.Walmsley (Capt.), J.Shaw (½ backs); W.Platt, E.Roscoe, J.Rockliffe, W.H.Carr, H.Richards, F.Mawdsley, G.E.Duxfield, R.Culshaw, H.Johnson (forwards)

1878/79

15/10/1878   **Walton (Away)**   **Lost - 0 v 1G, 1T, 1TIG, 6TD**
J.Halsall, B.Slack (full backs); R.Fletcher (Capt.), W.H.Ball (¾ backs); H.Walmsley,
J.Ellerby (½ backs); H.Johnson, E.Bridge, J.C.Wright, G.R.Duxfield, C.Andrews, J.H.Hollis,
J.Rockcliffe, W.H.Carr (forwards)

02/11/1878   **Litherland (Away)**   **Won - 1G v 1T, 1TD**
F.Pattison, G.Edge (full backs); W.Yates, R.Fletcher, R.E.Dickenson (¾ backs);
H.Walmsley, E.J.Thomas (½ backs); Andrews, Johnson, Richards, Duxfield, Ramsbottom,
Slack, Hollis, Bridge (forwards)

09/11/1878   **Chorley (Away)**   **Lost - 1TD, 1TIG v 2G, 2T, 3TD, 2TIG**
Raikes Hall Cup
F.Pattinson, C.Andrews (full backs); R.Fletcher (Capt.), J.R.Lonedale (¾ backs);
R.E.Dickinson, J.Shaw (½ backs); H.Johnson, J.Rockcliffe, J.Eastham, J.Ellerby, A.Hollis,
S.Radcliffe, J.E.Thomson, H.Richards, L.Conroy (forwards)

16/11/1878   **Fairfield (Away)**   **Won - 2G, 4TD v 1G, 2T, 1TD**
J.C.Wright, E.Bridge (full backs); R.Fletcher (Capt), W.H.Ball (¾ backs); F.Pattison,
J.Ellerby (½ backs); H.Johnson, G.Edge, J.Rockcliffe, J.Hollis, E.Rammsbottom, W.Carr,
H.A.Smith, R.J.Johnson, C.Andrews

21/11/1878   **PRESTON OLYMPIC (Home)**   **Lost - 1TD v 1G, 1T, 4TD**
Ball and Ellerby noted in the report. Full Line-Up Not Available.

31/11/1878   **FAIRFIELD WANDERERS (Home)**   **Lost - 0 v 1G,1TD**
No Line-up available

10/12/1878   **WATERLOO   (Home)**   **Draw - Nil v 1TD**
H.Richards, J.Halsall (full backs); R.Fletcher, W.Yates (¾ backs); J.Ellerby, Walmsley (½
backs); H.Johnson, W.Carr, J.Hollis, E.Ramsbottom, E.J.Thomas, E.Bridge, E.Jones,
F.Pattison, G.Edge (forwards)

21/12/1878   **ASHTON (Home)**   **Draw - 0 v 0**
J.Bullock, W.H.Ball (full backs); Wrench, R.Fletcher (¾ backs); S.Radcliffe, E.Bridge (½
backs); J.Rockliffe, G.Lloyd, Cliffe, Connor, J.Ball, Roberts, Barnes, E.J.Thomas, A.N.Other
(forwards)

22/02/1879   **WALTON (Home)**   **Lost - 1TD v 1G, 1T, 6TD**
H. Walmesley, R.Fletcher (Capt.) (full backs); E.Bridge, W.H.Ball (¾ backs); J.Ellerby,
F.Patterson (½ backs); S.Radcliffe, R.Marshall, E.Jones, J.Halsall, C.Andrews, Cliffe,
Ramsbottom, Ollis, W.H.Carr (forwards)

1879/80

04/10/1879   Walton (Away)   Lost - 2TD, 3 Dead balls v 2G, 4T, 4TD
H. Johnson (full back); J. Wrench, J.W.Ball (¾ backs); J.Butcher, J.Ellerby (½ backs); E.Roscoe, S.Radcliffe, E.Bridge, C.Andrews, Roberts, Barnes, R.Marshall (forwards)

11/10/1879   FAIRFIELD WANDERERS (Home)   Won - 4T, 2TD v 1 T
H.Johnson (full back); R.Fletcher, W.Ball (¾ backs); A.Walmesley, R.Dickenson, (½ backs); W.Carr, E.Bridge, T.Radcliffe, R.Parry, C.Andrews, T.Ball, J.Halsall, J.Barnes, E.Thomas (forwards)

18/10/1879   LIVERPOOL WANDERERS (Home)   Lost - 0 v 1G, 2T, 5TD
C.Andrews (full back); Ratcliffe, Parry, Edwards (¾ backs); Bridge, Clift (½ backs); Johnson (Capt.), W.H.Carr, Ramsbottom, Slack, T.Ball, J.Ball, J.Duxfield, F.Jones, Peterson, (forwards)

25/10/1879   LIVERPOOL RESISTANCE (Home)   Won - 2G, 2T, 4TD,1TIG v 0.
C.Andrews (full back); W.H.Ball, Parry, Wrench (¾ backs); E.Jones, Clift (½ backs); H.Johnson (Capt.), W.H.Carr, J.Ball, H.Roberts, S.Radcliffe, J.Duxfield, E.Thomas, W.Rimmer, R.Marshall (forwards)

01/11/1879   Ashton (Away)   Lost - 3TD v 1G, 2T, 1TD
three men short. No Line-Up Available

08/11/1879   North End (Preston) (Away)   Lost - 0 v 1T, 1DB, 3TD
No Line-up available

15/11/1879   St Ignatius, Preston (Away)   Lost - 0 v 1T
L.E.Johnson and J.G.Howards (of Victoria) played for Olympic as did W.H.Ball, H.Johnson, Parry. No Line-up available

22/11/1879   BOOTLE WASPS (Home)   Win   No score given
Walpole, Andrews (full backs); Ball, Wrench, (¾ backs);Clift, Ellerby, (½ backs); H.Johnson (Capt.), Bridge, Jones, Parry, Ball, Edge, Duxfield (forwards)

03/01/1880   ST IGNATIUS, PRESTON (Home)   Won - 1G, 1TIG, 4TD v 1T
S.Bramwell, C.Andrews (full backs); N.Howard, W.Ball (¾ backs); Ellerby, Bridge (½ backs);Johnson (Capt.), W.H.Carr, J.Ball, E.Jones, W.Rimmer, E.Thomas, R.Parry, J.Cliff, J.Duxfield (forwards)

17/01/1880   Fairfield Wanderers (Away)   Draw - 1TD v 0
S.Bramwell (full back); W.H.Ball, R.E.Parry (¾ backs); Bridge, Ellerby, (½ backs); H.Johnson (Capt.), E.Jones, J.Ball, J.Lloyd, J.Cliff, R.Slack (forwards)

01/02/1880   **Bootle Wasps (Away)**   **Won - 1G, 1T, 5M v 0**
No Line-Up Available

07/02/1880   **PRESTON OLYMPIC (Home)**   **Draw - 1TIG, 3TD v 1TD**
No Line-Up Available

21/02/1880   **SOUTHPORT (Home)**   **Won - 1G, 1TIG, 7TD v 0**
J.Eastham, J.Wrench (full backs); W.Ball, R.Fletcher (3/4 backs); J.Ellerby, E.Bridge (1/2 backs); H.Johnson (capt.), W.H.Carr, J.Barnes, E.Jones, R.Parry, G.Lloyd, Thomas, J.Rocckdliffe, J.Cliffe (forwards)

13/03/1880   **Preston Olympic (Away)**   **Draw - No score given**
J.Bullock, J.Parks (backs); W.Ball, E.Jones (3/4 backs); E,Thomas, E.Bridge, (1/2 backs); H.Johnson (Capt.), E.Bracewell, J.Cliffe, J.Lloyd, G.Wright, A.Wright, E.Parry, H.Connard, W.Rimmer

20/03/1880   **WALTON (Home)**   **Lost - 2TD v 1G, 3T,5M**
J.Halsall, E.Bridge (full backs); Rev. W.Williams, W.H.Ball, R.Dickenson (¾ backs); N Howard, J.Cliffe (½ backs); H.Johnson (Capt.), W.H.Carr, E.Jones, R.Parry, F.Jones, H.Conard, Barnes, Lloyd (forwards)

1880/81

02/10/1880   Resistance (Away)   Draw - 1TD v 1T
H.Johnson (full back); J.Morston, S.Workman (¾ backs); R.E.Parry, E.Bridge (½ backs);
S.Radcliffe, J.Parks, C.Andrews, W.Carr, G.Wright, T.Carr, R.Slack, J.Cliff, J.Bullock,
E.J.Thomas (forwards)

16/10/1880   WIGAN (Home)   Draw - 2TD v 0
H.Johnson (Capt.), C.Andrews (full backs); R.Parry, H.A.Smith, W.H.Ball (3/4 backs);
E.Thomas, Bridge (½ backs); W.H.Carr, Ball, Wright, Edge, Mounsden, Barnes, Cob,
Bullock, Parks (forwards)

23/10/1880   LITTLE LEVER (Home)   Lost - 2 dead balls v 2G, 2TD, 1 dead ball
Yates (full back); W.H.Ball, R.Fletcher (¾ backs); J.Ellerby, E.Bridge (½ backs) H.Johnson
(Capt.), W.H.Carr, J.Cliffe, Parley, J.Bullock, E.J.Thomas, C.Andrews, G.Wright,
F.Mawdsley, Barnes (forwards)

30/10/1880   Walton (Away)   Lost - 1TIG v 2G, 1TIG
J.Bullock, J.Eastham (full backs); R.E.Parry, W.H.Ball (¾ backs); Bridge, Ellerby (½ backs);
E.Thomas, J.Cliffe, F.Mawdsley, W.Wright, G.Lloyd, Mounsden, C.Andrews, Harkman,
Carrols.

06/11/1880   Freshfield College (Away)   Lost - 2T, 7TD v 1G, 2T, 5TD
No-Line Up Available

27/11/1880   St Ignatius Preston (Away)   Won - 1T, 1TD v 1T
Ball (full back); W.Yates, J.Barnes, Wrench (¾ backs); E.Bridge, J.Cliffe (½ backs);
H.Johnson (Capt.), G.Lloyd, J.Lloyd, R.Parry, J.Bullock, G.Wright, Mounsden, S.Radcliffe,
W.H.Carr (forwards)

11/12/1880   Waterloo (Away)   Result Not Given
H.Johnson (Capt.), W.H.Ball (full backs); J.Eastham, J.Barnes, H.A.Smith (¾ backs);
W.Rimmer, J.Cliffe (½ backs); W.H.Carr, W.Mounsden, S.Radcliffe, F.Mawdesley,
J.Hazlehurst, G.Wright, J.Lloyd, W.Walmesley, Richardson, W.H.Smith, E.Thomas, T.Ball,
E.Carr, C.Andrews, R.Parry (forwards)

01/01/1881   Birkenhead Rangers (Away)   Won - 1G, 1TD v 1TIG
*·*played 12 men to 13, but no line-up available*

05/03/1881   Liverpool Wanderers (Away)   Won - 1T, Several TD v 0
Report includes E.Thomas, Parry, H.A.Smith, W.H.Ball

19/03/1881   LEIGH (Home)   Won - 1G, 1T,6TD v 0
No Line-Up available

18/04/1881   HALIFAX FREE WANDERERS (Home)   Lost - 2G, 3TD v 1TD, 3 dead balls

W.H.Ball (full back); J.Eastham, R.Fletcher (¾ backs); J.Barnes, C.Davies (½ backs); H.Johnson (Capt.), R.E.Parry, G.Wright, J.Cliffe, G.Lloyd, E.J.Thomas, W.Rimmer, T.Ball, H.Haslehurst, E.Bridge (forwards)

1881/82

17/09/1881   BATLEY MOUNTAINEERS (Home)   Lost - 1TD, 1TIG v 2TD, 1 TIG
S.Radcliffe (full back); R.Fletcher, W.H.Ball, E.Thomas (¾ backs); E.Bridge, R.Parry (½ backs); H.Haslehurst (Capt.), T.Ball, J.Parks, H.Wignall, E.Wright, A.Wright, C.Andrews, W.Robinson, W.Carr (forwards)

01/10/1881   Wavertree (Away)   Won - 2G, 2T,2TD v2TD
Maffin (full back); S.Radcliffe, W.Rimmer, W.H.Ball (¾ backs); E.Bridge, R.Parry (½ backs); W.H.Roberts, T.Ball, J.Ball, R.Slack, H.Haslehurst (Capt.), J.Taylor, W.Robinson, T.Hooton, A.Wright (forwards)

08/10/1881   WALTON (Home)   Lost - 1TD v 3G, 5T, 9M
S.Radcliffe (full back); E.Thomas, H.Aughton, W.H.Ball (¾ backs); E.Bridge, R.Parry (½ backs); H.Haslehurst (Capt.), J.Parks, W.H.Carr, A.Wright, T.Hooton, W.Robinson, J.Taylor, G.Hollis, H.Wignall (forwards)

15/10/1881   LEIGH (Home)   Won - 3T, 5TD v 2TD
Ross, Parks, Parry, Slack included but no full Line-Up Available.

29/10/1881   Rochdale Hornets (Away) Lost - 1T,1TD, 1 dDB, 1TIG v 1G, 1T, 3TD, 2 dead balls
Ratclife (full back); J.Galvin, H.Aughton, W.H.Ball (¾ backs); T.Barrow, W.Rimmer (½ backs); R.E.Parry, G.Hollis, E.Bridge, G.Wright, R.Slack, W.Rimmer and W.Robinson (forwards)

05/11/1881   LITHERLAND (Home)   Won - 3G, 1 'poster', 2T, 9TD v 0.
S. Ratcliffe (full back); W.H.Ball (Capt.), H.Aughton, J. Cliffe (¾ backs); T.Barrow, W.Rimmer (½ backs); J.H.Hollis, G.Wright, E.Bridge, J.Parks, W.Rimmer, R.Slack, W.Robinson, R.Parry, D.Richardson (forwards)

12/11/1881   St Helens Recreation (Away)   Lost - 2TD v 1T, 1TIG
Played 2 men short - No Line-Up Available

19/11/1881   ASPULL (Home)   Lost - 1T,2TD v 0
A.Wright (full back); A.J.Ross, W.H.Ball, H.Aughton (¾ backs); H.Haslehurst (Capt.), R.E.Parry, E.Bridge, J.Parks, R.Slack, W.H.Carr, Wm.Rimmer, W.Robinson, Finney (forwards)

03/12/1881   ADLINGTON (Home)   Lost - 1TD v 1G, 1T, 3TD
R.E.Parry (full back); A.J.Ross, HAughton, J.Barnes (¾ backs); W.Rimmer, T.Barrow (½ backs); H.Haslehurst (Capt.), W.H.Carr, E.Bridge, J.Parks, Wright, W.Robinson, W.Rimmer, R.Slack, W.H.Roberts (forwards)

14/01/1882   WAVERTREE (Home)   Lost - 1T, 3TD v 1G, 2TD, 1T
A.Wright (full back); W.H.Ball, H.Aughton, T.Barrow (¾ backs); Hazlehurst, E.Bridge (½ backs); R.Parry, E.Jones, J.Parks, W.Rimmer, J.H.Hollis, W.Robinson, J.Bullock, S.Radcliffe, G.Wright (forwards)

21/01/1882   Walton (Away)   Draw - 1T, 2TD v 0
A.Wright (full back); T. Galvin, W.H.Ball, N.Howard (¾ backs); T.R.Barrow, W. Rimmer (½ backs); H.Haslehurst, E.Jones, E.Bridge, R.E.Parry, J.Parks, G.Wright, J.Bullock, W.Rimmer, R.Slack (forwards)

28/01/1882   Litherland (Away)   Draw - 2M v 2M
A.Wright (full back); N.Howard, T.Barrow, O.Clegg (¾ backs); W.Rimmer, E.Bridge, (½ backs); H.Haslehurst, R.Slack, G.Wright, R.E.Parry, E.Jones, W.Johnston, S.Ratcliffe, W.Rimmer, J.Bullock (forwards)

08/02/1882   SOUTHPORT HORNETS (Home)   Won, 1G, 6T, 12M v 1TD
Galvin, Parks, Barrow , Bullock, Rimmer noted in the report. Full Line-Up Not Available.

18/02/1882   LITTLE LEVER (Home)   Draw - 5M v 10M
*13 men v 15 men
O.Clegg (full back); N.Howard, W.H.Ball, R.E.Parry (¾ backs); T.R.Barrow, W.Rimmer (½ backs); H.Haslehurst, E.Bridge, J.Parks, G.Wright, E.Jones, W.Robinson, G.Lloyd (forwards)

18/03/1882   ST HELENS RECREATION (Home)   Won - 1G, 3T, 4TD v 0
S.Radcliffe (full back); O.Clegg, J.Barnes, N.Howard (¾ backs); W.Rimmer, T.R.Barrow (½ backs); H.Haslehurst (Capt.), J.Bullock, G.Wright, R.PE.arry, J.Parks, E.Jones, G.Lloyd, W.Rimmer, R.Marshall (forwards)

25/03/1882   Liverpool Old Boys (Away)   Draw - 2M v 2M
A.Wright (full back); N.Howard, W.H.Ball, O.Clegg (¾ backs); W.Rimmer, T.R.Barrow (½ backs); H.Haslehurst (Capt.), J.Parks, R.Parry, E.Jones, W.Rimmer, H.Johnson, G.Lloyd, G.Wright, R.Slack (forwards)

01/04/1882   LITTLE LEVER (Home)   Result Not Known
O.Clegg (full back); N.Howard, W.H.Ball, J.H.Britton (¾ backs); T.R.Barrow, W.Rimmer (½ backs); H.Haslehurst, William Rimmer, E.Jones, E.Bridge, R.E.Parry, J.Parks, G.Wright, R.Marshall

08/04/1882   ROCHDALE HORNETS (Home)   Draw - Score Not Known
N.Howard, W.Rimmer, W.H.Ball, H.Haslehurst, Wright

25/04/1882   SOUTHPORT HORNETS (Home)   Won - 1G, 1T, 8M v0
W. Rimmer, G.Wright, H.Haslehurst, R.E.Parry, A.Wright, O.Clegg

1882/83

16/09/1882   MARRIED v SINGLE   Result not known
Married: G.Edge (full back); O.Clegg, J.McIntyre, J.Sykes (¾ backs); H.Haslehurst (Capt.),
J.C.Wright (½ backs); H.Johnson, R.Brewer, G.Wright, R.Marshall, Wm.Rimmer,
W.Robinson, W.H.Carr, and Another (forwards)
Single: J.Salisbury (full back); W.H.Ball, R.E.Parry, H.Aughton (¾ backs); , R.Gregory,
J.Cliffe (½ backs); Rigby, J.Parks, F.Stead T.Rimmer, W.Tunstall, S.Radcliffe J.Thompson,
R.Ruscoe, R.Slack (forwards)

07/10/1882   Little Lever (Away)   Won - 1T v 2T, 2TD
G.Wright (full back); W.H.Ball, O.Clegg, R.Fletcher (¾ backs); W.Rimmer (Capt.), S.Rigby
(½ backs); Johnson, E.Bridge, Rimmer, R.E.Parry, J.Cliffe, W.H.Carr, J.McIntyre, J.Parks,
R.Marshall (forwards)

14/10/1882   WIGAN (Home)   Won - 3G, 3T, 8M v 0
G.Wright (full back); R.Fletcher, W.H.Ball, R.E.Parry (¾ backs); W.Rimmer, S.Rigby (½
backs); H.Haslehurst (Capt.), J.Parks, H.Johnson, W.Rimmer, J.Clift, E.Bridge, W.H.Carr,
R.Marshall (forward)

21/10/1882   Liverpool Gymnasium (Away)   Won - 1G, 2T, 7M v 0
G.Wright (back); W.H.Ball, R.E.Parry, E.Stead (¾ backs); W.Rimmer, S.Rigby (½ backs);
H.Haslehurst, H.Johnson, J.McIntyre, J.Parks, J.Clift, W.H.Carr, R.Slack, R.Ratcliffe,
H.Aughton (forwards)

28/10/1882   Rochdale Hornets (Away)   Lost - 3M v 1G, 6T, 5M
Parry (full back); W.H.Ball, R.Fletcher, F.Stead (¾ backs); W.Rimmer, S.Rigby (½ backs);
H.Haslehurst (Capt.), H.Johnson, R.Marshall, J.Cliffe, W.H.Carr, W.Rimmer, J.Parkes,
Right, Budge (forwards)

04/11/1882   LIVERPOOL GYMNASIUM (Home)   Win - 4T, 9M v 0
G.Wright (full back); W.H.Ball, H.Haslehurst, R.E.Parry (¾ backs); W.Rimmer, S.Rigby (½
backs); J.Parks, H.Johnson, R.Marshall, J.McIntyre, J.Cliffe, S.Radcliffe, E.Bridge,
W.H.Carr, J.C.Wright (forwards)
Tries: J.C.Wright, S.Ratcliffe, W.H.Ball, J.Parks

11/11/1882   Newton-Le-Willows (Away)   Draw - 1T, 5M v 1T, 3M
No Line-Up Available

18/11/1882   WAVERTREE (Home)   Won - 1G, 1TD v 1TD
G.Wright (full back); W.H.Ball, S.Rigby, R.E.Parry (¾ backs); H.Haslehurst (Capt.),
R.Gregory (½ backs); H.Johnson, E.Britton, R.Marshall, S.Radcliffe, J.Cliffe, G.Edge,
W.Rimmer, W.Robinson, H.Buxton (forwards)

27/01/1883   **FORMBY (Home)**   **Lost - 1T,3M v 1T, 8M**
G.Wright (full back); F.Stead, J.Cliffe, H.Walmesley (¾ backs); Lund, H.Haslehurst (Capt.) (½ backs); J.McIntyre, R.Slack, W.Rimmer, Yates, Ellis, Pasquil, S.Radcliffe, W.H.Carr, Gill, Neville (forwards)

03/02/1883   **SALE (Home)**   **Match Abandoned**
Score when abandoned due to injury of Sale player was 0 v 1G, 5T, Several M
No Line-up available

03/02/1883   **Wigan (Away)**   **Won - 2T, 5M v 1T 1M**
W.H.Ball, Hoban, Freeman, W.Rimmer, H.Haslehurst,

24/02/1883   **BIRKDALE FREE WANDERERS (Home)**   **Won - 1G,6T,12M v 1TD**
L.Connard, O.Clegg, Lund, F.Stead, H.Walmsley noted in the report. Full Line-Up Not Available.

03/03/1883   **ST HELENS RECREATION (Home)**   **Draw - 1G 3M v 1G 3M**
O.Clegg, Cliffe, R.Marshall, R.Gregory, W.H.Ball, J.Parkes, J.McIntyre, Anderton noted in the report. Full Line-Up Not Available.

24/03/1883   **ROCHDALE HORNETS (Home)**   **Lost - Few M v 2G, 1T, several M**
No Line-up given

26/03/1883   **ECCLES (Home)**   **Won - 1G 2T, 5M v 1G 4M**
Gregory, W.H.Ball, J.McIntyre included in report. No Line-Up available

1883/84

29/09/1883   St Helens (Away)   **Result Not Known**
Intended team: J.McIntyre, J.Cliffe, J.Hoban, H.Johnson, A.Ball, G.Wright, F.Stead, R.Slack, W.Lund, W.Rimmer, J.Ellerby, H.Shaw, W.H.Ball, A.Dalby, E.Bridge.

04/10/1883   BOOTLE (Home)   **Lost - 2M v 2G, 2T,5M**
No Line-Up Available

13/10/1883   Oldham (Away)   **Lost - 0 v 3G, 5T**
* Only 11 men available. No Line-Up Available

20/10/1883   Rochdale Hornets (Away)   **Lost - 4M v 1G, 5T, 4M**
T.Sellars (full back); J.Hoban, H.Aughton, W.Lund (¾ backs); W.Rimmer, J.Finney (½ backs); J.McIntyre, J.Cliffe, G.Wright, Haslehurst, R.Slack, Thornber, A.N.Other

27/10/1883   BURY (Home)   **Lost - 3M v 1G, 2T**
Stead, Marshall, Haslehurst, Lund, Sellars noted in the report. Full Line-Up Not Available.

03/11/1883   Litherland (Away)   **Won - 1G, 2T, 7M v 0**
T.Sellars (full back); W.Lund, J.Bellis, E.Stead (3/4 back); W.Rimmer, T.Finney (½ backs); J.McIntyre (Capt.), J.Clift, H.Johnson, J.Halsall, H.Haslehurst, R.Slack, W.Robinson, J.Halsall, F.Collins (forwards)

10/11/1883   CLIFTON (Home)   **Result Unknown**
No-Line-up Available

17/11/1883   SOUTHPORT FC   **Lost 0-2**
*Association rules.
No-Line-up Available

24/11/1883   Fairfield (Away)   **Lost - 1T, 9M v 1G *disputed**
T.Sellars (full back); Woodhouse, Bellis, Lund (¾ backs); G.Summers, W.Rimmer (½ backs); J.McIntyre, H.Johnson, J.Halsall, Mawdsley, Marshall, R.Slack (forwards)

01/12/1883   Wigan (Away)   **Lost - 1M v 1G, 5T, 13M**
*Played with 14 men
No Line-Up Available

08/12/1883   OLD BOYS, LIVERPOOL (Home)   **Draw - 4T v 0**
T.Sellars (full back); W.Lund, Dickinson, Bellis (¾ backs); W.Rimmer, G.Summers (½ backs); McIntyre (Capt.), H.Haslehurst, Marshall, Wright, Johnson, Halsall, Bimpson, Hankinson, Slack (forwards)

26/12/1883   RUNCORN (Home)   Lost - 0 v 6T, 3M
No Line-Up Available

29/12/1883   Liverpool Gymnasium (Away)   Lost - 3M v 1G, 3T, 3M
*Missing a number of first team men. No Line-Up Available

01/01/1884   SOUTHPORT FC   Result Not Known
Under Association Rules for the Benefit of the Infirmary

05/01/1884   ASHTON-UNDER-LYNE (Home)   Lost - 0 v 1T
*Team made up of spectators as captain received word at noon that 8 players could not play
No Line-Up Available

05/01/1884   PAGEFIELD (Home)   Lost - 2M v 1G, 1T, 4M
T.Hobler (back); A.Gill, L.Connard, J.W.Anderton (3/4 back); J.W.Worsley, C.Blundell (half backs); W.Hankinson, J.Sawyer, C.Ripley, A.Heckingbotham, J.W.Neville, H.Collins, P.Moorfield, F.Parry, C.Simm (forwards)

19/01/1884   STALYBRIDGE (Home)   Draw - 1M v 1T(Disputed), 5M
Sellars (full back); Bellis, Stead, Lund (3/4 back); Summers, Oliver (half back); Haslehurst,Johnson, Halsall, Colllins, Marshall, Robinson, Ellerby, Wright, Slack (forwards)

02/02/1884   SALE (Home)   Lost - 0 v 1T
T.Sellars (full back); J.Parks, J.Eastham, J.Wilkinson (¾ backs); G.Summers, L.Johnson (½ backs); H.Johnson, G.Wright, Halsall, J.McIntyre, Neville, Ripley, Collins, R.Marshall, R.Slack (forwards)

09/02/1884   Bury (Away)   Lost - 1G v 1G, 1T, 5M
T.Sellars (back); Lund, Eastham, Wilkinson, (¾ backs); G.Summers, L.E.Johnson (½ backs); Haslehurst, H.Johnson, Wright, Mason, Ripley, Halsall, Neville, McIntyre, Slack (forwards)

16/02/1884   ST HELENS (Home)   Lost - 4M v 1G, 2TD
T.Sellars (back); W.Lund, A.Jones, L.E.Johnson (¾ backs); H.Haslehurst, G.Summers (½ backs); H.Johnson, R.Marshall, J.Halsall, J.Neville, C.Ripley, G.Wright, J.Mason, J.McIntyre,R.Slack (forwards)

23/02/1884   Oldham (Away)   Result Unknown
T.Sellars (back); W.Lund, J.Parks, W.Rimmer (¾ backs); G.Summers, Dearden (½ backs); H.Haslehurst, H.Johnson, J.Ellerby, J.Halsall, J.McIntyre, L.E.Johnson, G.Wright, R.Slack, F.Stead (forwards)

01/03/1884   Fairfield (Away)   Won - 1G, 1T v 0
Sellars (back); Freeman, Hill, Parks (¾ backs); Summers, L.E.Johnson,(½ backs);
H.Johnson, J.Halsall, Ripley, Mason, Leonard, Clay, Grees, Goss, Slack (forwards)

22/03/1884   LIVERPOOL OLD BOYS (Home)   Lost - 1T v 3G, 2T (one disputed)
T.Sellars (back); Parkes, Rimmer, Gregson (¾ backs); Finner, Summer (half); Haslehurst
(Capt.), H.Johnson, L.Johnson, Halsall, Wright, Ellerby, Slack, McIntyre, Mason

29/03/1884   LIVERPOOL GYMNASIUM (Home)   Won - 4T v 0
Walmsley (back); W.Rimmer, Lund, H.Robinson (¾ backs); G.Summers, Sawyer (½
backs); Haslehurst, Mason, Neville, Hankinson, Halsall, Marshall, Wright, L.E.Johnson,
Slack

05/04/1884   Heaton (Away)   Lost - 1T v 2T
Slack noted in the report. Full Line-Up Not Available.

19/04/1884   MANCHESTER BUTTERFLIES (Home)   Draw - 1G, 1TD v 1G, 1T, 2TD
T.Sellars (full back); J.Parks, A.Gill, P.Barton (¾ backs); G.Summers, J.Sawyer (½ backs);
J.Halsall, J.McIntyre, L.Johnson, J.Mason, C.Bumpson, C.Ripley, W.Hankinson, R.E.Parry,
R.Slack (forwards)

26/04/1884   ROCHDALE HORNETS (Home)   Lost - 0 v 1G, 3T
P.Barton (back); W.Lund, J.Parks, A.Gill (¾ backs); Summers, Sawyer (1.2); H.Johnson,
L.E.Johnson, Wright, Ripley, Neville, Bimpson, Hankinson, Halsall, Slack

1884/85

13/09/1884   Tyldesley (Away)   Lost - 0 v 3G, 2T
W.Stevenson (full back); P.Barton, W.Lund, A.Gill (¾ backs); G.Summers, J.Sawyer (½ backs); J.Halsall, W.Hankinson, F.Stead, Heckingbottom, C.Ripley, J.Mason, Collins, Banghan, R.Slack (forwards)

20/09/1884   BRADFORD & CLAYTON (Home)   Draw - 0 v 8M
J.Sawyer (back); Gill, Sykes, Lund (¾ backs); Stephenson, G.Enoch, Sumners (½ backs); J.Halsall (Capt.), Ripley, Mason, Heckingbottom, Collins, Connard, Brooks, H.Wright, R.Slack (forwards)

27/09/1884   BIRCH (Home)   Lost - 1T, 2M v 2T, 10M
J.Hulmes (back); Lund, Gill, Dearden (¾ backs); Sawyer, Summers (½ backs); J.Halsall (Capt.), C.Ripley, Vaughan, Stewad, J.Mason, Collins, R.E.Parry, C.Bimpson, R.Slack (forwards)

04/10/1884   WIDNES WASPS (Home)   Won - 1G, 1T, 4M v 1T, 1M
Summers, Lund, Dearden noted in the report. Full Line-Up Not Available.

11/10/1884   ROCHDALE HORNETS (Home)   Lost - 1TIG v 4G, 6T, 12M
Sawyer (full back); Lund, Fletcher, Gill (¾ backs); Summers, Collins (½ backs); Halsall, Bennett, Dearden, Mason, Hankinson, Conars, Ripley, Hairean, Slack (forwards)

25/10/1884   Liverpool Gymnasium (Away)   Lost - 1T v 4T,6M
Sawyer (full back); Walter Rimmer, Heaton, Lund (¾ backs); Cragg, Summers (½ backs); J.Halsall, Bimpson, Ripley, Hankinson, Mason, Collins, Heckingbottom, J.Wilson, R.Slack (forwards)

08/11/1884   WIGAN (Home)   Lost - 0 v 3T
A.StClare (full back); J.Sawyer, Rimmer, Lund (¾ backs); Britton, Summers (½ backs); Halsall, Marshall, Wilson, Hankinson, Collins, H.Wright, Mason, Whiskers, R.Slack (forwards)

15/11/1884   Litherland (Away)   Won - 4 M v 1T Several M
W.H.Carr (full back); G.Summers, Lund, Freeman (¾ backs); Britton, Johnson (½ backs); Halsall, Spencer, Collins, Mason, Baughan, Parry, Hankinson, H.Wright, R.Slack (forwards)

22/11/1884   BURY UNITARIANS (Home)   Lost - 4M v 1T, 2M
Ripley (full back); Lund, Holder, Baughan (¾ backs); Summers, Wright (½ backs); Halsall, Mason, Wilson, Heald, Collins, F Parry, J Dearden, Marshall, R Slack (forwards)

20/12/1884   Bootle (Away)   **Lost - 1T v 3T**
No Line-Up Available * played 1 man short

26/12/1884   MANCHESTER GRASSHOPPERS (Home)   Draw – No Score Given
A.Fletcher (full back); W.Rimmer, W.Lund, P.Moorfield (¾ backs); J.W.Cavenay,
R.Gregory (½ backs); J.Halsall (Capt.), J.Heald, R.Slack, W.Hamkinson, J.Mason,
R.Marshall, C.Bimpson, C.Ripley, H.Collins (forward)

10/01/1885   LITHERLAND (Home)   **Draw - 1G, 4 M v 1G 4M**
Webster (full back); Lund, Holder, Smith (¾ backs); Gregory, Cavaney (½ backs); Halsall,
Mason, Collins, Baughan, Bell, Hankinson, Bimpson, Jones, Slack (forwards)

31/01/1885   Fairfield (Away)   **Draw - 1M v 5M**
J.H.Britton (full back); W.Freeman, G.Summers, T.Baughan (¾ backs); Gregory,
Leadbetter (½ backs); J.Halsall, J.Mason, J.Goss, J.Holden, Hankinson, Collins, Layfield,
Sefton, R.Slack (forwards)

05/02/1885   RADCLIFFE (Home)   **Lost - 3M v 3T, 4M**
J.H.Britton (full back); Russell, Summers, Moorfield (¾ backs); Cavaney, Gregory (½
backs); Halsall,Heald, Sefton, Collins, Mason, Bimpson, Wilson, Banhan, Slack (forwards)

14/02/1885   Pagefield (Away)   **Lost - 5M v 1T,5M**
J.H.Britton (full back); W.Lund, Freeman, T.Bangham (¾ backs); Gregory, Summers (½
backs); Halsall, Hall, Hankinson,Goss, Mason, Collins, Bimpson, Slack, A.N.Other
(forwards)

21/02/1885   FAIRFIELD (Home)   **Won - 1T v0**
J.Sawyer (full back); W.Lund, Abram Rimmer, T.Bangham (¾ backs); Gregory, Summers
(½ backs); Halsall, Mason, Hankinson, Bimpson, Sefton, Collins, Brown, Neville, R.Slack
(forwards)

07/03/1885   WAVERTREE (Home)   **Lost - 2M v 1T 1M**
J.H.Britton (full back); Russell, Lund, Abram Rimmer (¾ backs); Gregory, Summers (½
backs); Halsall, Hankinson, Bimpson, Bell, Sefton, Banhan, Mason, Wilson, R.Slack
(forwards)

21/03/1885   St Helens (Away)   **Lost - 1TD v 1G, 2T, 5TD**
W.Russell (full back); T.Bangham, H.Robinson,P.Moorfield (¾ backs); D.Moncur,
G.E.Summers (Capt) (½ backs); Neville, Harrison, Mason, Rigby, Bell, R.Slack, 3
substitutes

25/04/1885   BIRCH (Home)   **Draw - 1T, 2M v 1T, 2M**
Bell (full back); Lund, Holder, Abrams (¾ backs); Moncur, Summers (½ backs);
Marshall,Bangham, Ball, Parry, Ripley, Hankinson, Webster, Cavaney, Mason (forwards)

1885/86

12/09/1885   Wigan (Away)   Lost - 1T v 6T
Leadbetter, Freeman, Price mentioned in the report but no Line-up available

19/09/1885   HAIGH (Home)   Lost - 4M v 1G, 2T 6M
Sumner (full back); Rimmer (Capt), Price, Freeman (¾ backs); Sefton, Baugh (½ backs);
Slack, Brown, Rimmer, Mason, Webster, Bell, Sumner, Neville, Marshall (forwards)

26/09/1885   Pagefield (Away)   Won - 3G, 2T, 2M v 0
Price, Leadbetter, Lund, Summers, Marshall, Brown, Rimmer (Capt), Bangham
mentioned in report, no full line up available

03/10/1885   WAVERTREE (Home)   Won - 1T, 4M v 0
J.H.Brittan (full back); Price, Freeman, Lund (¾ backs); Summers, Leadbetter (½ backs);
Bell, Mason, Neville, Bangham, W.Rimmer(Capt), T.Rimmer, Brown, R.Marshall, Toole
(forwards)

17/10/1885   MANCHESTER GYMNASIUM (Home)   Win - 3T,3M v 3TD
Ball (full back); Price, Lund, Barnes (¾ backs); Leadbetter, W.Rimmer(Capt) (½ backs);
Neville, Slack, Baughan, Brown, T.Rimmer, Rigby, Toole, Bimpson, Marshall (forwards)

21/10/1885   Walton (Away)   Lost - 1T v2T
F.Ball (full back); W.Lund, W.Freeman, S.Rigby (¾ backs); W.Rimmer(Capt),
H.Leadbetter (½ backs); C.Bimpson, T.Brown, T.Rimmer, R.Marshall, R.Slack, T.Cross,
C.Bell, T.Webster, W.Sefton (forwards)

07/11/1885   LANCASTER (Home)   Won - 4T,5M v 1T, 3M
F.Ball (full back); W.Lund, Price, T.Banham (¾ backs); W.Rimmer (Capt), H.Leadbetter
(½ backs); Rimmer, Neville, Halsall, Webster, Brown, Marshall, Toole, Bimpson,
W.Sefton (forwards)

14/11/1885   Tuebrook (Away)   Draw - Score Unknown
*12 men
Webster (full back);H.Robinson, A.Gill (¾ backs); H.Price, W.Rimmer (½ backs); Brown,
Ball, Marshall, Rice, Neville, Sefton, Slack

21/11/1885   BRACKLEY (Home)   Lost - 5M v 2T, 2M
F.Ball (Full back); Robinson,Price, Lund (¾ backs); Rimmer, Leadbetter (½ backs); Bell,
T.Rimmer, Neville, Bangham, Mason, Slack, Brown, Webster, Sefton (forwards)

28/11/1885   Birch (Away)   Lost - 1T v 5 Disputed T, 5M
Holder (full back); Robinson, Price, Lund (¾ backs); Moncur, W.Rimmer (Capt) (½ backs); Brown, Ball, Bangham, Bimpson, Britton, Sefton, Webster, Marshall, Slack (forwards)

05/12/1885   SUTTON (Home)   Won - 1T, 2M v 0
F.Ball (full back); Lund, W.Rimmer (Capt), H.Robinson (¾ backs); Price, Murray (½ backs); T.Brown, R.Marshall, C.Bimpson, W.Sefton, T.Bangham, Webster, T.Rimmer, J.Mason, R.Slack (forwards)

19/12/1885   PEMBERTON (Home)   Won - 2G 3T v 0
F.Ball (full back); Lund, Price, Robinson (¾ backs); Leadbetter, Murray (½ backs); Sefton, Brown, W.Rimmer (Capt), Banham, J.Toole, R.Slack, Bimpson, Bell, Marshall

26/12/1885   Lancaster (Away)   Result Not Known
Ball (full back); Lund, Gill, Rimmer (¾ backs); Mocur, Holder (½ backs); Mason, Sefton, Slack, Bell, Toole, Marshall, Brown, Bangham, Bimpson (forwards)

02/01/1886   Aspull (Away)   Lost - 1 T v 1G 2T
*12 men
Fletcher (full back); Moorefield, W.Rimmer, Robinson (¾ backs); Sefton, Baughan (½ backs); Brown, Bell, Jones, Pennington, Mason, Slack (forwards)

09/01/1886   *Trial Match*
Marshall (possible) & Lund (probables) selected to play in trial match prior to the engagement of West Cumberland & District v West Lancs Border Union

23/01/1886   Pemberton (Away)   Lost - 0 v 1T 6M
No Line-Up Available

31/01/1886   ST HELENS RECREATION (Home)   Lost - 1T v 2T
H.Robinson (full back); Price, Lord, Gill (¾ backs); A.N.Other, Rimmer (½ backs); Webster, Banham, Toole, Slack, Rev. Rigbye, Marson, Meville, Brown and A.N.Other (forwards)

06/02/1886   ASPULL (Home)   Lost - 1T 3M v 2G 1T 2M
W.Worsley (full back); Mansfield, Holder, W.N.Bolton (¾ backs); Mouse, Cragg (½ backs); Wallwork, Corfield, Binks, Blundell, Hankinson, Rice, Rigby, Parry, T. Rimmer (forwards)

13/02/1886   WALTON (Home)   Won - 2T 6M v 2M
Lund, Banghan and Marshall noted in the report. Full Line-Up Not Available.

20/02/1886   PAGEFIELD (Home)   Won - 1G, 2T, 8M v 1G 2M
Price, Rimmer and Slack noted in the report. Full Line-Up Not Available.

27/02/1886   **Wavertree (Away)**   **No Result Given**

13/03/1886   ASPULL (Home)   **Lost - 2M v 1T 7M**
West Lancs Border Towns Cup
Aughton (full back); Lund, Booth, Gill (¾ backs); Rimmer, Moncur, Barnes (½ backs);
Toole, Marshall, Baughan, Hankinson, Summers, Webster, Neville, Bimpson (forwards)

20/03/1886   TUEBROOK (Home)   **Won - 5T v 1T**
No Line-Up Available

27/03/1886   MANCHESTER GYMNASIUM (Home)   Won - 1G 9M v 1M
T.Holder (full back); H.Robinson, Rimmer, Parks (¾ backs); Gee, E.Summers, D.Moncur
(½ backs); Marshall, Toole, Bimpson, Binks, Bell, Perry, Blundell, Webster, Neville
(forwards)

1886/87

16/09/1886   PEMBERTON (Home)   Lost - 1T v 2G, 1T
*Wareing (full back); Shaw, Lund, Robinson (¾ backs); Summers, Oliver (½ backs); Rice,
Toole, Halsall, Fletcher, Heckingbottom, Blundell, Webster*

25/09/1886   Radcliffe (Away)   Lost - 0 v 4T
*only 10 men
*Holder (full back), Ball, Robinson (¾ backs), Summers, Sub (½ backs); Halsall, Cobbles,
Toole, Rice, Bell, Fletcher, Webber and Sub (forwards)*

02/10/1886   LITHERLAND (Home)   Won - 1G, 4T, 4M v 2M
*Holder (full back); Gill, Lund, Robinson (¾ backs), Summers (Capt.), Shaww (½ backs);
Webster, Halsall, Toole, Slack, Steed, Blundell, Rice, Wright, Fletcher (forwards)*

16/10/1886   Tuebrook (Away)   Lost - 4M v 1T, 2M
*Summers (½ back) Webster, Toole, fletcher noted in the report. Full Line-Up Not
Available.*

30/10/1886   WATERTREE (Home)   Won - 2G, 5T, 7M v 2M
*Holder (full back); Lund, Gill, Robinson (¾ backs); Summers, Booth (Capt.) (½ backs);
Toole, Marrshall, Halsall, Fletcher, Webster, Slack, Neville, Hudsmith, Parry (forwards)*

6/11/1886   St Helens Recreation(Away)   Lost - 0 v 2G, 5T
*Holder (full back); Lund, Gill, Robinson (¾ backs); Summers, Booth (Capt) (½ backs);
Halsall, Fletcherm Webster, Slack, Hudsmith, Parry, 3 others not named*

20/11/1886   Ringley (Away)   Draw - 2M v 2M
*Holder (full back),Lund, Gill, Robinson (¾ backs); Booth, Summers (½ backs); Neville,
Webster, Hudsmith,Slack, Wright, Fletcher, Toole, Halsall, Rickerby.*

11/12/1886   SUTTON (Home)   Won - 2T, 5M v 0
*14 men - 20 minutes each way
*Holder (full back); Gill, Booth, Robinson (¾ backs); Lund, Summers (½ backs); Marshall,
Toole, Halsall, Webster. Neville, Rickaby, Wright, Slack (forwards)*
Tries: Summers, Gill

16/12/1886   Bruckley (Away)   Result Not Known
*Holder (full back); Lund, Robinson, Gill (¾ backs); Booth (Capt.), Summers (½ backs);
Toole, Halsall, Webster, Neville, Rickerby, Wright, Slack, Hudsmith, J.Blanchard
(forwards)*

25/12/1886 BLACKROD (Home)   **Result Not Known**
T.Holder (full back); Lund, Gill, Robinson (¾ backs); W.Rimmer, Summers (½ backs); Webster, Slack, Toole, Fletcher, Booth, Blanchard, Rickaby, Halsall, Neville, Wright (forwards)

27/12/1886 THE DISTRICT (Home)   **Won - 2G, 1T, 1M v 0**
Proceeds to the Lifeboat Disaster Fund
T.Holder (full back); Lund, Gill, Robinson (¾ backs), W.Rimmer, Summers (½ backs); Webster, Slack, Toole, Fletcher, Booth, Blanchard, Rickaby, Halsall, Neville, Wright (forwards)

22/01/1887 Litherland (Away)   **Lost - 1M v 1G, 4T, 10M**
Yates (full back); Lund, Gill, Holder (¾ backs); W.Lowe, Summers (½ backs); J.Toole, Booth, Halsall, Fletcher, Wright, Slack, Webster, Booth, J.Blanchard, Rickerby, Hankinson (forwards)

29/01/1887 ST HELENS RECREATION (Home)   **Draw - 1T v 1DG**
No Line-up Available

05/02/1887 Swinton 'A' (Away)   **Lost - 0 v 3T**
Holmes (full back); Lund, Gill, Robinson (¾ backs); Summers (Capt), Shaw (½ backs); Halsall, Toole, Hankinson, Blundell, Marshall, Wright, Rickerby, Slack, Webster

12/02/1887 Leigh (Away)   **Lost - 1G, 1T v 2G 1T**
*1 man short
Holmes (full back); Lund, Gill, Robinson (¾ backs); Summers, Shaw (½ backs);Bell, Webster, Rimmer, Wright, Rickerby, Hankinson, Horrocks, Holder (forwards)

19/02/1887 BIRKDALE (Home)   **Won - 1G, 4T, 7M v 1T, 1M**
Lund, Gill, Robinson (¾ backs); Summers, Shaw (½ backs); Webster, Marshall, , Neville, , Slack, fletcher, Rickerby (forwards)

26/02/1887 Walton (Away)   **Won - 1G,2T,6M v 2M**
Holmes (full back); Lund, Gill, Robinson (¾ backs); Summers (Capt), Shaw (½ backs); Fletcher, Webster, Blundell, Parry, Slack, Mason, Wallwork, Bell, Rimmer (forwards)

05/03/1887 Aspull (Away)   **Lost - 1G, 1M v 2G 2T, 2M After Extra Time**
West Lancashire Cup
Holmes (full back); Lund, Gill, Robinson (¾ backs); Summers, Shaw (½ backs); Slack, Rickerby, Marshall, Fletcher, Wright, Toole, Blundell, Rimmer, Webster (forwards)

19/03/1887   RADCLIFFE (Home)   **Won - 1G, 9M v 2T, 2M**
H.Robinson (full back); Lund, Holmes, Gill (¾ backs); Summers, Shaw (½ backs); Halsall, Webster, Toole, Slack, Marshall, Fletcher, Wright, Rickerby, W.Rimmer (forwards)

26/03/1887   LEIGH (Home)   **Lost - 1G, 1T v 2G, 2T**
H.Robinson (full back); Lund, Holmes, Gill (¾ backs); Summers, Rimmer (½ backs); Slack, Parry, Fletcher, Webster, Halsall, Wright, Toole, Rickerby, Jones (forwards)

02/04/1887   WARRINGTON (Home)   **Won - 2T, 5M V 1T, 3M**
H.Robinson (full back); Lund, Summers, Moorfield (¾ backs); Shaw, Rimmer (½ backs); Slack (Capt), Fletcher, Jones, Webster, Marshall, Toole, Rickerby, skipper, Halsall (forwards)

08/04/1887   STOCKPORT (Home)   **Draw - 2T v 2T**
No Line-Up available

09/04/1887   SWINTON 'A' (Home)   **Won - 1G, 1T v 1T**
Slack, Toole, Fletcher, Wareing noted in the report. Full Line-Up Not Available.

16/04/1887   Liverpool Wanderers (Away)   **Won - 5G 2T 5M v 1M**
Wareing (full back); Lund, Gill, Robinson (¾ backs); Shaw, Summers (½ backs); Slack (capt), Webster, Fletcher, Toole, Jones, Rickerby, Wallwork, Parry, Coupar (forwards)

23/04/1887   BRACKLEY (Home)   **Lost - 0 v 1T**
Coupar (full back); Robinson, Shaw, Gill (¾ backs); Summers, Lowe (½ backs); Slack, Toole, Jones, Rickerby, Webster, Ripley, Fletcher, Wareing, Wallwork

1887/88

27/08/1887   LOCAL PLAYERS (Home)   Result Not Known
J.Yates (full back); A.Gill, H.Robinson, Moorfield (¾ backs); Shaw, Wallwork (½ backs);
Webster, Moreton, Wright, Rickerby, Mason, Halsall, Toole, Blanchard, Slack

10/09/1887   WIDNES ST MARYS (Home)   Lost - 0 v 1G, 1T
W.Rimmer (full back); H.Robinson, R.Parry, P.Moorfield, (¾ backs); G.R.Summers,
W.Lowe (½ backs); R.Slack (Capt), J.Mason, J.Yates,O.Pennington, W.Wallwork,
E.Webster, Brookfield, Segar, Blanchard (forwards)

24/09/1887   LEVENSHULME (Home)   Won - 1T 4M v 1M
T. Holder (full back); Gill, Robinson, Summers (¾ backs); Lowe, Rimmer (½ backs); Slack
(Capt), Webster, Rickerby, Toole, Mason, Bell, Wright, Fletcher, Wallwork (forwards)

01/01/1887   Stockport (Away)   Lost - 3M v 2G, 2T, 3M
*11 men
Webster, Rickerby, Wright, Slack, Bell included In report but no Full Line-Up Available

08/10/1887   MILNROW (Home)   Lost - 1T v 1G, 1T
Holder (full back); Robinson, Webster, Gill (¾ backs); Lowe, Summers (½ backs); Slack
(Capt.), Bell, Toole, Yates, Mason, Walwork, Brookfield, Melrose, Bulock (forwards)

15/10/1887   BIRKENHEAD WANDERERS (Home)   Draw - 1T v 1T
Holder (full back); Robinson, Chew, Gill (¾ backs); Summers, Abrams (½ backs); Slack,
Bell, Rickerby, Mason, Walwork, Toole, Rimmer, Webster, Parkes (forwards)

22/10/1887   MANCHESTER ATHLETIC (Home)   Won - 1G, 1T v 1T
Holder (full back); Webster, Francis, Jones (¾ backs); Summers, Abrams (½ backs);
Toole, Slack, Walwork, Rickerby, Mason, Rimmer, Halsall, Bell

29/10/1887   Whitefield (Away)   Won - 1G, 1T, 5M v 1T, 3M
Holder (full back); Parks, Webster, Chew (¾ backs); W.Rimmer, Robinson (½ backs);
Slack (Capt.), Bell, Wallwork, Halsall, Rickerby, Mason, Bulock, F.Rimmer, Atherton

05/11/1887   WALTON (Home)   Won - 2G, 4T, v 1M
Barnes (full back); Webster, Fletcher, Robinson (¾ backs); W.Rimmer, Summers (½
backs); Slack, Bell, Wallwork, T.Rimmer, Rickerby, Mason, Jones, Poole, Atherton

12/11/1887   Walton (Away)   Won - 1G, 4M v 3M
T.Holder (full back); Robinson, Fletcher, Webster (¾ backs); Summers, Rimmer (½
backs); Slack (Capt), Bell, Atherton, Walwork, Mason, Jones, Rickerby, Parks, Gill
(forwards)

19/11/1887   WIGAN OLD BOYS (Home)   Won - 2G, 7T, 11M v 1M
Holder (full back); Fletcher, Webster, Robinson (¾ backs); Rimmer, Summers (½ backs);
Slack (Capt), Bell, Walwork, Jones, Rickerby, Gill, Toole, Atherton, Mason (forwards)

26/11/1887   Bolton   (Away)   Lost - 2T, 3TD v 1G 2 T 2TD
*13 men
Holder (full back); Webster, Fletcher, Robinson (¾ backs); Rimmer, Summers (½ backs);
Slack (Capt), Bell, Jones, Toole, Parks, Mason, Walwork, Atherton, Gill (forwards)

03/12/1887   Tuebrook (Away)   Lost - 0 v 1T
Holder (full back); Robinson, Webster, Fletcher (¾ backs); Summers, Lowe (½ backs);
Slack (Capt), Mason, Bell, Rimmer, Gill, Jones, Wallwork, Toole, Rickerby (forwards)

10/12/1887   MAYFIELD (Home)   Won - 1G, 2T, 7M v 4M
Rickerby (full back); Webster, Holder, Robinson (¾ backs); Gill, Summers (½ backs); Slack
(Capt), Mason, Bell, Toole, Jones, Walwork, Fletcher, Gill, Yates (forwards)

17/12/1887   BOLTON (Home)   Won - 1G, 1T, 3M v 1T, 3M
Rickerby (full back); Webster, Holder, Fletcher (¾ backs); Rimmer, Summers (½ backs);
Slack (capt), Bell, Toole, Jones, Walwork, Mason, Gill, Moorfield, Atherton (forwards)

24/12/1887   Ringley   (Away)   Lost - 1M v 1G 12M
*Played men short
Walwork (full back); Moorfield (¾ backs); Gill (½ backs); Slack, Summers, Coventry,
Bell, Bicks, Atherton, P.Rimmer, Jones, Mason (forwards)

26/12/1887   BARTON (Home)   Draw - 1T v 1T
Walter Rimmer noted in the report. Full Line-Up Not Available.

31/12/1887   BIRKDALE (Home)   Won - 5G, 7T, 6M v 1M
Rickerby, Webster, Holder, Moorfield, Rimmer, Gill, Slack, Bell, Mason, Jones, Summers,
Fletcher, Barnes, Atherton, Wallwork.

07/01/1888   Birkenhead Wanderers (Away)   Won - 1G, 6M v 2T, 1M
Rickerby (full back); Webster, Holder, Moorfield (¾ backs); Rimmer, Summers (½ backs);
Slack (capt), Bell, Mason, Parks, Binks, Fletcher, Jones, Walwork, Another (forwards)

14/01/1888   TUEBROOK (Home)   Won - 3T, 10M v 3M
Rickerby (full back); Webster, Holder, Moorfield (¾ backs); W.Rimmer, Summers (½
backs); Slack (capt), Bell, Jones, Binks, Aughton, Fletcher, Yates, Mason, Gill (forwards)

21/01/1888   **Litherland (Away)**   **Drawn - 4M v 4M**
Walwork (full back); Gill, Webster, Aughton (¾ backs); Slack (capt), Bell, Mason,
Fletcher, Binks, Jones, Barnes, Moorfields, Rickerby (forwards)

28/01/1888   **RINGLEY (Home)**   **Won - 1G, 3T,v 1T**
Walwork (full back); Webster, Holder, Britton (¾ backs); Summers, Gill (½ backs);Slack,
Bill, Mason, Fletcher, Jones, Moorfield, Aughton, Rickerby, Binks (forwards)

04/02/1888   **WIGAN OLD BOYS (Home)**   **Won - 2G, 3T, 6M v 1T, 1M**
Wallwork, robinson, Webster, Britton, Summers, A.Rimmer, Slack, Bell, Mason, Jones,
Moorfield, Parks, Rickerby, Gill, Binks

18/02/1888   **NEW BRIGHTON OLYMPIC (Home)**   **Won - 3T, 10M v 6M**
Walwork (full back); Ribonson, Britton, Webster (¾ backs); Summers, A.Rimmer (½
backs); Slack, Bell, Mason, Jones, Rickerby, Gill, Binks, Moorfield, P.Rimmer (forwards)

03/03/1888   **Wigan (Away)**   **Lost - 0 v 3G, 3T**
West Lancashire Cup
Britton (full back); Webster, Holder, Robinson (¾ backs); Rimmer, Summers (½ backs);
Slack (Capt), Mason, Jones, Binks, Walwork, Rickerby, Parks, Moorfield, Gill (forwards)

10/02/1888   **BLUNDELSANDS (Home)**   **Lost - 1G, 1T v 2G, 1M**
Britton (full back); Robinson, Webster, Holder (¾ backs); Rimmer, Wallwork (½ backs);
Slack (capt), Toole, Mason, Bell, Rickerby, Binks, Moorfield, Gill, Parks (forwards)

24/03/1888   **PEMBERTON (Home)**   **Draw - 0 v 1TD, 5DB**
Rickerby, Robinson, Holder, Webster, Summers, A.Rimmer, Slack, Bell, Toole, Moorfield,
Gill, Barton, Binks, Mason, Wallwork

30/03/1888   **WHITEFIELD (Home)**   **Won - 2T, 5M v 1T, 4M**
Britton, Webster, Holder, Robinson, Summers, Rimmer, Slack, Rickerby, Mason, Toole,
Barton, Binks, Wallwork, Gill, Moorefield

31/03/1888   **STOCKPORT (Home)**   **Lost - 0 v 2G, 4T**
No Line-Up Available

02/04/1888   **MANCHESTER ATHLETIC (Home)**   **Lost - 0 v 2T**
No Line-Up Available

14/04/1888   **Blundelsands (Away)**   **Lost - 1T v 2G, 2T**
No line-up available

21/04/1888   **SUTTON (Home)**   **Lost - 1T v 2T**
No Line-up available

1888/89

08/09/1888   GORTON (Home)   Won - 2G, 1T, 8M v 1T, 4M
Melrose (full back); Robinson, Webster, Faulkner (¾ backs); Wright, Summers (½ backs); Wallwork, Brookfield, Rimmer, Lee, Toole, Binks, Parry, Hutchinson, richardson

15/09/1888   Levenshulme (Away)   Draw - 1T v 1T
N.Melrose (full back); M.Robinson, A.Gill, A.N.Other (¾ backs); G.Summers, R.Abrams (½ backs); Webster (Capt), Walwork, Brookfield, Faulks, T.Rimmer, J.Lee, H.Wright, W.Wareing, F.Parry (forwards)

22/09/1888   Pemberton (Away)   Lost - 0 v 1G, 1T
Melrose (full back); Robinson, Webster, Wareing (¾ backs); Abrams, Wallwork (½ backs); Toole, Binks Wright,Mason, Parry, Lee, T.Rimmer, Brookfield, Slack (forwards)

29/09/1888   ROCHDALE ST ALBION'S (Home)   Draw - 1G v 1G
Melrose; W.Rimmer, Webster, Wareing, Robinson, Abrams, Wallwork, Brookfield, T.Rimmer, Lee, Toole, Binks, Parry, Slack, Wright

05/10/1888   Bolton (Away)   Draw - 1T v 1T
Melrose (full back); Webster (Capt), Wareing, Becket (3/4) Robinson, Summers (½ backs); Brookfield, Parry, Wallwork, Rimmer, Toole, Binks, Scott, Fletcher, Cowper

13/10/1888   POOLSTOCK (Home)   Won - 1G v 2T, 7M
Melrose, Webster, Wareing, Becket, Robinson, Summers, Brookfield, Wallwork, Rimmer, Toole, Binks, Lee, Fletcher, Parry, Scott

20/10/1888   GRANGE (Home)   Draw - 2T, 7M v 2T
Williamson, Allen, Jackson, Becket, Seddon, Abrams, P.Rimmer, Eastham, Scott, Todd, Lee, Withnell, Clark, Jonesm Ellis

27/10/1888   WOODMAN ROVERS (Home)   Lost - 0 v 2G, 2T
Melrose, Holder, Webster, Robinson, Summers, W.Rimmer, Brookfield, Wallwork, Toole, Binks, T.Rimmer, Lee, Parry, Fletcher, Wareing

24/11/1888   Birkenhead Wanderers (Away)   Lost - 0 v 1, 5T, 4M
Rickerby, Beckett, Barton, Carfield, Abrams, Webster, Brookfield, Walwork, Toole, Binks, Perry, Cooper, Scott, Mason

01/12/1888   WIGAN ROVERS (Home)   Lost - 2T v 1G,1T
Rickerby, Robinson, Barton, Harrison, Rimmer, Melross, Brookfield, T.Rimmer, Walwork Perry, Mason, Faulks, Faulks, Binks, Toole, Hodson,

08/12/1888   Lancashire A.V. (Away)   **Lost - 0 v 2T**

Rickerby, Robinson, Barton, Webster, Corfield, Becket, Brookfield, Walwork, Rimmer,
Mason, Melrose, Parry, Faulks, P.Rimmer, T.Hodson

15/12/1888   LITHERLAND (Home)   **Won - 1G v 1T**

Melrose, Barton, Harrison, Robinson, Becket, Rimmer, Webster, Parry, Walwork,
Brookfield, Rimmer, Wickham, Mason, Hibbs, Rickerby

22/12/1888   BIRKENHEAD GYMNASIUM (Home)   **Won - 2T v 1T**

Rickerby, Barton, Robinson, Harrison, Rimmer, Becket, Webster, Mason, Melrose, Hibbs,
Walwork, T.Rimmer, Hodson, Binks, Parry

30/12/1888   Blundelsands (Away)   **Lost - 2G v 3G 1T**

No Line-up available

05/01/1889   Litherland (Away)   **No Result Known**

S.Lea, Yates, Cooper, Carr, Rimmer, Seddon, Rimmer, Toole, Ellis, Withnell, Gill,
Hutchison, Sullivan, Todd, Allen

19/01/1889   BLUNDELSANDS (Home)   **Win - 1G 2T v 2T**

Rickerby, Harrison, Barton, Beckett, Webster, Brockfield, Mason, Wickham, Walwork,
Baughan, Blundell, Hodson, T Rimmer, Robinson, A.Rimmer

26/01/1889   New Brighton Olympic (Away)   **Lost - 1T 7M v 1G 1M**

Rickerby, Robinson, Barton, Harrison, Rimmer, Hibbs, Webster, Brockfield, Mason,
Hodson, Blundell, Rimmer, Wickham, Binks, Walwork

09/02/1889   Levenshulme (Away)   **Won - 1G 2T v 2T**

Rickerby, Robinson, Harrison, Barton, Rimmer, Yates, Webster, Mason, Brockfield,
Baughan, Wallwork, Wickham, Perry, Beckett, Hudson

02/03/1889   Blundelsands (Away)   **Lost - 1G 2M v 2G 2M**

No Line-up available

04/03/1889   Wigan (Away)   **Lost - 0 v 2G, 2T, 3M**
West Lancs Senior Cup

Rickaby (Capt.) (full back); Webster, Barton, Harrison (¾ backs); Johnson, Cowper (½
backs); F.Hodson, Wikham, Mason, Wallwork, Faulkner, Rimmer, Parry, Yates, Baughan
(forwards)

09/03/1889   Wigan Rovers (Away)   **Lost - 1M v 3G 1T 1M**

Rickerby, Webster, Barton, Harrison, Couper, Robinson, Hudson, Wickham, Brockfield,
Baughan, Warwick, Perry, Mason, Rimmer, Yates

23/03/1889   **ST HELENS 'A' (Home)**   **Lost - 0 v 1T**

Rickerby, Barton, Wright, Wareing, Couper, Robinson, Webster, Brockfield, Hodson, Mason, Peryy, Baughan, Rimmer, Walwork, P Rimmer

29/03/1889   **TUEBROOK (Home)**   **No Result Known**

Rickerby, Wareing, Barton, Webster, Robinson, Couper, Wickham, Brockfield, Parry, Mason, P Rimmer, Wallwork, Baughan, T Rimmer, Hudson

13/04/1889   **Mayfield (Away)**   **Lost - 1T, 4M v 1G, 1T, 1M**

No Line-up available

Results & Statistics - Association

The following chapters contain the results and line-ups of all fixtures traceable. Other fixtures may have been arranged but there appears to be no record published in any local newspapers to confirm that they took place

Southport (Association) Football Club

1881/82

08/10/1881   Burscough (away)   **Lost 1-3***
* "TB Burnett's Southport"
No line-up available

12/11/1881   BOOTLE (SECOND) (Home)   **Drew 1 - 1**
S.Platt (Goal); J.Howard, B.Pidduck (backs) J.Melross, F. Jackson, P.Edwards (½ backs); J.Topliss, J.Sykes, F.Holden, T.B.Burnett (Capt.), W.Platt (forwards)

19/11/1881   Burscough (Away)   **Lost 0 - 1**
T.B.Burnett (Goal); J.G.Howard, J.Bullock (backs); J.B.Richardson, A.Bimpson (½ backs); Sykes, Melross, Carruthers, F.Holden, J.R.Topliss, J.Hatch (forwards)

26/11/1881   BLACKBURN LAW (Home)   **Lost 0 - 7**
No line-up available

24/12/1881   BURSCOUGH (Home)   **Won 2-1**
J.H.Hollis (Goal); E.Ramsbottom, A.Irving, R.L.Rylance, H.Baxter (backs), J.Melross, J.Bullock, W.Platt, H.A.Smith, J.R.Topliss, T.B.Burnett (Capt.) (forwards).

01/01/1882   TRADESMEN OF SOUTHPORT (Home)   **Won 7 - 0**
T.Barrow (Goal); A.Irving, J.H.Hollis (backs); C.R.L.Rylance, H.Baxter (½ backs); H.A.Smith, W.Platt, J.Topliss, J.Melross, E.Ramsbottom, T.B.Burnett (Capt.) (forwards)
NB: B.Pidduck played for the Tradesmen

02/01/1882   Croston (Away)   **Lost 2 - 4**
J.H.Hollis (Goal); Pidduck, Blockley (backs); E.Ramsbottom, H.Baxter (½ backs); J.Melross, W.Platt, J.Topliss. H.A.Smith, A.N.Other, T.B.Burnett (Capt.) (forwards)

07/01/1882   LIVERPOOL EXELSIOR (Home)   **Won 7 - 0**
J.H.Hollis (Goal); E.Ramsbottom, R.C.Rylance, J.B.Richardson, J.Bullock (backs); A. Bimpson, J.Melross, T.Colman, J.Sykes, H.A.Smith, T.B.Burnett (Capt.) (forwards)

14/01/1882   Tranmere Rovers (Away)   **Won 3 - 0**
No line-up available

21/01/1882   TRANMERE ROVERS (Home)   **Won 3 - 0**
J. H. Hollis (Goal); J.B.Richardson, W.Kay, B.Pidduck, R.L.Rylance (backs); J.Melross, H.A Smith, A. Briggs, T.B.Burnett (Capt.), J.T.Woodhead, J.H.Stone (forwards)

28/01/1882   Blackburn Law (Away)   Lost 0-6
J.H.Hollis (Goal); W.Kay, B.Pidduck (backs); E.Ramsbottom, A.Irving (½ backs); J.Melross,
H.A.Smith, T.B.Burnett (Capt.), Ellis, J.H.Stone, J.B.Richardson (forwards)
NB: Rylance captained Blackburn Law

04/02/1882   WIRRAL (Home)   Lost 2 - 3
No line-up available

11/02/1882   Bootle Wanderers (Away)   Lost 0 - 2
No line-up available

18/02/1882   BOOTLE WANDERERS (Home)   Won 4 - 2
W.Platt (Goal); W.Kay, H.Baxter, R.L.Rylance, E.Ramsbottom (backs); J.B.Richardson,
J.H.Stone, A.Briggs, H.A.Smith, J.Melross, T.B.Burnett (Capt.) (forwards).

25/02/1882   Kirkdale St Mary's (Away)   Lost 0 - 8
No line-up available

1882/83

23/09/1882   LIVERPOOL ROVERS (Home)   Won 4 - 0
S.Platt (Goal); B.Pidduck, J.Hands, J.Briggs, T.Colman, E.Calvert, A.Dalby, A.Dalby, C.Ambler, T.B.Burnett, A.Irving

30/09/1882   Liverpool 'A' (Away)   Lost 0 - 1
Clark (Goal); W.Kay, B.Pidduck, R.L.Rylance, J.Melross, J.Briggs, T.Colman, A.Dalby, A.Dalby, C.Ambler, W.Platt

07/10/1882   LIVERPOOL RAMBLERS (Home)   Draw 1 - 1
FA Cup / 1
W.Platt (Goal); T.B.Burnett, B.Pidduck, E.Ramsbottom, R.L.Rylance, J.Briggs, T.Colman, A.Dalby, A.Dalby, E.Calvert, C.Ambler

14/10/1882   Bolton Olympic (Away)   Lost 1 - 5
W.Platt(Goal); W.Kay, T.B.Burnett; R.L.Rylance, A.Bimson, E.Ramsbottom; C.Ambler, A.Dalby, T.Colman J.Briggs, , R.Howard,

21/10/1882   STACKSTEADS WORKING MEN (Home)   Won 4 - 0
Lancashire Senior Cup / 1
S.Platt (Goal); W.Kay, B.Pidduck, R.L.Rylance, E.Ramsbottom, J.Melross, J.Briggs, T.Colman, E.Calvert, C.Ambler, T.B.Burnett

28/10/1882   Birkenhead (Away)   Draw 1 - 1
S.Platt (Goal); W.Kay, R.L.Rylance, E.Ramsbottom, J.Melross, J.Briggs, T.Colman, A.Dalby, E.Calvert, T.B.Burnett, R.Howard

04/11/1882   Liverpool Ramblers (Away)   Lost 0 - 4
FA Cup / 1R
T.B.Burnett (Goal); B.Pidduck, R.L.Rylance, E.Ramsbottom, J.Melross, J.Briggs, T.Colman, A.Dalby, A.Dalby, C.Ambler, W.Hatch

11/11/1882   Kirkdale St Mary's (Away)   Lost 0 - 7
S.Platt (Goal); W.Kay, E.Ramsbottom, J.Briggs, A.Dalby, C.Ambler, T.B.Burnett, Halsall, W.Platt, A.Bimson, R.Howard

18/11/1882   UNITED SCHOOLS (Home)   Lost 0 - 1
S.Platt (Goal); W.Kay, B.Pidduck, E.Ramsbottom, J.Melross, J.Briggs, A.Dalby, A.Dalby, C.Ambler, T.B.Burnett, R.Howard

25/11/1882   BOOTLE   Lost 0-7
W.Kay (Goal); T.Burnett, H.Baxter, J.Johnson, Parkes; J.Melross, ,Smalley, C.Ambler, R.Howard, P.Mellor, Briggs

02/12/1882   LINDON (Home)   **Won 4 - 1**
S.Platt (Goal); W.Kay, B.Pidduck, J.Hands, R.L.Rylance, E.Ramsbottom, J.Melross,
J.Briggs, P.Mellor, C.Ambler, T.B.Burnett

09/12/1882   Rishton (Away)   **Lost 4 - 5**
Lancashire Senior Cup / 2
S.Platt (Goal); W.Kay, H.Baxter, J.Hands, E.Ramsbottom, R.L.Rylance, J.Melross, J.Briggs,
P.Mellor, C.Ambler, T.B.Burnett

16/12/1882   BURSCOUGH (Home)   **Won 2-1**
W.Kay, H.Baxter, B.Pidduck, J.Melross, J.Briggs, P.Mellor, A.Dalby, C.Ambler, T.Burnett,
J.Johnson

23/12/1882   EVERTON (Home)   **Drew 2-2**
S.Platt (Goal); T.Iddon, W.Kay, E.Ramsbottom, J.B.Hands, H.Baxter, T.Briggs, T.Mellor,
A.Evans, A.B.Dalby, T.B.Burnett

31/12/1882   BLACKBURN LAW   **Won 4-3**
S.Platt (Goal); E.Rammsbottom, B.Pidduck, J.Heald, H.Baxter, J.Acton, W.J.Kay, J.Briggs,
T.Mellor, P.Hassall , T.B.,Burnett (Capt)

13/01/1883   Bolton Olympic (Away)   **Lost 1-3**
S.Platt (Goal); E.Ramsbottom, J.Parkes, R.L.Rylance, H.Baxter; C.Ambler, A.Dalby,
J.Briggs, R.Howard, J.R.Hatch, T.B.Burnett (Capt.)

03/02/1883   Tranmere (Away)   **Won 4-0**
S.Platt (Goal); A.B.Dalby, J.H.Johnson, M.Aughton, R.L.Rylance, J.Melross, J.R.Smalley,
J.Briggs, P.Mellor, C.Ambler, T.B.Burnett (Capt.)

10/02/1883   CROSTON (Home)   **Won 1-0**
S.Platt (Goal); J.H.Johnson, Whittaker, H.Baxter, R.L.Rylance; C.Ambler, J.Briggs,
E.Ramsbottom, Smalley, P.Mellor, T.B.Burnett

03/03/1883   DOVER FC (Home)   **Won 2-1**
*mixed 1st/2nd team fixture
Lawton (Goal); Howard, E.Ramsbottom, C.Ambler, P.Mellor, Hatch, Smith, Johnson,
Whittaker, Carter, Iddon

10/03/1883   St Benedicts, Liverpool (Away)   **Lost 1 - 8**
*Possibly a 2nd team game. Listed in Athletic News but not Southport Visiter or Guardian
Goal: Urmston
No Line-Up Available

24/03/1883   **BOOTLE (Home)**   **Lost 3-5**
S.Platt (Goal); H.Baxter, R.L.Rylance; E.Ramsbottom, Dalby; Briggs, Mellor, T.B.Burnett (Capt.), J.Howard, Hatch, J.Melross.

30/03/1883   **LIVERPOOL ROVERS (Home)**   **Won 3-2**
A.B.Dalby (Goal); W.Kay, W.Whittaker, M.Aughton, Johnson, Hatch (backs); Briggs, P.Mellor, Evans, J.Melross, T.B.Burnett (forwards)

14/04/1883   **MEADOW HEAD FORESTERS, BLACKBURN (Home)**   **Draw 1-1**
Ambler, Whittaker, Ramsbottom, Rylance, Hatch noted in the report. Full Line-Up Not Available.

21/04/1883   **ST BENEDICTS, LIVERPOOL (Home)**   **Won 5-1**
Kay (Goal); Whittaker, Johnson, Dalby, Baxter (backs); Ambler, Burnett, Briggs, Mellor, Barrow, Melross (forwards)

1883/84

01/09/1883   Southport Cricket Club (Away)   Won by 1 run (57 v 56)
*Cricket Game
T.B.Burnett, J Dickerson, P.Mellor, T.Morris, J.Hatch, W.Kay, T.Sellars, J.Woodhouse,
E.Houghton, J.Platt, Ramsbottom

04/08/1883   Southport Olympic (Away)   Result Not Known
No Line-Up Available

08/09/1883   Croston (Away)   Won 4 - 2
S.Platt (Goal); H.Baxter, R.L.Rylance, E.Ramsbottom, J.Melross, P.Mellor, Aughton,
W.Whittaker, C.Ambler, T.B.Burnett, E.Martin

15/09/1883   Everton (Away)   Lost 0 - 3
S.Platt (Goal); H.Baxter, R.L.Rylance, E.Ramsbottom, J.Melross, J.Briggs, P.Mellor,
W.Whittaker, C.Ambler, T.B.Burnett, E.Martin

22/09/1883   Meadow Head Foresters (Away)   Lost 0-9
No Line-Up Available

29/09/1883   Liverpool Rovers (Away)   Won 3-2
S.Platt (Goal); Pidduck, Whittaker (backs); Ramsbottom, Johnson (½ backs); Melross,
Martin (rights); Burnett, Morris (centres), Briggs, Mellor (lefts)

06/10/1883   BOLTON (Home)   Lost 0-5
Platt (Goal); Rylance, Whittaker (backs); Baxter, Ramsbottom (½ backs); Melross,
Martin, Briggs, Mellor, Burnett, Morris (forwards)

13/10/1883   HURST PARK ROAD (Home)   Won 3 - 0
Lancashire Senior Cup / 1
S.Platt (Goal); H.Baxter, R.L.Rylance, E.Ramsbottom, J.Melross, J.Briggs, P.Mellor,
W.Whittaker, C.Ambler, T.B.Burnett, T.Morris

20/10/1883   Blackburn Rovers (Away)   Lost 0 - 7
FA Cup / 1 (1500)
S.Platt (Goal); H.Baxter, R.L.Rylance, E.Ramsbottom, J.Melross, J.Briggs, P.Mellor,
W.Whittaker, A.Dalby, T.B.Burnett, T.Morris

27/10/1883   BIRKENHEAD (Home)   Won 4 - 0
S.Platt (Goal); H.Baxter, R.L.Rylance, E.Ramsbottom, J.Melross, J.Briggs, P.Mellor,
C.Ambler, T.B.Burnett, A.Bailey, T.Morris

03/11/1883   Bootle   (Away)   **Lost 0 - 2**
S.Platt (Goal); H.Baxter, T.B.Burnett (backs); Rylance (Capt.), A.Dalby, E.Ramsbottom, (½ backs); P.Mellor, J.Briggs, C.Ambler, T.Morris, J.Melross (forwards)

10/11/1883   Darwen Saxons (Away)   **Draw 1-1**
S.Platt (Goal); H.Baxter, Burnett (backs); Rylance, Ramsbottom, A.B.Dalby (½ backs); P.Mellor, C.Ambler (lefts); J.Melross, T.Morris (rights); J.J.Briggs (centre)

17/11/1883   SOUTHPORT OLYMPIC   (Home)   **Won 2-0**
S.Platt (Goal); H.Baxter, T.B.Burnett, Ramsbottom, A.B.Dalby, Heald (backs); Mellor, Ambler, Briggs, Melross, Morris (forwards)

24/11/1883   LIVERPOOL RAMBLERS (Home)   **Lost 2 - 4**
Liverpool Challenge Cup
S.Platt (Goal); H.Baxter, R.L.Rylance, J.Melross, J.Briggs, P.Mellor, W.Whittaker, A.Dalby, T.B.Burnett, E.Martin, T.Morris

01/12/1883   WHEELTON (Home)   **Won 4 - 3**
Lancashire Senior Cup / 2
S.Platt (Goal); H.Baxter, T.B.Burnett (backs); R.L.Rylance, A.B.Dalby, J.H.Johnson (½ backs); T.Morris, J.Melross, J.J.Briggs, P.Mellor, E.Martin (forwards)

13/12/1883   BLACKBURN ROVERS (Home)   **Lost 1-0**
S.Platt (Goal); T.B.Burnett, Baxter, Rylance, Dalby, Ramsbottom (backs); Morris, Melross, Briggs, Mellor, Martin

15/12/1883   LIVERPOOL ROVERS (Home)   **Won 2-0**
S.Platt (Goal); T.B.Burnett, H.Baxter (backs); R.L.Rylance, E.Ramsbottom (½ backs); A.B.Dalby, J.J.Briggs (centres); P.Mellor, E.Martin (lefts); J.Melross, T.Morris (rights)

22/12/1883   BLACKBURN OLYMPIC (Home)   **Lost 0 - 2**
Lancashire Senior Cup / 3
No Line-Up Available

29/12/1883   LEVENSHULME (Home)   **Won 5-0**
E.Stewart (Goal); W.Kay, W.Benyon (backs); J.H.Johnson, A.Bailey, J.Parks (half backs); J.Melross (Capt.), T.Morris (right); J.Mayall, P.Mellor (left); J.R.Hatch (Centre)

05/01/1884   BIRKENHEAD (Home)   **Result Not Known**
S.Platt (Goal); H.Baxter, T.Burnett (backs); E.Stewart, A.B.Dalby, R.L.Rylance (half backs); J.Worsley, C.Morris, J.Mayall, P.Mellor, J.J.Briggs (forwards)

12/01/1884 **CRESCENT (Home)** **Result Not Known**
S.Platt (Goal); Baxter, Burnett, Rylance, Dalby, Johnson, Mellor, Mayall, Briggs, Melross, T.Morris

19/01/1884 **Wigan (Away)** **Lost 2-3**
Platt (Goal); Baxter, Burnett, Rylance, Dalby, Jackson (backs); Morris, Melross, Briggs, Mellor, Mayall (forwards)

26/01/1884 **Birkenhead (Away)** **Result Not Known**
S.Platt (Goal); T.Burnett, H.Baxter (backs); R.Rylance (Capt.), A.B.Dalby, E.Stewart (half backs); T.Morris, J.Melross, J.J.Briggs, P.Mellor, J.Mayall

02/02/1884 **STRETFORD (Home)** **Result Not Known**
S.Platt (Goal); T.Burnett, H.Baxter (backs); R.L.Rylance (Capt.), A.B.Dalby, J.H.Johnson (half backs); J.Melross, T.Morris, J.J.Briggs, P.Mellor, Mayall

09/02/1884 **Birkenhead (Away)** **Won 2-0**
S.Platt (Goal); B.Pidduck, H.Baxter (backs); R.L.Rylance (Capt.), A.B.Dalby, J.H.Johnson (half backs); T.Burnett, T.Morris, J.J.Briggs, J.Mayall, P.Mellor

16/02/1884 **UNITED SCHOOLS (Home)** **Won 5-0**
Mayall (Goal); Baxter, Jackson (backs); Rylance, Dalby, Johnson (half backs); Morris, Melross, Briggs, Mellor, Burnett (forwards)

23/02/1884 **CROSTON (Home)** **Won 11-1**
S.Platt (Goal); T.Burnett, H.Baxter (backs); J.H.Johnson, A.B.Dalby, R.L.rylance (half); T.Morris, J.Melross, J.J.Briggs, P.Mellor, C.Morris

01/03/1884 **SOUTHPORT & DISTRICT (Home)** **Won 4-1**
S.Platt (Goal); T.Burnett, H.Baxter (backs); R.L.Rylance, A.B.Dalby, J.H.Johnson (half); T.Morris, J.Melross, J.J.Briggs, P.Mellor, C.Morris

08/03/1884 **LIVERPOOL RAMBLERS (Home)** **Lost 1-3**
S.Platt (Goal); H.Baxter, T.B.Burnett (backs); R.L.Rylance (Capt.), A.B.Dalby, J.H.Johnson (½ backs), J.J.Briggs (centre), T.Morris, J.J.Melross (right), P.Mellor, C.Morris (left)

15/03/1884 **Everton (Away)** **Draw 2 - 2**
S.Platt (Goal); H.Baxter, T.B.Burnett (backs); Ramsbottom, A.B.Dalby, J.H.Johnson (½ backs); E.Martin, P.Mellor, J.J.Briggs, J.Melross, J.Melross, T.Morris

22/03/1884 **WIGAN (Home)** **Won 3-0**
S.Platt (Goal); H.Baxter, T.B.Burnett (backs); Stewart, Dalby, Johnson (½ backs); T.Morris, J.Melross, J.J.Briggs, P.Mellor, J.Hatch

29/03/1884   **BOOTLE (Home)**   **Lost 0-1**
S.Platt (Goal); F.Jackson, J.H.Johnson (backs); J.Mayall, A.B.Dalby (Capt.), J.E.Marchant (half backs); J.Melross, T.Morris, P.Mellor, E.Martin, J.J.Briggs (forwards)

05/04/1884   **UNITED SCHOOLS**   **Result Not Known**
S.Platt (Goal); T.Burnett, H.Baxter (backs); J.H.Johnson, A.B.Dalby, Bailey (half backs); J.Melross, E.Martin, J.J.Briggs, C.Morris, J.Mayall

11/04/1884   **DARWEN SAXONS (Home)**   **Result Not Known**
J.Mayall (Goal); T.Burnett, H.Baxter (backs); E.Stewart, A.B.Dalby (Capt.), J.Bailey (half); T.Morris, J.J.Briggs, P.Mellor, C.Morris

12/04/1884   **LIVERPOOL ROVERS**   **(Home)**   **Won 4-1**
Mayall (Goal); T.Burnett, Baxter (backs); E.Stewart, Bailey, A.B.Dalby (half); T.Morris, Melross, Halsall, C.Morris, Mellor

14/04/1884   **EVERTON**   **Result Not Known**
No Line-Up Available

1884/85

06/09/1884   STOKE (Home)   Lost 0 - 2
S.Platt (Goal); H.Baxter, E.Ramsbottom, J.Melross, J.Briggs, P.Mellor, A.Dalby, T.Morris, A.Bailey, J.Johnson, Critchley

13/09/1884   SOUTHPORT WEDNESDAY (Home)   Won 4 - 0
S.Platt (Goal); H.Baxter, J.Melross, J.Briggs, P.Mellor, A.Dalby, T.Morris, J.Johnson, Jackson, W.Hodge, Critchley

20/09/1884   HORWICH (Home)   Won 3 - 1
Lancashire Senior Cup / 1
S.Platt (Goal); H.Baxter, E.Ramsbottom, J.Melross, J.Briggs, P.Mellor, A.Dalby, T.Morris, A.Bailey, J.Johnson, Critchley

04/10/1884   STANLEY (Home)   Lost 2 - 4
S.Platt (Goal); H.Baxter, E.Ramsbottom, J.Melross, J.Briggs, P.Mellor, A.Dalby, T.Morris, A.Bailey, J.Johnson, Critchley

11/10/1884   Accrington (Away)   Lost 0 - 3
FA Cup / 1
***Accrington Disqualified and Southport reinstated**
S.Platt (Goal); H.Baxter, E.Ramsbottom, J.Melross, J.Briggs, P.Mellor, A.Dalby, T.Morris, A.Bailey, J.Johnson, Critchley

18/10/1884   BOOTLE (Home)   Draw 0 - 0
S.Platt (Goal); H.Baxter, E.Ramsbottom, J.Melross, J.Briggs, P.Mellor, A.Dalby, T.Morris, A.Bailey, J.Johnson, Critchley

20/10/1884   SHEFFIELD (Home)   Lost 0 - 3
S.Platt (Goal); H.Baxter, E.Ramsbottom, J.Melross, P.Mellor, C.Morris, A.Dalby, T.Morris, A.Bailey, J.Johnson, Critchley

25/10/1884   Darwen Old Wanderers (Away)   Lost 2 - 6
S.Platt (Goal); H.Baxter, E.Ramsbottom, J.Melross, J.Briggs, A.Dalby, T.B.Burnett, T.Morris, A.Bailey, J.Johnson, Critchley

01/11/1884   PRESTON NORTH END (Home)   Won 1 - 0
Lancashire Senior Cup / 2
S.Platt (Goal); H.Baxter, E.Ramsbottom, J.Melross, J.Briggs, A.Dalby, T.B.Burnett, T.Morris, A.Bailey, J.Johnson, Critchley

08/11/1884   SOUTHPORT HIGH PARK (Home)   Won 4 - 1
Liverpool Challenge Cup
S.Platt (Goal); H.Baxter, E.Ramsbottom, J.Melross, P.Mellor, C.Morris, A.Dalby,
T.B.Burnett, T.Morris, A.Bailey, J.Johnson

15/11/1884   Liverpool Ramblers (Away)   Lost 0 - 3
S.Platt (Goal); H.Baxter, E.Ramsbottom, J.Melross, J.Briggs, P.Mellor, A.Dalby,
T.B.Burnett, T.Morris, A.Bailey, J.Johnson

22/11/1884   CLITHEROE LOW MOOR (Home)   Won 3 - 1
FA Cup / 2
S.Platt (Goal); H.Baxter, E.Ramsbottom, J.Melross, J.Briggs, P.Mellor, A.Dalby,
T.B.Burnett, T.Morris, A.Bailey, J.Johnson

29/11/1884   DARWEN (Home)   Lost 1 - 2
Lancashire Senior Cup / 3
S.Platt (Goal); H.Baxter, J.Melross, J.Briggs, P.Mellor, A.Dalby, T.B.Burnett, T.Morris,
A.Bailey, J.Johnson, R.Chadwick

13/12/1884   MELLOR VALE (Home)   Won 3 - 1
J.Mayall (Goal); H.Baxter, E.Ramsbottom, J.Melross, J.Briggs, P.Mellor, A.Dalby,
A.Bailey, J.Johnson, W.Hodge, T.Morris

19/12/1884   EVERTON (Home)   Lost 1 - 2
Liverpool Challenge Cup / 2
T.Parkes (Goal); S.Platt, H.Baxter, J.Melross, J.Briggs, P.Mellor, A.Dalby, T.B.Burnett,
T.Morris, A.Bailey, J.Johnson

03/01/1885   Church (Away)   Lost 0 - 10
FA Cup / 3
No Line-Up Available

10/01/1885   Sheffield (Away)   Draw 1 - 1
S.Platt (Goal); Baxter, Parks, Johnson, Ramsbottom (capt), Bailey, T.Morris, W.Hodge,
Burnett, Mellor, C.Morris

17/01/1885   WALLASEY & DISTRICT (Home)   Won 1-0
J.Mayall (Goal); Baxter, Burnett, A.B.Dalby (Capt), Bailey, Johnson, Hodge, Melross,
S.Platt, Briggs, Mellor

24/01/1885   Bootle   (Away)   Lost 1 - 3
S.Platt (Goal); H.Baxter, J.Griffiths (backs) J.Johnson, A.Dalby, H.B.Bailey (½ backs)
C.Morris, J.Melross (rights), J.Briggs (centre), P.Mellor, A.Hodge (lefts)

31/01/1885   LANCASHIRE & YORKSHIRE RAILWAY   Won - Score Not Known
Southport Charity Cup / 1st Round
S.Platt (Goal); Baxter, Griffiths, Dalby (Capt.),Bailey, Johnson, Morris, Melross, Briggs,
Mellor, Burnett.

07/02/1885   BLACKBURN NOMADS (Home)   Won 6-0
Platt (Goal), Baxter, Griffiths, Johnson, Bailey, Morris, Melross, Dalby, Burnett, Mellor,
Briggs

21/02/1885   SOUTHPORT WANDERERS (Home)   Won 2-0
Burnett (Goal); Baxter, Griffiths, Bailey, Johnson, Richardson, Morris, Melross, Dalby
(Capt.), Mellor, Hodge

07/03/1885   BIRKDALE AMATEURS   (Home)   Won - Score Not Known
Southport Charity Cup / 2nd Round
S.Platt (Goal); Baxter, Griffiths, Johnson, A.B.Dalby (Capt.), Bailey, Morris, Melross,
Mellor, Burnett, Hodge

14/03/1885   Wigan (Away)   Draw 0 - 0
S.Platt (Goal); H.Baxter, J.Melross, J.Griffiths, P.Mellor, A.Dalby, T.B.Burnett, A.Bailey,
J.Johnson, W.Hodge, T.Morris

21/03/1885   Wallasey (Away)   Won 6-1
Burnett (Goal); Baxter, Griffiths, Johnson, Bailey, Morris, Melross, Hodge, Dalby, Mellor,
Briggs

28/03/1885   CHRIST CHURCH (Home)   Won - Score Not Known
Southport Charity Cup / Semi-Final
S.Platt (Goal); Baxter, Griffiths, Bailey, Dalby (Capt.), Johnson, Morris, Melross, Mellor,
Briggs, Burnett

03/04/1885   MANCHESTER (Home)   Result Not Known
No Line-up available

04/04/1885   BURSCOUGH (Home)   Result Not Known
No Line-up available

06/04/1885   SOUTHPORT WANDERERS (Home)   Result Not Known
No Line-up available

11/04/1885   CRESCENT (Home)   **Won 5 - 0**
Southport Charity Cup / Final
S.Platt (Goal); H.Baxter, Griffiths, Bailey, A.B.Dalby (Capt.), Johnson, T.Morris, J.Melross, T.B.Burnett, Briggs, Mellor

18/04/1885   Oldham (Away)   **Draw 3-3**
Mayall (Goal);Baxter, Ramsbottom, Platt, Johnson, Bailey, Morris, Melross, Mellor, Briggs, Burnett

16/05/1885   DISTRICT   **Result Not Known**
J.Mayall (Goal); Baxter, Griffiths, Bailey, Platt, Johnson, Morris (Capt.), Melross, Dalby, Hodge, Mellor

1885/86

05/09/1885   TURTON (Home)   **Won 3 - 1**
J.Mayall (Goal); H.Baxter, J.Griffiths, J.Briggs, P.Mellor, C.Morris, T.Morris, A.Bailey,
J.Johnson, J.Halsall, W.Hodge

12/09/1885   Burscough (Away)   **Won 3 - 1**
Liverpool Challenge Cup / 1
J.Mayall (Goal); H.Baxter, J.Melross, J.Griffiths, J.Briggs, P.Mellor, C.Morris, T.Morris,
J.Johnson, W.Hodge, A.Bailey

19/09/1885   High Park (Away)   **Lost 1 - 2**
J.Mayall (Goal); H.Baxter, J.Melross, J.Griffiths, J.Briggs, P.Mellor, C.Morris, J.Johnson,
Gosson, W.Hodge, Critchley

26/09/1885   FISHWICK RAMBLERS (Home)   **Lost 0 - 7**
S.Platt (Goal); H.Baxter, J.Melross, J.Griffiths, J.Briggs, P.Mellor, C.Morris, W.Bailey,
W.Hodge, A.Bailey, T.Morris

28/09/1885   SHEFFIELD (Home)   **Lost 1 - 2**
E. Ramsbottom, Wright, J.Melross, J.Griffiths, P.Mellor, C.Morris, T.B.Burnett, T.Morris,
A.Bailey, J.Johnson, J.Richardson

03/10/1885   Darwen (Away)   **Lost 1 - 12**
Lancashire Senior Cup / 1
J.Mayall (Goal); S.Platt, H.Baxter, Wright, J.Griffiths, J.Briggs, C.Morris, J.Richardson,
T.Morris, A.Bailey, J.Johnson

10/10/1885   ASTLEY BRIDGE (Home)   **Lost 2 - 3**
FA Cup / 1
S.Platt (Goal); H.Baxter, J.Melross, J.Griffiths, J.Briggs, P.Mellor, C.Morris, A.Bailey,
J.Johnson, J.Richardson, T.Morris

17/10/1885   Southport Wanderers (Away)   **Won 4 - 1**
S.Platt (Goal); H.Baxter, J.Melross, J.Griffiths, J.Briggs, P.Mellor, C.Morris, W.Bailey,
A.Bailey, J.Johnson, T.Morris

24/10/1885   BURSCOUGH (Home)   **Won 1 - 0**
Liverpool Challenge Cup / 1
S.Platt (Goal); H.Baxter, J.Melross, J.Griffiths, J.Briggs, C.Morris, A.Bailey, J.Johnson,
W.Hodge, J.Richardson, T.Morris

31/10/1885   CAMBRIAN (Home)   Won 3 - 1
J.Mayall (Goal); H.Baxter, J.Griffiths, W.Morris, J.Richardson, T.Morris, T.Sellars, J.Johnson, J.Leadbetter, W.Hodge, T.Lea

07/11/1885   Everton (Away)   Lost 0 - 3
J.Mayall (Goal); H.Baxter, J.Griffiths, J.Briggs, P.Mellor, C.Morris, P. Hodge, W.Morris, J.Johnson, A.Bailey, T.Morris

14/11/1885   SOUTHPORT WANDERERS (Home)   Won 3 - 1
S.Platt (Goal); J.Mayall, J.Melross, J.Griffiths, J.Briggs, C.Morris, W.Morris, A.Bailey, T.Morris, J.Johnson, W.Hodge

21/11/1885   Stanley (Away)   Lost 1 - 5
J.Mayall (Goal); H.Baxter, J.Melross, J.Griffiths, J.Briggs, W.Morris, C.Morris, A.Bailey, J.Johnson, W.Hodge, T.Morris
Goal: A.Bailey

28/11/1885   Liverpool Ramblers (Away)   Draw 0-0
Platt (Goal); Baxter, Griffiths, Bailey, Johnson, Briggs, Mellor, Richardson, C.Morris, T.Morris, Gill

12/12/1885   BOOTLE (Home)   Lost 0 - 5
Liverpool Challenge Cup / 2
S.Platt (Goal); H.Baxter, J.Melross, J.Griffiths, J.Briggs, P.Mellor, C.Morris, W.Bailey, J.Johnson, J.Richardson, T.Morris

19/12/1885   BURSCOUGH (Home)   Won - Score Not Known
No Line-Up Available

25/12/1885   HIGH PARK (Home)   Won 1 - 0
Hesketh (Goal), Burnett, Griffiths, Johnson, Briggs, Bailey, Melross, R.Dutton, C.Morris, P.Mellor, W.Morris

26/12/1885   WIGAN (Home)   Won 6 - 1
J.Morris (Goal); Burnett, Mayall, Bailey, Briggs (Capt.), Johnson, Melross, Dutton, C.Morris, Mellor, W.Morris

01/01/1886   NEWTON HEATH (Home)   Won 2 - 1
J.Mayall (Goal); S.Platt, H.Baxter, J.Melross, J.Briggs, P.Mellor, C.Morris, T.B.Burnett, D.Dutton, W.Hodge, T.Morris

02/01/1886   Liverpool Ramblers (Away)   Won 2 - 0
J.Mayall (Goal); S.Platt, H.Baxter, J.Briggs, P.Mellor, C.Morris, W.Morris, T.B.Burnett, W.Bailey, D.Dutton, T.Morris

16/01/1886   SOUTHPORT WANDERERS (Home)   Lost 2 - 3
S.Platt (Goal); J.Melross, J.Briggs, P.Mellor, C.Morris, C. Riley, A. Dalby, A.Bailey,
D.Dutton, T.Morris   , J.Johnson

23/01/1886   Liverpool Cambrian (Away)   Result Not Known

30/01/1886   Newton Heath (Away)   Lost 0 - 4
J.Mayall (Goal); J.Melross, P.Mellor, J.Sykes, W.Morris, C.Morris, T.B.Burnett, W.Bailey,
J.Johnson, W.Hodge, D.Dutton

06/02/1886   ECCLES BOROUGH (Home)   Draw 0 - 0
J.Mayall (Goal); Ormerod, J.Melross, P.Mellor, Walmsley, W.Morris, T.B.Burnett,
W.Bailey, T.Morris, J.Johnson, D.Dutton

13/02/1886   Fishwick Ramblers (Away)   Lost 2 - 5
No Line-Up Available

20/02/1886   Wigan (Away)   Result Not Known

27/02/1886   SOUTHPORT WANDERERS (Home)   Won 4 - 0
J.Mayall (Goal); S.Platt, H.Baxter, P.Mellor, C.Morris, W.Morris, T.B.Burnett, W.Bailey,
J.Johnson, D.Dutton, T.Morris

06/03/1886   LIVERPOOL RAMBLERS (Home)   Result Not Known
*At Sandringham Road School
No Line-Up Available

13/03/1886   BOOTLE (Home)   Draw 1 - 1
No Line Up Given

20/03/1886   Everton (Away)   Lost 2 - 8
J.Mayall (Goal); H.Baxter, J.Briggs, P.Mellor, W.Morris, C.Morris, T.B.Burnett, A.Bailey,
J.Johnson, D.Dutton, T.Morris

27/03/1886   BURSCOUGH (Neutral)   Draw 1 - 1
Southport Charity Cup
No Line-Up Available

03/04/1886   STANLEY (Home)   Won 2-0
T.B.Burnett (Goal); J.Mayall, J.Griffiths; J.Melross, Bailey, J.Briggs, P.Mellor, W.Morris,
C.Morris, D.Dutton, T.Morris

10/04/1886   **BURSCOUGH (Home)**   **Won 7 - 0**
Southport Charity Cup / 1
J.Mayall (Goal); S.Platt, J.Melross, J.Briggs, C.Morris, W.Morris, T.B.Burnett, W.Bailey, J.Johnson, D.Dutton, T.Morris

17/04/1886   **LIVERPOOL RAMBLERS (Home)**   **Won 2 - 0**
Platt (Goal); Clare, Mayall (backs); Johnson, Briggs, Bailey (½ backs); Mellor, Dutton, T.Morris, C.Morris, W.Morris (forwards)

23/04/1886   **HIGH PARK (Home)**   **Won 2 - 0**
No Line-Up Available

01/05/1886   **CHRIST CHURCH (Home)**   **Won 2 - 1**
Southport Charity Cup / SF
J.Mayall (Goal); H.Baxter, J.Briggs, P.Mellor, W.Morris, C.Morris, T.B.Burnett, W.Bailey, J.Johnson, D.Dutton, T.Morris

08/05/1886   **SOUTHPORT WANDERERS (Home)**   **Won 4 - 0**
Southport Charity Cup / Final
J.Mayall (Goal); H.Baxter, J.Briggs, P.Mellor, W.Morris, C.Morris, T.B.Burnett, W.Bailey, J.Johnson, D.Dutton, T.Morris

Southport Wanderers

1884/85

13/09/1884   Halliwell (Away) Lost   Lost 0 - 20
Kay (Goal); Parks, Griffiths, Travelorge, Tattersall, Haselhurst, Morris, Walmsley, McIntyre, Farrer, Marti

11/10/1884   Lancashire & Yorkshire Railway (Away)   Draw 1-1
No Line-Up Available

18/10/1884   Bickerton House (Away)   Lost 1-2
No Line-Up Available

25/10/1884   Farington (Away)   Won – Score Not Known
No Line-up available

29/10/1884   SOUTHPORT WEDNESDAY (Home)   Won   2-1
Parks,Griffiths, McIntyre, Wright, Wardley, Halsall noted in the report. Full Line-Up Not Available.

08/11/1884   EVERTON A (Home)   Won 2-0
Moorhead (Goal); Parks, Griffiths, Sellars, McIntyre, Tunstall, Kay, Parkes, Martin, Wright, Stead

06/12/1884   SOUTHPORT CRESCENT (Home)   Won 2-1
W.Kay (Goal); J.Parkes, McMillan, W.Marshall, J.Turvey, T.Sellars, E.Martin, E.Dickenson, E.Stead, T.Parks, Theirns.

13/12/1884   CROSSENS (Home)   Won 5-0
No Line-Up Available

03/01/1885   FARINGTON (Home)   Won 2-0
Moorhead (Goal); McMillan, W.Kay, McIntyre, T.Wright, T.Sellars, Farrar, Walmsley, Martin, Dickinson, Stead

10/01/1885   SOUTHPORT CRESCENT (Home)   Won 3-1
Moorhead (Goal); McMillan, Kay, J.McIntyre, J.Clift, T.Sellars, Walmsley, Farrar, T.Wright, Clark, T.Martin

24/01/1885   LANCASHIRE & YORKSHIRE RAILWAY (Home)   Draw 1-1
No Line-Up Available

31/01/1885   **PRESTON ZINGARI (Home)**   **Lost 0-2**

Moorhead (Goal); McMillan, J.Parks, McIntyre, Wright, Sellars, Martin, T.Parks, Stead, Kay (Capt), Walmsley

04/02/1885   **PRESTON ASSOCIATION (Home)**   **Draw 2-2**

Moorhead (Goal); Parks, Baxter, Bailey, Bowman, McIntyre, Marchant, Halsall, Parks, Wardley, Love

21/02/1885   **Southport (Away)**   **Lost 0-2**

Moorhead (Goal); J.Parks, McMillan, Sellars, Clift, Wardley, Martin, T.Parks, Gill, C.Morris, Halsall

28/02/1885   **BLACKBURN SWIFTS (Home)**   **Won 2-0**

W.Kay (Goal) (Capt); McMillan, J.Parks, McIntyre, J.Clift, T.Sellars, W.Wardley, J.Halsall, T.Parks, T.Martin, E.Stead

28/03/1885   **THE SOUTHPORT CLUBS (Home)**   **Won 2-1**

R.E.Dickenson (Goal); McMillan, W.Kay, C.Parkinson, J.Clift, T.Sellars, W.Walmsley, J.Parks, T.Parks, E.Martin, E.Stead

06/04/1885   **Southport (Away)**   **Result Not Known**

No Line-Up Available

09/05/1885   **CHRIST CHURCH (Home)**   **Lost 1-2**

Kay (Goal); J.Parks (Capt.), A.N.Other, T.Holder, C.Parkinson, W.Marshall, E.Martin, T.Parks, W.Lund, A.Gill, W.Halsall (Crescent)

28/05/1885   **3ᴿᴰ L.A.V. (Home)**   **Lost 1-3**

Hesketh (Goal); Marsden, J.McIntyre, J.W.Liptrot, Taylor, T.Sellars, W.Lund, T.Parks, Hill, Halsall, J.Parks

1885/86

05/09/1885   Blowick (Away)   Drew 2-2
No Line-Up Available

12/09/1885   BOLTON WANDERERS RESERVE (Home)   Lost 0 - 16
No Line-Up Available

23/09/1885   Southport Wanderers and Southport Crescent agree to merge.

26/09/1885   BRINSCALL (Home)   Draw 0-0
Lancashire Junior Cup
No Line-Up Available

03/10/1885   Brinscall (Away)   Lost 3-8
Lancashire Junior Cup Replay
J.Parks (Goal) (capt), R.Aitken, W.Kay, J.Liptrot, J.Shorrock, T.Sellars, R.Halsall, W.Halsall, T.H.Lea, T.Lea, J.Leadbetter

10/10/1885   Burscough (Away)   Won 7-2
Parks (Goal); Kay, Aitken, Sellars, Sharrock, Liptrot, R.Halsall, T.H.Lea, J.Leadbetter, T.Lea, E.Stead

17/10/1885   SOUTHPORT (Home)   Lost 1-4
W.Kay (Goal); Parks, Berry, Sellars, Liptrot, Shorrock, R.Halsall, W.Halsall, E.Stead, Leadbetter, T.Lea

24/10/1885   EVERTON   Lost 1-3
Liverpool Senior Cup / 1
Kay (Goal); Parker, Rimmer, Sellars, Shorrock, Liptrot, Leadbetter, Lea, Stead, R.Halsall, W.Halsall

07/11/1885   Bootle Wanderers (Away)   Draw 1-1
Kay (Goal); Parks, Rimmer, Sellars, Shorrock, Liptrot, Leadbetter, Lea, Stead, W.Halsall, R.Halsall

14/11/1885   Southport (Away)   Lost 1-3
W.Kay (Goal); Parks, Rimmer, Shorrock, Sellars, Liptrot, W.Halsall, R.Halsall, Stead, Lea, Leadbetter

21/11/1885   WIGAN (Home)   Won 4 - 1
Dunkerley (Goal); Kay, Rimmer, Sellars, Shorrock, Liptrot, Leadbetter, T.Lea, T.H.Lea, W.Halsall, R.Halsall

28/11/1885   **BURSCOUGH (Home)**   **Won 3-1**
Kay (Goal); Parks, Rimmer, Sellars, Shorrock, Liptrot, Leadbetter, T.Lea, Stead, H.Halsall, W.Halsall

12/12/1885   **HIGH PARK (Home)**   **Won 2-1**
Kay (Goal); Parks, Rimmer, Sellars, Liptrot, Shorrock, Leadbetter, T.Lea, Moss, R.Halsall, W.Halsall

26/12/1885   **BURSCOUGH (Home)**   **Won 3 - 2**
Dunkerley (Goal); Baxter, Parks, Liptrot, Ramsbottom, Sellars, R.Halsall, Graham, Shorrock, T.H.Lea, T.Lea

01/01/1886   **HALLIWELL ROVERS (Home)**   **Draw 0 - 0**
No Line-Up Available

02/01/1886   **High Park (Away)**   **Lost 0 - 6**
J.Dunkerley (Goal); J.Parkes, W.Rimmer, F.Ramsbottom, J.Liptrot, R. Halsall, W.Halsall, W.Barton, J.Leadbetter, T.Lea, T.Sellars

16/01/1886   **LINACRE (Home)**   **Result Not Known**

23/01/1886   **New Springs (Away)**   **Won 1 - 0**
No Line-Up Available

30/01/1886   **HALLIWELL ROVERS (Home)**   **Lost 0 - 3**
W.Kay (Goal); J.Parkes, J.Rimmer (backs); Frost, T.Sellars, J.Liptrot (½ backs); R. Halsall, W.Halsall, H.Lea, J.Leadbetter, A.N.Other (forwards)

06/02/1886   **BLACKBURN SWIFTS (Home)**   **Result Not Known**
W.Kay (Goal); Parks (Capt.), Rimmer (backs); Liptrott, Sellars, Ramsbottom (½ backs); A.Halsall, W.Halsall, Lea, Leadbetter, Shorrock (forwards)

13/02/1886   **Fairfield (Away)**   **Won 9 - 0**
No Line-Up Available

13/03/1886   **New Springs (Away)**   **Draw 2 - 2**
J.Dunkerley (Goal); J.Parkes, F.Berry, J.Liptrot, H.Lea, W.Halsall, A.Halsall, J.Rimmer, B.Aitken, T.Lea, T.Sellars

20/03/1886   **Burscough (Away)**   **Lost 2 - 4**
Brough (Goal); J.Liptrot, R. Halsall, H.Haslehurst, W.Halsall, C. Riley, W.Kay, B.Aitken, J.Leadbetter, T.Lea, T.Sellars

03/04/1886   ASTLEY BANK (Home)   Won 5 - 0
J.Parkes (Goal); J.Liptrot, R. Halsall, H.Haslehurst, W.Halsall, H.Lea, W.Kay, J.Rimmer,
J.Leadbetter, B.Aitken, T.Lea

17/04/1886   CHURCHTOWN CONGREGATIONAL (Neutral)   Won 4-2
Charity Cup 1
J.Parkes (Goal); F.Berry, J.Liptrot, H.Haslehurst, W.Halsall, H.Lea, W.Kay, J.Rimmer,
J.Leadbetter, T.Lea, T.Sellars

08/05/1886   Southport (Away)   Lost 0-4
Southport Charity Cup / Final
Parkes (Goal); Rimmer, Griffiths, Sellars, Farrar, Liptrot, Leadbetter, Halsall, Haslehurst,
T.Lea, T.H.Lea.

Southport Crescent

1882-83

25/11/1882   Dover (Away)   Draw 2-2
E.Blundell (Goal); H.A.Critchley, W.Halsall (backs); J.C.Dean, T.Blundell, R.Lund,
Cheetham, W.Morris, J.Hilton, C.Morris (Capt.), J.Shorrock (forwards)

06/02/1883   southport 2ⁿᵈ   (Away)   Won 8-1
R.Halsall (Goal); W.Blundell, H.A.Critchley (backs); W.Halsall, W.Morris (½ backs);
T.Bailey, R.Lund, J.Shorrock, G.Aspinall, C.Morris, T.Morris (Capt.) (forwards)

17/02/1883   DOVER (Home)   Won 1-0
Cheetham (Goal); W.Blundell (Capt.), H.A.Critchley (backs); Evans, F.Stratham (½ backs);
G.Aspinall, J.Shorrock, C.Morris, R.Halsall, A.Bailey, W.Halsall (forwards)

03/03/1883   BURSCOUGH 'A' (Home)   Draw 2-2
R.Halsall (Goal); W.Blundell, H.A.Critchley (backs); W.Morris, F.Hilton (½ backs);
G.Aspinall, W.Halsall, P.T.Pierpoint, R.Lund, C.Morris, T.Morris (Capt.) (forwards)

1883-84

20/10/1883 Crossens (Away) Won 3-0
*J.R.Dean (Goal); Haworth, Critchley (backs); Boyle, Holden (½ backs); Halsall,
W.Morris(rights), C.Morris, J.Shorrock (Centres), Liptrot, Lund (lefts)*

27/10/1883 Lancashire & Yorkshire Railway (Away) Won 3-0
*P.Halsall (Goal); Critchley, Haworth (backs); Boyle, W.Morris (½ backs); W.Halsall,
H.Halsall, Shorrock, C.Morris, Liptrot, Lund*

17/11/1883 LANCASHIRE & YORKSHIRE RAILWAY (Home) Won 4-0
*P.Halsall (Goal); H.A.Critchley, K.Knight (backs); R.Lund, J.H.Dean (½ backs); R.Halsall,
W.Halsall (rights), J.W.Liptrot, W.Morris (lefts), C.Morris, J.Shorrock (centres)*

24/11/1883 Linacre Wanderers (Away) Won 2-1
*P.Halsall (Goal); Critchley, Knight (backs); W.Morris, Haworth (½ backs); R.Halsall,
W.Halsall, C.Morris, Shorrock, Liptrot, Lund*

01/12/1883 UNITED SCHOOLS (Home) Won 1-0
*P.Halsall (Goal); Critchley, Night (backs); Holden, Lund (½ backs); Holden, Lund (rights),
W.Halsall, R.Halsall (lefts), W.Morris, Liptrot (centres)*

08/12/1883 BOOTLE YMF SOCIETY (Home) Lost 0-2
*P.Halsall (Goal); H.A.Critchley, H.Knight (backs); H.Lund, A.Howarth, J.Shorrock (½
backs); R.Halsall, W.Halsall, C.Morris, A.Briers, J.W.Liptrot*

12/01/1884 Southport (Away) Result Not Known
No Line-up Available

02/02/1884 LANCASHIRE & YORKSHIRE RAILWAY (Home) Won 1-0
No Line-Up Available

16/02/1884 CROSSHILL, BLACKBURN (Home) Lost 0-2
*Morehead (Goal); Critchley, P.Halsall (backs); Holden, Farrar (half backs); R.Halsall,
W.Halsall, C.Morris, Shorrock, Liptrot, Lund*

08/03/1884 LINACRE WANDERERS (Home) Won 1-0
*P.Halsall (Goal); Critchley, Heyworth (backs); Knight, Lund, Holden (half backs);
R.Halsall, W.Halsall, Shorrock, Bryers, Liptrot*

15/03/1884 CROSTON (Home) Lost 0-2
*Griffin (Goal); Critchley, Haworth (backs); Holden, Dean, Knight (half); R.Halsall,
W.Halsall, Shorrock, Lund, Bryers (forwards)*

22/03/1884   **LANCASTER ROAD, PRESTON**   **Draw 2-2**
Kay (Goal); Critchley, Bailey (backs); Shorrock, Holden, Lund (half); R.Halsall, W.halsall, C.Morris, Briars, Farrar

29/03/1884   **Cross Hill, Blackburn (Away)**   **Won 2-1**
Kay (Goal); Bailey, Critchley (backs); Shorrock, Liptrot, Lund (half); W.halsall, R.Halsall, C.Morris, Farrar, Bryers

19/04/1884   **CHRIST CHURCH (Home)**   **Lost 1-2**
No Line-Up Available

03/05/1884   **CHRIST CHURCH and ROVERS**   **Won 3-1**
No Line-Up Available

1884-85

04/10/1884   STRATHMORE HOUSE (Home)   **Won 2-0**
Gordon (Goal); Heyworth, Griffiths, Rimmer, Shorrock, Liptrot, R.Halsall, W.Halsall, C.Morris, Bryers, Leadbetter

11/10/1884   BIRKDALE AMATEURS (Home)   **Won 4-1**
R.Lund (Goal); Hayworth, Rimmer, Holden, Liptrot, Shorrock, R.Halsall, W.Halsall, C.Morris, Bryers, Leadbetter

18/10/1884   Lancashire & Yorkshire Railway (Away)   **Won 2-0**
No Line-up available

25/10/1884   HIGH PARK (Home)   **Lost 0-2**
F.Traveloni (Goal); J.Griffiths, W.Aughton, Rimmer, Liptrot, Shorrock, W.Halsall, R.Halsall, Bryers, J.Leadbetter, C.Morris

15/11/1884   Burscough (Away)   **Won 2-1**
Traveloni (Goal); W.Rimmer, Griffiths, R.Rimmer, Shorrock, Liptrot, Leadbetter, Bryers, Morris, W.Halsall, R.Halsall

22/11/1884   CROSTON (Home)   **Won 2-0**
No Line-up available

06/12/1884   Southport Wanderers (Away)   **Lost 1-2**
Traveloni (Goal); Griffiths, Rimmer, Rimmer, Shorrock, Liptrot, Halsall, W.Halsall, H.Leadbetter, Bryers, Morris

13/12/1884   Birkdale Amateurs (Away)   **Won 6-0**
Traveloni (Goal); Griffiths, W.Rimmer, Liptrot, Alty, R.rimmer, Leadbetter, Bryers, Shorrock, Morris, W.Halsall (Capt)

03/01/1885   LANCASHIRE & YORKSHIRE RAILWAY (Home)   **Lost 2-5**
No Line-up available

24/01/1885   ROYAL (Home)   **Won 4-1**
No Line-Up available

07/02/1885   Christ Church (Away)   **Won 1-0**
No Line-up available

14/02/1885   BURSCOUGH (Home)   **Won 2-1**
No Line-up available

21/03/1885   HIGH PARK (Home)   **Won 3-1**
Charity Cup Semi Final
No Line-up available

04/04/1885   CHRIST CHURCH (Home)   **Won 1-0**
Dawson (Goal); R.rimmer, P.Halsall, R.Lund, Shorrock, J.W.Liptrot, W.Halsall (Capt),
A.Johnson, C.Morris, J.Leadbetter, W.Morris

11/04/1885   Southport (Neutral)   **Lost 0-5**
Charity Cup Final
Dawson (Goal); W.Rimmer, R.Rimmer, Liptrot, Sharrock, W.Morris, R.Halsall, W.Halsall,
C.Morris, A.Bryers, J.Leadbetter

14/05/1885   Christ Church (Away)   **Lost 0-1**
Lund (Goal); Griffiths (Southport FC), R.Aitken, J.Liptrot, J.Shorrock, R.Rimmer,
J.Leadbetter, Bryers, R.Halsall (Capt), W.Morris, C.Morris

1885-86

23/09/1885   **Southport Wanderers and Southport Crescent agree to merge.**

26/09/1885   **SOUTHPORT OLD BOYS**   **(Home)**   **Lost 0-1**
No Line-Up Available

Southport Football Club*

Note that whilst the 1886/87 season was started as Southport Wanderers, after 2 games the club was re-named Southport Football Club

1886/87

18/09/1886   ANTLEY (Home)   Won 4 - 0*
S.Platt (Goal); T. Parkes, J. Kerr, J.Griffiths, P.Mellor, C. Riley, W.Morris, T.Lea, T.Sellars, J.Johnson, Hindley
*As Southport Wanderers

25/09/1886   SKELMERSDALE UNITED   (Home)   Won 2 - 1*
S.Platt (Goal); J.Melross, J.Griffiths, J.Briggs, P.Mellor, W.Morris, T.Lea, J.Johnson, Hindley, T.Sellars, Cookson
*As Southport Wanderers

02/10/1886   BOLTON ROVERS (Home)   Lost 1 - 3
Lancashire Junior Cup / 1
S.Platt (Goal); J.Melross, J.Griffiths, J.Briggs, P.Mellor, W.Morris, T.Lea, J.Johnson, T.Sellars, Hindley, Cookson

09/10/1886   PEEL BANK ROVERS (Home)   Lost 0 - 3
S.Platt (Goal); T. Parkes, A.Haworth, J.Griffiths, J.Briggs, P.Mellor, W.Kay, W.Graham, Hindley, Cookson, T.Lea

13/10/1886   Birkdale (Away)   Result Not Known
Southport Charity Cup
A. Guest (Goal); W.Rimmer, F. Barry, T.Halliwell, C.Duncan, A.Haworth, W.Graham, Forshaw, A.Halsall, T.Lea, W.Hodge

16/10/1886   HAYDOCK (Home)   Lost 1 - 2
Liverpool Challenge Cup
S.Platt (Goal); T.Parkes, H.Baxter, J. Kerr, J.Briggs, P.Mellor, A.Halsall, T.Lea, J.Leadbetter, Hindley, Cookson

23/10/1886   Walmer Bridge (Away)   Won 3 - 2
S.Platt (Goal); J.Kerr, J.Griffiths, J.Briggs, P.Mellor, W. Graham, A.Halsall, Coupar, Hindley, Cookson, T.Lea

30/10/1886   LINACRE WANDERERS (Home)   Won 3 - 1
S.Platt (Goal); J.Griffiths, J.Briggs, P.Mellor, A.Halsall, Illingworth, T.Lea, Hindley, T.Sellars, Cookson, J.Leadbetter

06/11/1886   FISHWICK RAMBLERS (Home)   **Lost 1 - 5**
T. Parkes (Goal); J.Griffiths, J.Briggs, P.Mellor, Illingworth, J.Rimmer, T.Lea, T.Sellars, Hindley, Cookson, J.Leadbetter

20/11/1886   Lytham (Away)   **Lost 1 - 7**
T. Parkes (Goal); T.B.Burnett, Cookson; Hindley, T.Sellars, Graham; J.Melross, P.Mellor, Illingworth, A.Halsall, T.Lea

27/11/1886   EVERTON 'A' (Home)   **Lost 1 - 2**
T. Parkes, J.Briggs, P.Mellor, W. Graham, T.Lea, T.Sellars, Cookson, T.H.Lea

11/12/1886   Everton Swifts (Away)   **Lost 0 - 1**
S.Platt (Goal); J.Griffiths, J.Briggs, P.Mellor, A.Halsall, W. Graham, W.Hodge, T.Sellars, Cookson, J.Leadbetter, T.Lea

18/12/1886   NEW SPRINGS   **No Result Known**
No Line-Up Available

25/12/1886   SOUTHPORT RECREATION (Home)   **Won 2 - 1**
No Line-Up Available

27/12/1886   BLACKBURN OLYMPIC (Home)   **Lost 2 - 5**
No Line-Up Available

22/01/1887   BURSCOUGH (Home)   **Won 4-1**
T.Parkes (Goal); Cookson, Griffiths, Halliwell, Briggs, Sellars, Lea, A.Graham, P.Mellor, Hodge, Leadbetter

05/02/1887   Southport Old Boys (Away)   **Lost 1-3**
Southport Charity Cup / 1
S.Platt (Goal); Griffiths, Cookson, Briggs (Capt.), Sellars, Halliwell, Leadbetter, Halsall, Hodge, Lea, Graham

19/02/1887   OAKFIELD ROVERS (Home)   **Lost 0-1**
Guest (Goal); Cookson, Griffiths, Sellars, Briggs, Halliwell, Hodge, T.Lea, Mellor, T.H.Lea, Graham

26/02/1887   Liverpool Ramblers (Away)   **Won 1-0**
*10 men a side
Kay (Goal); Cookson, Griffiths, Halliwell, Briggs, Sellars, T.H.Lea, A.Graham, Leadbetter, T.Lea

05/03/1887   LYTHAM (Home)   Draw 1 - 1
Parkes (Goal); Cookson, Griffiths, Sellars, Briggs, Halliwell, T.H.Lea, Graham, Mellor, Leadbetter, T.Lea.

12/03/1887   LIVERPOOL RAMBLERS (Home)   Won 10-0
Parkes (Goal); Cookson, Griffiths, Sellars, Briggs, Halliwell, T.H.Lea, Graham, T.Lea, Leadbetter, Mellor

19/03/1887   CHURCHTOWN (Home)   Won 3-1
Parkes (Goal); Cookson, Griffiths, Halliwell, Briggs, Sellars, T.H.Lea,, Graham, T.Lea, Leadbetter, Mellor

26/03/1887   Linacre (Away)   Won 4-1
Cookson, Griffiths, Halliwell, Briggs, Sellars, T.H.Lea, W.Forshaw, Lea, J.Rimmer,

08/04/1887   SOUTHPORT RECREATION (Home)   Won 3-1
No Line-Up Available

09/04/1887   EVERTON 'A' (Home)   Won 2-0
No Line-Up Available

11/04/1887   BLACKBURN OLYMPIC (Home)   Won 2-1
Parkes (Goal); Griffiths, Cookson, Halliwell, Aitken, Taylor, Graham, Lea, Mellor, Leadbetter, Farrar

1887/88

18/08/1887   SOUTHPORT & DISTRICT (Home)   Lost 3-5
*Hesketh (Goal); Aitken, Cookson, Pasquill, Dutton, Rimmer, Whittaker, G.Halsall,
Graham, T.H.Lea, T.Lea*

24/09/1887   Birkenhead Argyle (Away)   Lost 3-4
*Harrison (Goal); Aitken, Berry, Forshaw, A.N.Other, Duncan, Lea, Whittaker, Hilton,
Rimmer, G.Halsall*

01/10/1887   St Mary's Kirkdale (Away)   Lost 1-3
No Line-Up Available

01/10/1887   LIVERPOOL RAMBLERS (Home)   Won 3 - 2
*10 men each
Harrison (Goal); Berry, Aitken, Sellars, Briggs, Graham, Lea, Hilton, Forshaw, G.Halsall

Southport Recreation amalgamate with club

08/10/1887   Bromborough Pool (Away)   Lost 1-2
Liverpool & District Senior Cup 1st Round
*Harrison (Goal); Aitken, G.Halsall, Sellars, Briggs, Pasquill, Lea, Sutton, Rimmer,
F.Blackledge, Briers.*

15/10/1887   Ten Acres (Away)   Lost 0 - 2
*No Line-Up Available - Team noted as being weakened by absences of key men,
including Briggs (Capt.)*

22/10/1887   LIVERPOOL GYMNASIUM (Home)   Won 3-1
*Tynsley (Goal); Aitken, Baxter, Pasquill, F.Rimmer, Sellars, Bryers, Blackledge, T.Lea,
Leadbetter, T.H.Lea*

29/10/1887   BIRKDALE (Home)   Draw 1-1
*Tynsley (Goal); H.Baxter, R.Aitken, Pasquil, J.J.Briggs, Halliwell, T.H.Lea, A.Graham,
T.Lea, Blackledge, Leadbetter*

05/11/1887   BOOTLE RESERVE (Home)   Lost 0-5
*Tynsley, Sellars, Forshaw, Blackledge, G.Halsall, T.Lea, Briers, Aitken, T.H.Lea and
Briggs, A.N.Other*

19/11/1887   Bolton Wanderers Reserves (Away)   Lost 0 - 2
*Tynsley (Goal); Berry, Aitken, Thompson,Rimmer, Sellars, G.Halsall, Geeson, Daniels,
Rimmer, Pasquill*

03/12/1887   Southport Old Boys (Away)   Draw 0-0
G.Halsall, Aitken, T.Lea noted in the report. Full Line-Up Not Available.

07/12/1887   BLACKPOOL (Home)   Draw 2 - 2
Sloane (Goal); Baxter, Aitken, Duncan, Pasquill, G.Halsall, Bryers, Blackledge, T.Lea,
Rimmer, Briggs

17/12/1887   High Park (Away)   Lost 0-1
Tynsley (Goal); Baxter, Aitken, Halsall, Pasquill, Bryers, Blackledge, Lambs, Rimmer,
T.Lea, Farrar

24/12/1887   SOUTHPORT OLD BOYS (Home)   Lost 1-2
Tynsley (Goal); Baxter, Aitken, Farrar, Pasquill, Geeson, Blackledge, Rimmer, Bryers,
T.Lea, Halsall

31/12/1887   CHURCHTOWN (Home)   Draw 1-1
Tynsley (Goal); Aitken, Halsall, Farrar, F.Rimmer, Duncan, T.Morris, Sutton, Blackledge,
Pasquill, T.Lea

7/01/1888   Churchtown (Away)   Lost 1-3
Guest (Goal); Aitken, Halsall, Pasquill, F.Rimmer, Sellars, Farrar, Sutton, Blackledge,
Rimmer, Blackledge

21/01/1888   SOUTHPORT OLD BOYS   (Home)   Draw 1-1
Tynsley (Goal); Aitken, Halsall, Rimmer, Pasquill, Leadbetter, Blackledge, Berry, Sutton,
T.Lea, Hoban

04/02/1888   BIRKDALE (Home)   Won 6-0
Harrison (Goal); Baxter, Aitken, Leadbetter, F.Rimmer, Pasquill, Blackledge,Bryers,
Sutton(Briggs), T.Lea, Forshaw

11/02/1888   Liverpool Gymnasium (Away)   Lost 3 - 5
Tynsley (Goal); Halsall, Wright, Leadbetter, F.Rimmer, Sutton, Blackledge, Hilton, Briggs,
Forshaw, T.Lea

21/02/1888   SCRATCH XI (in place of the OLD SOUTHPORTONIONS) Won 7-2
Tynsley, Halsall, T.Hesketh, F.Rimmer, Pasquill, Leadbetter, Forshaw, J.Rimmer,
Blackledge, Bryers
V: Briggs, Smith, Berry, J.H.Johnson, Taylor, Kay, S.Platt, W.Hodge, Sellars, Blackledge,
R.Rimmer

25/02/1888   **Southport Old Boys (Away)**   **Won 4 - 1**
Southport Charity Cup
Tynsley (Goal); Aitken, Baxter, Pasquill, Leadbetter, Forshaw, T.Lea, Bryers, Blackledge,
Briggs, Rimmer

03/03/1888   **EVERTON RESERVE (Home)**   **Draw 1-1**
Tynsley (Goal); H.Baxter, Aitken, Leadbetter, F.Rimmer, Pasquill, Smith, Blackledge,
Briggs, Forshaw, Halsall

10/03/1888   **BOLTON WANDERERS RESERVES (Home)**   **Lost 1 - 5**
Tynsley (Goal), Baxter, Aitken, Pasquill, F.Rimmer, Leadbetter, Forshaw, Hilton, Sellars,
Blackledge, Bryers.

30/03/1888   **OLD BOYS (Home)**   **Lost 0-5**
No Line-Up Available

02/04/1888   **NEWCASTLE SWIFTS (Home)**   **Lost 1-3**
Pasquill, O'Brien and Aitken noted in the report. Full Line-Up Not Available.

07/04/1888   **Hesketh Park (Away)**   **Won 3-0**
Leadbetter, Rimmer noted in the report. Full Line-Up Not Available.

14/04/1888   **HIGH PARK (Sports Ground)**   **Won 3-2**
Southport Charity Cup Semi Final
Tynsley (Goal); Aitken, Baxter, Leadbetter, Pasquill, Forshaw, T.Lea, Bryers, Blackledge,
Briggs, Rimmer

21/04/1888   **CHURCHTOWN**   **Draw 2 - 2**
Southport Charity Cup / Final
Tynsley (Goal); Baxter, Aitken, Leadbetter, Pasquill, Rimmer, Bryers, Blackledge, Briggs,
T.Lea, Forshaw

28/04/1888   **CHURCHTOWN**   **Draw 3 - 3 AET**
Southport Charity Cup / Final Replay
Tynsley (Goal); Baxter, Aitken, Pasquill, Leadbetter, Forshaw, T.Lea, Blackledge, Bryers,
Briggs, Rimmer

05/05/1888   **CHURCHTOWN**   **Won 4 - 1**
Southport Charity Cup / Final Second Replay
Tynsley (Goal); Baxter, Aitken, Pasquill, O'Brien, Forshaw, T.Lea, Blackledge, Bryers,
Briggs, Rimmer

Southport Central Football Club

1888/89

01/09/1888   STANLEY (Home)   **Lost 1 - 4**
L.Tyldesley (Goal); F.Horton, W.Akeroyd, D.Graham, Walsh, J. Farrar, G.Duncan, Taylor, J.Sourbutts, B.Aitken, T.Lea

08/09/1888   SOUTHPORT OLD BOYS (Home)   **Won 6 - 0**
L.Tyldesley (Goal); F.Horton, W.Akeroyd, D.Graham, Walsh, J. Farrar, G.Duncan, Taylor, J.Sourbutts, B.Aitken, T.Lea

15/09/1888   LONG EATON ATHLETIC (Home)   **Lost 2 - 3**
L.Tyldesley (Goal); Blenkhorn, Shaw, Horton, Akeroyd, Farrar, Sourbutts, T.Lea, Taylor,Graham, , Duncan

22/09/1888   ST HELENS (Home)   **Won 9 - 2**
Tyldsley (Goal); Joy, Shaw, Farrar, Akeroyd, Horton, Duncan, Graham, Taylor, T.Lea, Sourbutts

29/09/1888   CHORLEY (Home)   **Won 6 - 0**
L.Tyldesley (Goal); F.Horton, Shaw, W.Akeroyd, J.Sourbutts, T.Lea, T.Morris, H.Hunter, D.Graham, G.Duncan, Taylor

06/10/1888   Irwell Springs (Away)   **Won 5 - 4 AET**
FA Cup / 1Q
Tyldesley (Goal); Walsh, Baxter, Shaw, Akeroyd, Horton, Duncan, Graham, Sourbutts, T.Lea, Dodd

06/10/1888   WHISTON (Home)   **Lost 1 - 3**
Liverpool Challenge Cup
*2nd Team fulfilled fixture
Guest (Goal), Pasquill, Walmsley, F.Rimmer, Evans, Blundell, Blackledge, Brighouse, Forshaw, Hibbs, J.Rimmer

13/10/1888   HAYDOCK ST JAMES (Home)   **Won 4 - 1**
Lancashire Junior Cup / 1
Tyldesley (Goal); Barrow, Shaw, T.Lea, Akeroyd, Horton, Duncan, Graham, Sourbutts, Dodd, Taylor

20/10/1888   STANLEY (Home)   **Won 3 - 0**
L.Tyldesley (Goal); F.Horton, Shaw, F.Rimmer, W.Akeroyd, D.Graham, G.Duncan, B.Aitken, Taylor, Cheetham, T.Lea

27/10/1888   South Shore (Away)   **Lost 1 - 7**
FA Cup / 2Q
L.Tyldesley (Goal); F.Horton, Shaw, F.Rimmer, W.Akeroyd, Blinkhorn, T.Lea, D.Graham,
G.Duncan, Taylor, J.Sourbutts

03/11/1888   Bootle Wanderers (Away)   **Won 5 - 3**
Lancashire Junior Cup / 2
Tyldesley (Goal); Aitken, Pasquill, Horton, Rimmer, Evans, T.Lea, Forshaw, Taylor,
Sourbutts, Graham

10/11/1888   PRESTON ST JOSEPH'S (Home)   **Draw 0 - 0**
Ingram (Goal); Taylor, Sourbutts, Duncan, Akeroyd mentioned in report but No Line-Up
Available

17/11/1888   BLACKBURN OLYMPIC (Home)   **Won 3 - 1**
Ingram (Goal); Shaw, Blenkhorn, Akeroyd, Horton, T.Lea, Taylor, Mullin, Sourbutts,
Graham, Duncan

24/11/1888   FISHWICK RAMBLERS (Home)   **Won 3 - 0**
Ingram (Goal); Blenkhorn, Shaw,T.Lea, Akeroyd (Capt), Horton, Duncan, Graham,
Mullin, Taylor, Sourbutts

27/11/1888   BLACKBURN DISTRICT (Home)   **Won 7 - 0**
Ingram (Goal); Shaw, Robinson, Blenkhorn, Joy, T.Lea, Duncan, Graham, Mullin, Milne,
Taylor

01/12/1888   Stanley (Away)   **Won 3 - 1**
Ingram (Goal); Blenkhorn, Aitken, Horton, Akeroyd, T.Lea, Sourbutts, Taylor, Graham,
Mullen, Duncan

08/12/1888   ASTLEY BRIDGE (Home)   **Won 2 - 0**
Ingram (Goal); Aitken, Shaw, T.Lea, Akeroyd, Horton, Duncan, Graham, Taylor, Mullin,
Halton

15/12/1888   Hindley (Away)   **Lost 1 - 3**
Ingram (Goal); Aitken, Shaw, Horton, Akeroyd, T.Lea, Duncan, Graham, Harrison, Taylor,
Mullin

22/12/1888   LYTHAM (Home)   **Lost 1 - 3**
Ingram (Goal); Aitken, Thompson, T.Lea, Horton, Akeroyd, Mullin, Graham, Taylor,
Sourbutts, McKecknie

25/12/1888   HEYWOOD CENTRAL (Home)   Draw 2 - 2
Burnett (Goal); Forshaw, Aitken, Horton, Akeroyd, T.Lea, Mullin, Cronshaw, Sourbutts, Duncan, Taylor

26/12/1888   ULSTER (Home)   Won 6 - 2
Ingram (Goal); Aitken, Evans, Burnett, Horton, T.Lea, Duncan, Graham, Mullin, Sourbutts, Taylor

29/12/1888   BURY (Home)   Won 2 - 1
Ingram (Goal); F.Horton, Shaw, W.Akeroyd, Taylor, D.Graham, J.Sourbutts, G.Duncan, Mullins, B.Aitken, T.Lea

01/01/1889   HIGH PARK (Home)   Lost 3 - 4
Ingram (Goal); F.Horton, W.Akeroyd, G.Duncan, D.Graham, B.Aitken, Taylor, J. Farrar, T.Lea, J.Sourbutts, Mullins

05/01/1889   FLEETWOOD RANGERS (Home)   Lost 0 - 2
Lancashire Junior Cup / 4
Voss (Goal); F.Horton, Shaw, F.Rimmer, Evans, W.Akeroyd, E.Graham, T.Lea, D.Graham, Taylor, J.Sourbutts

12/01/1889   WITTON (Home)   Draw 1 - 1
Ingram (Goal); W.Hodgkinson, F.Horton, Shaw, W.Akeroyd, Heslop, T.Lea, Taylor, D.Graham, G.Duncan, Mullins

19/01/1889   High Park (Away)   Draw 1 - 1
Southport Charity Cup
Ingram (Goal); F.Horton, Shaw, Evans, T.Lea, Walsh, Taylor, D.Graham, J.Sourbutts, G.Duncan, Mullins

25/01/1889   BLACKPOOL (Home)   Draw 2 - 2
Ingram (Goal); W.Hodgkinson, F.Horton, Shaw, W.Akeroyd, Blinkhorn, Hothersall, D.Graham, Taylor, G.Duncan, Mullins

02/02/1889   Chorley (Away)   Won 2 - 0
Ingram (Goal); W.Hodgkinson, F.Horton, Shaw, W.Akeroyd, Hothersall, Mullins, Taylor, D.Graham, G.Duncan, T.Lea

09/02/1889   HINDLEY (Home)   Won 2 - 1
Ingram (Goal); W.Hodgkinson, F.Horton, Shaw, W.Akeroyd, Hothersall, Taylor, D.Graham, Mullins, G.Duncan, T.Lea

16/02/1889   Blackpool (Away)   Lost 0 - 5
Ingram (Goal); W.Hodgkinson, F.Horton, Shaw, W.Akeroyd, Hothersall, Taylor,
D.Graham, Mullins, G.Duncan, T.Lea

23/02/1889   Heywood (Away)   Won 4 - 2
Ingram (Goal); W.Hodgkinson, Shaw, W.Akeroyd, Blinkhorn, Hothersall, Taylor,
D.Graham, G.Duncan, Mullins, T.Lea

27/02/1889   EVERTON (Home)   Lost 1 - 2
Ingram (Goal); W.Hodgkinson, F.Horton, Shaw, J.Milne, Hothersall, G.Duncan, T.Lea,
Mullins, Taylor, D.Graham

02/03/1889   CHURCHTOWN   Won 4 - 1
Southport Charity Cup / Final
Ingram (Goal); W.Hodgkinson, F.Horton, Shaw, W.Akeroyd, Hothersall, Taylor,
D.Graham, Mullins, G.Duncan, T.Lea

09/03/1889   Bury (Away)   Lost 4 - 5
Ingram (Goal); W.Hodgkinson, F.Horton, Shaw, W.Akeroyd, Hothersall, Taylor,
D.Graham, Mullins, G.Duncan, T.Lea

16/03/1889   Fishwick Ramblers (Away)   Lost 0 - 2
Ingram (Goal); W.Hodgkinson, F.Horton, Shaw, W.Akeroyd, Hothersall, Taylor,
D.Graham, Mullins, G.Duncan, T.Lea

23/03/1889   CHURCHTOWN (Home)   Draw 2 - 2
Ingram (Goal); W.Hodgkinson, F.Horton, Shaw, Abbott, W.Akeroyd, Taylor, D.Graham,
G.Duncan, Mullins, T.Lea

27/03/1889   Everton (Away)   Lost 1 - 4
J. Gee (Goal); W.Hodgkinson, F.Horton, Shaw, C.Weir, W.Hewitt, H.Fecitt, T.Lea,
D.Graham, G.Duncan, Mullins

30/03/1889   Heywood Central (Away)   Lost 0 - 3
J. Gee (Goal); W.Hodgkinson, Shaw, C.Weir, W.Akeroyd, C.Gee, W.Hewitt, Taylor,
Mullins, A.Halsall, Walsh

06/04/1889   Higher Walton (Away)   Lost 0 - 2
Ingram (Goal); W.Hodgkinson, F.Horton, Shaw, W.Akeroyd, Hothersall, Walsh, Taylor,
D.Graham, G.Duncan, Mullins

13/04/1889   HIGHER WALTON (Home)   Won 3 - 2
Ingram (Goal); W.Hodgkinson, F.Horton, Shaw, C.Weir, W.Akeroyd, F.McGuinnes,
R.Watson, Mullins, D.Graham, Taylor

19/04/1889   OSWALDTWISTLE ROVERS (Home)   **Won 3 - 0**
Ingram (Goal); W.Hodgkinson, F.Horton, Shaw, C.Weir, W.Akeroyd, R.Watson, Mullins, D.Graham, G.Duncan, Taylor

20/04/1889   HEYWOOD CENTRAL (Home)   **Lost 1 - 2**
Ingram (Goal); W.Hodgkinson, F.Horton, Shaw, C.Weir, W.Akeroyd, R.Watson, Mullins, D.Graham, G.Duncan, Taylor

22/04/1889   ROSSENDALE (Home)   **Lost 1 - 3**
Ingram (Goal); W.Hodgkinson, F.Horton, Shaw, C.Weir, Evans, W.Akeroyd, Bryers, R.Watson, G.Duncan, Taylor

13/05/1889   PRESTON NORTH END Home)   **Lost 2 - 4**
J. Gee (Goal); W.Hodgkinson, J. Forbes, C.Weir, W.Akeroyd, J. Southworth, R.Watson, D.Graham, Mullins, B. Townley, T.Lea

Christ Church / Southport Recreation

1882/83 (Rugby)

03/02/1883   St Josephs, Birkdale (Away)   Won - 3T, 1TIG, 1DB v 1TIG, 1DB
*Rugby Rules
D.Quayle (full back); J.Ingham, F.Traveloni, J.Whittaker (¾ backs); R.Blackledge,
G.Rockliff (½ backs); G.W.Hesketh, Fred. Blundell, J.Blackledge, H.Blundell, J.Evans,
H.Wainwright, J.Robinson, A.N.Other.

1883/84 (Association)

29/12/1883   ST JOSEPHS (Home)   **Lost 0-1**
F.Traveloni (goal); G.Hesketh (Capt.), D.Quayle (backs); R.Sawyer, J.Robinson (half backs); H.Wainwright, N.Rimmer (rights); R.Blackledge, F.Lund (lefts); J.Evans, G.Halsall (centres)

05/01/1884   CROSSENS (Home)   **Lost 0-3**
F.Traveloni (goal); Hesketh, Rimmer (backs); Porter, Rimmer, Quayle (half backs); Blackledge, Lunt (left); Wainwright, Halsall (right); Porter (centre)

19/01/1884   High Park Ramblers (Away)   **Draw in favour of High Park**
both sides played with 12 men
F.Traveloni (Goal); T.Mayo, F.Sheridan, John Ball, W.Evans, T.Sawyer, G.Hesketh, R.Johnson, A.Blackledge, S.Houghton, Tushy, J.Rimmer, J.Robinson

02/02/1884   SOUTHPORT ROVERS (Home)   **Draw 1-1**
10 men
F.Travloni (Goal); P.Rimmer, J.Ball (backs); J.Evans, D.Quayle (½ backs); H.Wainwright, (Capt.), N.Rimmer, G.Halsall, F.Lunt, R.Blackledge

09/02/1884   ST JOSEPHS   **Lost 0-3**
F.Traveloni (Goal); F.Berry, J.Ball (backs); J.Robinson, J.Evans, D.Quayle (half backs); N.Rimmer, G.Halsall, H.Wainwright (Capt), R.Blackledge, T.Porter

16/02/1884   Lancashire & Yorkshire Railway (Away)   **Won 2-0**
F.Traveloni (Goal); J.Evans,G.Hesketh (backs); D.Quayle, T.Porter, Robinson (half backs); H.Wainwright (Capt). N.Rimmer, G.Halsall, R.Blackledge, F.Lunt

23/02/1884   HARMONIC (Home)   **Draw 1-1**
F.Traveloni (Goal); G.Hesketh, R.Rimmer (backs); D.Quayle, G.Evans, G.Robinson (½ backs); H.Wainwright, (Capt.), N.Rimmer, G.Halsall, F.Lunt, T.Porter

08/03/1884   Crossens (Away)   **Draw 1-1**
F.Traveloni (Goal); G.Hesketh, P.Rimmer (backs); T.Porter, J.Evans, D.Quayle (half); D.Blackledge, N.Rimmer, G.Halsall, H.Wainwright, F.Lunt

15/03/1884   HARMONIC (Home)   **Won 5-0**
F.Traveloni (Goal); P.Rimmer, G.Hesketh (backs); R.Rimmer, T.Porter, J.Robinson (half); N.Rimmer, H.Wainwright (Capt.), G.Halsall, J.Evans, R.Blackledge

22/03/1884   Burscough 2nd   (Away)   **Won 1-0**
F.Traveloni (Goal); G.Hesketh, R.Rimmer (backs); D.Quayle, J.Evans, J.Robinson (half); H.Wainwright (Capt.), N.Rimmer, T.Porter, F.Lunt, R.Blackledge

29/03/1884 BURSCOUGH (Home) Lost 0-2
F.Traveloni (Goal); G.Hesketh, P.Rimmer (backs); J.Robinson, D.Quayle, J.Evans (half); T.Porter, D.Blackledge, F.Lunt, H.Wainwright, N.Rimmer

05/04/1884 ROYAL (Home) Won 3-1
F.Traveloni (Goal); H.Hesketh, R.Rimmer (backs); T.Porter, J.Evans, D.Quayle (half); G.Halsall, R.Blackledge, F.Lunt, H.Wainwright (Capt.), N.Rimmer

12/04/1884 BAMBER BRIDGE (Home) Won 3-1
F.Traveloni (Goal); G.Hesketh, P.Rimmer (backs); J.Evans, T.Porter, J.Robinson (half); R.Blackledge, F.Lunt, H.Wainwright (Capt), G.Halsall

19/04/1884 CRESCENT Won 2-1
F.Traveloni (Goal); H.Aughton, W.Blundell (backs); J.Robinson, D.Quayle, G.Hesketh 9half); H.Wainwright, W.Leadbetter, W.Rimmer, D.Blackledge, F.Lunt

1884/85

20/09/1884   Lonton Martyrs (Away)   Lost 0-4
*R.Rimmer (Goal); G.Halsall, W.Moore, J.Robinson, G.Hesketh, D.Quayle, H.Wainwright
(Capt.), W.Brewer, J.Evans, R.Dutton, N.Rimmer*

27/09/1884   LONGTON (Home)   Draw 1-1
*F.Traveloni (Goal), W.Blundell, W.Moore, J.Robinson, G.Hesketh, R.Rimmer,
R.Blackledge, N.Rimmer, H.Wainwrihgt, W.Brewer, G.Halsall*

11/10/1884   BAMBER BRIDGE (Home)   Won 1-0
*F.Traveloni (Goal); W.Blundell, W.Moore, D.Quayle, G.Hesketh, J.Robinson,
H.Wainwright (Capt.), R.Rimmer, R.Blackledge, J.Evansm G.Halsall*

18/10/1884   Bamber Bridge (Away)   Won 2-1
*G.Hesketh (Goal); W.Moore, G.Rockcliffe, D.Quayle, R.Rimmer, J.Robinson,
H.Wainwright (Capt), J.Evans, R.Blackledge, R.Dutton, N.Rimmer*

25/10/1884   BANKS (Home)   Won 2-0
*G.Hesketh (Goal); W.Moore, H.Moore, J.Robinson, G.Rockcliffe, R.Rimmer, M.Rimmer,
H.Wainwright, R.Blackledge, R.Dutton, G.Halsall*

01/11/1884   PRESTON PARISH CHUCH (Home)   Won 1-0
*G.Hesketh (Goal); H.Moore, W.Moore, D.Quayle, G.Rockliff, J.Evans, R.Blackledge,
R.Dutton, H.Wainwright (Capt)., R.Rimmer, G.Halsall*

15/11/1884   Skelmersdale Temperance (Away)   Lost 0-1
*Hesketh 9Goal); H.Moore, W.Moore, J.Robinson, N.Evans, N.Rimmer, G.Rockliffe,
R.Blackledge, R.Rimmer, G.Halsall, H.Wainwright (Capt)*

22/11/1884   BURSCOUGH 2nd (Home)   Won 2-1
*Hesketh (Goal); W.Moore, H.Moore, J.Robinson, G.Rockliff, N.Rimmer, R.Blackledge,
R.Dutton, R.Rimmer, H.Wainwright (Capt), J.Evans*

29/11/1884   SKELMERSDALE ROVERS (Home)   Won 5-0
*G.Hesketh (Goal); H.Moore, W.Moore, N.Rimmer, G.Rockliffe, J.Robinson, J.Evans,
R.Rimmer, G.Halsall (Capt), R.Blackledge, R.Dutton*

06/12/1884   St James's, Westhead (Away)   Lost 0-1
*G.Hesketh (Goal); H.Moore, W.Moore, N.Rimmer, G.Rockliffe, J.Evans, H.Wainwright
(Capt), R.Rimmer, R.Blackledge, R.Dutton, G.Halsall*

13/12/1884   **SKELMSERSDALE TEMPERANCE (Home)**   **Won 1-0**
G.Hesketh (Goal); W.Moore, H.Moore, J.Robinson, G.Rockcliffe J.Evans, H.Wainwright (Capt), R.Rimmer, G.Halsall, R.Dutton, R.Blackledge

20/12/1884   **Blackburn Crosshill (Away)**   **Lost 1-8**
G.Hesketh (Goal); W.Moore, P.Rimmer, J.Robinson, G.Rockliffe, J.Evans, H.Wainwright (Capt), R.Rimmer, N.Rimmer, R.Blackledge, R.Dutton

26/12/1884   **PRESTON PARISH CHURCH (Home)**   **Draw 0-0**
G.Hesketh (Goal); H.Moore, W.Blundell, N.Rimmer, J.Evans, G.Halsall, H.Wainwright (Capt), R.Rimmer, P.Rimmer, R.Dutton, T.Lea

10/01/1885   **SOUTHPORT ROYAL (Home)**   **Draw 0-0**
J.Evans (Goal); W.Moore, H.Moore, N.Rimmer, G.Hesketh, J.Robinson, HWainwright (Capt), G.Halsall, G.Rockliffe, P.Rimmer, R.Dutton

17/01/1885   **Churchtown Congregational (Away)**   **Won 1-0**
Hesketh (Goal); H.Moore, W.Moore, R.Rimmer, J.Evans, G.Halsall, H.Wainwright (Capt), R.Dutton, P.Rimmer, J.Robinson, N.Rimmer

24/01/1885   **CROSSENS (Sports Ground)**   **Won 3-1**
Southport Charity Cup 1st Round
Hesketh (Goal); H.Moore, W.Moore, J.Evans, Rimmer, Robinson, Wainwright, Blackledge, Halsall, Dutton, Rockliffe

31/01/1885   **ORMSKIRK 2nd (Home)**   **Won 1-0**
J.Evans (Goal); W.Blundell, G.Hesketh, P.Rimmer, J.Blackledge, J.Robinson, G.Halsall, F.Lunt, N.Rimmer, R.Blackledge, R.Dutton

07/02/1885   **CRESCENT (Home)**   **Lost 0-1**
No Line-Up Available

14/02/1885   **WESTHEAD (Home)**   **Won 1-0**
Heaketh (Goal); W.Moore, H.Moore, N.Rimmer, J.Evans, T.Porter, H.Wainwright, G.Halsall, G.Rockliffe, R.Blackledge, R.Dutton

28/02/1885   **Banks (Away)**   **Draw 1-1**
Heaketh (Goal); H.Moore, W.Moore, J.Robinson, P.Foster, J.Evans, R.Blackledge, G.Halsall (Capt), R.Rimmer, G.Rockliffe

07/03/1885   **Ormskirk 2nd (Away)**   **Lost 0-1**
G.Hesketh (Goal); W.Moore, P.Rimmer, J.Robinson, J.Evans, D.Quayle, R.Rimmer, T.Porter, R.Blackledge, R.Dutton, G.Rockliffe

03/04/1885   CRESCENT (Home)   Lost 0-1
G.Hesketh (Goal); H.Moore, W.Moore, C.Taylor, J.Robinson, R.Rimmer, R.Dutton,
R.Blackledge, J.Evans, G.Halsall, H.Wainwright (Capt)

04/04/1885   BLACKBURN DISTRICT (Home)   Draw 0-0
Hesketh (Goal); H.Moore, W.Moore, J.Robinson, R.Rimmer, T.Lea, R.Dutton,
R.Blackledge, J.Evans, G.Halsall, H.Wainwright (Capt)

09/05/1885   Southport Wanderers A (Away)   Won 2-1
Hesketh (Goal); H.Moore, W.Moore, J.Robinson,G.Rockliffe, R.Rimmer, G.Halsall,
R.Blackledge, J.Evans, R.Dutton, H.Wainwright (Capt)

14/05/1885   CRESCENT (Home)   Won 1-0
Heskath (Goal); H.Moore, W.Moore, J.Robinson, J.Evans, R.Rimmer, R.Blackledge,
G.Halsall, R.Dutton, H.Wainwright (Capt), T.Porter

20/06/1885   BLACKBURN CROSS HILL (Home)   Won 3-1
Hesketh (Goal); H.Moore, W.Moore, R.Rimmer, J.Robinson, J.Evans, R.Blackledge,
C.Morris (Crescent FC), R.Dutton, H.Wainwright (Capt), F.Rimmer

**Final Reported Record: Played 28, 16 Won, 6 Lost, 6 Drawn, 32 Goals For, 26 Goals
Against**

1885/86

19/09/1885   BIRKDALE (Home)   Won 3-0

Hesketh (Goal); H.Moore, G.Halsall, W.Sloane, J.Robinson, J.Seddon,H.Wainwright (Capt), R.dutton, J.Evans, R.Rimmer, F.Rimmer

26/09/1885   Churchtown Roamers (Away)   Lost 1-3

Hesketh (Goal); H.Moore, Blundell, Robinson,Rimmer, Blackledge, Dutton, Sloan, Keen, Wainwright (Capt), F.Rimmer.

03/10/1885   Southport Wanderers A (Away)   Won 3-0

G.Hesketh (Goal); H.Moore, G.Halsall, J.Robinson, W.Sloane, R.Rimmer, R.Blackledge, J.Evans, F.Rimmer, R.Dutton, H.Wainwright(Capt)

10/10/1885   ST MARYS, BLACKBURN   (Home)   Won 4-1

G.Hesketh (Goal); H.Moore, W.Moore, R.Rimmer, J.Evans, J.Robinson, G.Halsall, R.Blackledge, R.Dutton,

17/10/1885   OAKFIELD ROVERS, LIVERPOOL (Home)   Won 3-0

G.Hesketh (Goal); H.Moore, W.Moore, R.Rimmer, J.Evans, J.Robinson, R.Dutton, H.Wainwright (Capt), R.Blackledge, G.Halsall, F.Rimmer

**24/10/1885   BOOTLE WANDERERS (Wanderers' Ground)   Won 2-1
Liverpool and District Cup 1st Round**

G.Hesketh (Goal); H.Moore, W.Moore, J.Robinson, J.Evans, R.Rimmer, R.Blackledge, G.Halsall, R.Dutton, H.Wainwright (Capt), F.Rimmer

31/10/1885   BRECK ROVERS, LIVERPOOL (Home)   Won 2-0

G.Hesketh (Goal); H.Moore, P.Foster, J.Robinson, R.Rimmer, R.Blackledge, J.Evans, H.Wainwright (Capt), R.Dutton, F.Rimmer

07/11/1885   EARLESTOWN WANDERERS (Home)   Draw 1-1

Hesketh (Goal); H.Moore, W.Moore, Evans, R.Rimmer, Robinson, Rimmer, Dutton, Wainwright, Blckledge, Halsall

**14/11/1885   Earlestown Wanderers (Away)   Lost 0-7
Liverpool Cup**

Hesketh (Goal); H.Moore, W.Moore, J.Robinson, J.Evans, R.Rimmer, H.Wainwright, R.Dutton, F.Rimmer, R.Blackledge, G.H.Halsall

21/11/1885   High Park (Away)   Lost 3-4

G.Hesketh (Goal); H.Moore, W.Moore, Robinson, Evans, Porter, R.Blackledge, G.Halsall, Dutton, Wainwright, F.Rimmer

05/12/1885   Liverpool Arkles (Away)   Won 1-0
Played with 9 men
G.Hesketh (Goal); G.Halsall, J.Robinson, J.Evans, R.Blackledge, T.Porter, R.Dutton,
H.Wainwright (Capt), F.Rimmer

12/12/1885   Ormskirk (Away)   Won 2-0
Hesketh (Goal); Halsall, Evans, Keen, J.Carr, N.Rimmer, R.Blackledge, T.Porter,F.Rimmer,
R.Dutton, H.Wainwright (Capt)

19/12/1885   St Josephs, Preston (Away)   Lost 0-2
No Line-Up Available

25/12/1885   SOUTHPORT OLD BOYS   Draw 0-0
G.Hesketh (Goal); W.Moore, H.Moore, Robinson, Evans, Halsall, R.Dutton,
H.Wainwright (Capt), J.Lea,R.Blackledge, T.Porter

01/01/1886   Ashton Recreation (Away)   Draw 3-3
Hesketh (Goal); Halsall, Moore (backs); J.J.Keen, J.Robinson (½ backs); R.Blackledge,
T.Porter, W.Moore, F.Rimmer, H.Wainwright (forwards)

02/01/1886   CHURCHTOWN ROAMERS (Home)   Won 2-1
Hesketh (Goal); G.Halsall, H.Moore (backs); T.Porter, J.Evans, J.Robinson (½ backs);
A.Bryers, R.Blackledge, W.Moore, F.Rimmer, H.Wainwright (forwards)

09/01/1886   Oakfield Rovers (Away)   Lost 0-1
Hesketh (Goal); R.Pasquill, G.Halsall (backs); W.Evans, JJ Keen, J Robinson (½ backs);
H.Wainwright (Capt.), T.Porter, R.Blackledge, T.Lea, F.Rimmer (forwards)*
*from Southport Wanderers

23/01/1886   BRIDGEWATER, WIGAN (Home)   Won 4-0
Hesketh (Goal); H.Moore, G.Halsall (backs); J.Robinson, J.Evans, W.Moore (½ backs);
H.Wainwright, F.Rimmer, R.Blackledge, A.Bryers, T.Porter (forwards)

30/01/1886   ASHTON RECREATION (Home)   Won 3-1
Hesketh (Goal); H. Moore, G.Halsall (backs); J.Robinson, J.Evans, P.Rimmer (½ backs);
R.Blackledge, T.Porter, C.Forrest, H.Wainwright, F.Rimmer (forwards)

06/02/1886   Breck Rovers, Liverpool (Away)   Won 5-1
R. Parkinson (Goal); H.Moore, G.Halsall (backs); H.Quale, W.Rimmer, G.W.Hesketh (½
backs); T.Porter, J.Evans, J.J.Keen, H.Wainwright (Capt.), F.Rimmer (forwards)

13/02/1886   ARKLES (Home)   Won 1-0
G.Hesketh (Goal); H.Moore, J.Evans (backs); J.Robinson, W.Moore, J.Evans (½ backs);
R.Blackledge, A.Bryers, F.Rimmer, T.Porter, H.Wainwright (forwards)

20/02/1886   BIRKDALE (Home)   Won 4-0
G.W.Hesketh (Goal); H.Moore, G.Halsall (backs); J.Robinson, J.Evans, R.Rimmer (½ backs); T.Porter, H.Wainwright, R.Blackledge, F.Bailey, F.Rimmer (forwards)

06/03/1886   Birkdale (Away)   Result Not Known
No Line-Up Available

20/03/1886   CHURCHTOWN ROAMERS (Home)   Won 7-0
Hesketh (Goal); H.Moore, G.Halsall (backs); R.Pasquill, J.Evans, W.Moore (½ backs); A.Bryers, R.Blackledge, F.Rimmer, T.Porter, H.Wainwright (forwards)

03/04/1886   Burscough (Away)   Won 1-0
G.Hesketh (Goal); H.Moore, G.Halsall (Capt.) (backs); W.Moore, R.Rimmer, J.Evans (½ backs); R.Blackledge, R.Pasquill, T.Porter, P.Rimmer, F.Rimmer (forwards)

10/04/1886   ST JOSEPH'S PRESTON (Home)   Lost 0-6
G.Hesketh (Goal); H.Moore, G.Halsall (Capt.) (backs); R.Pasquill, J.Evans, T.Sellars* (½ backs); T.Porter, J.Leadbetter*, F.Munro, R.Blackledge, T.Lea (forwards)
* Southport Wanderers

17/04/1886   HIGH PARK (Sports Ground, Sussex Road)   Won 2-0
Charity Cup 2nd Round
G.Hesketh (Goal); H.Moore, G.Halsall (backs); R.Pasquill, J.Evans, W.Moore (½ backs); T.Porter, H.Wainwright (Capt.), F.Rimmer, R.Blackledge, A.Bryers (forwards)

01/05/1886   SOUTHPORT (Wanderers Ground)   Lost 1-2
Charity Cup Semi Final
Hesketh (Goal); H.Moore, Halsall, J.Evans, R.Pasquill, W.Moore, H.Wainwright (Capt.), T.Porter, A.Bryers, Blackledge, F.Rimmer

20/05/1886   Southport (Away)   Won 4-0
*Benefit Match for Bailey
Hesketh (Goal); Halsall, Moore, Evans, Rigby, Pasquill, Wainwright, Porter, F.Rimmer, Blackledge, Bryers

1886/87

04/09/1886   CROSSE HALL, CHORLEY (Home)   Won 2-1
G.W.Hesketh (Goal); H.Moore, G.Halsall (backs); J.Evans, C.Blundell, R.Pasquill (½ backs); H.Wainwright, H.Dutton (Capt.), R.Blackledge, A.Bryers, F.Rimmer (forwards)

11/09/1886   Salford (Away)   Lost 3-1
A.N.Other (Goal); R.Pasquill, G.Halsall (backs); J.Evans, R.Dutton (Capt.), C.Blundell (½ backs); W.Geeson, E.Rimmer, H Wainwright, W.Halsall, F.Rimmer (forwards)

18/09/1886   ST PETER'S LIVERPOOL (Home)   Won 3-1
Campbell (Goal); H.Moore, R.Pasquill (backs); W.Geeson, J.Evans, C.Blundell (½ backs); A.Bryers, R.Blackledge, F.Rimmer, R.Dutton (Capt.), H.Wainwright (forwards)

25/09/1886   Churchtown (Away)   Won 3-2
Campbell (Goal); H.Moore, R.Pasquill (backs); J.Evans, F.Briggs, W.Geeson (½ backs); H.Wainwright, R.Dutton (Capt.), R.Blackledge, A.Bryers, F.Rimmer (forwards)

09/10/1886   Liverpool Police Athletic Club (Away)   Won 2-1
Liverpool Cup
G.W.Hesketh (Goal); H.Moore, Halsall (backs); J.Evans, W.Geeson, R.Pasquill (½ backs); R.Dutton (Capt.), H.Wainwright, F.Rimmer, A.Roberts, R.Blackledge (forwards)

6/11/1886   Old Boys (Away)   Won 2-1
Benefit Match for T Porter
No Line-Up Given

13/11/1886   Skelmersdale United (Away)   Draw 0-0
G.W.Hesketh (Goal); H.Moore, J.Evans (backs); P.Foster, R.Pasquill, A.Roberts (Capt.) (½ backs); F.Rimmer, R.Blackledge, H Wainwright (forwards)

27/11/1886   LINACRE (Home)   Draw 1-1
Campbell (Goal); H.Moore, G.Halsall (backs); R.Pasquill, J.Evans, W.Geeson (½ backs); H.Wainwright, R.Dutton (Capt.), R.Blackledge, J.J.Keen, F.Rimmer (forwards)

04/12/1886   BIRKDALE (Home)   Lost 1-4
Ingham (Goal); R.Pasquill, G.Halsall (backs); J.Evans, G.W.Hesketh, J.Robinson (½ backs); H.Wainwright, W.Geeson, R.Blackledge, F.Rimmer (forwards)

11/12/1886   BURSCOUGH (Home)   Lost 1-2
*10 men each
G.W.Hesketh (Goal); H.Moore, W.Rimmer (backs); J.Evans, Halsall (Capt.), J.Carr (½ backs); W.Geeson, J.J.Keen, R.Blackledge, F.Rimmer (forwards)

22/01/1887   Haydock (Away)   Lost 1-8
G.Hesketh (Goal); H.Moore, G.Halsall, W.Geeson, J.Evans, R.Pasquill, H.Wainwright, R.Dutton, F.Rimmer,A.N.Other, sub, R.Blackledge

29/01/1887   Tranmere Rovers (Away)   Lost 0-2
Liverpool & District Cup / 3rd Round
G.W.Hesketh (Goal); H.Moore, G.Halsall, R.Pasquill, H.Thompson, G.Evans, E.Sutton, R.Dutton (Capt),W.Geeson, R.Blackledge, F.Rimmer

19/02/1887   HIGH PARK (Home)   Draw 0-0
Southport Charity Cup / 1st Round
Hesketh (Goal); Halsall, Moore, Evans, Geeson, Pasquill, Wainwright, Dutton, Blackledge, W.Evans, F.Rimmer

26/02/1887   HIGH PARK (Neutral)   Lost 2-4
Southport Charity Cup / 1st Round Replay
Hesketh (Goal); Halsall, Moore, Evans, Geeson, Pasquill, Wainwright, Dutton, Blackledge, W.Evans, F.Rimmer

19/03/1887   Southport Old Boys (Away)   Draw 2-2
*Benefit Match for G.W.Hesketh. No Line-up Available

08/04/1887   Southport (Away)   Lost 1-3
No line-up Available

16/04/1887   Churchtown (Away)   Lost 1-2
No line-up Available

07/05/1887   Park Lane Wanderers (Away)   Draw 1-1
Harrison (Goal); Halsall, Cookson, F.Rimmer, Thompson, Robinson, Corry, Wainwright, W.Rimmer, Pasquill, Blackledge

At the end of the 1886-87 season their record read Played 22, Won 11, Lost 6, Drawn 5.

About the Author

I grew up in Ormskirk but my father was Liverpool born and therefore Liverpool was his club. I tagged along and I guess it never occurred to me to support anyone else.

My first football experience was being taken to Anfield to watch Liverpool take on Lech Poznan in the European Cup in 1984. Being only 3, I don't have any memories of that game, but I do have fond memories of visiting Anfield with my father on other occasions, standing on the Kop (well, sitting on the crush barriers so I could see!) to watch the great Liverpool sides of the late 80s.

My love affair with Southport did not begin until 1992 but the seeds had been sown back in April 1989. My father had bought two tickets for Liverpool's FA Cup Semi Final against Nottingham Forest at Hillsborough, with the intention of taking me to the game. I, however, had other plans and decided that a day trip with the Beaver Scouts to Jungle Jim's underneath Blackpool Tower was where any self-respecting 8-year-old should be. With what happened at Hillsborough on that fateful day, in hindsight it was probably the smartest decision I have ever made.

In 1992, for reasons completely unbeknown to me, I found myself at a Southport v Marine game at Haig Avenue with my father and a family friend, Henry Nutter. I'm convinced that prior to setting foot in the ground I did not even know it was there - at only 11 years old, I had no knowledge of anything below the First Division. That season Southport won the Northern Premier League, and I became a regular from 1993 alongside my father, Southport's first season in the G.M. Vauxhall Conference.

As an enthusiastic student at Ormskirk Grammar School, I became the creator and editor of the first Southport Football Club website in 1996 and have held a number of voluntary roles with the Club, including Press Officer, in the years since. Rather than stay on to complete my A-Levels in familiar surroundings, I chose to move to King George V Sixth Form College in Southport. My time at KGV coincided with the Sandgrounders taking a trip to Wembley for the FA Trophy Final and I spent much of my break and leisure time at the ground helping Commercial Manager Kevin Warburton with preparations, rather than on the college campus.

In the early 2000s my father moved to Glasgow and began to work for The Celtic Football Club, a club steeped in history and tradition. I stayed at home in Aughton with my mum and attended Edge Hill University to study Communication and Media. It was there, in my second year of study, that I met Becky.

In 2006, Becky and I got married, and two years later we had our first child, Olivia. In 2010, we added Cameron to our clan, and he has attended games with me at Haig Avenue frequently since he turned five or six. He enjoys his football even more than I do and spends a lot of time with Becky's family - his Grandad Steve and Uncle James - watching Wigan Athletic, in addition to the Sandgrounders.

Ever since I had first read the opening chapter of 'the book' (as the Complete League History of Southport FC by Wilde and Braham is most often referred to) in the mid-90s I had been fascinated with the early history of Southport Football Club, and seeing the way that Celtic embraced and celebrated its history made me even more keen to see Southport celebrate its own.

I'm very fortunate that over the years, as my own interests grew, and I started to keep my own Southport FC records, Geoff and Michael indulged by enthusiasm.

I have worked as a Business Analyst in the Financial Services industry since 2005. My analytical mindset lends itself to research work and in 2019 I started the Southport FC Former Players Association to help promote the history and heritage of the club, and to recognise the hundreds of players that have made their contributions, big or small, along the way.

I've spent a number of years researching the very early years of Southport Football Club and have contributed a number of articles to the Club's match day programme, Club website and to the Former Players Association's website, but, encouraged by Michael Braham, decided that it was perhaps about time I wrote a book!

Printed in Great Britain
by Amazon

18084837R00208